Ancient monuments in the countryside:
an archaeological management review

English ⌗ Heritage

Archaeological Report no 5

Ancient monuments in the countryside:

an archaeological management review

by Timothy Darvill

for the Ancient Monuments Division of English Heritage

Historic Buildings & Monuments Commission for England

1987

First published 1987 by
Historic Buildings and Monuments Commission for England
Fortress House, 23 Savile Row, London W1X 2HE

Printed by Derry & Sons Ltd, Nottingham, England

British Library Cataloguing in Publication Data

Darvill, T.C.
Ancient monuments in the countryside: an archaeological management review. — (English Heritage archaeological report; no. 5).
1. Historical sites — England — Conservation and restoration   2. England — Antiquities — Conservation and restoration
I. Title   II. English Heritage. *Ancient Monuments Division*
III. Series
936.2   DA90

ISBN 1-85074-167-0

Contents

I   Archaeology and management

II   Archaeology in the countryside 1: Semi-natural landscapes

III   Archaeology in the countryside 2: Man-made landscapes

IV   Looking forward

List of figures

List of tables

Foreword

by Lord Montagu of Beaulieu, Chairman of English Heritage

The English countryside is one of the nation's most valued and cherished assets. For thousands of years, successive generations have gradually shaped it and moulded it into what we see today, and we in our turn will add our own distinctive marks before passing it on to future generations. The countryside has always been changing, and will continue to do so, but many now feel that the speed and extent of change is out of control and that it is time to take stock both of what resources the countryside contains, and of how, as a responsible society, we can best approach the future control or management of those resources.

This volume is a contribution towards the development of a more enlightened approach to the future management of one particular aspect of the countryside heritage – the archaeological resource. Our concern is with the whole range of monuments in rural areas, from prehistoric sites, such as barrows and hillforts, through to more recent traces of man's activities, such as the industrial remains, parks, and gardens of the last century.

The intention is to set out the main issues relating to the conservation of these monuments, so that they can be appreciated by everyone with an interest in the countryside. Given that the greatest portion of the nation's ancient monuments lie in the countryside, it is perhaps easy to see why English Heritage believes that it is crucial to secure the preservation and well-being of sites in rural areas.

We are not advocating the conservation of monuments for their own sake, or for the indulgence of a few individuals. The ancient monuments in the countryside are a valuable resource, part of the history of our islands, which chart the story of society's past development, growth, and change. This is a story which should be of interest and value to the nation as a whole. Our aim is to help that value to be realized and to ensure that money, time, and effort devoted to the ancient monuments in the countryside are well spent and represent a sound investment for the future.

The development of a coherent framework for the enjoyment, preservation, and conservation of ancient monuments, or archaeological resource management as it is commonly known, is a relatively new field for archaeologists working in Britain, and this volume marks the first detailed treatment of the subject. In some other countries, notably the United States of America, Denmark, and Japan, this form of management has been an important component of national policies for their cultural heritage for some years.

This volume has three main goals. First, it aims to present the background to the recognition, investigation, and management of the archaeological resource. Second, it attempts to review what is known of the resource, the threats currently posed to it, and the ways in which it can be exploited and conserved. Finally, it looks towards the development and promotion of a secure future for ancient monuments in the countryside.

1 Introduction

1.1 Ancient monuments and the changing countryside

Much of England's rich archaeological heritage lies in the countryside. The burial mounds, hillforts, Roman villas, deserted villages, and industrial ruins left by our ancestors are often familiar features of the landscape, crowning hills in skyline splendour, nestling in sheltered valleys, or sprawling across open country. Many more sites, far less clear on the surface but no less important, lie buried or only partly visible. Countless generations of people lived, worked, and died in the English countryside, and have all left behind traces of their activities. The cumulative effect is the landscape we know today in which the historical dimension is an integral part of the valued whole (Fig 1).

By its very nature, England's archaeological heritage is a finite and non-renewable resource. Over the last two decades or so, preserving monuments has been a difficult task in the face of constant pressures from farming, industry, and commerce to maximize the return on investment from every available piece of land. Many ancient monuments in the countryside have been damaged or lost completely. Detailed surveys of areas as far apart as West Penwith, Cornwall, and the Cheviots, Northumberland, and as diverse in landscape character as the wet Levels of Somerset and the dry chalk Downs of Sussex, show that this is not a localized phenomenon but one which is widespread in its extent and devastating in its impact. Later chapters describe and document the main threats currently facing ancient monuments in the countryside.

While monuments are still being lost and damaged at an alarming rate, there are encouraging signs that attitudes are beginning to change in the wake of growing support for nature and countryside conservation. Recent changes in agricultural policy to reduce problems of over-production have additionally opened the way for less intensive farming operations and the more flexible use of land. While this could have its dangers for conservation, it may also allow greater scope for the preservation of our remaining heritage. A well-maintained landscape, which retains as much of its historical dimension, wildlife, and natural beauty as possible, is probably regarded as desirable by most people in England today, but the practicalities and benefits of achieving this need to be set out clearly and presented to a wide audience. This volume owes its inception to the desire to fulfill that need with reference to ancient monuments.

The development of a coherent strategy for the preservation of archaeological sites on a large scale is now critical in order to take advantage of the tide of change taking place in the way the countryside is managed. Britain has a long history of protecting and caring for its ancient monuments, but the experience of the last two decades makes it clear that more must be done *now* to ensure that even a small sample of what remains is preserved for our own and future generations to enjoy. To be successful means striking a balance between the demands of farming and development and those of conservation. Balancing the many, sometimes conflicting, demands affecting the archaeological resource, and developing a positive approach to its preservation and conservation, are known as archaeological resource management — the focus of this book. The intention is to help and inform those involved with, or interested in, the archaeology of the countryside, whether as landowner, tenant, contractor, administrator, planner, or member of the general public. It sets out to illustrate the wealth and variety of archaeological remains in the countryside, and to suggest a framework for decision-making in relation to those remains.

1.2 Archaeological interests in the countryside

The widespread distribution of archaeological remains and the public interest in them mean that a large number of organizations are directly or indirectly involved in their management. Centrally, English Heritage,[1] established under the National Heritage Act 1983, is responsible both for the management of those monuments which are in State care and more generally for the protection and preservation of the vast majority of monuments which remain in private ownership (HBMC 1984a).

English Heritage works closely with other national bodies such as the Royal Commission on the Historical Monuments of England, the Countryside Commission, and the Nature Conservancy Council whose interests interrelate. The Council for British Archaeology, which is independent of direct government support, is concerned with many aspects of archaeological work in Britain and also has important representational and coordinating roles at national level with over 350 member organizations. The National Trust owns and manages many archaeological monuments on its extensive land holdings-across the country.

At a local level archaeological coverage is more complicated and rather uneven. All county councils and National Park authorities are involved with archaeology to a greater or lesser extent through the administration of planning legislation and the provision of public services such as museums, country parks, and leisure facilities. Many county councils employ a county archaeological officer, and some undertake or sponsor excavations, surveys, and management work. District councils are also involved with archaeology through the administration of planning legislation and the provision of public services, and a few operate or fund various archaeological units which provide advice on archaeology and planning matters. In addition, there are independent archaeological trusts or units in some counties, or serving more than one county. Again, these units and trusts undertake excavations, surveys, and management work.

Every county in England is covered by some form of Sites and Monuments Record, mostly operated by county councils, but in some cases maintained by independent county-based or regional archaeological trusts and units. At the time of writing some of these records are far from complete, and it will be some years before every county can boast a comprehensive and fully retrievable set of records as a database for archaeological resource management (Burrow 1985; Fraser 1986)

Mention may also be made of the many voluntary bodies, local societies, and interest groups wholly or partly concerned with archaeological matters which are spread widely throughout the country.

Archaeology is also a well-developed academic discipline. At the time of writing there are 33 universities and university colleges teaching archaeology in the British Isles, and most are also actively involved in archaeological research.

Most important of all, however, are the thousands of landowners and land-users in the countryside who are in effect, sometimes unwittingly, custodians and guardians of over 95% of the nation's archaeological heritage. Only through their

Figure 1   Maiden Castle, Dorset: a multi-period hilltop settlement site and defended enclosure, lying in the midst of today's busy agricultural landscape

interest, sympathy, and continued support can the nation's archaeological heritage be properly managed and maintained.

1.3 Historical background

The development and application of archaeological resource management in the English countryside springs from a long tradition of archaeological work in rural areas and a wealth of practical experience in dealing with ancient monuments of widely different types. Interest and curiosity about the prehistoric monuments of the countryside can be detected in England as far back as Tudor times, and from the mid sixteenth century onwards antiquaries published accounts of monuments known to them. In 1533 John Leland was appointed King's Antiquary by Henry VIII and was granted a commission to search the length and breadth of England and Wales for surviving antiquities and monuments of all types (Marsden 1983, 1–3). This post did not continue after Leland, but royal interest was maintained; Charles II, for example, ordered a discourse on Avebury from the Wiltshire antiquary John Aubrey (M Hunter 1975, 158–9).

On these foundations a strong tradition of field archaeology developed, including the careful recording of monuments by maps and plans and their investigation by excavation. Archaeology has changed considerably over the last 200 years, in terms both of an improved understanding of the remains themselves and of many refinements in the ways that they can be investigated (Ashbee 1972; Daniel 1967; 1975; 1981; P Fowler 1980). Archaeology in Britain today is an exacting, professional discipline.

One concern that has pervaded archaeological work over the last century or so has been the preservation of monuments. Among the most outspoken advocates of legislative protection for ancient monuments in the late nineteenth century was Sir John Lubbock (later Lord Avebury). In a seminal speech to the International Congress on Prehistoric Archaeology at Norwich in August 1868 Lubbock expounded his thinking to a large audience and attracted considerable interest from leading archaeologists of the time (M Thompson 1977, 58–9). Later, as a Member of Parliament, Lubbock introduced a series of private bills concerned with ancient monuments and, though these were unsuccessful, he later persuaded the Government to introduce a bill which in October 1882 became the Ancient Monuments Protection Act 1882 (M Thompson 1977, 60).

The main concern of this first Act was for prehistoric monuments, principally because, it was believed, they were relatively cheap to maintain. Many people at the time, however, found it extraordinary that in a Christian country protection should be accorded only to pagan monuments on grounds of economy (M Thompson 1977, 60). The main limitation of this first Act was that for sites to be protected ownership or title to the monuments had to be transferred to a body acting in the name of the State. This was of course a very sensitive issue in Victorian England as it appeared to interfere with the rights of private property. It is therefore to the great credit of the first Inspector of Ancient Monuments, Lieutenant-General Pitt Rivers, that he managed to acquire 43 monuments for the State between 1883 and 1890, among them such well-known sites as the West Kennet long barrow, Wiltshire, and the stone circle known as Long Meg and her Daughters, Cumbria. Monuments acquired in this way were included on a Schedule, and, in addition to these sites, Section 10 of the Act allowed that 'Her Majesty may, from time to time, by Order in Council, declare that any monument of a like character to the monuments described in the Schedule hereto, shall be deemed to be an ancient monument to which this Act applies.'

From the late nineteenth century onwards successive parliaments have amended and expanded upon the Ancient Monuments Protection Act 1882. The Ancient Monuments Consolidation and Amendment Act 1913 provided an important extension of existing powers by the introduction of Preservation Orders, which allowed monuments 'in danger of destruction or removal or damage from neglect or injudicious treatment' to be placed in the protection of the Commissioners of Works. The single most important qualification for this treatment was that the preservation of the monument in question was considered to be of national importance (Section 6.2). This factor has remained a feature of all subsequent legislation. Section 12 of the Act provided for the Commissioners of Works to prepare and publish a list of ancient monuments the preservation of which was considered of national importance. Any ancient monument could be considered for inclusion on this list, not just those in the Guardianship of the State, and this meant that for the first time legislative protection could be applied on a large scale. The distinction between Guardianship Monuments and what later became known as Scheduled Monuments was thereby established. An Ancient Monuments Board was formed to advise the Commissioners of Works on the selection of monuments, and to advise owners of ancient monuments on the treatment of the monuments.

Later, in the Ancient Monuments Act 1931, the protection of monuments included on the list (or Schedule) was extended by the introduction of a notification system, whereby owners of monuments had to give the Commissioners of Works three months' notice in writing of any works affecting the monument (Section 6.2). This was a system which remained in use until 1979.

Alongside the development of legislation for ancient monuments, a number of background strategies were prepared by various organizations concerned with ancient monuments. Each of course reflected slight changes in emphasis according to the development of the discipline and the interests of its practitioners at the time. Immediately after the Second World War, for example, a committee was established to look into the existing state and future direction of archaeological work in Britain, the results of which were published in 1948 as *A survey and policy of field research in the archaeology of Great Britain* (CBA 1948). The main thrust of this document was towards the gaining of more information about the past in order to fill gaps in knowledge.

In the Historic Buildings and Ancient Monuments Act 1953 ancient monuments legislation was extended to cover historic buildings. The use of Preservation Orders for ancient monuments was extended, and Interim Preservation Notices were introduced to provide a rapid way of preventing damage to monuments until the importance of the site could be assessed.

These Acts provided the legislative framework current throughout the 1950s and 1960s. In 1966 a committee was formed under the chairmanship of Sir David Walsh to assess the arrangements for the protection of ancient monuments; the findings were later published (Walsh 1969). In retrospect, perhaps the most formative and far-sighted recommendation in this report was that local authorities should compile consolidated records of all known ancient monuments, if they were not already doing so, and, at the same time, should consider whether adequate professional archaeological

Figure 2   The Nine Ladies stone circle on Stanton Moor, Derbyshire: the monument is well managed and the land-use is sympathetic to its long-term preservation; situated in a woodland clearing, the site is kept under grassland, lightly grazed by sheep

assistance was available to them. Some local authorities responded to this call, but many ignored it at the time, only to find themselves in need of such records and assistance by the end of the 1970s (Burrow 1985). Little of what was said in the report was translated into new legislation, the main exception being the introduction, in the Field Monuments Act 1972, of a system of acknowledgement payments to owners of Scheduled Monuments. These payments were primarily intended to discourage activities within a prescribed area that were damaging to the monuments, especially ploughing and forestry, by compensating farmers for consequent loss of income. The main drawback of such an approach was that it encouraged a rather negative attitude towards monument protection, and sites were often left to take care of themselves.

In 1979 the existing ancient monuments legislation was consolidated and amended by the Ancient Monuments and Archaeological Areas Act 1979. This Act, which is discussed in detail in chapter 5, represented a much needed strengthening of the previous legislation, and included provisions for management agreements in place of acknowledgement payments and a Scheduled Monument Consent system in place of the notification procedure.

The 1979 Act came into force in stages between 1979 and 1982, and so at present it is still too early to assess its full impact. One of its successes may, however, be that it has rejuvenated interest in the preservation and conservation of monuments. This can be clearly seen in the various policy statements issued by archaeological organizations over the last few years. In 1983, the preservation of monuments and academic interests were given equal treatment in the section relating to the countryside in the volume entitled *Research objectives in British archaeology* published by the Council for British Archaeology (Thomas 1983). The same concerns appear in discussion documents prepared by the Prehistoric Society (1984) and the Society for the Promotion of Roman Studies (1985).

Policy for the preservation of sites to date, however, has tended to treat monuments in isolation, with little regard to the differing conditions in which such monuments have survived, the wider archaeological importance of the landscape in which they lie, and related countryside interests. For farmers, foresters, other landowners, and conservationists, it is the nature of the countryside and the pressures on it which determine the scope for changes in management practice. This volume attempts to approach archaeology from this wider perspective.

1.4   A basis for archaeological resource management today

The underlying philosophy of archaeological resource management is not, as some might think, that everything old is good and should therefore be retained. Rather it is an adaptation of the World Conservation Strategy (IUCN 1980) to archaeological conservation, reflecting the concern that archaeological sites represent a resource which is already, and may continue to be, useful to mankind for various purposes and therefore requires to be maintained.

Unlike natural flora and fauna, the archaeological resource is non-renewable because it cannot reproduce itself, recolonize decimated areas, or be transplanted. Precious reserves must therefore be preserved *in situ*, and the temptation to squander them for short-term gains resisted. Archaeological sites represent one of man's most enduring contributions to the environment, and concern for them is largely motivated by their human interest and the recognition and appreciation of the achievements and endeavours of past generations. That archaeological sites can be preserved and conserved within a dynamic, working landscape is demonstrated by monuments where appropriate management strategies are already in operation (Fig 2).

There is naturally much common ground here with the aims of other conservation interests, especially wildlife conservation (Ratcliffe 1977; Lambrick 1985a). The preservation of the human environment must be seen in terms of its contribution to an overall strategy for the conservation of the whole landscape.

1.5 Scope and definitions

This book is primarily concerned with the countryside of England, the open landscape of farmland, moors, rivers, lakes, coasts, and woods which today comprises over 85% of the total land area. Archaeology is taken to mean the study of past human activities through material remains; archaeological sites are places where traces of these activities still survive. Specific definitions used in current ancient monuments legislation are covered in chapter 5.

Archaeological sites in the countryside, particularly those visible on the ground surface as earthworks, are usually called field monuments because of their situation. Some standing ruins or uninhabited buildings, such as castles, abbeys, and priories, especially those associated with buried features, also fall within the scope of this volume. Occupied areas and buildings, however, including farms, hamlets, villages, towns, and cities, are not covered here as they require separate detailed treatment, although there is of necessity some overlap and mention of such areas is made where appropriate.

No rigid date range is imposed, but for practical purposes the span covered stretches from earliest prehistoric times through to the period of the Second World War.

1.6 Arrangement and content

This volume is arranged in four main sections. First, the nature of archaeological evidence in the countryside and approaches to its management are considered. This is followed by two sections covering the archaeology of types of semi-natural landscape and of man-made landscape respectively. The volume concludes with a section on the future of archaeological interest in the countryside.

I Archaeology and management

The following four chapters provide a background to archaeological work in the countryside and discuss the principles and practicalities of archaeological resource management as it will be applied in parts II and III. Chapter 2 deals specifically with the nature, extent, and character of the archaeological resource in the countryside, and describes the main ways in which sites are recognized, recorded, and investigated. Chapter 3 provides a chronological summary of the way the countryside has developed in the hands of man since the last Ice Age. Chapter 4 takes the present pattern of rural land-use as the basis for developing the theme of archaeological resource management proper. Chapter 5 rounds off part I with a review of the present legislation which has a bearing on ancient monuments in countryside areas.

2 Archaeological evidence

2.1 Extent and diversity

Almost every parish in England contains one or more archaeological sites, which might be known as anything from the findspot of a few ancient objects to the extensive remains of an ancient farm or settlement covering many hectares. Nobody knows exactly how many sites there are, but at present over 650,000 have been recorded in greater or lesser detail in England as a whole (HBMC 1984b).

Every archaeological site represents the remains of, or setting for, some past activity. Throughout the time that man has lived in England the land has been exploited in one way or another, and traces of these activities have become imprinted on the landscape. Thus the remains of settlements, farms, fields, burial grounds, quarries, industrial areas, ritual places, and many other aspects of everyday life are represented in more or less detail.

Past societies made use of the whole landscape, but it is crucial to realize that each different kind of activity leaves behind evidence which is proportional to its scale and intensity. In order to understand the past, all aspects of life have to be considered, and all types of site taken into account. Field systems, for example, may cover several hectares with widely spaced lynchets and boundaries, which at first sight may seem rather uninteresting. But field systems were important to the economy of the communities who used them and, in piecing together a picture of the past, they are just as relevant as settlements where perhaps much activity was concentrated in a very small area and relatively rich archaeological deposits accumulated. The distribution of sites is uneven across the landscape. Some areas, such as fertile agricultural land or places with good communication links, have naturally tended to attract settlement over and over again throughout prehistoric and historic times. As a result, evidence for many phases of activity spanning thousands of years may be superimposed – a palimpsest landscape as these areas are often called (Fig 3).

Elsewhere, man's activity was often intermittent, determined perhaps by environmental conditions, changes in climate, or special economic or social circumstances. Thus, much of the heavy clay land in southern England was not extensively occupied until later prehistoric times, while in the uplands of northern and western England the extent of settlement fluctuated with changes in climate and in accord with population growth in lowland areas.

At a local level the variations in the intensity of archaeological finds is greater still. The landscape has influenced man's activities since earliest times, to the extent that some slopes have always been too steep and some land always too wet to cultivate, and some ridges always too exposed to choose as sites for dwellings. Thus, although the whole countryside has been in continuous use by man over the centuries, some areas have been more heavily exploited than others, and some places have never been used in a way which leaves tangible archaeological remains.

2.2 The nature of the evidence

The ways in which man has left his mark on the landscape vary greatly according to the types of activity, the length of time during which they were undertaken, and their intensity. Some archaeological sites represent deliberate constructions, as in the case of barrows, enclosures, defences, houses, and boundaries. Others are the by-products of particular activities, for example pits and spoil tips, which are the result of quarrying for natural resources, or lynchets, caused by the build-up of soil on the edge of cultivation plots. Yet other kinds of site came about through accidents and processes over which people at the time had little or no control, as when lost or discarded objects became incorporated into the accumulating layers of a peat bog or a partly-silted ditch, or when the line of a trackway became etched into the landscape simply by continuous use over a long period. It was by these same sorts of processes that bones, seeds, insect remains, and pieces of charcoal became preserved in a variety of different types of archaeological and naturally accumulating deposits. Studies of the way archaeological sites came into existence and have survived to the present day are known as 'site formation studies' (Schiffer 1976).

In terms of the surviving remains commonly encountered in the countryside, three general types of evidence can be recognized:

i   Standing remains: built structures, ranging from the upstanding walls of buildings, or field boundaries, through to stone constructions such as stone circles, standing stones, or burial chambers. These constitute some of the most visually impressive sites in the landscape.

ii   Earthworks: soil-covered remains of any sort, which can be seen as surface undulations at ground level. These include the covered remains of ruined buildings or their foundations, as well as banks, mounds, lynchets, dykes, ramparts, ditches, gullies, and hollows.

iii Buried features: soil-covered remains which have no visible surface trace at ground level. The depth of burial varies greatly, not necessarily according to the age of the features, but as a consequence of the circumstances under which the evidence became buried.

Figure 3   Barrow Hills, near Abingdon, Oxfordshire: an aerial view of cropmarks reflecting activities on the site during many episodes of use; the rectangular feature bottom right is a Neolithic barrow, the circles are Bronze Age burial monuments, some of the linear features are field boundaries, and the dark rectangular blobs are Saxon houses; the cluster of circular pits (top right) results from ornamental tree-planting in the nineteenth century

Each of these types may, in one sense, be considered as a stage in the decay of a site. From their prime condition as foci of activity, all archaeological sites pass through a phase of ruination, collapse, soil coverage, stabilization, and eventually perhaps levelling and complete burial. The speed at which this happens depends upon the type of site, the materials used for its construction, the history of land-use after its abandonment, and the action of natural processes of erosion. Models of the cumulative effects of these decay processes on archaeological deposits over the course of time have been proposed for Dorset by Groube (1978; Groube and Bowden 1982, ch 3) and for upland areas by Darvill (1986a, ch 5).

In the countryside as a whole, at any given time, there will be sites in many different states of preservation. Round barrows serve as a particularly good example. These monuments were built in many parts of the country as burial places between about 2500 and 1500 BC. They usually comprise one or more burials in pits or cists covered by a mound or cairn constructed from material quarried from a surrounding ditch, or scraped up from around them. In upland areas, such as Dartmoor or the Pennines, stone boulders were used to build the barrow mound and, because land-use since prehistoric times has been at a relatively low level of intensity, these monuments are thought to survive today very much as they were seen by their builders. In contrast, communities living in some lowland areas, such as the Thames valley, constructed their barrows out of gravel and soil, and most are now badly denuded because the monuments themselves were not very robust and subsequent land utilization has been intensive. Aerial surveys have shown (RCHME 1960, 16–23) that the only surviving traces of many round barrows in these areas are the buried quarry ditch which once encircled the mound, and the bottom of the central grave pit cut down into the subsoil. Nothing visible remains on the surface.

2.3   Recognizing and recording archaeological sites

Different types of site can be recognized in different ways depending upon their size, their form, and the present land-use.[2] Many monuments, especially standing remains and substantial earthworks, are obvious even to the untrained eye and can be seen from ground level. Some guidance as to the signs which betray the existence of sites in different parts of the landscape are given in parts II and III, but uneven ground and unnatural looking slopes always require close attention, as they may indicate the presence of an archaeological site of some description.

Less well-preserved sites – for example very slight earthworks – can usually only be recognized at ground level with practice and experience. Buried sites are still more difficult to locate and often come to light purely by chance, when the ground is disturbed, or when conditions are right for the application of one or other of the specially developed techniques of reconnaissance used in field archaeology today.[3]

The following sections briefly summarize the main ways in which archaeological sites are recognized and recorded.

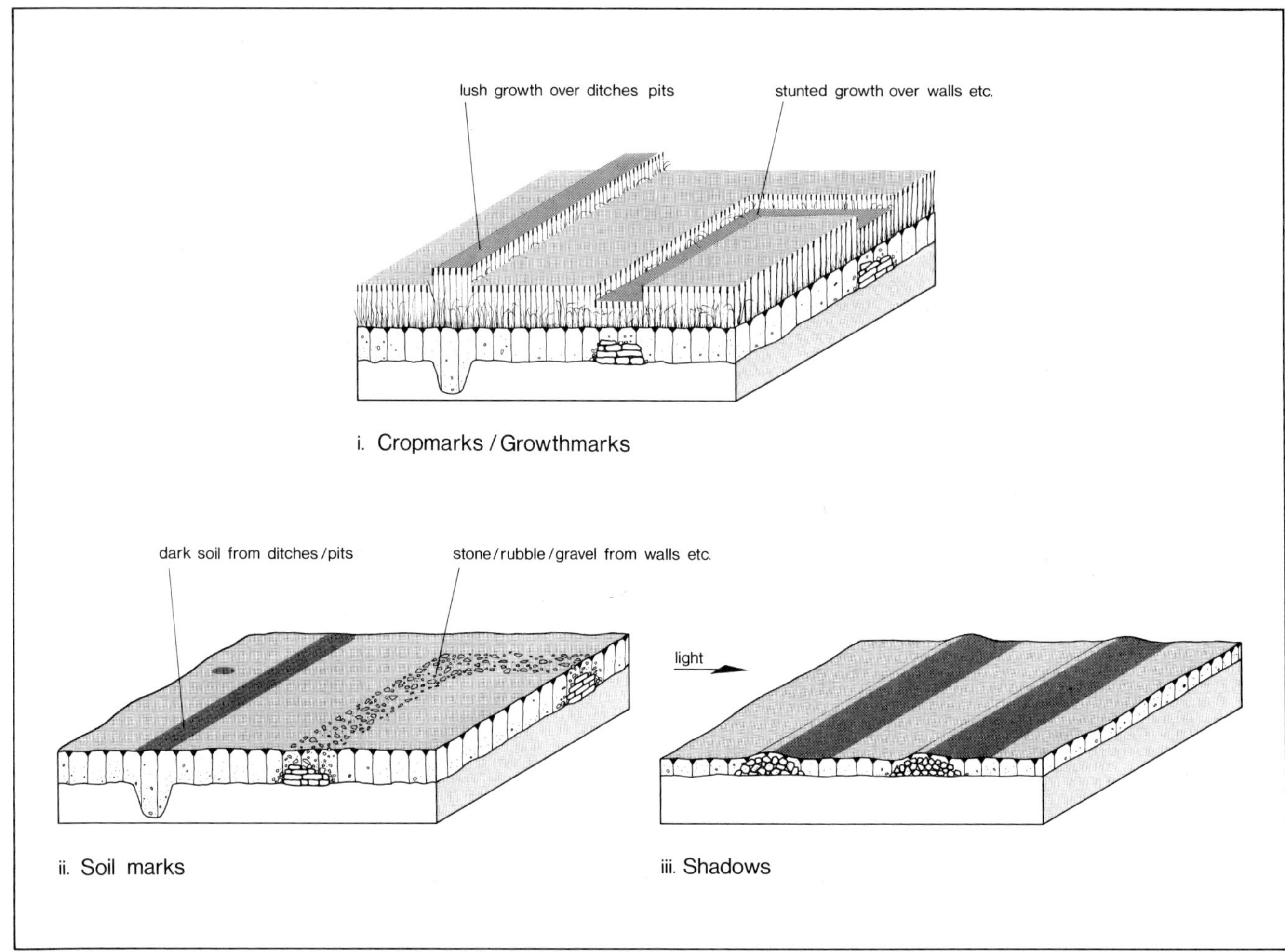

Figure 4   Diagram illustrating the three main ways in which archaeological features can be recognized from conventional aerial photographs

Chance finds

Wherever the ground is disturbed, either deliberately through engineering or cultivation works, or accidentally through land-slip or stock erosion, there is the possibility that objects or traces of structures may be revealed and so betray the existence of a site in the vicinity. Potsherds, flint tools, metal objects, coins, animal bones, worked stone, mortar, charcoal, and even human remains may come to light in this way. The finder should ideally take the pieces to a local museum or archaeological unit for identification and recording, otherwise the full significance of the finds may never be known.

It is always important to record the circumstances under which chance finds were made, their position within the plot of land in which they were found (a map is useful here), their depth below the ground surface, the type of soil they were in, and their association with other finds or structures still left in the ground.

Observations

When ground disturbance is going to take place in an area suspected as being of archaeological interest, a skilled archaeologist may watch the work being undertaken and be on hand to record and advise on anything that comes to light. When something of interest does turn up unexpectedly, most contractors or workmen will halt work for a time while photographs are taken, a drawing made, or finds collected and recorded. When important finds are made, perhaps human burials or a substantial structure, work may need to be halted for a longer time.

Trial trenching

Exploratory excavations are sometimes undertaken to confirm the presence or absence of buried features or visible earthworks, and if necessary to assess their date, extent, and condition of preservation. Potentially interesting humps and bumps sometimes turn out to be natural formations, while on other occasions quite unpromising sites turn out to be well preserved and very extensive.

Trial trenches are planned to examine small areas, with the aim of gaining the maximum information about below-ground deposits with the minimum of disturbance.

Aerial photography

This has long been recognized as a useful and rapid way of surveying large areas of open countryside, where sites lie on or near the ground surface, and there is no masking vegetation cover like woodland or scrub. A number of general accounts of the methods and potential of aerial photography in

Figure 5 Geophysical survey: A (above) fluxgate gradiometer survey in progress; B (below) plot of results from a geophysical survey at Coneybury Henge, Wiltshire; the area shown is 60m square and was surveyed in two strips each 30m wide; the roughly circular ditch with an entrance at the top can be clearly seen, and traces indicative of a large pit may be noted near the left margin at the top; the sharp, narrow spikes are caused by pieces of recently-deposited iron in the ploughsoil

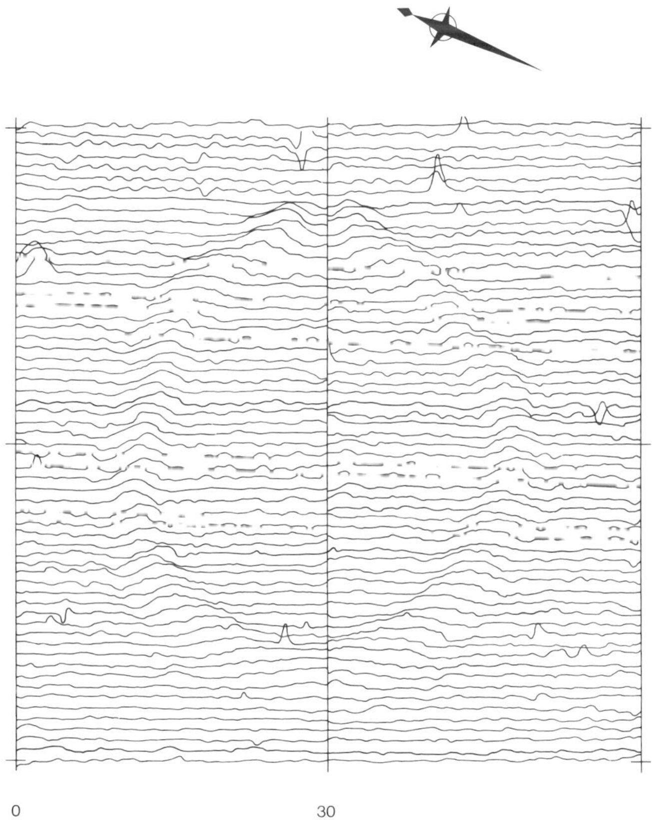

archaeology are available (Allen 1984; Hampton and Palmer 1977; Maxwell 1983; Riley 1982; D R Wilson 1975a; 1982).

Archaeological sites are recognized on conventional photographs in a number of different ways (Fig 4). Earthworks, even those of very low relief, can be identified and recorded when the circumstances are favourable, for example when there is oblique sunlight or a sprinkling of snow to accentuate shadows. Changes in soil colour over archaeological sites, or the presence of scatters of stone on field surfaces, can sometimes be meaningful and will be seen most clearly immediately after ploughing. In the spring and in late summer, differential crop growth over infilled ditches or pits can be clearly seen from high above. Infra-red photography allows the identification of sites through the differential heat retention of disturbed ground or buried features (Baker 1975). Computer enhancement and image plotting techniques allow accurate analysis of aerial photographs (R Palmer 1977).

Field survey

This involves the careful scrutiny of the ground surface for traces of archaeological sites, such as earthworks, walls, hollows, and ditches. Any features found in this way are then plotted onto a large-scale map and, if appropriate, a detailed plan is drawn. Field survey is now widely used in Britain and abroad (Macready and Thompson 1985), and in certain cases may also include the scrutiny of river banks and the sides of drainage channels, because they can provide a glimpse of features which lie below ground level (Pryor 1985a).

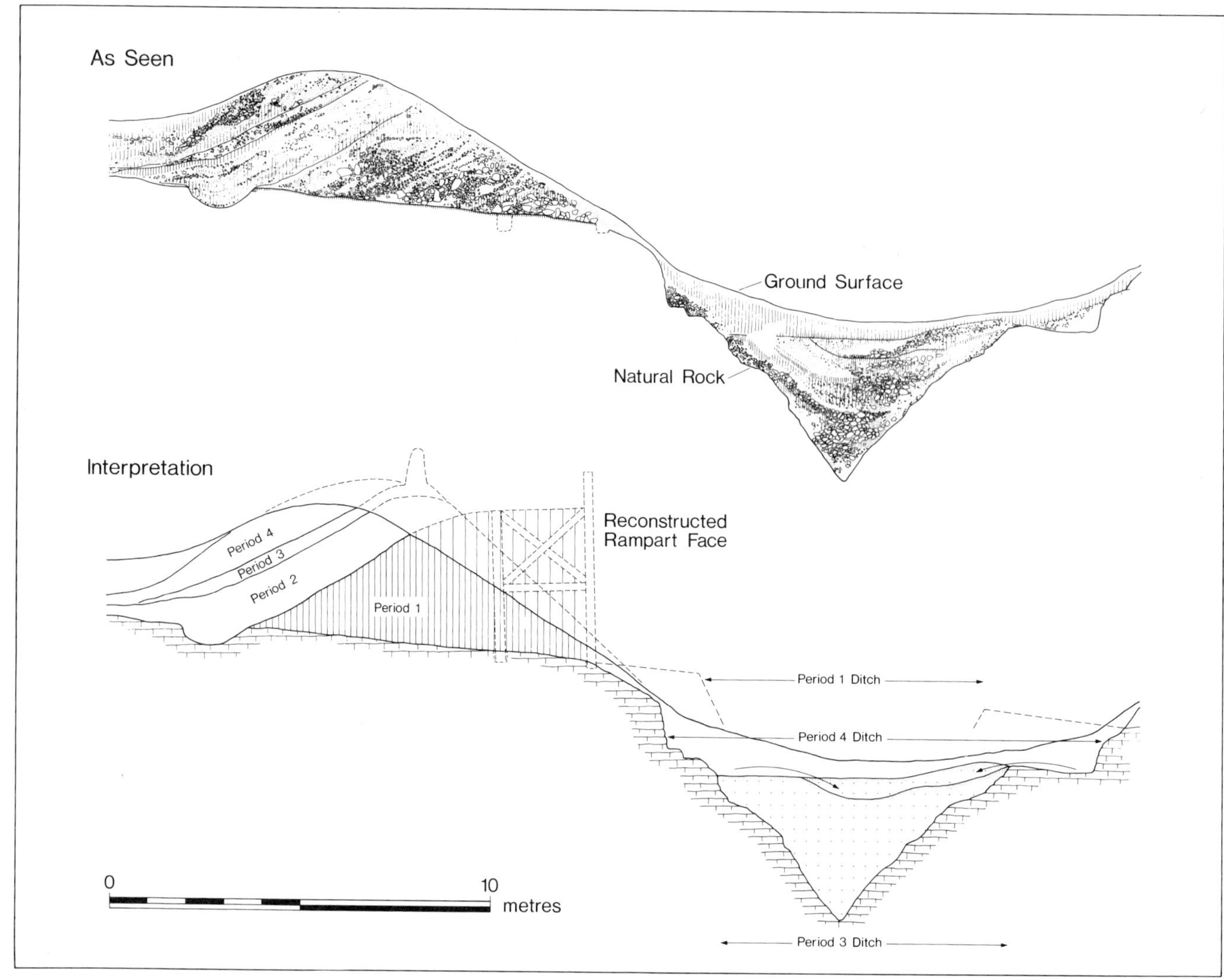

Figure 6   Drawing of archaeological deposits represented in the side of an excavation through the rampart of Danebury hillfort, Hampshire, as recorded (upper) and interpretation (lower) (after Cunliffe 1984, figs 3.4, 3.5, and 3.6)

Fieldwalking

This is the systematic recovery of artefacts from the surface of disturbed ground, usually ploughed fields or land cultivated for afforestation. By carefully plotting the position of all the finds recorded from the exposed ground surface, it may be possible to work out the position and extent of buried features, or identify past activity areas which could not otherwise be discerned from surface remains.

Although fieldwalking has been used as an archaeological technique for many years, only recently has much attention been given to improving the methodology of survey itself and the interpretation of the results (Darvill 1984a; Fasham *et al* 1980; Haselgrove *et al* 1985; Hayfield 1980; Shennan 1985).

Historical records

Written records, including old maps and charters, provide information for many periods after the Roman occupation (Aston and Rowley 1974; Hoskins 1970; C Taylor 1974). These are most plentiful and informative for the medieval and more recent periods, but all early records are of vital importance, because they may show sites which have since disappeared. Place-names and field-names can be very informative about past land-use. Written records can also help in the interpretation of visible features.

When any sort of detailed survey has been undertaken, the results are usually deposited in the appropriate county-based Sites and Monuments Record (SMR), and/or in the National Monuments Record (NMR) maintained by the RCHME. Sometimes the results of a survey are published.

2.4   Archaeological investigation

Investigation is a more thorough process than identifying, verifying, and recording the existence of sites, and is not necessarily consequent upon a previously unknown site being discovered. There has to be a good reason for an investigation to be undertaken, perhaps because a site cannot be preserved and will be destroyed, or because of a need for academic research. Before any site is investigated, detailed non-destructive surveys should be undertaken. These can often bring to light unsuspected details about the site, which can be useful at a preliminary stage of planning an investigation. In addition to the application of the techniques already described,

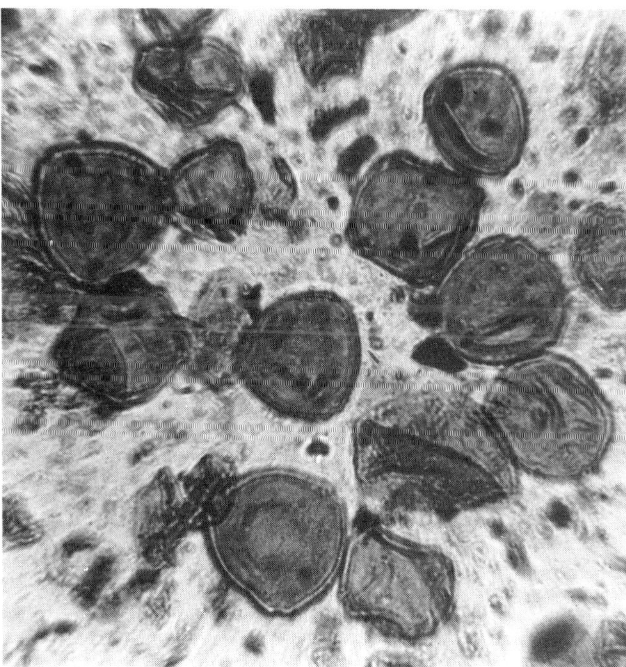

Figure 7   Post-excavation analysis of finds: A (top) sorting fragments of broken medieval window glass; B (bottom left) pollen grains seen under a microscope; C (bottom right) conserving the body found in Lindow Moss, Cheshire, by freeze-drying

the site itself should be recorded by measured drawings, elevations, contour surveys, plans, and photographs. Following this, geophysical and phosphate surveys may yield valuable information without any sub-surface damage to the site.

Geophysical survey

These techniques rely upon differences in the magnetic properties or the electrical resistance of the soil in buried features to build up a picture of pits, ditches, hollows, walls, and surfaces below ground level (Fig 5). The range of techniques available is considerable, but most have limitations on their application; Tite (1972, ch 2) provides a useful general introduction, while A Clark (1975) provides numerous examples of successful surveys.

Phosphate survey

Differences in soil phosphate levels can reflect differences in the type and intensity of past activity, enabling, for example, areas of animal penning to be distinguished from cultivation plots. Small soil samples are taken at regular intervals so ground disturbance is very slight. Gurney (1985) and Craddock *et al* (1985) provide general accounts of the techniques and their applications, with examples from work in the Welland Valley, Cambridgeshire, and elsewhere.

With the results of detailed surveys to hand an excavation strategy can be developed to maximize the effectiveness of the work.

Excavation

This is the most intensive method of investigation used in archaeological work today. The aim is normally to examine one layer or deposit at a time to build up a picture of the sequence of deposition, so that the finds, objects, and structures can be related to one another. Detailed records in the form of plans, sections (Fig 6), photographs, and written descriptions of the layers investigated are made as work progresses. Barker (1977; 1986) provides general introductions to the techniques of archaeological excavation.

The size of an excavation depends upon the scale of the problem under investigation and the resources available. However, it is always important to bear in mind that because excavation involves the removal of deposits it destroys sites, or parts of sites, in the process. Even when parts of a structure are left standing after an excavation, the layers which documented its history and abandonment will probably have been removed.

Post-excavation analysis

Archaeological investigations do not finish with the end of an excavation. Analysis of the finds and the records of structural evidence has to be undertaken, so that the site as excavated can, as it were, be reconstructed on paper. Technical studies of the finds (Fig 7A) and other materials sampled during the excavation provide further details of the date and nature of past activities on the site.[4] Studies of the soils, animal bones, seeds, insect remains, and pollen (Fig 7B) collected during an excavation provide information on the environment and economy of the site and its immediate area.[5] In some cases, finds from an excavation are so fragile that they have to undergo special conservation to arrest decay and prevent further deterioration (Fig 7C). Often, all this work takes longer than the excavation itself.

An important aspect of any archaeological investigation is setting the site in the context of its contemporary landscape. Whenever possible, studies of the local environment should also be undertaken to determine the nature of the surrounding vegetation cover before, during, and after the use of the site, the extent of any flooding if a site is near a river, or the relationship of the site to nearby natural resources and other sites in the neighbourhood. This work may involve surveys of various sorts, trial trenching, and the sampling of naturally formed sediments and soil accumulations for environmental evidence.

Overall, the results of archaeological investigations allow a picture of the landscape at different times to be built up. One of the great attractions of archaeological research is that, because many different periods are represented, a dynamic picture of the changing landscape and the evolution of the countryside can be established.

3 The development of the countryside

3.1 People and past landscapes

In its present form, the English countryside represents the product of many thousands of years of gradual evolution and change, involving natural and human agencies of weathering, erosion, and modification. Often the natural features of the landscape are emphasized with little reference to the effects of man, but archaeological evidence makes it clear that the soils, flora, fauna, and vegetation of today are in large measure the result of man's activities whether in the uplands of the north and west (J G Evans *et al* 1975), or in the lowlands of the south and east (Limbrey and Evans 1978).

Most of what is known about the development of the landscape since the last Ice Age derives from archaeological evidence, supplemented by the results of work on environmental indicators, such as pollen, sediment profiles, and molluscan (snail shell) remains. Some of the basic techniques of recording archaeological evidence in the field have already been touched upon in chapter 2. Technical studies of objects and structures, and the careful piecing together of scraps of evidence collected from many sources, represent the forensic side of archaeological investigations; the aim is always to say something about the people and societies of the past (Fig 8), their activities, and their ways of life. No written records exist from prehistoric times, and even those remaining from Roman and Saxon times are of limited value. It is not until the medieval and post-medieval periods that documentary evidence begins

to make a major contribution to our knowledge of the development of the landscape.

Archaeological evidence can be very difficult to date. The greatest problems are encountered when dealing with features such as banks and ditches which have been constructed in much the same way for thousands of years. The recognition of monuments of such distinctive type as long barrows or round barrows can prove difficult in areas where quarry mounds and waste heaps abound. Ideally some identifying characteristic of the monument itself, or a datable object unequivocally derived from it, is needed before a site can confidently be assigned to a particular period.[6] Thus, trial excavations are sometimes necessary to give substance to a suggested interpretation.

From Roman times down to the present day, our familiar calendar of years and centuries AD provides the chronological framework within which archaeological information is described. When specific dates cannot be determined, terms such as the Saxon period, Tudor times, or the Victorian era provide useful short-hand to refer to general periods. For pre-Roman times, our knowledge of basic chronology is often rather more hazy. Radiocarbon dating provides absolute dates for organic materials preserved in archaeological deposits (Gillespie 1984), and, as more determinations become available, a sound chronological framework is gradually building up (Megaw and Simpson 1979; Darvill 1987). For convenience, however, the prehistoric period is traditionally divided into five basic units or ages, and, as with more recent historical periods, these provide a useful short hand.[7] In chronological order, these are: the Palaeolithic (before 10,000 bc), the Mesolithic (10,000–3500 bc), the Neolithic (3500–2000 bc), the Bronze Age (2000–650 bc), and the Iron Age (650 bc–AD 43) (*see*

Figure 8   Thwing, Humberside: Saxon cemetery under excavation, showing intercutting graves all on a common orientation

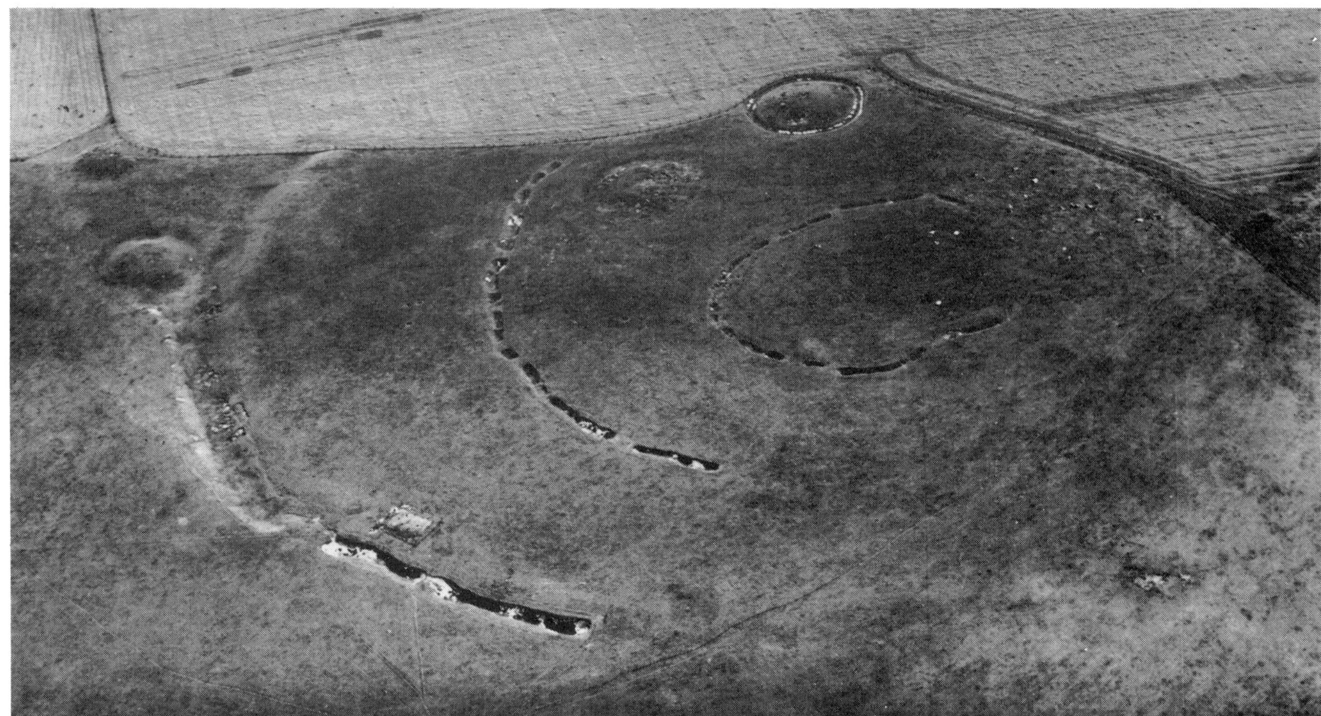

Figure 9   Windmill Hill, Wiltshire: one of a number of Neolithic enclosures known in England which were occupied between about 3000 and 2500 bc by early farming communities; these enclosures seem to have variously served as villages, or ceremonial centres, or both

Glossary under Radiocarbon dating for an explanation of the use of 'bc'). The end of the Iron Age is traditionally marked by the Roman invasion, which began in AD 43 but did not affect northern and western areas until some decades later.

In the following sections, a few of the main trends and developments within prehistoric and later periods are picked out as a background sketch to the information which follows in parts II and III. Attention is here specifically directed towards the appearance of the countryside and man's activities within it. More detailed accounts of the history of the countryside from a variety of different standpoints are provided by C Taylor (1983a), Aston (1985), Rackham (1986), and M Jones (1986).

3.2   The early hunters and gatherers

There is no certainty about when man first arrived in the land now known as Britain, but it was probably between a quarter and a half a million years ago, at a time when the northern hemisphere was experiencing the Pleistocene Ice Age (Wymer 1981). This was not simply a single massive advance and retreat of the polar ice cap, but a series of perhaps five or more successive expansions of the ice caps, separated by periods of retreat when the climate was at least as good as that of today. It was during these warmer, inter-glacial, spells that Palaeolithic people came to Britain as hunters and gatherers in pursuit of herds of wild animals such as horse, deer, bison, wild cattle, and elephant. Some communities may also have visited Britain during the colder spells, but the evidence is very slight.

Hunting and gathering require very little equipment and leave very little trace. Settlements were short-lived, often temporary river-side or lake-side camps, or occupation inside a suitable cave (Roe 1981). Hunting territories were large, and there were undoubtedly long periods when nobody visited Britain at all.

Much of our evidence for these Palaeolithic communities has been disturbed by later glacial advances as the size of the ice caps fluctuated, so that now it is mixed up in river gravels, especially those of large rivers such as the Thames, the Severn, and the Trent. Only very exceptionally have sites been preserved *in situ*, for example in some caves, such as Kent's Cavern in Devon, or where thick mantles of soil and rock covered an occupation site before the next glacial advance had a chance to scour it, for example at Boxgrove, Sussex (Bedwin *et al* 1985, 32–4).

After the retreat of the last ice cap from Britain around 12,000 bc, the picture of settlement becomes rather clearer, not least because the evidence more often survives undisturbed (Campbell 1977). Hunting and gathering remained the mainstay of the economy, and groups were still highly mobile, for Britain was joined to Europe by dry land which is now under the North Sea and the English Channel. Thus hunting bands could roam freely across the whole north European plain.

After 10,000 bc, the arctic conditions associated with the last glacial episode began to change (I Simmons *et al* 1981). The climate became warmer, and by about 9000 bc the vegetation had changed from tundra to a closed woodland, comprising mostly pine and birch. Alongside the development of this woodland, soils improved in quality. These changes traditionally mark the beginning of the Mesolithic period.

Changing landscape meant changing food resources available to the communities exploiting the area, and their technology also changed in order to cope with hunting woodland animals such as red and roe deer, wild boar, brown bears, and cattle, rather than those of the open tundra. Occupation sites, such as coastal settlements convenient for the exploitation of marine resources, and upland hunting camps based on the exploitation of herds of animals grazing the less wooded or open high ground, can be recognized (Jacobi 1978b; 1979). In the course of time, the annual range of seasonal movement undertaken by these groups decreased.

Until 6000 bc, human groups seem to have accepted their environment as they found it, taking the resources it offered and adapting to natural changes. But as groups came to rely on a smaller range of resources, and perhaps as population increased, attempts began to be made to modify or control the environment. In the Peak District, pollen records from the vicinity of settlement sites of later Mesolithic date indicate that substantial areas of forest were being burnt down, probably to concentrate herds of red deer into forest clearings, and to improve the browsing by stimulating the growth of fresh young shoots in the wake of the clearance (Mellars 1976). The full extent of these activities countrywide has yet to be determined.

One factor which may have contributed to the need for attempts to manipulate the environment was the rise in sea level which occurred between about 7000 bc and 5000 bc and caused Britain to be cut off from the continent (I Simmons *et al* 1981, 83). As a result communities in Britain became more insular, using distinctive tool types and a fairly restricted range of animal and plant resources (Jacobi 1976). Groups who had occupied areas covered by the sea must have been forced to move into already settled areas, thereby increasing pressure on the available natural resources (Jacobi 1978a; 1979).

By 3500 bc there was a fairly extensive scatter of hunter-gatherer groups dependent largely on red deer, aurochs, wild boar, and, on the coast, marine resources. Some small-scale clearances in the post-glacial climax forest certainly existed, but the country was still largely wooded.

3.3 Prehistoric farming groups

Possibly the most influential event in the history of the English countryside took place between about 3500 and 2900 bc; it was during this period that farming was adopted as the basis of the subsistence economy. This marks the beginning of the Neolithic period (Whittle 1977). The effects of this change must be seen not so much in the inevitable abandonment of earlier types of tools and weapons, appropriate for hunting and gathering, and the development of new types of object, such as axes, pottery containers, and quernstones, appropriate for farming, as in the changing relationship between man and the countryside.

Figure 10   Winterbourne Stoke crossroads, near Amesbury, Wiltshire: a linear barrow cemetery, comprising a Neolithic long barrow and a variety of Bronze Age round barrows; this cemetery was probably in use from about 2700 through to 1500 bc

Figure 11   Fisherwick, Staffordshire: plan of Iron Age enclosures and field boundaries beside the River Tame, as revealed by excavation and aerial photography (after C Smith 1979, fig 4)

The manipulation of plants and animals with the purpose of providing a predictable and sustainable supply of food led to greater control of the environment (*see* P Fowler 1983; Mercer 1981c). Farming could be more easily undertaken in cleared areas, and from about 3200–2900 bc pollen diagrams from many parts of the country record clearance episodes and the establishment of grassland. Evidence for cereal cultivation, and the attendant weeds of cultivation, can also be found in these pollen records (A Smith 1981). Cultivation marks of third millennium bc date, probably made by an ard, have been recorded as linear grooves scored into the natural subsoil in a criss-cross pattern below the South Street long barrow, Wiltshire (P Fowler 1971; Ashbee *et al* 1979).

Not all of the landscape was, however, settled by early farming groups. Attention at first focused on well-drained, easily cultivated land, such as may be found in the major river valleys, on the downlands of central and southern England, and the coastal fringes. The uplands were apparently only used for occasional hunting forays and as the source of fine stone for the manufacture of tools and weapons.

Farming brought changes in the social structure and organization of the population. Whereas previously life had depended upon the availability of constant supplies of natural foodstuffs, plants, and animal herds, and the skill of the hunter, land and sufficient hands to work it now became valued resources. Ties to the land meant that settlements became more permanent, some of them developing into massive causewayed enclosures, such as the one on Windmill Hill, Wiltshire (Fig 9). This permanence is also reflected in the burial grounds of the early farmers, for many were elaborated by the construction of monumental mounds and cairns of various sorts – long barrows and megalithic tombs as they are generally known (Daniel 1950; Darvill 1982; Ashbee 1984).

Thus, the countryside not only began to lose its natural clothing of woodland, but for the first time artificial constructions began to appear (S Piggott 1981; Megaw and Simpson 1979, ch 3). Barrows and settlements have already been mentioned. Mines for flint and stone caused quarry scars and waste heaps, trackways were built in wet areas to facilitate communications (wheeled vehicles were unknown at this time), land was enclosed, clearance cairns grew, fields were established, and farmyard waste was spread over the arable plots.

Most areas experienced changing fortunes during the course of time, and by about 2000 bc the distribution of farming groups had changed quite markedly. Agriculturally less rich areas had been brought into use, while more specialized economies, involving the seasonal movement of people and stock, spread through upland areas (Darvill 1986a, ch 4). Fluctuations in settlement intensity can often be glimpsed in many areas (Whittle 1978; Darvill 1984b). The climate between about 2500 and 1500 bc was warmer and drier than that of today, and the mid second millennium represents a zenith in the distribution and intensity of prehistoric farming (Burgess 1980).

The introduction of metalworking about 2000 bc, which traditionally marks the start of the Bronze Age, had little effect on farming since most of the early products were probably luxury items, such as daggers, trinkets, and ornaments, along with a few woodworking and craftsmens' tools, many of which appear to have ended up as grave goods for the wealthy. Round barrows, sometimes clustered together as impressive cemeteries (Fig 10), replaced long barrows as burial places. Rapidly changing styles of metalwork and pottery may be taken to reflect the opulence of the time, where access to exotic goods and fashion seems to have counted for much (Bradley 1984, ch 4).

Areas like Dartmoor, the North York Moors, and the Cheviots were extensively farmed, and the overall impression gained from the available evidence for this period is of a densely populated and well-organized landscape (Fleming 1982). Isolated farms and scattered clusters of houses were the norm over most of England, although the range of crops grown and the balance between crops and animals in the economy naturally varied from region to region (Burgess 1980, ch 5). Woodland management was well developed by the Bronze Age, after over 1000 years of experience in coppicing and pollarding (Rackham 1977).

The later part of the second millennium, the middle and late Bronze Age, appears to have been a time of change over much of the country (*see* papers in Barrett and Bradley 1980). Signs of trouble may be seen in settlements enclosed by palisades, earth ramparts, or stone walls. By 1000 bc many upland areas were in serious decline; some had been abandoned, and blanket bog was already forming over uncultivated fields and deserted settlements (J Turner 1981, 256). Why this should have happened is a matter for much debate. It has been claimed by some that a deterioration in the climate was largely to blame, while others point to soil exhaustion after nearly 500 years of continuous exploitation in fragile environments (A Harding 1982). Whatever the reason, the effects were widespread. Arable cultivation declined in many areas, and there is some evidence for the widespread adoption of cattle herding, even in places such as Wessex where arable agricultural practices had become fossilized in the landscape as Celtic field systems, some of which are still visible today. There were social consequences too. Population was forced into small areas, and there was greater competition for resources. The result was considerable tension. Metalworkers were turning out very large quantities of weapons, especially swords and spears, and there is some evidence from human bodies found with weapons still embedded in them that these products were used in anger.

By 800 bc hillforts, defended villages perched on strategic hilltops, were being built, and by 500 bc several thousand were established across western, central, and northern England, while defended enclosures were becoming more common in other areas (Cunliffe 1978a). These nucleated settlements appear to herald a phase of increased autonomy of small social groups, which were probably almost self-sufficient. Iron began to be exploited after about 650 bc, a date which traditionally marks the beginning of the Iron Age. This metal was widely available, in contrast to copper, tin, and lead which had to be obtained from distant sources in order to make bronze. Moreover, iron became used for making basic farming equipment and tools,

Figure 12   Bancroft Roman Villa, Buckinghamshire: site under excavation, showing circular and rectangular buildings

Figure 13   Motte-and-bailey castle at Yielden, Bedfordshire, built by the Trailly family shortly after the Norman conquest; the motte mound and wide moat around the bailey can be seen

such as sickles, hooks, plough tips, mattocks, chisels, hammers, and knives, as much as for weapons.

Settlement and economy during the Iron Age followed regionally diverse patterns (Cunliffe 1978a). The landscape itself was probably extensively occupied, and although large areas of woodland undoubtedly still existed, in comparison with earlier times the landscape was decidedly open in aspect. By 300 bc the climate was probably very similar to that of today (J Turner 1981, 261).

In the west and north, small autonomous family groups seem to have been the norm, and are represented archaeologically by numerous single farmsteads which were well adapted to locally variable farming practices. In the south and east a basic hierarchy in settlement, and by implication in social organization, can be seen with major hillforts and small villages representing nucleated occupation and around them numerous smaller dispersed farmsteads and hamlets (*see* papers in Cunliffe and Miles 1984). The landscape itself continued to be well ordered, with fields defined by hedges and ditches, trackways linking settlements, and unenclosed grazing areas beyond the more intensively-used enclosed land (Fig 11).

This was largely the situation before the Roman conquest, although in some parts of south-eastern England leaders who were strongly influenced by the affluence and culture of the Roman world tried to emulate Mediterranean custom by acquiring, through trade, exotic eating and drinking equipment, wine, and luxury food, perhaps in return for slaves, silver, corn, iron, and hunting dogs. In these areas coins were used, and the beginnings of a market economy may have been established by the time of the Roman conquest (Cunliffe and Rowley 1976).

3.4   The Roman countryside

The landscape which the Romans took over was already well laid out and, for the most part, productive. Many farmsteads continued much as before, although the influence of Roman lifestyles had made their mark on most sites by about AD 100. Villa estates developed in the south and east, while in the north and west native farmsteads continued along traditional lines (Rivet 1964; 1967).

The major changes wrought by the Romans lay in the reorganization of the political and economic infrastructure (Frere 1967; Salway 1981; Wacher 1979). A strict hierarchical government was imposed on what had previously been a politically fragmentary society. Status was determined by position within this new hierarchy; property and wealth were qualifications for power and status and could bring the benefits of Roman styles of civilization. In this way, some pre-existing Iron Age farmsteads became the centres of villa estates soon after the conquest, while others simply disappeared. Villas were, however, more than just well-appointed residences for the wealthy (Rivet 1969). They were the centres of sometimes very extensive estates, and, in addition to the domestic quarters, there were usually offices and agricultural buildings (Fig 12).

Substantial towns were established across the country, providing administrative, political, and market centres (Wacher 1974). In some cases, these towns were near pre-existing centres of population, large hillforts, and *oppida* sites. In other cases, towns were established adjacent to major forts.

Small towns developed in the countryside, often at road junctions, as markets and resting places for travellers (Finch Smith 1987). In addition to the farmsteads, hamlets, and villas, there were also temples and shrines to serve the religious needs of the population (Rodwell 1980).

Among other changes in the countryside was a dramatic increase in nucleated rural industry (Miles 1982). Some, such as brick and tile works and stone quarries, were new developments to serve Roman tastes in building style. Others, such as metal mines for silver, lead, and iron, were operated on a scale far greater than in previous centuries, and some of the mineral wealth at least was destined to be transported back to the Mediterranean, rather than for use in Britain. Ironworking and pottery production, the latter especially concentrated in areas such as the New Forest, Nene Valley, the Oxford region, and southern Dorset, were also major rural industries in Roman times.

The uplands, which had been only sparsely occupied when the Romans arrived, were opened up principally as sources of raw materials, especially metals, but also as military training areas and frontier zones. Perhaps the most important such area was around Hadrian's Wall in Northumberland and Cumbria, but there were also notable military installations along the Welsh Marches and in the south-west. Elsewhere too the military presence must have been felt, as both permanent installations and practice works were established amongst civilian settlements (Clack and Haselgrove 1982 on northern England).

Whereas communications had been essentially local in the Iron Age, the new organization imposed by the Romans required an altogether different type of road network, much of which still survives within the present day road system (Margary 1973). River works, canals, bridges, harbour works, and lighthouses were also products of Roman engineering skills.

3.5 The medieval countryside, AD 450–1700

Traditionally, the centuries immediately after the collapse of the Roman administration in the fifth century AD are known as the Dark Ages, but recent archaeological work, usefully summarized by Sawyer (1978), Hodges (1982), and Arnold (1984), has shed much light on events during the period between the fifth and the seventh centuries. It is now clear that the greatest effect of the Roman collapse was the loss of the organizational side of economic and political life. Without the market system and the demand for goods to be shifted about the country, patterns of settlement and land-use became rather more simplified, localized, and in many respects rather like conditions before the Roman invasion.

Figure 14   Laxton, Nottinghamshire: a rare example of an open-field system surviving from medieval times, when this sort of landscape would have been the norm rather than the exception; the photograph shows the south field with its original strips separated by furrows (visible as cropmarks) grouped together in recent times, but remaining unenclosed except for the hedged field in the centre; at the bottom of the picture, along the stream, is part of the common land

Small, essentially self-sufficient, farmsteads and villages became the main centres of population, towns fell out of use, and there was probably an overall decrease in population. Some earlier hillforts were reoccupied (Burrow 1981). In many areas woodland probably expanded after its heavy use during Roman times and as agricultural land was abandoned. Demand for timber for building remained high, however, as stone was no longer used. The uplands were almost deserted at this time (Mytum 1986).

The late Roman and immediate post-Roman period saw a great many population movements in northern Europe. During the fifth century, Angles and Saxons started to establish themselves in eastern England, heralding a period of close contact between England and the Germanic tribes across the North Sea and English Channel (Dixon 1976).

By the ninth century, a pattern of small villages and farmsteads was well established. Christianity had become widely adopted, and there was an increasing number of ecclesiastical landholdings. Political unity developed first through the development of tribal units and later through the emergence of ruling families at the head of regional kingdoms (*see* papers in D M Wilson 1976).

By the tenth century, some of these kingdoms in the south of England had become very powerful, with the system of feudal control over landholdings and labour (Hinton 1977). Industries were once again expanding, and stone began to be used again for important buildings. Continental trade increased, and ports and trading posts prospered. In the north, raids by Vikings and Norsemen from about AD 790 onwards posed a special threat, which resulted in greater attention to defence. Although place-names suggest considerable Viking settlement

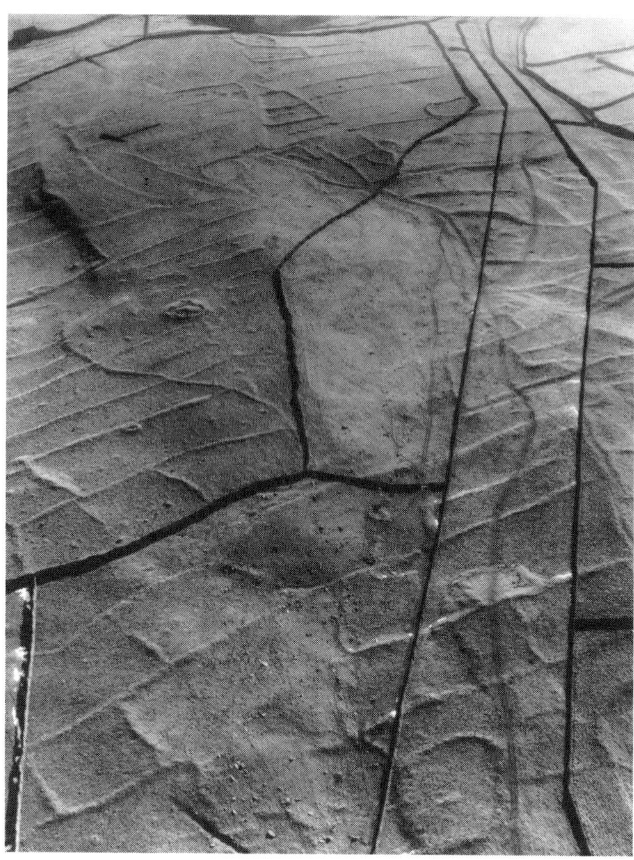

Figure 15   Medieval and post-medieval enclosure: A (left) Chelmorton, Derbyshire; two phases of enclosure can be seen in the pattern of field boundaries; near the village, the fields are long, narrow plots or crofts which were probably first set out in the medieval period, each plot being attached to one of the houses; further out are roughly square and rectangular fields, and these represent the enclosure of the former common fields and pasture in 1809; B (right) Grassington, North Yorkshire; post-medieval field boundaries cross-cutting late prehistoric fields

(M Gelling 1978, ch 9), and Viking graves and weapons are known, there is at present little archaeological evidence for actual Viking occupation sites.

The Norman conquest of 1066, and the events immediately thereafter, produced little immediate effect on the landscape (Loyn 1962). The pre-existing feudal system lent itself to the imposition of Norman knights and barons in positions of importance.

One new feature in many areas was the construction of castles as strongholds for noblemen (Fig 13). At first these were confined to areas of unrest, but later became widespread as symbols of the power of their feudal owners (Renn 1968; R Brown 1976). The Church also gained much land in the years after the conquest and established itself as a major landholder. Royal estates and Royal forests represented land managed in new ways according to strict laws (Young 1979).

Towns expanded as commercial, political, and religious centres, by the twelfth century reaching similar proportions to the towns of Roman times (Platt 1976). Markets were important for the redistribution of foodstuffs to the growing urban population, and to channel food and raw materials from the producers to traders and craftsmen (Britnell 1981).

The majority of the population remained in rural areas, and many communities were largely self-sufficient (C Taylor 1983a; Aston 1985). Their need for a range of resources is reflected in the shape and size of medieval parishes, which often mirrored the manor or estate landholding. Typically, parishes include meadow land, arable, pasture, and woodland. Fields were unenclosed and cultivated on a communal basis, each individual having a number of strips of land scattered among the fields (Rowley 1981; A Baker and Butlin 1973). At Laxton, Nottinghamshire, an example of the type of early medieval field system common in midland England is still preserved (Fig 14). Rural industries were small in scale, usually to meet local needs. Population probably increased between the eleventh and the thirteenth centuries, and there is some evidence for the expansion of settlement into less fertile areas. The uplands in particular were extensively occupied at this time, on a scale not seen since the Bronze Age (Moorhouse 1986).

Throughout the Middle Ages there were fluctuations in fortune and great regional variations in prosperity (Sawyer 1976; Platt 1978; Cantor 1982). A major trend, however, was the gravitation of land into the hands of fewer people, especially the Church, the Crown, and favoured important families. With high population levels in rural areas, farming and rural industry was labour intensive, and great skill in managing and exploiting the landscape developed, especially in the case of woodland management (Rackham 1976; 1980). The introduction of rabbits in the twelfth century and the establishment of extensive deer parks and hunting forests provided new avenues for employment. The twelfth and thirteenth centuries were boom periods in rural areas, and the large agricultural surpluses were used to finance the building or rebuilding of many great castles, churches, abbeys, and manors.

Rural prosperity reached a peak in the early fourteenth century. Demesne farming, under the direct control of estates, gave way to tenant farming. Landlords thus reaped the benefits at the expense of those actually working the land. Enclosure of land first started at this time, and in many areas there was a swing from arable to pasture. The Black Death in the early fourteenth century dealt a major blow to many areas, and it was over the ensuing decades that many villages were either deserted or shrunk to a fraction of their former size (M Beresford and Hurst 1971).

The stabilization of life in the countryside from the fifteenth century onwards provides the origin for many familiar features. Parish boundaries, field boundaries, woods, ponds, mill streams, and trackways, fossilized at this time, remained unchanged for centuries.

Although the Stuart and Tudor periods were politically important, since they saw Britain rise to a position of power in Europe, in the countryside change was slow and unspectacular. Enclosure continued, and rural populations declined as the towns grew. Less labour-intensive farming, especially pastoral farming, became widespread. The single most significant event was the Dissolution of the monasteries in the mid-sixteenth century, when the very extensive landholdings of the Church were broken up and divided between the Crown and favoured statesmen (Platt 1978, ch 7). By the end of the sixteenth century, interest in the potential of farming was increasing and heralded a new age of experimentation and wealth, which in time changed the face of the countryside.

3.6 The post-medieval countryside, AD 1700–1900

The eighteenth and nineteenth centuries witnessed major changes in the countryside. The processes of development, which began in the late seventeenth century, gathered momentum, and produced the effect which has been described as the agricultural revolution (Chambers and Mingay 1966; Mingay 1981). Drainage schemes, new crops, new breeds of livestock, and labour-saving machines lay at the heart of the changes in farming practice, but these could not have been introduced had it not been for important changes in landscape organization and increased capital investment in landscape management. The enclosure of land transformed the appearance of the countryside (Tate 1967; M Turner 1980) and, for the first time in many centuries, parcelled the land into more usable units (Fig 15).

Employment in farming decreased, but while many people no doubt moved to the cities, which lay at the hub of the industrial revolution, there were also new opportunities in the countryside. Market gardening was one growth area, as too was the creation and management of country houses, parks, and gardens. Engineering and building work also increased, for, while those living and working in the medieval countryside had tended to develop management skills appropriate to the landscape, by the nineteenth century the landscape had to be adapted wherever possible to suit the new farming practices. This often meant drainage, the creation of water meadows, river works, and of course the construction of new barns, animal shelters, and equipment stores.

The industrial revolution also had its effect on the countryside (Ashton 1948; Mathias 1969). Indeed many of the industries relying on fast-flowing streams to drive water wheels initiated the industrial changes within an essentially rural setting. Raw materials were also taken from the countryside for processing in the towns. The uplands were particularly heavily exploited for metal ores, minerals, and stone (Collins 1978, 18). The scale of these workings was unprecedented. Timber was also used in very large quantities, but many of the skills of woodland management common in earlier periods were in decline, and stocks were not replenished in many areas.

Some rural industries such as flour-milling, paper-making, fulling, woodworking, brickmaking, quarrying, and agricultural engineering expanded, creating in the process their own distinctive archaeological monuments (Buchanan 1972).

The other great change was the opening up of the countryside through the construction of railways, canals, and roads. Thousands were employed in this work and the effect on the landscape was startling. Even upland areas did not escape, for the new lines of communications went wherever there were goods, resources, or people to be moved.

3.7 The countryside in the twentieth century

Since 1900, the speed and intensity of change in the countryside, in terms of the development of the landscape, has been greater than at any previous time (Blunden and Curry 1985, ch 2). The effects of economic and political decisions have also been more decisive than ever before. The need to produce more food during both the world wars stimulated the development of a more efficient agricultural industry. Government interventionism through the Agriculture Act 1947, and subsequent price support systems, have encouraged the expansion of productivity and promised sufficient capital for improvement works as well as research and development. The result has been a second revolution in farm practice, with highly mechanized farms predominating in many areas.

The impact of new farming systems on the landscape derives mostly from the scale of the operations now possible, perhaps most clearly exemplified by the changes in ploughing technology this century (Fig 16). Land which only 100 years ago was considered unproductive can now be improved through the use of chemicals and, perhaps more important from the archaeological viewpoint, through the use of massive tractors and machines that can clear ground on steep slopes, remove huge boulders, and plough heavy ground to improve drainage. Naturally there is still much regional variation in the extent and impact of these changes, but the establishment of special status areas, such as the Less Favoured Areas defined by the European Economic Commission, spread the resources for improvement schemes more widely. Since the last war, emphasis in the private sector has been placed upon livestock and cereals, with a consequent decline of the skills needed to use and manage other types of landscape, such as woodland and wetland. The Forestry Commission, established in 1919, has largely been responsible for replenishing stocks of timber which had declined during the late medieval and post-medieval periods (Forestry Commission 1978).

Alongside the changes in farming, rural industries have declined and, in some cases, died completely. In their place, the extraction of mineral resources, notably gravels, sand, stone, minerals, coal, and metals, has increased. Associated secondary working and processing of these materials have tended to be focused in urban and urban fringe locations. In contrast to earlier times, extraction has concentrated on a few sites at an enormous scale.

Figure 16 Changes in ploughing and traction 1850–1986: A (top) ploughing with horses at Lockinge, Berkshire, late nineteenth century; B (bottom) steam ploughing with a traction engine during the First World War; C (opposite top) tractor and plough of the 1930s at Burford, Oxfordshire; D (opposite below) tractor and reversible plough of the 1980s at Dover, Kent

Figure 16 C (top) and D (bottom); caption opposite

Concern to ensure orderly and controlled planning in urban and built-up areas, enunciated in the early Town and Country Planning Acts passed in the 1930s and 1940s, was not widely applied in the countryside (Blacksell and Gilg 1981).

Since the late 1970s, the range and scale of demands for which the countryside can be exploited has changed again. Leisure interests and tourism are the biggest growth sectors at present, but the demands of military training, water catchment, waste disposal, and urban expansion must also take their place alongside farming and forestry. Such demands have been made before, but because viability and profitability are now often only measured in terms of growth and expansion, rather than sustainability, the competition for space in the countryside has become acute.[8] The countryside is, of course, always changing, and will continue to do so as long as man continues to use it. Accepting this is the key to developing strategies for the future of the archaeological heritage. The way forward must lie in an integrated approach to the use and management of the countryside, which will ensure that archaeological factors are recognized in the constant reshaping of our surroundings.

4 Archaeological resource management

4.1 The meaning of management

As the balance of interests in the countryside becomes more complex, and as there is increasing pressure placed on rural resources for their economic and amenity value, the need for positive management of the landscape as a whole becomes more acute. Since the archaeological heritage is a non-renewable and irreplaceable resource, its care needs to be integrated with the overall management of the countryside on a scale not previously attempted in England.[9]

The development of effective archaeological resource management in the countryside has three main objectives:

i   To retain the rich diversity of archaeological remains that is known to exist in the landscape

ii   To make the archaeological heritage satisfy the demands made upon it by society as a whole

iii   To reconcile conflict and competition for the use of land containing ancient monuments

Often such objectives find common ground with the aims of other countryside interests, for example the conservation of old pasture on archaeological sites for its wildlife habitat value, or the maintenance of wetlands for their flora, fauna, and landscape value (P Fowler 1968; Countryside Commission 1980c; Lambrick 1985a). In other cases, overlap with the development of sporting, amenity, leisure, and recreational services may be found. Such cases are dealt with more fully in parts II and III of this volume.

Archaeological resource management applies to all identified sites, not simply the best known, most spectacular, or potentially picturesque examples (Morgan Evans 1986, 9). The notion of identifiable 'historic landscapes', which has become a popular term in recent years (Polytechnic of North London 1978; Wager 1981; Swanwick 1982; Haynes 1983), is misleading and inappropriate, in all but a few contexts, for three main reasons. First, all landscapes are historic in the sense that, as they appear today, they are the products of periods of development and evolution. Second, all types of landscape include some historic features, despite the fact that in some areas they are better preserved than in others. Third, there is no single universal management strategy that can be applied to all archaeological sites. Each needs to be managed within the context of the landscape in which it is situated, taking full account of ownership, prevailing land-use, and land potential.

One of the axioms of effective management is that the landscape is not fossilized in any sense but is allowed to change over time, just as it always has done. The term 'historic landscape' should be reserved for the very few areas of the countryside which have been preserved as time capsules, comprising earlier landscapes almost untouched by subsequent land-use.

The term 'site' is also one that needs defining when used in the context of archaeological management. As will have already become clear, archaeological remains in the countryside represent many different past activities, and these can differ greatly in scale from a few accidentally lost objects spread over a few square metres, through to field systems with associated settlements and burial grounds occupying perhaps several hectares. All may be described as sites in the general sense, but, at the same time, a large and complex site may be made up of several elements, of which perhaps only a small proportion can be seen above ground. Where large areas of landscape have been investigated, it is often difficult to sort out which sites were in use at the same time, and where one site ends and another begins (Fig 17). Thus, although the term 'site' is used to describe any area of land containing archaeological remains, in practice the term needs to be qualified with some sort of assessment of what is actually represented.

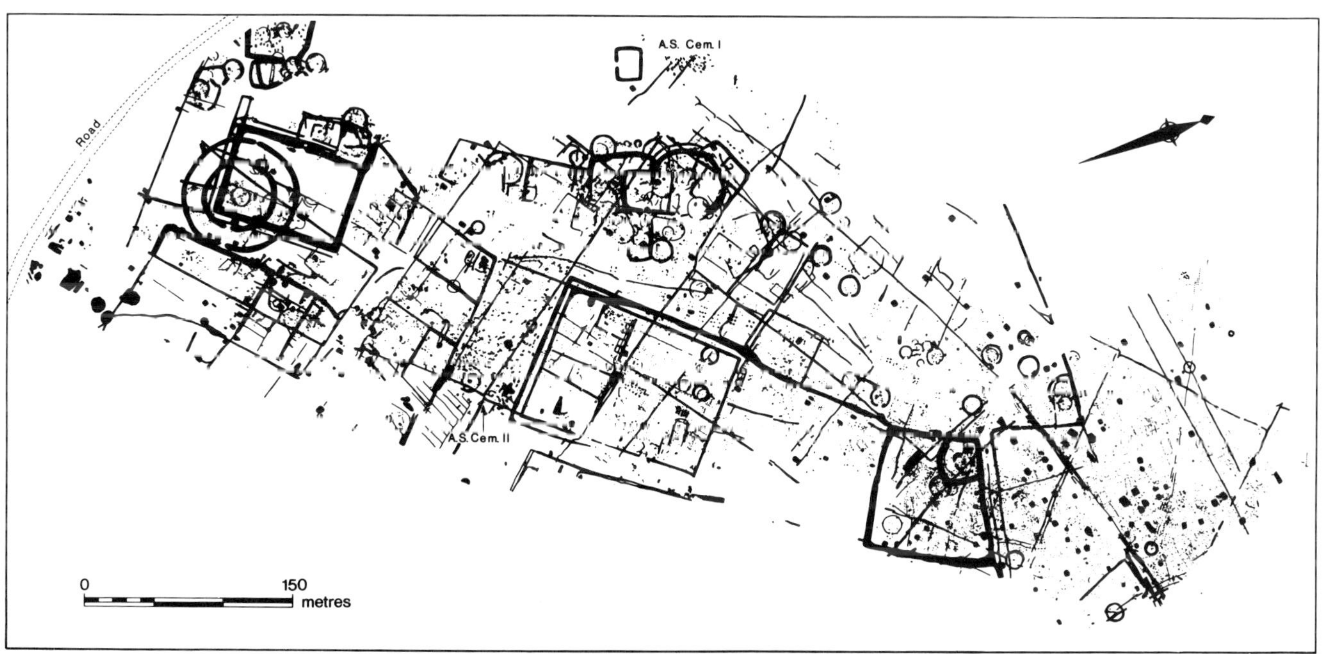

Figure 17   Mucking, Essex: occupation of the same gravel terrace for thousands of years has resulted in the build-up of a palimpsest landscape, comprising many overlapping sites relating to different periods and different activities (after Haigh et al 1983, fig 62)

Management of the archaeological resource may be orientated specifically towards one or more of the three general objectives set out above, and these may be pursued in isolation, in series, or in parallel with one another. The main ways in which these objectives are achieved fall into three groups and may be summarized as follows.

Curatorial management

The main aim here is to arrest the natural and man-induced processes of decay affecting the long-term well-being of a site, and, through whatever measures are considered appropriate, prolong its life. There are two basic approaches: conservation and protection.

Conservation is not so much a technique or a methodology, but rather a philosophy which promotes a positive relationship between change and preservation (Green 1981). No specific provision is made for particular eventualities; rather, day-to-day activities are undertaken and planned with the care of the known resource to the fore. Thus, if a new access road is needed, it is planned precisely to avoid the position of known remains, and if land needs improving, those areas free of known features are selected. If accidental damage to a known feature is noted, for example the erosion of a site by livestock or visitors, remedial action is taken (Fig 18). In this way, the archaeological resource is never actually under threat, because problems are dealt with before they become serious.

Protection is slightly different from conservation, as it essentially involves the recognition, or anticipation, of a range of specific threats, and the main aim of any action taken is to avert them. By its very nature, protection involves close definition both of the designated area and of the threats against which it is shielded.

Exploitation

The archaeological resource can be used for public enjoyment through interpretation and display, or for academic interest through investigation and excavation. Such uses almost inevitably alter the character of the site (Beazley 1971, 142), and sometimes contribute to its decay or destruction (Fig 19).

Presentation and display may take many forms. At the most simple, a site may be cleared to make it visible, and a path made round it to allow access. Alternatively, on a site expected to command greater interest and a higher level of visitor attention, displays, explanations, and visitor facilities may be provided. In exceptional cases, excavations may be undertaken specifically to expose interesting or significant detail. Safety considerations have to be taken into account, and some of a site's authenticity may be lost through strengthening and repair work, and through trying to show more than one phase of a site's development at once.

Rescue excavation

Archaeological remains cannot normally be removed without destroying them, or at least destroying the relationships which existed between components of the monument and the surrounding landscape. In exceptional circumstances, when preservation is no longer possible, because the value of the archaeological resource is outweighed by some other factor, a

Figure 18   Conservation work on archaeological monuments: A (left) returfing an eroded rampart at Barbury Camp, Wiltshire; B (right) investigating and restoring a collapsed section of Hadrian's Wall, Northumberland

Figure 19 Stonehenge, Wiltshire: until recently this well-known site was fully accessible, but, with over 650,000 visitors a year, erosion of the monument and over-crowding led to the central area being closed off. The site is currently the subject of a special study to find new and appropriate ways of displaying and interpreting it; as a well-known monument, it highlights the problems connected with managing the exploitation of the archaeological heritage

site may be excavated to record as much as possible of its structure and form (Fig 20), and thus in effect preserve it on paper (HBMC 1986b). Such work must form a valuable contribution to our understanding of the past, and the selection of sites to be treated in this way is partly conditioned by academic priorities at the time (HBMC 1986a). There are insufficient resources to excavate all the sites which need rescuing. Nevertheless, the underlying aim is to rescue evidence that would otherwise be lost. If full-scale excavation is not possible, then observation work may be undertaken to record evidence as it is disturbed (*see above*, chapter 2.3).

4.2 Management in practice and the development of management plans

In practical terms, the management of archaeological sites can only be undertaken efficiently with commitment on the part of the landowner and land-user, and the integration of management needs with all other demands placed on the land. Some financial assistance may be available through management agreements for capital works or continuous maintenance, and these are considered further in a later section. It has been found that where the management of sites is integrated with existing land-use practice, little or no cost is incurred in their maintenance (Gosling 1985).

It is recommended that a management plan for the archaeological heritage of any land containing monuments is drawn up by, or on behalf of, the landowner (Morgan Evans 1986). This need not be elaborate, but ideally it should form part of a wide-ranging farm or estate plan. Figure 21 shows the main steps in drawing up a management plan with reference to the archaeological heritage, but it must always be remembered that such a plan is only a tool for administration, and that its exact nature will depend upon individual needs and controls. A number of general discussions of management plans, and their construction and use, are available (Margules and Usher 1980; J Wood and Warren 1978; Countryside Commission 1986; Leavy *et al* 1986).

Management plans drawn up by public bodies tend to be very formal and detailed, so that everyone concerned knows exactly what is involved. Rather less formal plans are usually appropriate for private holdings, but if they are drawn up as part of an application for an improvement grant, or some other similar purpose, they may have to conform to certain standards set down by MAFF or the Forestry Commission.

The value of management plans lies primarily in the fact that their preparation serves to focus attention on the implications of the archaeological resource for land-use in general. In addition, such plans provide a quarry of detailed information for decision-making in the course of day-to-day activities and serve also to promote continuity by emphasizing the long-term strategy.

Before any management plan can be drawn up, or any management implications considered, some basic information on the nature, scale, and distribution of the archaeological resource needs to be collected. Such information may already exist in greater or lesser detail in the local county Sites and Monuments Record. Every county in England now has provision for a Sites and Monuments Record, with qualified staff able to help with both general and specific enquiries relating to management and planning (see Appendix A). Experience suggests that it is often useful for a qualified archaeologist to visit and inspect the land being considered for a management plan, not least so that the need for more detailed surveys and possible sources of practical and financial assistance can be discussed. County archaeological officers can usually arrange such a visit.

At an early stage in developing a management plan it is often helpful to know something of the importance of the archaeological resource in question. Again, the county SMR should be able to help here. At present, four categories of monument can be defined:

1   Sites of national importance, usually Scheduled Monuments or ancient monuments in the process of being scheduled

2   Sites of regional or county importance

3   Sites of district or local importance

4   Sites which are not authentic antiquities, or are so badly damaged that too little now remains to justify their inclusion in a higher grade

Figure 20   Rescue excavation: A (top) excavations at Stanwick, Northamptonshire in advance of gravel quarrying; B (bottom) excavation of a Bronze Age ring-ditch threatened by the realignment of the A30 near Exeter, Devon; C (opposite) Iron Age chariot burial, one of three discovered during gravel extraction at Wetwang, Humberside, in 1984

Figure 20C (caption opposite)

Some local authorities have begun designating sites of regional or county importance within their areas, but it should be emphasized that all sites within categories 1–3 are important.

In addition, some areas of the countryside can be identified as being potentially high in archaeological value. Such areas may at first sight appear devoid of much known archaeological evidence, but their situation, proximity to known sites, or the ground conditions in the area make them of interest. Sometimes, and this applies especially in the uplands, the lack of known archaeological sites is attributable to the fact that nobody has ever checked the area on the ground with a view to recording them

Once information about the nature of the resource to be managed has been gathered, the formulation of the management plan itself may be undertaken. The first step is to set out clearly the objectives of management, for example preservation or exploitation, and the implications for land-use. This process may in itself be enough to highlight what needs to be done, and the ways in which it can be achieved. It is more likely, however, that management of the archaeological resource will have to be balanced against the requirements of other resources and a compromise worked out. From this, the plan will probably develop three main themes:

i   Immediate works to streamline existing arrangements in a way appropriate to the aims of the plan

ii   Short term principles to be applied to day-to-day working, for example specific rotations, maintenance tasks within the annual cycle of work, and perhaps a few 'dos' and 'don'ts' for specified areas

iii   Long-term principles for developing the potential of the landholding, probably through a set of options dependent upon short-term performance and return

Once established, such a plan needs to be carefully implemented by explaining it to those actually working on the land, including contractors who may be periodically engaged. A set of maps is often very useful to summarize proposals in graphic terms and portray constraints where necessary. Typically, one such map would summarize the archaeological components of the management strategy.

Above all, management plans must be flexible. There must be scope to take account of fluctuations in the rate of return from a piece of land, changes in technology and techniques, and of course the vagaries of quotas and imposed practice.

Stages   **External input**

1   The plan in outline

Having decided that a management plan would be useful, determine what form it should take, whether it should be solely concerned with the archaeological side of management or whether it should be a multi-purpose farm plan.

2   Survey

Undertake or commission an evaluation of the archaeology of the land being made the subject of the plan, noting expecially advice the nature and extent of any features of historic/ archaeological interest, and their importance. It may be useful to mark known archaeological features on a large scale map.

Obtain advice from HBMC and/or your county archaeologist

3   Assessment

Determine the objectives of management for each monument/ area (eg conservation, exploitation etc) and the ideal land-use appropriate to that objective.

Obtain advice from HBMC and/or your county archaeologist

4   Discussion and debate

Consider other demands on the land and the extent to which these conform or conflict with the ideal land-use for each area determined during stage 3. Attempt to reconcile conflicts by balancing advantages against disadvantages. Once this has been done, an integrated plan can be developed which makes provision for initial works and future land-use. It may be useful at this stage to prepare a land-use/constraint map and an outline calendar of activities.

Input from other management plans, eg farming, woodland, shooting, recreation, and wildlife

5   Getting going

Undertake any necessary capital works to make the proposals in the plan work efficiently, for example constructing new tracks, fences, boundaries, or gates, diverting footpaths, tree planting, clearance, etc.

Check with HBMC, MAFF/ADAS, and your local authority about grants

6   Implementation and review

Day-to-day management following the pattern established in the plan. An annual review of the objectives, and the means by which they are achieved, provides a useful way of monitoring the effectiveness of the plan.

Check with HBMC, MAFF/ADAS, and your local authority about grants

7   Long-term future

The plan itself must be sufficiently flexible to accommodate changing circumstances, but to ensure continuity it should, ideally, be tied to the land so that some long-term security for the archaeological monuments is provided.

Figure 21   Flow diagram summarizing the main stages in the formulation and implementation of a management plan for archaeological sites

Table 1 Archaeological landscape categories in England

Category	Area (km²)	%of total
A Semi-natural categories		
1 Wetland	1360	1.04%
2 Coastland	3228	2.47%
3 Rivers, lakes, and alluvium	3478	2.66%
B Generalized man-made categories		
4 Arable and short ley	51987	39.85%
5 Pasture (>5 years old)	31706	24.30%
C Specialized man-made categories		
6 Woodland	9450	7.24%
7 Upland moor	12950	9.90%
8 Lowland heath	2250	1.72%
9 Parkland and ornamental gardens	1340	1.02%
10 Urbanized/built-up	12690	9.80%
Total	130439	100.00%

Some provision for formal periodic review may be appropriate in some cases and will allow the fine tuning of principles and practices to achieve the desired results. There also needs to be some provision to allow the integration of sites which come to light after the initial formulation of the plan.

4.3 Management and the landscape

The management needs of each site have to be assessed on their merits and against the background of available resources and the aims of management. However, a crucial point about all management is that it takes place within the context of the present-day countryside. While it may be of academic interest to know what the landscape was like when a particular site was in use, its continued survival and potential for exploitation largely depends on current and anticipated land-use patterns. Moreover, the recognition and character of the evidence preserved varies according to existing and recent land-use and landscape type.

For archaeological purposes, nine categories of landscape can be defined (Table 1). Of these, three are essentially semi-natural landscapes which have been modified by human agencies, and six, in their present form at least, are artificial or man-made. This distinction is important because it greatly influences the type and scale of management necessary for the continued survival of the monuments. Each of these landscape categories is dealt with individually in parts II and III of this volume, and specific management recommendations for monuments in each are made.

The defined landscape categories are not completely spatially exclusive, and there will always be some overlap, for example between arable and wetland. Also, there is no segregation country-wide. Even within quite small areas, a variety of landscape types can usually be found, each with slightly different management implications and demands. Most counties in England may contain seven or eight of these landscape categories, but many contain areas of all nine. Even within a single estate or landholding there may be three or four different categories.

Although each landscape category has different management needs, sites of different dates within each require broadly the same treatment. Thus, an earthwork under pasture presents the same management problems, whether it is of later prehistoric or later medieval date.

Some landscape categories are very extensive, for example arable land, which accounts for nearly 40% of the total land area. Other categories have a restricted distribution – wetlands, for example, only cover about 1% of England. Clearly, when assessing the importance of sites and their overall value as managed resources, the relative scarcity of the particular conditions within which they can be preserved has to be taken into account.

Sites are more completely preserved in some landscapes than others. In general, the lower the intensity of land-use and the lower the extent of sub-surface disturbance, the greater the potential for the survival of archaeological remains. Such matters are considered in detail in later chapters, but it is important to note that effective management of the archaeological resource in some landscape categories is easier and cheaper than in others. If the current land-use can be changed to one with better potential for preservation, then, in general, the burden of management is reduced.

4.4 Management in context

Effective management requires local initiative and a commitment on the part of those actively engaged in working and using the land. It is only at such a level that the well-being of the archaeological heritage can be assured. Management schemes need not be conceived or executed in isolation, however, for there is much interest and help available from regional and national authorities (*see* Gosling 1985).

Management must however be undertaken within the context of existing legislation, and this is the subject of chapter 5.

5 The legislative background

5.1 Introduction and definitions

In England today there is a considerable body of legislation relevant to the management of ancient monuments in the countryside, and a number of organizations variously involved in its implementation. Something of the historical background to the present situation has been set out in chapter 1, and the wider context of the legislation is discussed elsewhere (O'Keefe and Prott 1984; Harte 1985). The purpose of this chapter is to outline the main provisions of the legislation and the responsibilities of the bodies concerned with its implementation. Appendix B provides detailed references to the individual Acts of Parliament mentioned in this chapter.

The expressions 'monument', 'scheduled monument', and 'ancient monument' are statutorily defined in the Ancient Monuments and Archaeological Areas Act 1979 as follows:

Monument: (a) any building, structure, or work, whether above or below the surface of the land, and any cave or excavation; (b) any site comprising the remains of any such building, structure, or work, or of any cave or excavation; and (c) any site comprising, or comprising the remains of, any vehicle, vessel, aircraft, or other movable structure or part thereof, which neither constitutes nor forms part of any work which is a monument within paragraph (a) above.[10] The site of a monument includes not only the land in or on which it is situated, but also any land comprising or adjoining it which is essential for its support and preservation.

Scheduled Monument: any monument which is, for the time being, included in the Schedule. (The Schedule of Ancient Monuments is compiled and maintained by the Secretary of State for the Environment.)

Ancient Monument: any Scheduled Monument, and any other monument, which, in the opinion of the Secretary of State, is of public interest by reason of the historic, architectural, traditional, artistic, or archaeological interest attaching to it. (In certain contexts, it is the opinion of HBMC which determines the matter.)

5.2 Responsibilities

Historic Buildings and Monuments Commission for England

The Historic Buildings and Monuments Commission for England (HBMC)[11] was established under the National Heritage Act 1983, and commenced its public functions on April 1 1984. It inherited most of its functions from the Secretary of State for the Environment. Its general duties are, as far as is practicable, to:

i secure the preservation of ancient monuments and historic buildings situated in England

ii promote the preservation and enhancement of the character and appearance of conservation areas situated in England

iii promote the public's enjoyment of, and advance their knowledge of, ancient monuments and historic buildings situated in England and their preservation

More specifically, HBMC's functions, which are discussed more fully later in this chapter, are:

— managing and presenting some 400 monuments and buildings on behalf of the Secretary of State for the Environment

— making grants to individuals and other bodies in respect of historic buildings, conservation areas, town schemes, ancient monuments, and for archaeological investigations

— acquiring (including through the acceptance of gifts), or becoming guardian of, ancient monuments

— advising the Secretary of State for the Environment on the selection of buildings for inclusion in the list of buildings of special architectural or historic interest, on the monuments to be added to the Schedule of monuments, and on the designation of Areas of Archaeological Importance

— advising the Secretary of State on applications for permission to carry out works to listed buildings and Scheduled Monuments

— carrying out research or helping others to do so

— undertaking archaeological investigation, and publishing the results

— providing educational facilities and services

— making and maintaining records

— advising any person in relation to ancient monuments, historic buildings, and conservation areas

Secretary of State for the Environment

The functions retained by the Secretary of State for the Environment in relation to ancient monuments include the compilation of the Schedule of ancient monuments, determinations of Scheduled Monument Consent applications, consent for HBMC to acquire or take into Guardianship any monument, and consent for HBMC to carry out emergency works to monuments.

Other bodies with archaeological responsibilities may be mentioned here.

Royal Commission on the Historical Monuments of England

The Royal Commission on the Historical Monuments of England was first constituted by Royal Warrant in 1908 to make 'an inventory of the Ancient and Historical Monuments and Constructions connected with or illustrative of the contemporary culture, civilization and conditions of life of the people in England...and to specify those which seem most worthy of preservation.' The original intention was that the

Figure 22   Survey by the Royal Commission on the Historical Monuments of England in progress

inventory would be concerned solely with 'monuments and constructions' dated before 1700. However, the terms of the Warrant were subsequently extended to 1714, and latterly to 'such further Monuments and Constructions subsequent to that year as may seem...to be worthy of mention...' (Croad and Fowler 1984).

Various other duties have subsequently been laid upon the Royal Commission, including the assessment and surveying of archaeological remains threatened with destruction, the recording of Listed Buildings when consent has been given for their total or partial demolition, and the creation and curation of the national public archive for archaeological monuments and historic buildings, which is called the National Monuments Record. This record comprises an Archaeological Records Section (including the National Archaeological Record, based on the records compiled by the Ordnance Survey up to 1983), an Air Photographic Section, and an Architectural Records Section. The Commissioners regard the National Monuments Record as the inventory which they are required to make under the terms of the Royal Warrant. Archaeological sites which are recorded by the Royal Commission, and which appear to be worthy of preservation, are identified in *White Papers*.

The staff of RCHME carry out archaeological surveys (Fig 22) and architectural recording from regional offices, while the National Monuments Record is based in London and Southampton.

Local authorities

Local authorities have a number of powers at their disposal to protect and conserve ancient monuments, both through the ancient monuments Acts and the town and country planning legislation. Most county councils, and a few district councils and National Park authorities, operate some kind of archaeological service to provide specialist input to planning work and to give advice to landowners and the general public. The archaeological policies and intentions of local authorites are set out in their structure plans and, in more detail, in local plans or subject plans.[12]

Other bodies

Many large public and private landowners take an active interest in the ancient monuments on their estates, and some, such as the National Trust (Thackray 1986), engage archaeological staff to provide the necessary specialist input to the management of their properties.

5.3   Ancient monuments legislation

The principal statute governing the protection and preservation of ancient monuments is the Ancient Monuments and Archaeological Areas Act 1979, as amended for England by the National Heritage Act 1983.[13] Broadly speaking, the statutory provisions fall into three groups. First, the statutory protection of monuments against damaging activities. Second, the encouragements to landowners to protect, conserve, and, if appropriate, present monuments. Third, the investigation, recording, and assessment of sites of archaeological importance.

Statutory protection

Statutory protection is extended to archaeological sites and historic structures principally by scheduling (Fig 23). Under the 1979 Act, the Secretary of State for the Environment is required to keep a Schedule of monuments considered to be worthy of protection because of their national importance. In compiling this Schedule, the Secretary of State must have regard to the advice of HBMC, and in fact most schedulings originate with the Commission. It is, however, open to any person to recommend that a site should be scheduled.

A Scheduled Monument may comprise any monument from a single burial mound up to a large tract of landscape containing many individual sites, and from buried prehistoric remains to upstanding buildings or structures as recent in date as the twentieth century AD. Monuments in, on, or under the sea bed and within territorial waters may be included.[14] Buildings in use as dwellings, other than by a caretaker, and those in regular ecclesiastical use do not, however, qualify.

At present, there are over 12,800 Scheduled Monuments, of which about 30% are buildings and the rest field monuments (Fig 24). Scheduling is a continuous process, and it is expected that many more monuments will be added to the Schedule over the next ten years or so, as the direct result of a systematic assessment of all known monuments to identify those of national importance. This will redress certain imbalances in the range of monuments represented, and take into account recently discovered monuments (HBMC 1984b). Even at the end of this resurvey, however, the total number of Scheduled Monuments in England is unlikely to represent more than about 10% of all known ancient monuments recorded in the county Sites and Monuments Records.

Owners and occupiers of monuments are usually notified and given the opportunity to comment before their property is included on the Schedule. There is no appeal against the addition of a monument to the Schedule, and, once scheduling has taken place, a charge is registered in the local land registry.

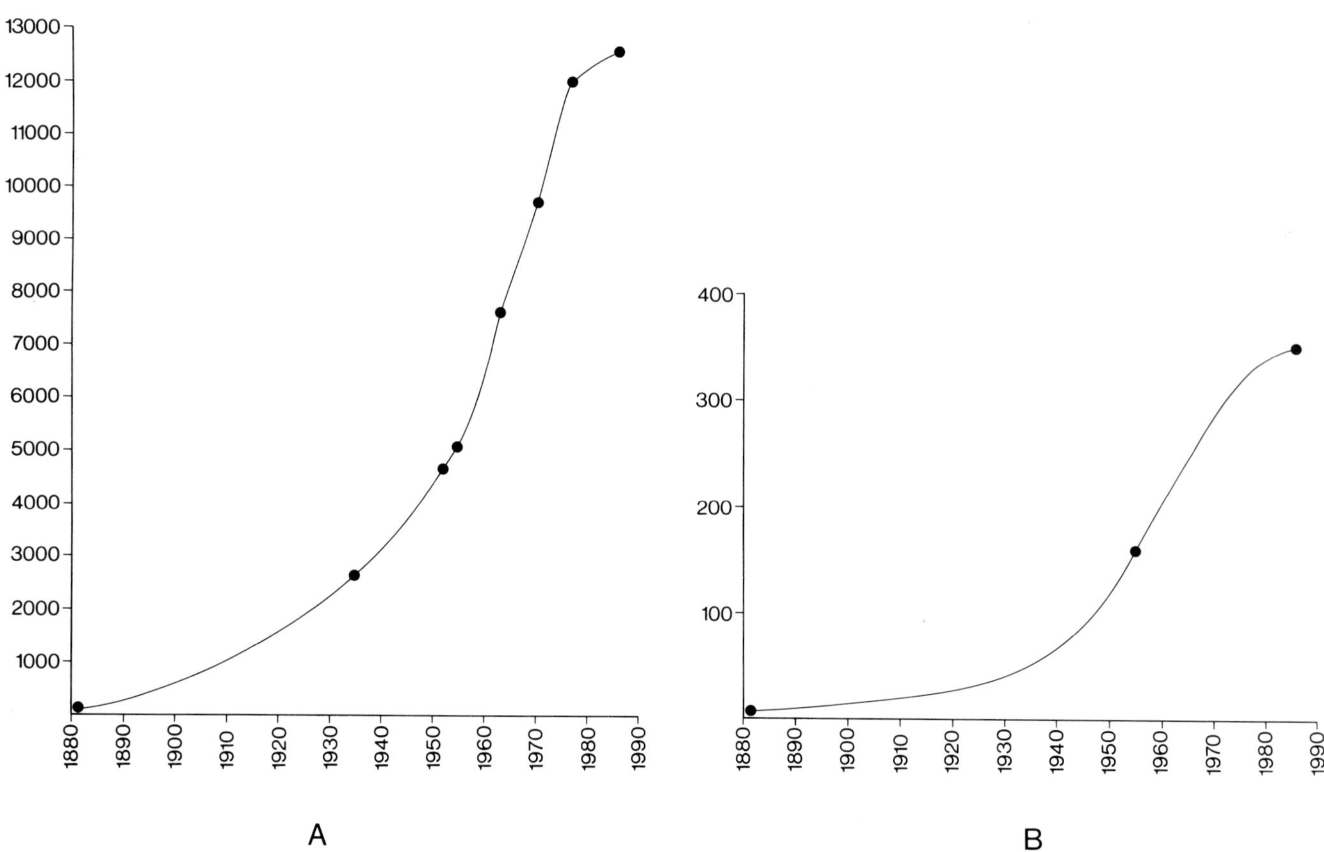

A

B

Figure 23   Graphs showing the increase in A) the number of scheduled monuments, and B) the number of monuments in Guardianship since 1882

Non-statutory criteria have been developed for assessing whether monuments are schedulable (DoE 1983). These may be summarized as follows:

i   Survival/condition: the survival of the monument's archaeological potential both above and below ground is a crucial consideration and needs to be assessed in relation to its present condition and surviving features

ii   Period: it is important to consider for preservation all types of monument that characterize a category or period

iii   Rarity: there are some monument categories which in some periods are so scarce that all of them which still retain any archaeological potential should be preserved. In general, however, a selection must be made which portrays the typical and commonplace, as well as the rare. For this, account should be taken of all aspects of the distribution of a particular class of monument, not only in the broad national context, but also in its region

iv   Fragility/vulnerability: highly important archaeological evidence from some field monuments can be destroyed by a single ploughing, or by unsympathetic treatment; these monuments would particularly benefit from the statutory protection which scheduling confers. There are also standing structures of particular form or complexity, where again their value could be severely reduced by neglect or careless treatment, and which are well suited to protection by this legislation, even though they may also be listed historic buildings

v   Diversity: some monuments have a combination of high quality features; others are chosen for a single important attribute

vi   Documentation: the significance of a monument may be given great weight by the existence of records of previous investigation or, in the case of more recent monuments, by the support of contemporary written records

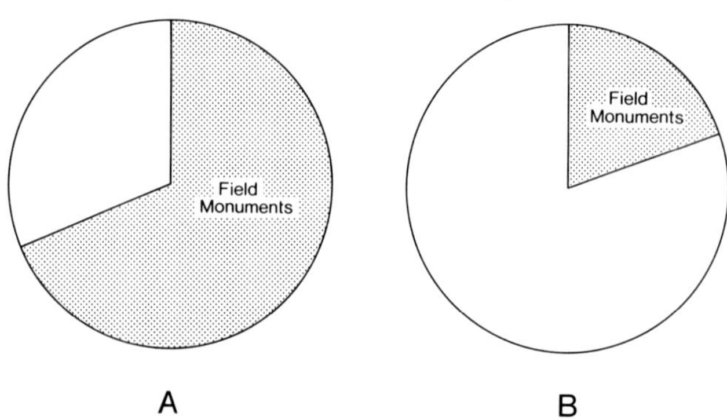

Figure 24   Pie-charts showing the relative proportions of buildings and field monuments covered by A) Scheduling, and B) Guardianship

vii Group value: the value of a single monument (such as a field system) is greatly enhanced by association with a group of related contemporary monuments (such as a settlement and cemetery), or with monuments of other periods. In the case of some groups, it is preferable to protect the whole, including the associated and adjacent land, rather than to protect isolated monuments within the group

viii Potential: on occasion the nature of the evidence cannot be precisely specified, but it is possible to document reasons for anticipating its probable existence and importance, and so demonstrate the justification for scheduling. This is usually confined to sites, rather than upstanding monuments

Of the monuments of national importance, some 400 are in the care of central government. Of these, all but the Royal Palaces (including the Tower of London) have been transferred from the Department of the Environment to the management of HBMC. Some of these monuments are owned by the State, others have been taken into Guardianship with the transfer of responsibility for their maintenance and management, but not ownership, to the State. Of the 400 monuments in the Guardianship of HBMC, about 80% are buildings, the remainder being field monuments of various sorts (Fig 24), including many well-known sites such as Stonehenge, Wiltshire, Grimes Graves, Norfolk, and Maiden Castle, Dorset.

State care remains an option of last resort for monuments of supreme national importance, whose future cannot otherwise be secured. Local authorities too have powers to take sites into care, and in fact look after many important monuments. The preservation of the great majority of monuments, even Scheduled Monuments, will, however, always remain the responsibility of private and other owners.

Once a monument is scheduled, it is an an offence to carry out certain works to it, or affecting it, without the written consent – known as Scheduled Monument Consent – of the Secretary of State for the Environment. The Secretary of State is required to consult HBMC before deciding whether Scheduled Monument Consent should be given, and, if so, whether conditions should be attached to such consent. Conditions may, for instance, relate to prior recording of any part of the monument to be altered, or the precise methods to be adopted for carrying out the work. Scheduled Monument Consent applications may be the subject of a hearing or public inquiry, if either party so wishes. Once given, consents remain valid for five years unless modified or revoked. In certain circumstances, notably where planning permission was granted prior to scheduling, refusal or the conditional grant of Scheduled Monument Consent may give rise to compensation, as may the modification or revocation of consent once given.

Scheduled Monument Consent for classes or descriptions of works may be granted by an order made by the Secretary of State. At present, there are six categories of class consent.[15] Class I is of particular importance to farmers.

Class I: Agricultural, horticultural, or forestry works, being works of the same kind as works previously executed in the same field or location during the five years immediately preceding the coming into operation of the Ancient Monuments (Class Consents) Order 1981; but not including subsoiling, drainage works, the planting or uprooting of trees, hedges, or shrubs, or any other works

likely to disturb the soil below the maximum depth affected by normal ploughing.

Class II: Works executed more than ten metres below ground level by the National Coal Board, or any person acting under a licence granted by the National Coal Board.

Class III: Works executed by the British Waterways Board in relation to land owned or occupied by them, being (a) works of repair or maintenance not involving a material alteration to a monument; (b) works which are essential for the purpose of ensuring the functioning of a canal.

Class IV: Works for the repair or maintenance of machinery, being works which do not involve a material alteration to a monument.

Class V: Works which are essential for the purposes of health or safety.

Class VI: Works executed by the Historic Buildings and Monuments Commission for England.

Special procedures apply to monuments on crown property which are covered by the spirit, but not the letter, of the law. Legislation governing the activities of statutory bodies also contains specific provisions for the protection of Scheduled Monuments (see Appendix B).

Scheduled Monuments are regularly inspected by Field Monument Wardens. These are part-time employees of HBMC, whose duty it is to report back to the Commission on the condition of the monuments.

Reports of damage or unauthorized works to monuments are investigated by the Commission, who may try to secure that legal proceedings are initiated against the offender.[16] It is open to any person or body to prosecute offenders, and the Commission also looks to local authorities and the police to take action where appropriate.

Encouragements for positive conservation measures

There are several means available to HBMC and other authorities to give owners or occupiers more positive encouragement to conserve, or in some cases to develop, their monuments in a sympathetic manner.

HBMC and local authorities both may offer occupiers (who may of course be owners) management agreements to secure the satisfactory management of the monument. These agreements replace the system of acknowledgement payments made under previous legislation.

A monument does not need to be scheduled to be eligible for a management agreement, but where the agreement is to be financed by HBMC, the monument will be of national importance and will normally be scheduled. Payments under such agreements are only made in respect of the management of the land, and are not made merely as an acknowledgement of the presence of a monument, or for inconvenience caused by a monument; moreover, they are not intended as compensation for loss of profits. Two sorts of work can be distinguished: capital works, such as fencing or an action which puts a monument in suitable condition for further management, and regular management works over and above normal practice, such as maintaining a healthy grass cover or keeping the monument under agreed conditions. Agreements are designed to meet problems peculiar to individual monuments and can include surrounding land, where this is felt to be appropriate (HBMC 1984e; Wainwright 1985). Agreements may be made for the maintenance and preservation of the monument and its amenities; carrying out any required work to the monument; allowing public access to a monument or land; the provision of facilities and services for the use of the public; and restricting the use of a monument or land.

The period covered by a management agreement varies, but is likely to be between five and seven years. Management agreements concluded with local authorities are broadly similar to those established by HBMC, but are based on one of a range of powers, according to precise circumstances.[17] Both HBMC and local authority agreements are subject to the availability of funds at any given time.

In addition to payments under management agreements, HBMC may provide grant aid for the acquisition, repair, maintenance, and management of ancient monuments. The bulk of expenditure is on the repair or consolidation of upstanding monuments, but HBMC's powers can be used to repair damage to field monuments, or, very rarely, to help some other body acquire a site or structure at risk. When funds are available, grant aid may be extended to cover capital expenditure required to improve access or presentation.

Under the Capital Transfer Tax Act 1984, which amended and consolidated earlier legislation, conditional exemption from Capital Transfer Tax may be given for land of outstanding scenic, historic, or scientific interest, including created landscapes. The conditions of exemption require that reasonable steps will be taken for the maintenance of the land and the preservation of its character, and for securing reasonable public access. This is normally achieved through implementing a detailed management plan (H M Treasury 1980; Quest 1982; Countryside Commission 1986). Applications are made to the Capital Tax Office, which refers requests to the Inland Revenue. Normally, advice is taken from HBMC, the Countryside Commission, and the Nature Conservancy Council about the national importance of the land in question, and the Forestry Commission, the Royal Botanic Gardens, Kew, and MAFF may also be consulted where appropriate. A number of exemptions have been granted wholly or partly because of the importance of the archaeological remains contained within the estate. Among such sites is Bransdale Moor, North Yorkshire (Statham 1982).

Two other important provisions relating to archaeological remains are contained in the Capital Transfer Tax Act 1984. First, Capital Transfer Tax is not payable on gifts of land or buildings of outstanding scenic, historic, or scientific interest made over to a body not established or conducted for profit, which includes HBMC, the National Trust, and any local authority. Second, maintenance funds can be established to protect and preserve the character of the land.

Financial assistance may occasionally be available from the National Heritage Memorial Fund. The fund sees its role very much as a safety net, covering crises beyond the power of other government agencies. It will not therefore normally give funds for purposes which could be met by HBMC, and it cannot give assistance to private owners, only to public bodies or charitable trusts.

More generally, as already indicated, HBMC has powers to advise, educate, and inform the public. In many cases, this is as important as financial assistance in helping other authorities, and owners, to recognize the importance of sites, and to develop means for their better management.

Investigation, assessment, and recording

HBMC has powers of access to record and investigate monuments, as also does RCHME as part of its designated responsibilities. These functions are important, given the need to record those aspects of the archaeological heritage which are disappearing in a rapidly changing landscape.

Where it is impossible to preserve a monument *in situ*, detailed recording is undertaken when practicable and within the constraints of available finance. For field monuments this usually means excavation – rescue excavation. Under the 1979 Act, HBMC or a local authority may contribute towards or defray the costs of an archaeological investigation.[18] Where Scheduled Monument Consent is sought, applications frequently include details of relevant provisions for dealing with the archaeology, and may be refused for not doing so. Where planning permission is required, provisions for archaeology may also be negotiated or included as conditions of consent (DoE 1985, 60–1).

In some cases, rescue excavations are carried out directly by the Central Excavation Unit of HBMC (HBMC 1986b), but more often grants are made to recognized regional or county-based archaeological organizations to enable them to undertake the work. Funds are often channelled through county council based archaeological bodies.

HBMC expenditure on rescue excavation, survey, post-excavation research contracts, and publishing has increased greatly over the last decade or so (HBMC 1984c; Wainwright 1984). In 1972–3, rather less than £500,000 was spent nationwide on rescue work, but by 1986–7 this figure had risen to £5.74 million (Fig 25). Funds do not, however, cover all demands and, accordingly, the allocation of resources is based on the merits of each proposal within the context of a broad national research framework, focusing on particular themes or deficiencies in existing knowledge (HBMC 1986a).

In order to evaluate and assess the impact of development on ancient monuments in the countryside, various records are maintained. HBMC is establishing a comprehensive computer-based record of Scheduled Monuments, and has certain powers of entry to land containing, or thought to contain, ancient monuments for the purposes of recording them and obtaining information for their records.[19] In addition, HBMC has encouraged the development of a network of county-based Sites and Monuments Records, which provide comprehensive coverage of known scheduled and non-scheduled monuments in each respective area. The information on Scheduled Monuments which is held by HBMC, and that on non-scheduled sites which is held by local authority Sites and Monuments Records, is complemented by the RCHME's National Archaeological Record section of the National Monuments Record. In the countryside, investigation and recording by RCHME is undertaken by survey and aerial reconnaissance. The Royal Warrant gives extensive powers in connection with compiling surveys. In the past, RCHME carried out surveys on a county by county basis, and the results were published in printed inventories. RCHME now conducts thematic surveys, in addition to specific field surveys, which are sometimes requested by other bodies. RCHME no longer publishes county inventories; instead detailed results are incorporated in the National Monuments Record and in county Sites and Monuments Records. The results of surveys are published in volumes of synthesis.

Part II of the 1979 Act contains special provisions for the investigation of areas designated as Areas of Archaeological

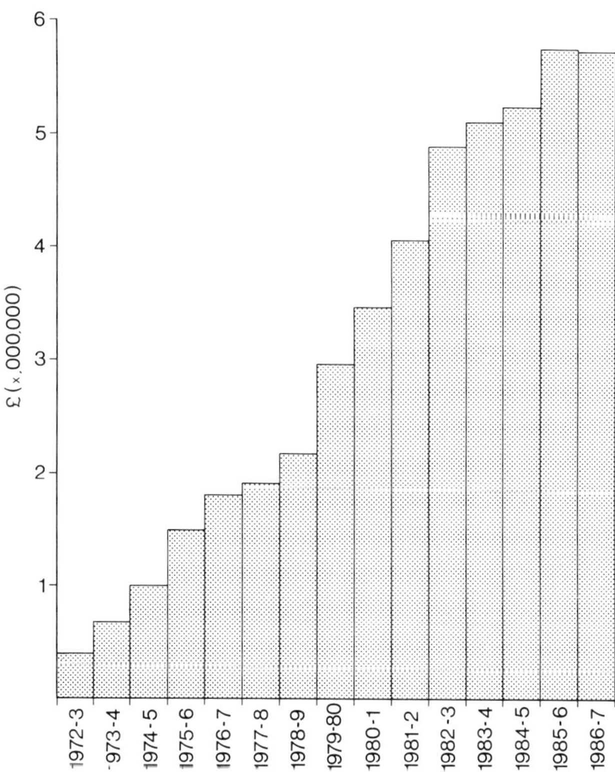

Figure 25   Graph showing the increase in rescue funding 1972–87

Importance. These are areas containing extensive concentrations of archaeological deposits and were introduced primarily as a way to improve the recording of urban sites in advance of redevelopment. Agricultural and mineral-bearing lands were excluded from the initial scope of the legislation, and accordingly its provisions are not discussed further here.

Mineral operators do, however, have a very noticeable impact on the countryside, and have subscribed to a voluntary code of practice to allow time for archaeological investigation in advance of mineral extraction. This code is set out in Appendix C. When followed, it provides a valuable framework for cooperation between all the parties involved.

5.4   Finds and Treasure Trove

Under Common Law in England, objects which are physically within the soil become part of the soil and are therefore the property of the landowner (O'Keefe and Prott 1984; Harte 1985). In the case of finds recovered during excavations, observations, or examinations carried out during the exercise of any powers of entry established under the Ancient Monuments and Archaeological Areas Act 1979, the author-ized person may take temporary custody of the finds and remove them from the site for the purpose of examining, testing, treating, recording, or preserving them. The objects may not, however, be retained beyond such period as may be reasonably required for these purposes, and, for this reason, it is particularly important that the treatment of finds recovered during excavations or archaeological investigations is clearly understood by all parties before work begins.

The only exception to these generalities lies in the case of Treasure Trove. This is a most ancient law, dating back to before 1276 (N Palmer 1981; Sparrow 1982), and is intended to provide for the acquisition by the Crown of any items of gold or silver which were in the past deliberately hidden with the intention of being recovered, but which were not recovered and of which the owner cannot now be traced. Items of gold or silver lost or deposited without intent to recover are not Treasure Trove, and are normally returned to the finder.[20] If the finder of Treasure Trove reports the find immediately to the police, either he is allowed its full value, or alternatively the articles are returned to him. Difficulties naturally arise in determining whether objects were deliberately deposited or accidentally lost, or, in the case of grave goods accompanying burials, deposited deliberately but without intent to recover. There are also difficulties over the definition of what constitutes gold and silver. The case law to 1980 has been discussed by N Palmer (1981).

The use of metal detectors on Scheduled Monuments is prohibited, unless permission has been obtained in writing in advance from HBMC,[21] and many local authorities have recently introduced by-laws imposing similar restrictions on land in their ownership.

5.5   Archaeology and other countryside legislation

In addition to the direct references to ancient monuments in the statute book, there are a number of pieces of legislation which indirectly promote the preservation and conservation of the archaeological heritage. The main impact of these derives from the provision of tighter planning controls, increased forward planning, and the greater availability of management advice, grants, and management agreements within designated areas.

Conservation areas

Although conservation areas, designated by local authorities under the Town and Country Planning Act 1971, are normally within built-up areas of towns and cities, they can also be applied to rural areas where appropriate. Such designation effectively restricts the scale and nature of redevelopment and promotes the general enhancement of the area through conservation schemes. Among rural areas designated in this way, wholly or partly because of their archaeological value, are the upper Wey valley in Hampshire (Bird 1986), and some village fringes in north Oxfordshire.

National Nature Reserves and Sites of Special Scientific Interest

These two classes of protected area may be designated by the Nature Conservancy Council under the National Parks and Access to the Countryside Act 1949, and the Wildlife and Countryside Act 1981, as amended by Section 2 of the Wildlife and Countryside (Amendment) Act 1985, and are primarily intended for the conservation of areas of special interest for plants, animals, their natural habitats, and geological and physiographical features. Many NNRs and SSSIs contain archaeological features, and management as a result of NNR and SSSI status can provide effective protection, as demonstrated by Lambrick's (1985b) review of ancient monuments in Oxfordshire. Such cases may include cave deposits, peat/wetland deposits, and natural drift deposits containing archaeological material. The preservation of working water meadows may also be better achieved in the context of a Nature Reserve or SSSI than through scheduling under the 1979 Act, because here it is a working practice which requires to be maintained.

Areas of Outstanding Natural Beauty

These areas were first established under the National Parks and Access to the Countryside Act 1949, but have since been variously extended, and new areas have been added. There are currently 32 AONBs in England, and these cover approximately 16,252 square kilometres (Countryside Commission 1983a). Further areas are awaiting designation.

The purpose of AONB designation is to conserve the natural beauty and character of the area so designated, including protecting flora, fauna, and geology, as well as landscape features. AONB status thus makes it less likely that government or public agencies will propose major new intensive developments; strengthens the hand of planning authorities in rejecting proposals for new urban development which would be out of character; makes it more likely that funds will be found for conservation measures, including management agreements; encourages the appointment of ranger services; and increases the chances that owners may gain relief from capital transfer tax.

HBMC and other archaeological bodies are consulted when extensions and additions are proposed, and the archaeological potential of an area is one of the factors which might help decide the line of the boundary, if not the area chosen.

National Parks

There are seven National Parks in England, established between 1950 and 1955 under the National Parks and Access to the Countryside Act 1949. Collectively they cover approximately 9501 square kilometres (CNP 1984a). All are essentially upland regions, and all contain a wealth of archaeological remains. There is much variation in the way different park authorities choose to use their powers. From the archaeological standpoint, the main benefits of National Park designation lie in the provision of more intensive management schemes (Fig 26), tighter control on development and changes in land-use, and the provision of tourist and visitor facilities. The extension of Landscape Area Special Development Orders (LASDOs) to all National Parks means that the siting and design of new agricultural buildings and roads is subject to special consultation procedures. MAFF grant procedures mean that damaging activities within National Parks are more likely than in other areas to be prevented through consultation prior to implementation.

Two parks, Dartmoor and Peak District, employ archaeological officers; the other parks rely on the services of the relevant county archaeological officers.

The Countryside Act 1968 makes special provision for the establishment of study centres and other facilities for learning within national parks. Archaeological and historical interest is among the themes explicitly covered by this provision.

Local authority initiatives

Many local authorities, whether National Parks, county councils, or district councils, designate special areas of various sorts, within which greater attention is given to conservation.

The Heritage Coasts, jointly promoted by the Countryside Commission and local authorities, are examples of such areas.

In Hampshire, the county council's Countryside Heritage Policy (Hampshire County Council 1984) provides for the definition of County Heritage Sites, which the authority then uses its powers to protect and conserve. In Somerset, the county council has designated non-statutory Areas of High Archaeological Potential in the Levels and Moors, while in Cornwall and Wiltshire, county-wide Countryside Heritage Plans have been established as thematic local plans, providing special protection for defined archaeological areas.

Some county councils are currently developing general policies which will ensure that potential developers, in particular mineral operators, carry out assessments of the archaeological implications of proposals submitted for planning permissions, in much the same way as drainage and transport have to be assessed.

Military remains

The Protection of Military Remains Act 1986 aims to secure the protection from unauthorized interference of the remains of military aircraft and vessels that have crashed, sunk, or been stranded, and of any associated human remains. In the countryside, the Act mainly applies to military remains under 200 years old, which have been designated for protection by the Secretary of State. Once they are designated, it becomes

Figure 26   Workmen re-erecting Marchants Cross at Meavy, Devon, for the Dartmoor National Park

an offence to tamper with, damage, move, or unearth the remains, unless the Secretary of State has issued a licence authorising such things to be done.

Agriculture Act 1986

This Act contains two important sections relevant to the archaeological heritage in the countryside, and is the first piece of legislation which integrates conservation with farming practice. Section 17 imposes a duty on the Minister of Agriculture Fisheries and Food to balance the interests of maintaining an efficient and stable agricultural industry with economic, social, and conservational interests in the countryside, including features of archaeological interest. Section 18 provides for the designation and management of 'Environmentally Sensitive Areas' (ESAs). These areas may be defined where it appears to the Minister that it is particularly desirable to: (a) conserve and enhance the natural beauty of the area; (b) conserve the flora, fauna, or geology of physiographic features of an area; or (c) protect buildings or other objects of archaeological, architectural, or historic interest. Funds are available within the defined areas to encourage or maintain particular agricultural methods which are likely to facilitate conservation, enhancement, or protection of these various facets of the landscape. At the time of writing, five areas have been identified for designation — the South Downs, the Somerset Levels and Moors, the Pennine Dales, the Broads, and West Penwith — but it remains to be seen how the scheme will work, and how big a contribution it can make to the better management of ancient monuments.

II   Archaeology in the countryside 1: Semi-natural landscapes

The following three chapters detail the archaeology of landscape categories which are essentially natural in origin, although variously modified by human activity. The preservation conditions and management requirements of the archaeological sites in each category are largely determined by the natural environment and thus grouped together. Each chapter deals with the reasons why monuments in the particular landscape category are important, the development of the landscape category itself, the kinds of archaeological features represented, the main threats posed to them, and current approaches to their management.

6   Wetland

6.1   Archaeological importance

The English wetlands are areas in which environmental factors have promoted the development of wet-ground vegetation. This has led to the accumulation of organic deposits, over the underlying mineral substratum, in conditions of waterlogging that are essentially anaerobic. During these processes, which have taken place over many millennia, archaeological material has become covered or trapped within the developing peat. Today, wetland areas are characterized by organic soils with a high water table, in which anaerobic conditions prevail beneath the ground surface.

Wetlands have attracted a great deal of attention from archaeologists (Coles 1984; Coles and Lawson 1986) and are important because of the types of sites represented and the exceptional preservation offered by anaerobic conditions. This may be reviewed under four headings:

i   Organic materials: wood, leather, textiles, basketry, and other perishables (including animal and human tissue in some circumstances), which do not normally survive on dry-land sites, are often preserved in the wetlands. This allows insights into the form of otherwise unknown classes of artefacts and structures.

ii   Inorganic materials: pottery, stone, glass, and other inorganic materials are often preserved with associated organic materials, and often in better overall condition on wetland sites than on dry-land sites. This allows a more complete understanding of the way artefacts were made and used.

iii   Environmental indicators: evidence of the environment on and around a site before, during, and after its use can be derived from studies of pollen, wood, leaves, seeds, fungi, beetles, mollusca, and other invertebrate remains trapped in the peat as it formed. This provides insights into vegetation history and local hydrology, which is important for understanding the effects of man on the environment and the constraints governing activities in the area (Godwin 1981; Coles 1984, 59–68).

iv   Stratigraphy and landscape: because, in very general terms, peat bogs accumulate relatively uniformly and rapidly, the evidence preserved comprises a series of superimposed and successive horizons. This provides invaluable insights into the way things changed over time (vertical dimension), and also the disposition of activities across the landscape at a single point in time (horizontal dimension).[22]

Wetlands cover approximately 1360 square kilometres of England, about 1% of the total land area (Fig 27). They are mostly confined to the north and west, although the largest single block of approximately 530 square kilometres (39% of all wetland) lies in eastern England around the Wash. A national peat inventory is currently being prepared by the Soil Survey of England and Wales (Burton and Robson 1985), which will eventually provide a more accurate picture of the distribution of wetlands. In archaeological terms, small areas of wetland, covering perhaps less than 1ha, can be just as important for the information they contain as the large wetland areas such as the fens of East Anglia or the Somerset Levels (Bewley 1986).

As defined here, the wetlands fall into four groups: raised mires, basin mires, blanket mires, and valley mires.[23] Rivers, lakes, and alluvium deposits are covered in chapter 8. Stagnopodzols, wet flushes, and localized waterlogging are not discussed here, because their archaeology and management do not merit special treatment outside the landscape categories in which they occur.

Although the wetlands may appear to present ideal circumstances for the survival of archaeological evidence, there are three important limitations. First, there is considerable variation in the quality of preservation offered by the many different types of wetland. Second, the evidence recovered from wetland sites relates to highly specialized environments, which were not necessarily settled or exploited in the same way as other areas of the landscape. Third, some generally common types of site do not occur in wetland areas.

6.2   Origin and distribution

The formation of mires is a complex process rooted in the balance between water supply (rivers, run-off, and rain) and water loss (drainage, run-off, and evaporation). Ratcliffe (1977, 250–60) provides a detailed account of wetland formation, but, in general terms, wetlands are either *ombrogenous*, caused by high effective wetness from rainfall, or *topogenous*, where local relief results in a permanently high water table. The cause of waterlogging in any given wetland area has important implications for the preservation of archaeological material, especially organic materials.

Ombrogenous mires, often called bogs, are usually acid, because the rainwater which supplies them is itself acidic. Topogenous mires, variously called marshes, swamps, and fens, depending upon the degree of wetness and their soil chemistry, rely on ground water and tend to be either alkaline or only mildly acidic. To complicate matters, topogenous mires may become bogs during the course of their growth, if the peat builds up to such a level that the effects of ground water are cancelled and the system becomes dependent upon rainfall.

The acidity of wetlands is one of the most important factors

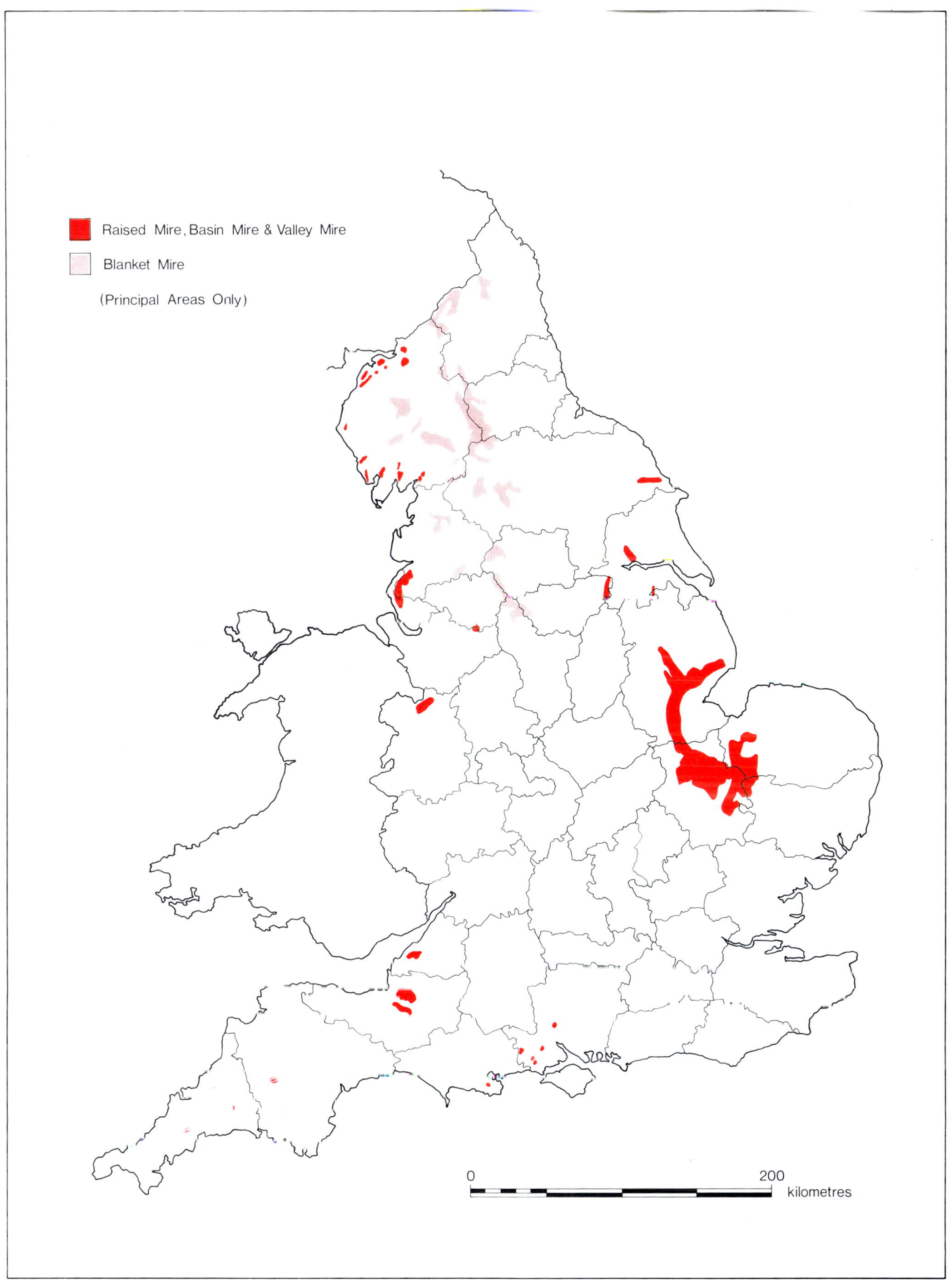

Figure 27   Map showing main areas of wetland landscape in England

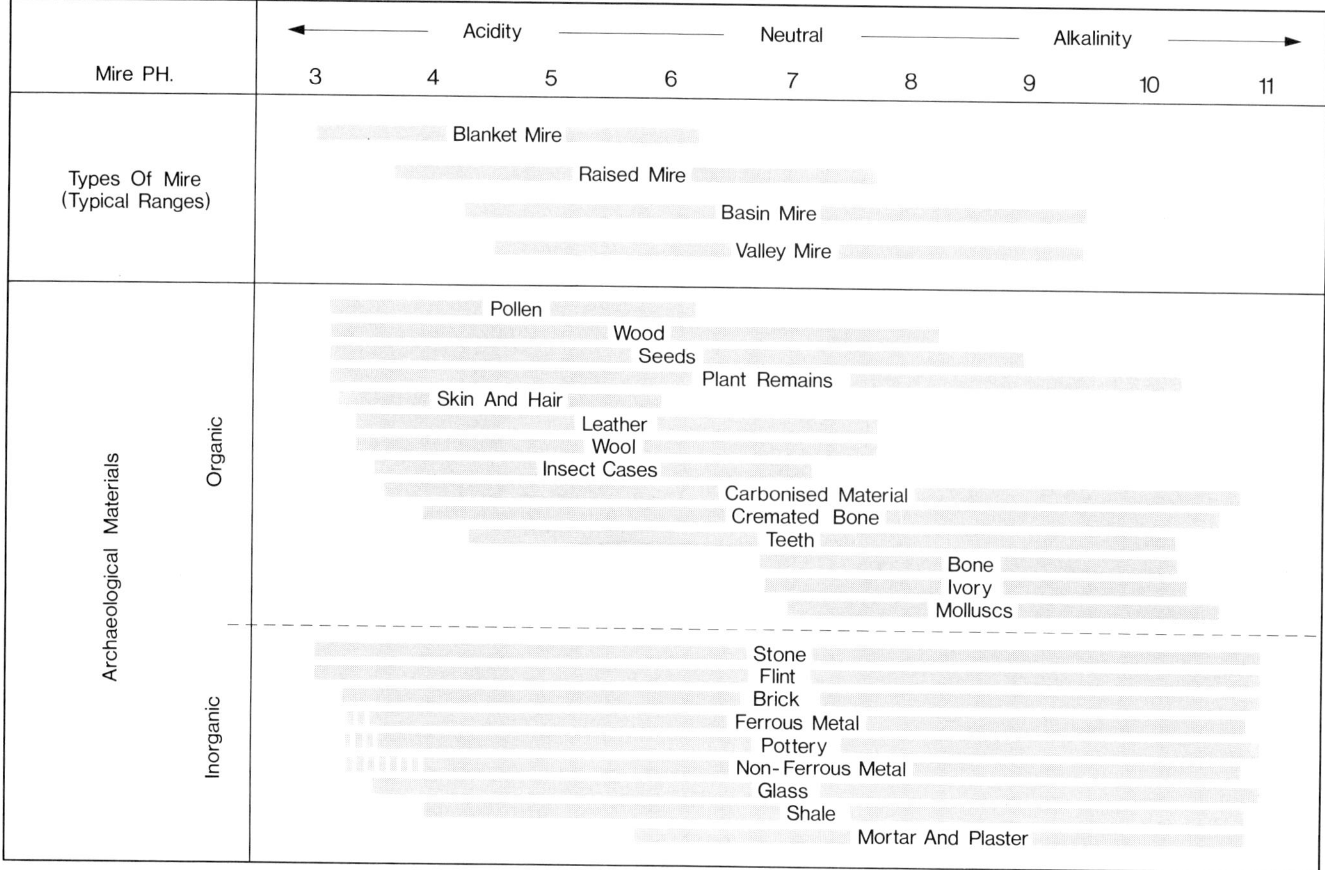

Figure 28　*Mire acidity and generalized preservation of archaeological materials in anaerobic conditions*

determining the range of archaeological material preserved (Fig 28). A change in acidity might be detrimental to material already stabilized within a mire.

The origins of the four main types of mire are considered in the following sections.

Raised mires

This is the most widespread class of wetland, being especially common in lowland areas adjacent to major river valleys and coasts. Principal areas include the Somerset Levels, the peat fens of East Anglia, the mosses of the Solway Plain, and the mires around Morecambe Bay.

Most raised mires began as topogenous mires. The Somerset Levels, for example, started to develop soon after 4000 bc, when the sea retreated from the area leaving a swampy estuarine basin soon colonized by reeds.[24] As the mat of dead reeds grew thicker, fen woodland, dominated by birch and alder, colonized the drier, higher areas of the swamp, the dead leaves and branches contributing to the peat growth. By 3500 bc, fen wood had almost totally replaced the reed swamp, but was in turn replaced by *sphagnum* moss, cottongrass, and heather as the surface of the mire rose above the natural water level and was then supplied by rainfall. Between 3500 bc and AD 400, when the bog stopped growing, up to 10m of peat accumulated.

The fens of East Anglia have a broadly similar story, with peat formation beginning in flooded woodland perhaps as early as 6660 ± 160 bc (Q-588), according to a radiocarbon date from near the bottom of the peat at Shippea Hill,

Cambridgeshire (J G D Clark and Godwin 1962). As the peat developed, so the mires expanded to smother areas of the surrounding landscape.

Few raised mires are still growing, but their great size and depth of deposits make them valuable records of human activity over wide areas.

Basin mires

These are topogenous mires, developed in enclosed waterlogged depressions, which became colonized by peat-forming vegetation. They are generally small, perhaps 200m or less across, and occur mainly in areas of glacial deposition, where local irregularities of relief provide the necessary environment of hollows with closed drainage.

The principal concentrations are in north Shropshire, Cheshire, and Lancashire. In Cheshire, a recent vegetation survey by the county council[25] has revealed 36 basin mires and raised mires within the county, in all covering an estimated 179.6ha. Almost every parish in lowland areas of Cheshire contains at least one mire, and there is no reason to doubt a similar distribution over other parts of the Cheshire Plain. Isolated examples of basin mires are known outside the glaciated parts of England, including recently investigated instances in Hampshire and Dorset (Waton 1982; 1983).

Since basin mires have fairly steep and well-defined edges, are often very deep, and have usually been accumulating since early post-glacial times, they are especially important as records of local environment. Something of the scale of these deposits can be glimpsed from the site of Wem Moss, Shropshire, where even after drainage and peat cutting a 10m thick peat deposit survived, altogether spanning the period from late glacial through to post-medieval times (F Slater 1972). The lower levels of a comparable profile recorded at Crose Mere, Shropshire, were radiocarbon dated to 10,310 ± 210 bc (Q-1240) (Beales 1980).

Valley mires

This type of mire occurs in small shallow valleys or channels which are rarely enclosed. They are characteristic of parts of southern England and East Anglia, and were first described in the New Forest, where they are numerous (Ratcliffe 1977, 258 for full discussion).

The peat is often shallow, and the date of initiation varies greatly from one deposit to the next.

Blanket mires

These are ombrogenous mires which are widespread in the uplands of northern England, as well as on Dartmoor, Bodmin Moor, and other parts of the south-west peninsula. Their formation depends upon impeded drainage, so they are rarely found on steep slopes or soft bedrock. The peat is usually shallow, mostly less than 4m thick. Because of their origin, blanket mires are generally acidic.

Blanket mire is highly variable in age. In a few parts of Britain it evidently began to form at the onset of the Atlantic period about 5000 bc, possibly because of a climatic deterioration (Conway 1954). Elsewhere its development began much later, and was possibly accelerated or even initiated by intensification of land-use in the uplands during the third and second millennia bc (Moore 1973; Merryfield and Moore 1974). Later prehistoric blanket mire formations are known to cover Bronze Age landscapes on Dartmoor (Fleming 1978, 99) and Bodmin Moor (Mercer 1970). Still more recent deposits, such as at Blackstone Edge, Lancashire (Walker 1984), and Tintagel, Cornwall (Thomas and Fowler 1985), are probably stagnopodzols and stagnogleys, giving rise to organic topsoils.

Many blanket mires have peat with a basal layer, containing the remains of trees and tall shrubs which grew on the underlying mineral soil.

Wetland development

Few, if any, wetland areas have undergone continuous uninterrupted development. Periods of desiccation are evident

Figure 29   Flag Fen, near Peterborough, Cambridgeshire: general view of the site under excavation, showing the north wall of a wooden house with a large threshold plank in position; a small yoke with a perforation at either end lies near the threshold plank. The site dates to the late Bronze Age, about 800 bc (scale in centimetres)

Figure 30 Eclipse Track, Somerset: a trackway constructed of wooden hurdles which runs out into the wet Levels south-westwards from Meare island; this structures dates to about 2000 bc. The figure stands in a recent peat cutting lined with stacks of peat blocks (mumps) set out to dry

in the stratigraphy of most mires, and episodes of both rapid and slow peat growth can usually be detected from the texture and colour of the peat. In Somerset, these differences are reflected in local names for different peat beds, for example 'upper light' and 'top black' (Curtis *et al* 1976, 242).

In extensive wetland areas, such as the fens of East Anglia or the Somerset Levels, mire development was complicated by occasional incursions of the sea, which gave rise to deposits of marine clay within the peat (Pennington 1974, 117; Godwin 1978). Naturally, these provide useful chronological horizons, but they also represent discontinuities in the sequence. The greatest complexity in peat stratigraphy occurs at the junction of dry land and wetland, or where rivers cross wetland areas. Moreover, islands of higher, drier, ground occur within most large wetland expanses, and these often formed the focus of early settlement.[26]

6.3 The archaeology of the wetlands

Archaeological evidence from the wetlands naturally falls into three subdivisions, according to position: below the peat, within the peat, and above the peat. These three zones may be considered separately.

Below the peat

Wherever peat has developed over a previously inhabited land surface, evidence of past activities will be preserved beneath the peat. This is most common under blanket mire, raised mire, and valley mire. The antiquity of the preserved remains depends of course upon the date of peat initiation.

Mesolithic sites beneath blanket mire in the Pennines are known from scatters of flintwork recovered from eroding sections at Cross Fell and Knocks Fell, among other places (Radley *et al* 1974). A Neolithic enclosure sealed beneath a combination of peat and alluvium has recently been excavated at Haddenham, Cambridgeshire (C Evans and Hodder 1985), and, at the same site, Bronze Age burial monuments have been located because their crowns now protrude through the shrunken peat. Similar barrow fields have been discovered at Anwick Fen and Walcott (Chowne and Healy 1983). Other Bronze Age sites include the settlement at West Row, Mildenhall, Suffolk (Martin 1985). This site was situated on a dry island within a raised mire, but some time after its abandonment peat rose up over the island and covered it. Some of the extensive later prehistoric field systems on Dartmoor were similarly covered in peat after their abandonment in the early first millennium bc (Fleming 1978, 99).

More recent sites sealed beneath peat include parts of the Iron Age and early medieval settlement at The Berth, Baschurch, Shropshire (P Gelling and Stanford 1965).

During their life, all these sites were on dry land, and thus the full range of wetland evidence cannot be expected. Preservation is, however, generally good, because the peat overburden has protected the archaeological deposits from destructive processes which would otherwise have damaged them.

Detecting the existence of sites sealed beneath peat is most difficult. Chance finds account for much of the evidence, but where the peat is thin, systematic field and aerial survey allows protruding earthworks and drier islands to be identified in cultivated areas, through differential shrinkage and soil marks (D Hall 1981). In areas with deeper peats, such as the Fens, and in areas of permanent pasture in the Somerset Levels, drainage ditch surveys have proved productive, where such ditches occur and are subject to regular cleaning operations (Pryor 1983a; 1983b; 1985a; Coles and Orme 1983a; 1983b). Survey techniques involving the recording of mineral magnetism within and below peat, using specially developed probes, have

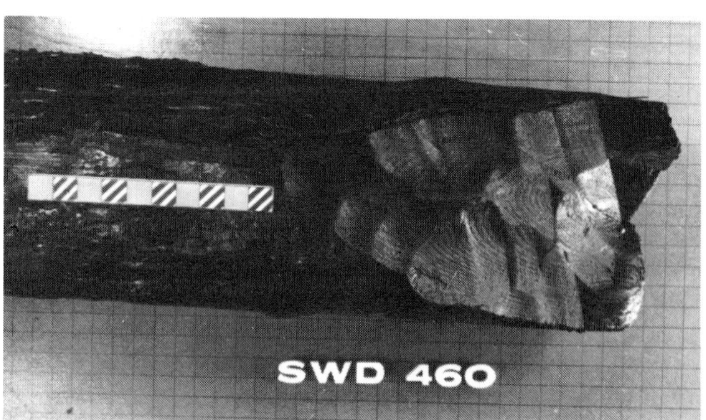

Figure 31 Ashwood peg from the Sweet Track, Somerset, showing facets made by sharpening with a stone axe, dated to about 3200 bc (scale totals 10cm)

been tested in Lancashire, Cumbria, and Cambridgeshire with promising results (Oldfield *et al* 1985).

Within the peat

Evidence from within peat deposits relates to the settlement and exploitation of mires during their growth. For this reason, the evidence is often environmentally specific.

A wide range of activities is represented by artefacts and structures recovered from within peat deposits. Many of these probably relate to seasonal use of wetland areas for grazing, collecting fuel and materials, and hunting. In deep mires, the date range of these activities is equally impressive. It is important to remember that, when deposited, these artefacts and structures were on the surface of the peat and only became incorporated within it as the mire grew higher.

The largest category of evidence comprises stray finds, many of which presumably resulted from casual losses during everyday activities. Flint tools, such as sickles, axes, arrowheads, and knives, pottery, and wooden tools including spears, a reed fork, and a mallet, have turned up in various mires over the last few decades (Coles and Hibbert 1972; Coles and Orme 1980). Two wooden longbows recovered from Meare Heath in the Somerset Levels have been radiocarbon dated to about 2600 bc (J G D Clark 1963).

Prehistoric settlements on the edge of mires, and even within developing mires, are well known, and are of especial interest because of the wide range of domestic and environmental evidence preserved. Among the earliest wetland settlements known is Star Carr, North Yorkshire, where a platform over marshy ground beside a lake was built about 7500 bc by Mesolithic hunters (J G D Clark 1954). Similar sites have been excavated at Seamer Carr, also in Yorkshire (Schadla-Hall 1986; forthcoming), and Williamson's Moss in Cumbria (Bonsall *et al* forthcoming). Neolithic wetland settlements include the well-known site at Ehenside Tarn, Cumbria, discovered in the early 1870s, when a mire was being drained (Darbishire 1874). Later prehistoric wetland settlements were more extensive than their predecessors. At Flag Fen, Cambridgeshire, a Bronze Age site, dated to about 700 bc, was located during a dyke survey in 1982 (Pryor 1983b; 1985b). Augering suggests that the site covers an area of over 15,000 square metres, and excavations have revealed the remains of timber buildings (Fig 29). In Somerset, the Iron Age 'lake villages' of Glastonbury and Meare each covered over 14,000 square metres (Coles and Coles 1986, 153–83).

Traversing wetland posed a major problem throughout prehistoric and recent times. Numerous timber trackways and platforms variously constructed from planks, hurdles, or brushwood are known from the Somerset Levels (Fig 30) and range in date from 3200 bc for the Sweet Track, through to late Iron Age times (Coles and Coles 1986). Associated with these tracks are artefacts and environmental evidence for conditions in the vicinity. The wood used in trackway construction provides information on woodworking techniques (Fig 31; Coles *et al* 1978) and woodland management (Rackham 1977). Trackways are also known in Lincolnshire (May 1976, 112–13), and in Cheshire (R Turner 1986, 11). They must be expected in other wetland areas too.

In very wet areas, boats were widely used. Mesolithic paddles are known from Star Carr (J G D Clark 1954, fig 77), but the earliest intact boats are log-boats of Bronze Age date. Log-boat building continued down into early medieval times, and over 50 examples, of widely varying date, have been found in English wetlands, including the Fens, Somerset Levels, Lancashire, and Shropshire (McGrail 1978). A fairly sophisticated log-boat, probably of Roman date, was excavated at Hasholme, Humberside, in 1984 (Fig 32; McGrail and Millett 1985).

Among the most spectacular finds from wetland areas are the ritual or votive deposits. Much of the finest metalwork produced during the middle and late Bronze Age was deposited in wet places. One collection, from Edington Burtle, Somerset, comprised four bronze palstaves, four bronze sickles, and eight bronze ornaments including finger rings, armlets, and torcs. It had been buried in a maplewood box about 1100 bc (M Smith 1959, 144). Other notable finds include a pair of gold torcs from Hampton, Cheshire (J J Taylor 1976, 62 and 78), and the Bishop's Castle hoard of bronze swords and spearheads, found during the draining of a mire at Lyndham Heath, Shropshire (Burgess *et al* 1972, 240).

It is not known whether any of these objects accompanied burials or were offerings for some other purpose. Animal carcases, largely undated, and over 100 human bodies, in various states of preservation, have been found in peat bogs, many of them discovered during the mid-nineteenth century when peat cutting was done manually (R Turner and Briggs 1986). When discovered, many of these bog-bodies were in such good condition that they were thought to be modern, possibly the remains of murder victims or tramps. The most recent bog-body finds come from Lindow Moss, Cheshire (Stead *et al* 1986). The first of these, which came to light in May 1983, was a female, probably of Roman date, but only the head survived. The second find, in August 1984, was a male, rather more completely preserved than the first find (Fig 33). Detailed examination of the remains revealed that he was well-built, in his mid-twenties, and about 1680mm tall. Prior to death, he seems to have been stripped naked apart from a fox-fur band on his left arm, then, while standing or kneeling, struck from behind twice on the top of the head with a narrow-bladed axe-like weapon, and, perhaps at the same time, once in the back, which broke one of his ribs. Following this, he was strangled and his neck broken by a garrotte. His throat was then cut and the body dropped face down into a shallow pool on the mire. The exact date of the body is not yet clear, but it is probably Iron Age or Romano-British.

The preservation of archaeological finds in mires is largely governed by the acidity of the deposit and the extent and duration of waterlogging. Where desiccation has taken place, the recorded archaeological evidence may be subject to marked post-depositional changes. This is clearly illustrated at the Meare lake village, Somerset, where at first the houses appeared to have been built on raised clay mounds. These 'mounds' later proved to be nothing more than islands of firm deposits which had been left standing proud by the shrinkage of the surrounding peat (Orme *et al* 1981, 67).

Locating and recording finds from within peat deposits is subject to the same difficulties as for finds sealed beneath them. Chance finds are important, and it is notable that the bog-bodies from Lindow Moss, and most of the trackways and stray finds from the Somerset Levels, came to light during peat cutting. Systematic surveys of peat cutting areas and drainage works provide another source of evidence (Coles and Orme 1983b), and on cultivated land fieldwalking and aerial survey can reveal sites within the peat, owing to differential shrinkage and the migration of artefacts to the surface (D Hall 1981). Augering and coring are slow but effective ways of determining the limits of buried sites, and can often shed light on the state of preservation.[27] However, the picture so far recovered by survey work is very incomplete.

Figure 32   Hasholme, Humberside: a wooden boat, probably of late Iron Age date, under excavation

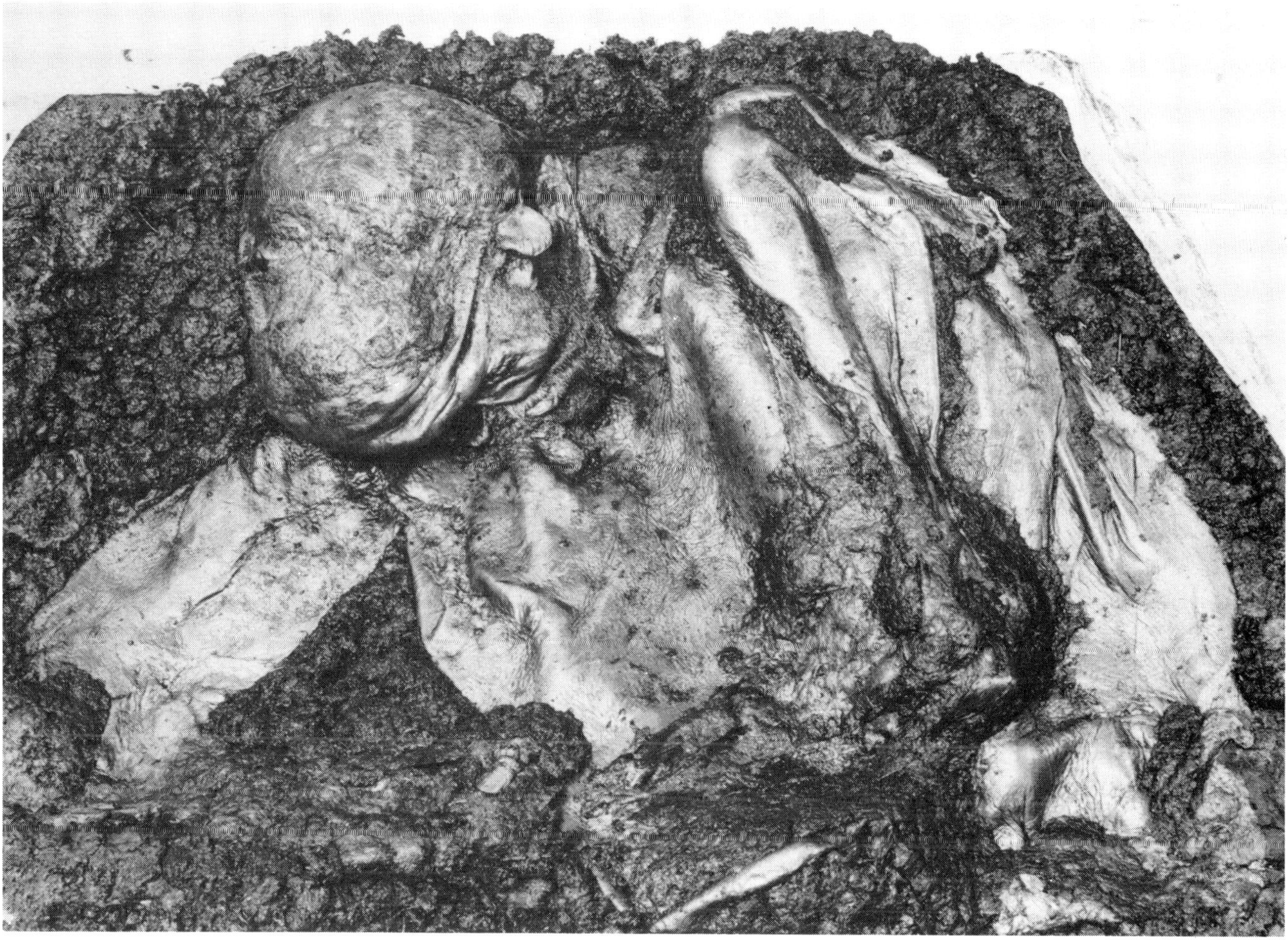

Figure 33   Lindow Man – a late Iron Age or Romano-British bog-body found during peat-cutting on Lindow Moss, Cheshire; the photograph shows the front of the body with the head sunk forward looking into the right shoulder; traces of facial hair can be seen

Above the peat

The preservation of archaeological remains above wetland deposits varies greatly, being largely determined by current and past land-use.

Drainage of some areas of the Fens and the Somerset Levels in Roman times provided areas for settlement and cultivation, which have left tangible traces (*see* papers in C Phillips 1970). Fieldwalking and aerial photography are the main methods of locating these sites, although in predominantly pastoral areas the task is much more difficult. Drainage works of Roman, medieval, and post-medieval date are themselves of interest (Darby 1956; M Williams 1970), and many of the parish boundaries around wetland areas are of considerable antiquity.

Peat cutting was widespread throughout the medieval and post medieval periods. On Bodmin Moor, Cornwall, and a few other upland areas, traces of peat drying platforms alongside cutting areas (turbaries) have been recorded during field survey by the Cornwall Archaeological Unit and RCHME.

6.4   Threats

Over the last few centuries, the wetlands have been exploited to provide a wide range of resources, including peat for fuel, rushes, bog-iron, and grazing. However, much of this exploitation was small-scale and seasonal. It is notable that many of the known finds from wetland areas came to light in the nineteenth century, when peat cutting and drainage works were undertaken by hand. When coal became widely available, peat cutting for fuel declined, and so too did the flow of archaeological discoveries.

Land-use in wetland areas today varies considerably. Since the last war, large areas of the East Anglian fens, previously under pasture, have been brought into cultivation to provide one of the richest arable areas in England. Large open fields and extensive farms predominate. In contrast, the Somerset Levels are still mostly under pasture, with numerous small fields and farms. The upland blanket mires mostly lie within unimproved moorland. It is important to realize, however, that a significant fraction of wetland areas consists of small isolated pockets, usually valley or basin mire, and these are largely integrated within mixed farming regimes.

Given this diversity of land use directly affecting wetland areas, there is a wide range of threats which must be taken into account when seeking to preserve archaeological remains. The following may be singled out for special attention.

Drainage

By far the most widespread and most damaging threat is drainage of wetland areas for cultivation and flood prevention. On a regional scale, water boards and river authorities are

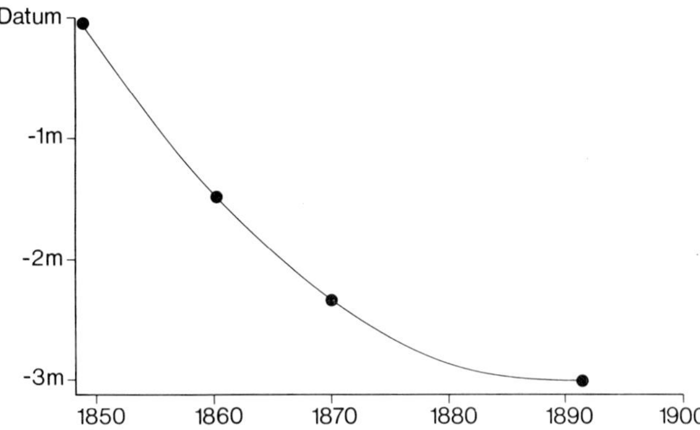

Figure 34   Graph showing the shrinkage rate of the peat at Whittlesey Mere, Cambridgeshire, during drainage operations over the period 1848–1892 (data from Godwin 1978)

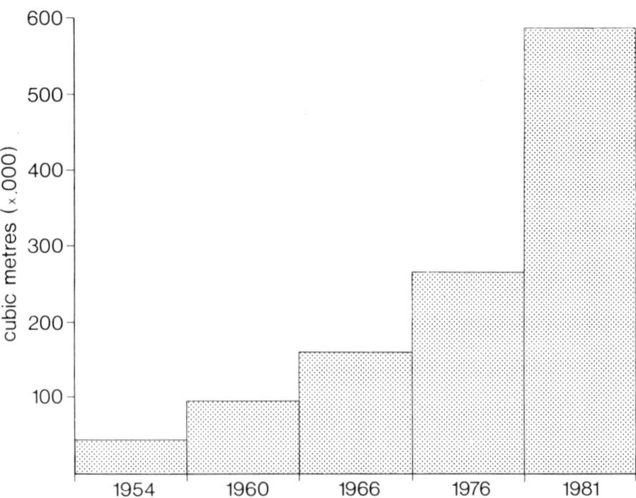

Figure 35   Graph showing the increased rate of peat extraction in Somerset between 1954 and 1981 (data from Somerset County Council 1983a)

gradually lowering water tables. Localized arterial and field drainage schemes can be just as damaging, especially when applied to small wetland areas outside the control of larger authorities.

Desiccation of peat, even for short periods, causes shrinkage and allows biological organisms and small animals to invade the peat through cracks.[28] This accelerates decay.

Since the mid-nineteenth century, the East Anglian fens have been lowered by well over 3m through shrinkage and intensive cultivation. This is graphically illustrated by the lowering of the ground surface over the period 1848 to 1892, during a single episode of drainage at Whittlesey Mere, Cambridgeshire (Fig 34; Godwin 1978).

The effects of drainage on archaeological sites are devastating. Desiccated wetland sites are generally of less value archaeologically than dry-land sites.

Cultivation

As wetland areas are drained, many are taken into cultivation, because organic soils are very attractive for agriculture. There are, however, marked regional variations. In the Fens, some 95% of the land is now under arable cultivation, compared with only 10% about 50 years ago. On King's Sedgemoor, Somerset, only 10% is under cultivation today, although this is increasing.

Cultivation exposes the land to wind erosion, which remains a very serious problem especially in the Fens (ADAS 1985). As soil is blown away, so the water table has to be lowered to maintain its level relative to the ground surface. This accelerates shrinkage and areas of pre-fen surface are now protruding through the peat (B Simmons 1980a; D Hall 1981).

The effects on buried archaeological remains of the phosphates and nitrates added to organic soils as fertilizers has not been fully explored.

Peat extraction

This is a serious but localized problem. The Somerset Levels produces about one-fifth of UK peat output, mostly for horticultural use.[29] Smaller operations exist in Cheshire and other parts of north-west England.

Although peat extraction has increased considerably over the last 50 years (Fig 35), and is expected to increase still further, most peat companies are very cooperative about the investigation of archaeological evidence before it is destroyed. Many chance finds result from vigilant peat cutters, but, as peat cutting becomes more mechanized (Fig 36), there are fewer opportunities to see archaeological objects coming out of the ground.

Burning

In upland areas, accidental and deliberate burning of blanket mire (muirburn) to control vegetation damages, if not destroys, archaeological evidence within the peat. It also accelerates erosion.

Acid rain

Large areas of blanket mire in northern England are being killed by acid rain (Fry and Cooke 1984). This in turn leads to erosion of the peat and exposure of any archaeological remains within or under the deposit.

Figure 36   Mechanized peat extraction in the Somerset Levels

Figure 37   Meare Village West, Somerset: excavation of an Iron Age marshland/lake settlement in progress

6.5   Management

Archaeological remains in wetland areas are especially fragile and vulnerable. Many areas of wetland containing a wealth of evidence have been lost over the last century or so, and special attention to the conservation and management of remaining wetlands is therefore essential.

In formulating management strategies for archaeological sites in wetland areas, two important factors must be taken into account:

i   Scale of the threats: in many cases, responsibility for the major threats to the well-being of archaeological remains lies outside the control of the landowners and land-users. Management agreements in such cases are therefore of limited use.

ii   Cost of works: conservation projects involving major changes to established water regimes are extremely costly to implement. Likewise, excavation of wetland sites is very expensive both in on-site costs of examination and recovery, and in post-excavation costs of specialist analysis and conservation (Coles 1984, 36–68).

More often than not, there is an overlap of interests between archaeological management schemes in wetland areas and those of other countryside bodies, particularly the Nature Conservancy Council.[30]

Curatorial management

Maintaining high water tables is of paramount importance in preserving wetland remains. Despite the fact that the water authorities are required by the Water Act 1973[31] to have regard to the desirability of protecting features of archaeological interest which might be affected by water schemes, very little has been done to safeguard wetland sites.

English Heritage, in conjunction with the NCC, has recently taken the lead in long-term management schemes, by establishing a preservation plan for a 550m length of the Sweet Track in the Shapwick Heath Nature Reserve, Somerset (Coles and Orme 1983b). This track is of Neolithic date and is the oldest recorded such monument in England. In 1982, the site was purchased by the NCC with a grant from the National Heritage Memorial Fund. A clay barrage has been built round the site to reduce water loss, and electric pumps have been installed to maintain water levels within the reserve. It is still too soon to assess the long-term efficiency of this scheme.

At present there are approximately 50 Scheduled Monuments in wetland areas,[32] including the length of the Sweet Track in Somerset, already mentioned, and the Glastonbury and Meare Iron Age lake villages, also in Somerset.

Selecting wetland sites of national importance is especially difficult, because of inadequate knowledge of what lies hidden within and below peat deposits. Lack of disturbance to mire stratigraphy, structure, and hydrology will, however, be an important consideration for their survival and will condition requirements, not least with a view to minimizing expense in maintaining water levels. Structures and sites of most periods are represented in the wetlands, and all are equally important for the evidence they hold, but the range of site types known in the wetlands is not especially wide. Preservation of less well-represented types will therefore be important. All wetland sites are extremely fragile, but those near the surface are most vulnerable and require special treatment. Sites displaying a range of typical wetland features are likely to be settlement or occupation foci, comprising habitation, exploitation, and communications evidence. Few wetland sites have much documentary evidence. Sites which have been partly excavated may still contain valuable evidence, but each must be assessed on individual merits. Related, or successive, sites occur in both the vertical and the horizontal stratigraphy of wetland areas. Sites with sub-surface chemistry compatible with good preservation of a wide range of archaeological material must be given priority for preservation.

In Somerset, the stock of statutorily protected sites is supplemented by a series of recently identified *Areas of High Archaeological Potential* (AHAPs), defined by Somerset County Council (1983a; 1983b). Within these areas, a voluntary notification system operates to alert the county archaeological officer to operations such as earthmoving, new ploughing of old pasture, ditch clearance, and new drainage schemes. An assessment of the likely archaeological impact can then be made, and any necessary preliminary or concurrent action taken.

The needs of archaeological conservation can easily be served locally through sympathetic management of wetland areas. Particularly important are the numerous small areas of wetland, where drainage can be controlled by the landowner, and where peat cutting has not penetrated medieval and earlier deposits. Traditional grazing practices and periodic harvesting of reeds will more than adequately preserve sealed landscapes and peat-bound archaeological remains. Trees should not normally be encouraged, because of the very large quantities of water they consume, apart from the fact that their roots penetrate and disturb buried deposits. In upland areas, burning of peat bogs should be avoided where archaeological remains are likely to be jeopardized.

Special attention should be given to protecting the edges of wetland areas, as these are at greatest risk of desiccation and are likely to contain some of the best archaeological evidence. Old land surfaces beneath peat deposits over 2m thick are likely to be relatively safe, except from prolonged episodes of drainage.

The chemistry of any water used to supplement natural supplies in order to keep archaeological sites wet must be carefully checked to ensure its similarity with the prevailing sub-surface conditions.

Demonstration farms at Tealham Moor, Somerset, Catsholme Farm, Norfolk, and Five Mile Farm, Norfolk, include the conservation of archaeological features (mostly surface features) within their management plans (Cobham 1984; Somerset County Council 1983a, 8.08).

Recording

Since chance finds contribute such a large part of the recovered evidence from wetlands, landowners and land-users should be alerted to the archaeological potential and implications of certain operations (particularly drainage) and encouraged to report finds, so that these can be properly recorded and, if necessary, conserved.

In formulating management plans, it is important to determine the age, extent, character, depth, and degree of waterlogging of wetland deposits. This information will allow an assessment of the value and potential of the deposit. The source of the water supply should also be identified, so that it can be retained in any alterations to natural drainage in the vicinity.

Exploitative management

The public display of *in situ* wetland archaeological remains is rarely practicable at present, although conservation of objects and structures from wetland excavations has been encouraged, and many museums now exhibit material from wetland areas.

Among the existing visible attractions are the reconstructed timber trackways near the Somerset Levels Museum on Shapwick Heath, Somerset, and the Abbots Fish-house at Meare, Somerset. The latter is an English Heritage Guardianship monument.

Academic interest in wetland sites is high, because of their exceptional state of preservation. Excavation projects of both rescue and research types have been especially numerous in the Somerset Levels (Fig 37) and the fens of East Anglia, because of the difficulties of preserving sites from desiccation and destruction. The nature of the archaeological deposits, however, makes such archaeological investigation, and subsequent analysis of the results, extremely expensive, and requires the commitment of a wide range of scarce specialist services. One of the most difficult problems can be coping with ground water (Fasham 1984).

7   Coastlands and estuaries

7.1   Archaeological importance

The coastlands and estuaries of England comprise the seashore, inter-tidal zone, river estuaries, and a belt of land immediately behind this frontage, where a harsh oceanic environment gives rise to mud-flats, slacks, salt-marsh, and sand dunes. Some small off-shore islands fall entirely within this definition.

Today, the coastlands display a great variety of scenery (Steers 1946). High cliffs accompanied by a narrow coastal belt prevail in some areas, especially where hard rocks predominate, while elsewhere low-lying land often gives rise to a wide coastal belt. Of all the landscape environments considered in this volume, the coastlands are most subject to rapid and dramatic changes and modifications through natural forces. Little or no practical control can be exercised over these changes, and this must be borne in mind throughout the following discussion.

Archaeologically the coastlands are important because of the specialized types of site represented and the diversity of remains preserved. This may be reviewed under five headings:

i   Coastally specific sites: because Britain is an island, the coastline has served many roles; as a barrier, a boundary, a place of entry and exit, a highway and means of communication, an easily accessible source of raw materials, and as a source of natural on-shore and off-shore food resources. Thus, sites on the coast tend to be specialized, in the sense that the range of activities undertaken at them could not have taken place inland. Off-shore islands such as the Scilly Isles, Lundy, or Lindisfarne represent microcosms for archaeological study.

ii   Organic remains: waterlogging and inundation with fine silts and clays often promote localized anaerobic conditions and sometimes permit the survival of organic remains, especially wood. Sites found in such conditions are likely to be relatively well preserved.

iii   Environmental indicators: the rapidly changing geo-morphology of coastal areas sometimes provides good conditions for the preservation of a wide range of environmental indicators. In waterlogged areas, such as coastal peat beds, salt marshes, and slacks, pollen is likely to survive if sub surface acidity is high. In dry areas, such as sand dunes, mollusca may be preserved in calcareous sediments. The value of this evidence is clear from work in East Anglia (Murphy 1984b) and south-west England (Bell 1984).

iv   Landscape and stratigraphy: along some coastlines ancient land surfaces have been drowned by the sea and are now only partially visible at low tide. In other areas, the deposition of sand, alluvium, or shingle has smothered considerable tracts of ancient landscape, providing valuable insights into the spread of activities across a given area. When such inundation has a long history, several successive landscapes may be stratified, one above another, within a single deposit.

v   Interpretative value: many areas of coastland provide good opportunities for sensitive archaeological inter-pretation and presentation, not least because the quality of the preserved evidence is high, and many lengths of coastline are already managed as recreational areas.

The length of the coastal frontage of England has been estimated at about 3228km (Countryside Commission 1968). The coastal belt, dominated by a harsh oceanic environment, averages about 1km wide, although in practice it ranges from less than 100m to several kilometres even over short distances. Defined in this way, the coastlands comprise about 3228 square kilometres, about 2.5% of the land area of England (Fig 38).

For archaeological purposes, three main types of coastland may usefully be identified on the basis of the prevailing long-term geomorphological trends: accretional coasts, where natural processes are causing the extension of dry land over previously sea-covered areas; erosional coasts, where land is being lost to the sea; and neutral coasts, which are broadly stable. Along some rapidly expanding accretional coasts, archaeological sites and monuments at one time near or on the coast may now lie several kilometres inland, as for example with sites in the Fens, or the Cinque ports of Sussex. Where such monuments now lie within altogether different landscape environments, they are discussed in other chapters. Areas of ancient coast now permanently submerged by the sea lie outside the scope of this volume.

Although the highly dynamic nature of coastland environments may appear to militate against the survival and effective maintenance of archaeological evidence, this is not so. A surprising number of sites are already known, and many more await discovery. Moreover, because coastal areas are among the most intensively managed landscape environments in the country, there is every hope that, where natural forces permit, sites can be preserved for future generations to enjoy.

7.2   Coastal history, dynamics, and distribution

Broadly speaking, the modern coastline had its origins about 8000 years ago, when the water locked up in the ice caps of the last glacial period was released into the sea, dramatically raising sea-levels and flooding many areas of land which had previously been inhabited. Among such areas were large tracts now under the North Sea and the English Channel.

Over the last 8000 years or so, the coastline has been far from stable. Long-term processes of adjustment have altered the relative levels of land and sea, making the dividing line between them oscillate to and fro. Especially influential has been the gradual rising of some land and the accompanying down tilting of other areas after the disappearance of the ice sheets (*isostatic readjustment*). Another factor has been the continual change in the level of the sea (*eustatic fluctuation*).[33] Environmental studies have shown that, alongside physical changes, there have also been variations in the vegetation cover characteristic of coastal areas (Spencer 1975; J G Evans 1979).

Both isostatic readjustment and eustatic fluctuation have important implications for the preservation of archaeological evidence, especially on low-lying coasts where a change of just a few metres in the relative levels of land or sea can mean the drowning or exposure of large areas. A particularly notable episode of flooding (marine transgression) took place about 2000 bc around much of southern and south-eastern England. Large areas of landscape containing Neolithic and early Bronze Age sites were covered by the sea (Fig 39). This old ground surface is generally known as the Lyonesse surface and is

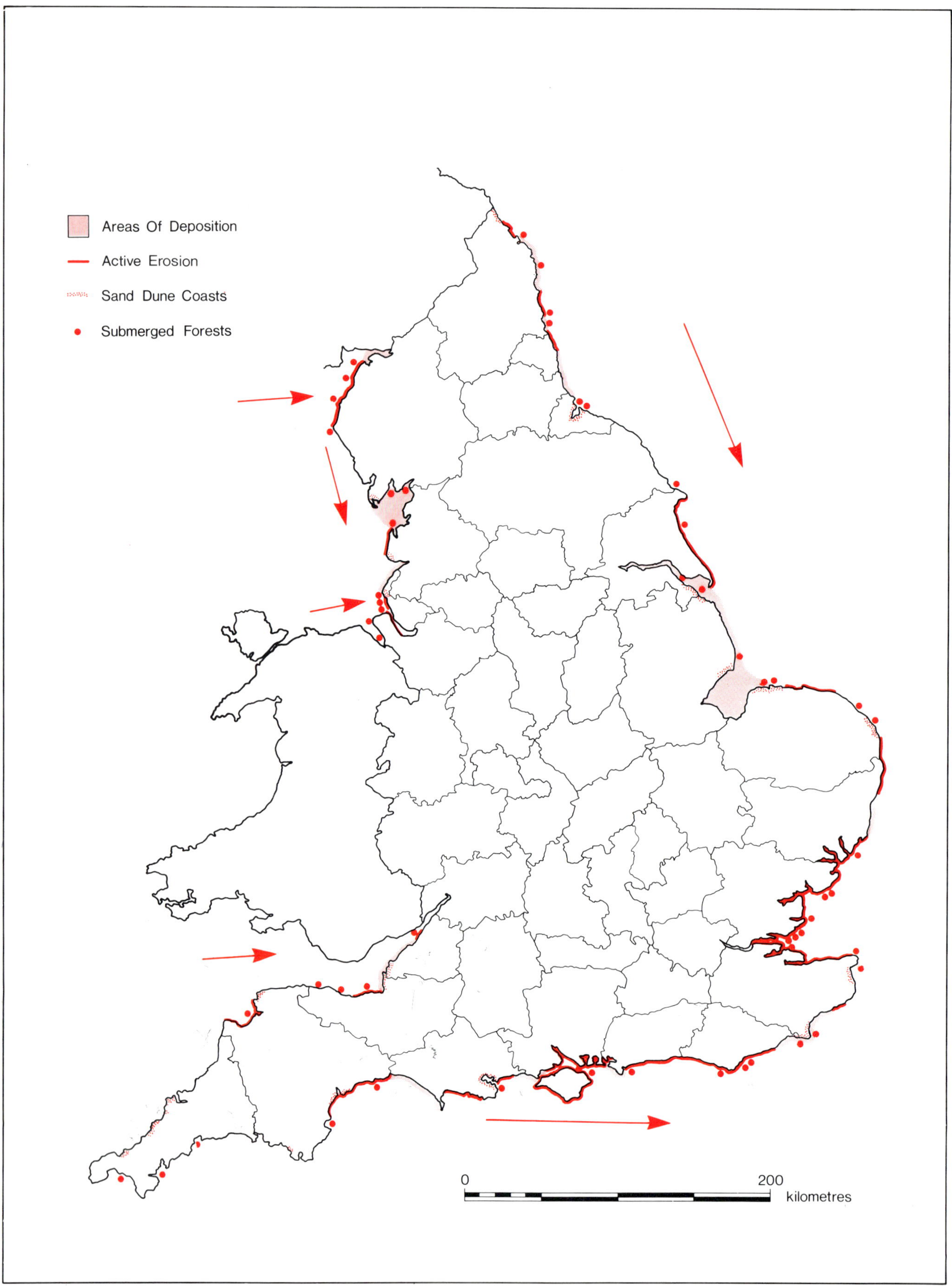

Figure 38   Map showing the main categories of coastland, the distribution of submerged forests (after Godwin 1975), and the principal areas of sand dunes; the large arrows indicate the direction of movement or 'pebble streams'

Figure 39   Prehistoric structures revealed at low tide around the Essex coast: A (above) wooden hurdle structure exposed by current erosion on the foreshore in the Blackwater Estuary (scale totals 50cm); B (right) wooden paddle of Bronze Age date found on the foreshore during survey work in the Hullbridge Basin (scale totals 2m)

especially well documented in Essex (Warren *et al* 1936; I Smith 1955) and Kent (Burchell and Piggott 1939; Burchell 1957; J H Evans 1953). Many of the submerged forests around the coast represent the remains of landscapes flooded at about the same time (Godwin 1975, 20).

To complicate matters, these long-term trends which affect large areas are accompanied by more localized, but no less important, processes of erosion and deposition caused by wave action, storms, riverine deposition, and tidal movement. These bring about the formation of cliffs, caves, promontories, stacks, arches, beaches, bars, spits, and tombolos. They also influence the micromorphology of individual stretches of coast. The operation of these processes also determines the range of archaeological evidence likely to be preserved (Fig 40).

Accretional coasts

These occur wherever the boundary between the land and sea is retreating seaward, either through the combined effects of isostatic readjustment and eustatic fluctuations, or because tidal action is causing the deposition of sediments to build up new land. In the case of the former, emergent land may contain ancient sites, which effectively lose their protective covering when out of the water and are then subject to desiccation or erosion by storms and wind.

Only in the north-west of England, around the Solway Firth, are the effects of isostatic uplift overcoming eustatic fluctuation to reveal land previously sea-covered (Tooley 1980).

Areas of deposition are widespread round the coast.

Wherever currents or waves suffer a reduction in velocity, sediment held in suspension or in movement by long-shore drift will be dumped. Among the most notable areas of deposition are Selsey Bill, Sussex, Chesil Beach, Dorset, Morecambe Bay, Lancashire, the Humber Estuary, Humberside, and the Wash. Investigations on Romney Marsh, Kent, have revealed the approximate positions of earlier coastlines (Cunliffe 1980) and serve to underline the fact that on coasts undergoing active deposition only very recent sites will lie near the present shoreline; the more ancient sites will now lie well back from the frontage, and probably for this reason are relatively well preserved.

Erosional coasts

These are areas where the boundary between land and sea is advancing landward, either through isostatic readjustment and eustatic fluctuation allowing marine transgression, or through mechanical weathering of the shoreline through wave action. It may also be noted that human agencies, such as agricultural activity, visitor erosion, and directional sea defences, can prompt or exacerbate mechanical weathering. In either case, archaeological evidence is probably being destroyed or damaged, even if what remains is later submerged. Only where a marine transgression has been fairly rapid do archaeological sites benefit from this process through better preservation.

Among the most spectacular examples of marine transgression drowning significant area of landscape are the Isles of Scilly (P Fowler and Thomas 1979; Thomas 1985). Here what

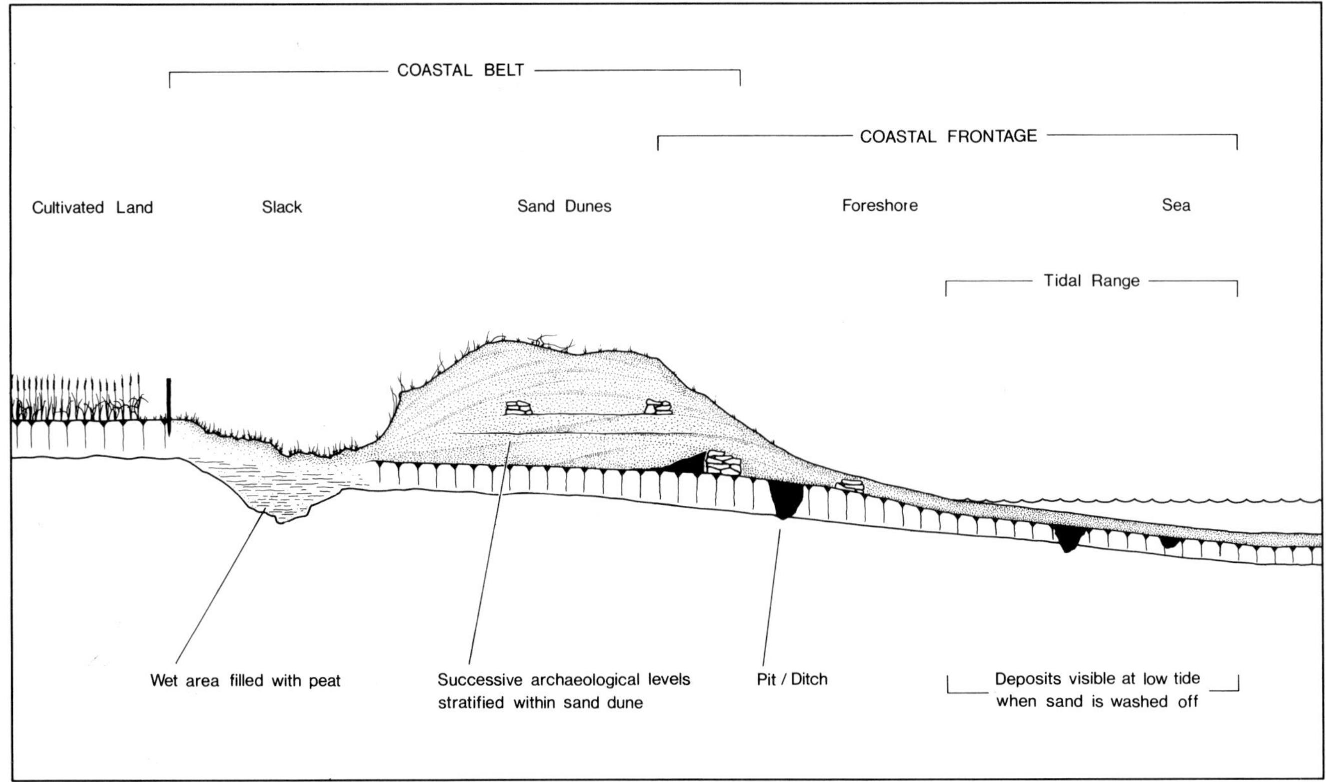

Figure 40   Idealized cross-section through a low-lying coastline, showing the variety of preservation contexts present and the main areas of erosion

was once probably a single island has been drowned, leaving only the higher ground as separate islands in an archipelago. Prehistoric field boundaries can be seen on some beaches at low tide and seem to be linked with comparable boundaries on dry land. It seems that, in this area, the major phase of drowning began in the medieval period and is still continuing at a rate of about 0.25m every century (Thomas 1985, 8).

Active mechanical erosion is taking place along stretches of the English coastline. It is particularly destructive where the coastline is flanked by soft rocks, for example in East Anglia and parts of the east coast, where whole villages are known to have been lost since medieval times. Hornsea Beck, Humberside, is one such site. Its existence was recorded in 1367, but it was last mentioned about 1747 (Loughlin and Miller 1979). How many pre-medieval sites have been lost is impossible to guess.

Even where relatively hard rocks, such as chalk, flank the coast, the erosive power of the sea can be considerable. In some parts of south-eastern England, chalk cliffs are being eaten away at a rate of up to 2m a year (Bradley 1970a).

Neutral coasts

Large parts of the English coastline are fairly stable, neither drastically eroding, nor being subject to active deposition. These areas include the hard rock edged coasts of the south-west penisula and the north-east. However, within areas of essentially neutral coast, localized erosion or deposition does take place, and this may be important from the archaeological standpoint.

Sand dunes

Quite separate from the processes of marine erosion and deposition around the coast is the formation of sand dunes. These are mounds or hills of sand deposited by the wind. They have a widespread occurrence on the coast simply because of strong winds and abundant unconsolidated sediment. Dunes may reach heights of 30m or more, and are important archaeologically because they sometimes cover and protect coastal sites. Moreover, they often form over very long periods, with many providing the setting for successive phases of activity which, because of the steady rate of formation, have become interstratified within the dune. Dunes are, however, unstable and susceptible to erosion by mechanical weathering and wind erosion, which may result in what are known as 'blow-outs'. Dunes also move their position to the extent that sites can be buried and then later exposed again, as at St Pirans Oratory, Perranzabuloe, Cornwall (N Johnson 1981, 216).

The complexity of coastal dynamics results in a variety of situations in which archaeological deposits can be preserved. These include burial beneath sand or silt, and submergence below the sea or below marshland. In some cases, the same site or ancient landscape may be preserved in different ways, even within quite a small area (Fig 40).

7.3   The archaeology of coastlands

Archaeological sites in coastland areas can be divided into two groups. First, there are coastally specific sites, whose existence is in some way reliant on being at the coast and which are therefore only found on or very near the coast. Second, there are coastally situated sites, which were not on the coast when they were in use but have since become coastal through subsequent changes in coastline. Both groups are equally deserving of proper management, but may be described separately.

Coastally specific sites

The main types of site found exclusively on the coast are those connected with the settlement, exploitation, and defence of the coastal littoral, and those connected with trade, communications, and the use of the coast as a barrier or boundary. Stray finds along coastal areas are common, but their interpretation is often difficult because of possible displacement by tides, cliff falls, and slumping. The dumping of ballast and other waste by passing ships and the possibility that material from shipwrecks has washed ashore also complicate the interpretation of material recovered as stray finds.

Settlements, both permanent and seasonal, are well represented all around the coast, especially those of prehistoric date. At Brean Down, Somerset, for example, a series of at least six occupation levels from the early Bronze Age to the Saxon period has been revealed stratified within sand dunes (Fig 41; ApSimon et al 1961; Bell 1985). Settlements on the Lyonesse surface of Essex date from the Neolithic and Bronze Age, and include well- preserved wooden structures (Warren et al 1936; I Smith 1955; Warren and Smith 1954). In south-west England, cliff castles represent a distinctive form of enclosed later prehistoric settlement (Fig 42).

Less permanent coastal settlement is represented by the short-term occupation of caves, as at Ash Hole, Brixham, Devon, which was occupied in the middle Bronze Age to judge from the pottery found at the site (ApSimon 1968), and cooking sites comprising little more than a midden and a hearth as at Braunton Burrows, Devon, thought to date to the eleventh and twelfth centuries AD (P Smith et al 1983). Many of the late Mesolithic coastal sites, so common in Cornwall (N Johnson and David 1982), Dorset (S Palmer 1970), and Northumberland (Buckley 1925), may have been seasonal sites. In Sussex, field survey has led to the identification of a number of marshland camps along the coast. These mostly date to the Neolithic period, although later examples are known. All yield distinctive types of flint tools, including notched and hollow scrapers, presumably related to hunting and gathering activities (Bedwin 1980).

Closely associated with some coastal settlements are cemeteries, barrows, and ritual sites. These tend to be identical with examples found inland, although when sealed below sand dunes they can be very well preserved.[34]

Ports and harbours occur in a wide variety of forms at

Figure 41   Bronze Age coastal settlement under excavation at Brean Down, Somerset: the site is preserved under a sand dune, but is threatened by erosion on this stretch of coast (scales each total 2m)

Figure 42   The Rumps, Cornwall: Iron Age cliff-castle on the north Cornish coast

different dates all round the coast. Among the earliest known is Hengistbury Head near Christchurch, Dorset (Cunliffe 1978b). This site was a focus for foreign trade from the late Iron Age period into early Roman times, and was probably one of a series of similar sites facing the continent in later prehistory. Harbours are also associated with some of the cliff castles in the south- west, and, from Roman times onwards, harbours and ports incorporated a greater range of engineering works, including jetties, quays, dockyards, and harbour walls. Lighthouses and beacons were also built along the coast from at least Roman times onwards.

Fortifications to defend the coast as a boundary are perhaps the most spectacular of all archaeological monuments in the coastlands, often comprising substantial structures at regular intervals to form a defensive chain. Among the earliest recorded defensive work is the coastal extension of the Hadrian's Wall frontier for over 25km along the Solway coast of Cumbria to protect England from barbarian raids (G Jones 1982). Of slightly later date, probably third century AD in origin, are the nine or ten so-called Saxon shore-forts along the south and east coast from Brancaster, Norfolk, to Portchester, Hampshire (S Johnson 1976). These were built to defend harbours and river estuaries, and to garrison troops connected with the channel fleet. Of the original sites, one has probably been totally lost to the sea, two are partially destroyed by the sea, and three are now some way inland because of coastal reclamation and accretion since Roman times. Later defensive works of special note include the Henrician forts, built in the sixteenth century at intervals all around the coast, the Martello Towers of the south coast, built during the Napoleonic wars, the Palmerstonian and First World War defences, and the widespread Second World War coastal works, including pill-boxes (Fig 43; Wills 1985), gun emplacements, and anti-tank traps.[35]

Transportation in coastal areas leaves a variety of archaeological evidence. The Royal Military Canal between Folkestone and Rye in Kent is closely connected with the defensive works of the Napoleonic wars, but of more prosaic origin are numerous causeways across tidal flats and narrow inter-tidal channels. One example, brought to light by engineering works at Mersea, Essex, was 500m long and comprised 15–20 rows of oak piles. Dendrochronology of the timbers dated its construction to between AD 684 and 702 (Crummy et al 1982).

Figure 43   Type 22 pill-box at Highcliffe, near Bournemouth, Dorset; note how cliff falls are gradually submerging the monument

Shipwrecks on beaches, or in inter-tidal waters, are also well represented,[36] and range from massive galleons, such as the *Amsterdam* on the beach at Hastings, Sussex, to small cargo vessels, such as the one revealed in 1985 on the beach at Minehead, Somerset (Fig 44).

Possibly the largest single class of evidence from coastal areas is that connected with the exploitation of on-shore and

Figure 45   Aerial view of the medieval salterns at Marsh Chapel, Lincolnshire: in the grass field (centre foreground) are the remains of medieval salterns or islands separated by narrow watercourses; the salterns in adjacent fields are in the course of being levelled by ploughing. The present shoreline lies just beyond the top left corner of the picture

off-shore resources. Temporary campsites from Mesolithic times to the post-medieval period have already been mentioned and were undoubtedly connected with the seasonal use of the various resources available in the vicinity. The collection of minerals and rocks, such as flint, amber, chert, coal, and shale, leaves very little trace, but one of the most widespread coastal activities was saltmaking (*see* papers in de Brisay and Evans 1975).

Mounds of burnt clay, often up to 25m across, and briquetage, a coarse ceramic fabric used to make porous containers in which to boil down concentrated brine to extract the salt, usually betray the presence of salt extraction from seawater. The earliest examples so far recorded date to the late Bronze Age, but similar sites continued in use well into the post-medieval period. Relatively recent examples are often surrounded by leats and shallow ponds, in which the preliminary concentration of seawater by natural evaporation took place. Especially well documented are the 'red hills' of Essex, of which over 175 examples have been recorded (de Brisay 1975). Many other areas, including Cumbria, Dorset, Hampshire, Sussex, Kent, Somerset, Lincolnshire, and Lancashire can also boast large numbers of saltworks (Fig 45). Around the Adur estuary above Shoreham, Sussex, for example, fieldwork revealed 130 examples (Holden and Hudson 1981). Salterns are not only confined to low-lying coasts; in Dorset, examples are known on cliff-lined coasts (Bradley 1975).

Pottery production is associated with some salterns, and was again probably a seasonal activity undertaken in the summer months (Bradley 1975). In the Upchurch Marshes of Kent,

Figure 44   Shipwreck revealed at low tide on the beach at Madbrain Sands, near Minehead, Somerset

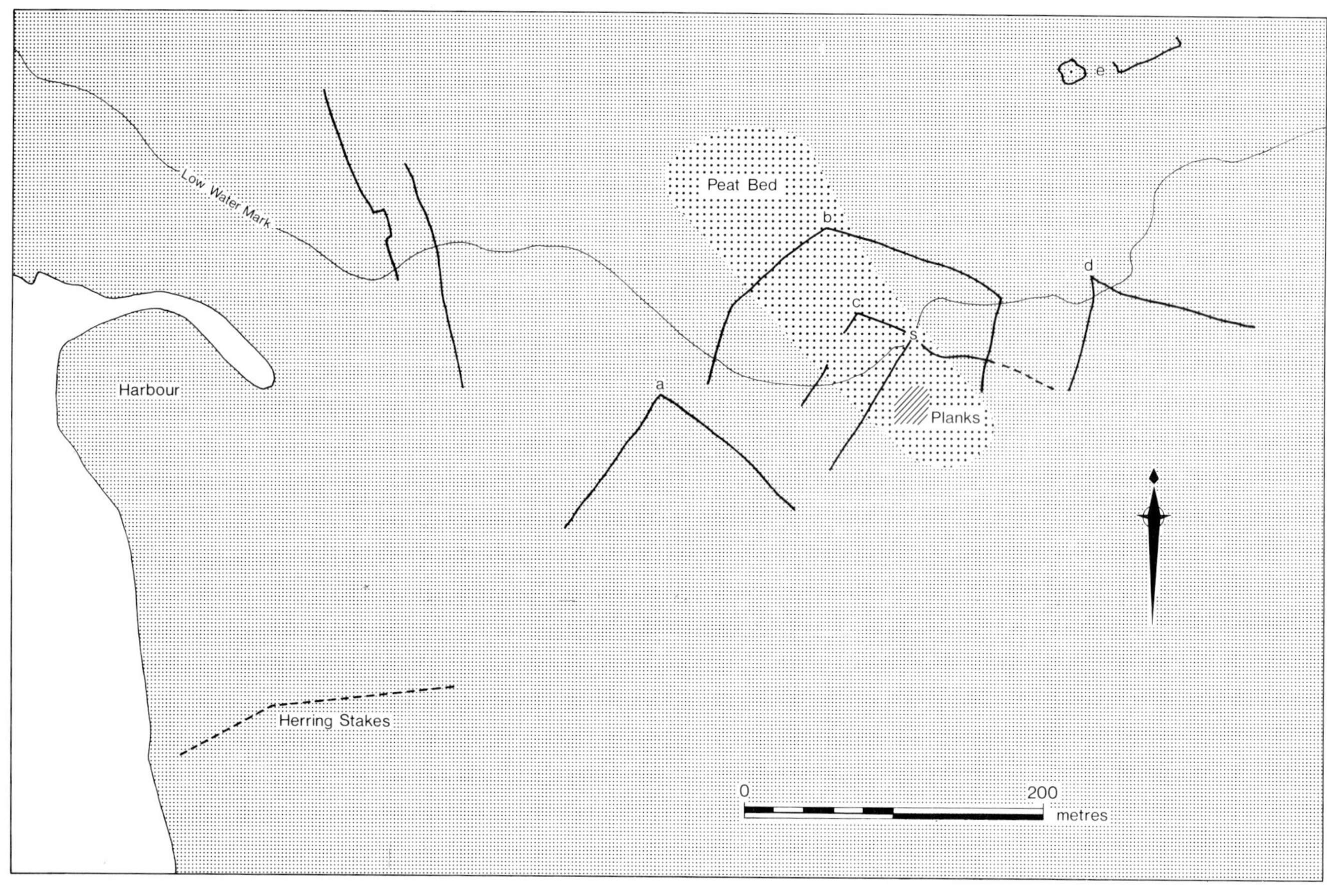

Figure 46   Minehead, Somerset: plan of tidal fishweirs along the inter-tidal zone; fish caught in the walled enclosures when the tide goes out can be simply picked up by hand at low tide. Two of the weirs (A and B) are still operational, but C and D have been disused for some time; a pile of stones at S may have been used to repair the weirs from time to time; a congar heap (eel trap) is situated further out from the shore at E (after survey by E Dennison for Somerset County Council)

pottery was produced on a considerable scale in Roman times (Monaghan 1982).

Fishing was another widespread coastal activity and, although hard to detect archaeologically, elaborate fish traps comprising stone-walled enclosures, interconnected with sluices and weirs are known in the inter-tidal zones of some beaches (McDonnell 1980). Among the best preserved examples are those at Minehead, Somerset (Fig 46), some of which are still in use. They comprise long lines of beach boulders forming drystone walls with pebble and larger stone infill. They all form a 'V' shape with the apex pointing out to sea. The method of operation is relatively simple: a net is stretched across the neck of the weir, so that any water trapped inside as the tide recedes has to pass through the net. At low tide the trapped fish are removed.

Coastal peat beds were extensively cut for fuel, as with inland peat beds. The Norfolk Broads owe their formation to exceptionally heavy and widespread peat extraction (Lambert and Joyce 1960). Tide-mills, and their associated ponds and leats, are known at the head of many creeks and small estuaries and represent a special adaptation of the water-mill principle to the coastal situation (Syson 1965). On the Isle of Sheppy, Kent, another adaptation to coastal circumstances can be seen in the form of low mounds, constructed as refuges for livestock grazing the coastal marshes at times of flood (Wood 1972, 197).

Along many low-lying coasts, sea walls or earthworks have been constructed to protect farmland and settlements from high tides. Some of these are of considerable antiquity. In Essex, early examples are known at Barking and Dagenham (Wood 1972, 196). In some cases, old sea defences have been left high and dry by later coastline changes, as with the Rhee Wall on Romney Marsh, which is probably Roman in origin, and is now between 3 and 12km inland (Cunliffe 1980). One potentially important feature of coastal defences of this sort is the area of old ground surface preserved beneath them.

In general, the identification of coastally specific sites is easiest on eroding coasts, where wave action and tidal flow regularly bring new evidence to light. The wide tidal range common round the English coasts (often up to $+$ 3m) allows scrutiny of large inter-tidal areas by careful field survey and aerial photography. Projects have recently been undertaken around the Hullbridge Basin, Essex (Wilkinson and Murphy 1984, with earlier refs), the Chichester Harbour area of Sussex (Fig 47; Cartwright 1984), and the Portsmouth Harbour area of Hampshire (Bradley and Hooper 1973), and all serve to highlight the wealth of evidence along the coastal frontage. Many types of site have distinctive earthworks or above-ground components, and therefore should be recognizable on neutral coasts and some accretional coasts.

Coastally situated sites

Most Palaeolithic and early Mesolithic sites now on the coast were in altogether different situations when occupied. The settlement on Hengistbury Head, dated to about 1200 bc, overlooked a river valley when in use; now it overlooks Poole Harbour (Barton and James 1983). Other coastal Palaeolithic sites include Rainbow Bar in the Solent (Shackley 1981, 6). Whenever early prehistoric coastal settlements are investigated, close attention must be given to researching contemporary sea-level, to check whether the site was coastal at the time of its use or not (Churchill 1965; Butcher 1978).

Rapidly eroding coastlines may also bring sites into closer contact with the sea than they were in antiquity. The beaker settlement at Belle Tout, Sussex (Bradley 1970a; 1970b) and the Roman villa at Folkestone, Kent (Winbolt 1925), for example, are both now partly lost to the sea, but were well inland when occupied.

Marine transgressions can also create a false impression of the position of sites. On Scilly, the fields now partly submerged were sufficiently well back from the coastline to allow their use for cultivation or grazing in prehistoric times (P Fowler and Thomas 1979). The many submerged forests which have been identified around the coast were, of course, on dry land when alive (Reid 1913; Godwin 1943; 1975, fig 6). Again, special attention has to be given to establishing the contemporary environment of these sites.

Recognizing coastally situated sites follows broadly the same pattern as for coastally specific sites. Eroding coasts again provide most evidence, but only because traces can be most readily recognized.

Table 2   Land-use of the coastal frontage in England[*]

Land use	Length of frontage (km)	% of all frontage
Open and agriculture etc	2072	64.2%
Built-up, industrial, etc	857	26.6%
Government and MOD lands	160	4.9%
Nature reserves and similar	89	2.7%
Golf courses, commons, etc	50	1.6%
Total	3228	100.0%

[*] Data from Countryside Commission (1968)

7.4   Threats

The greatest threat to the archaeology of the coastlands always has been, and always will be, the effects of the natural processes of weathering and erosion. Increasingly, however, the coastlands are being exposed to man-made threats, as more demands are placed upon the coastal landscape.

Until the last century, the coastlands were fairly isolated areas, largely used for the small-scale, often seasonal, exploitation of natural resources, for fishing and fowling, and as a strategic line of defence during times of war. The harsh environment precluded much agricultural activity, although low density grazing was widespread.

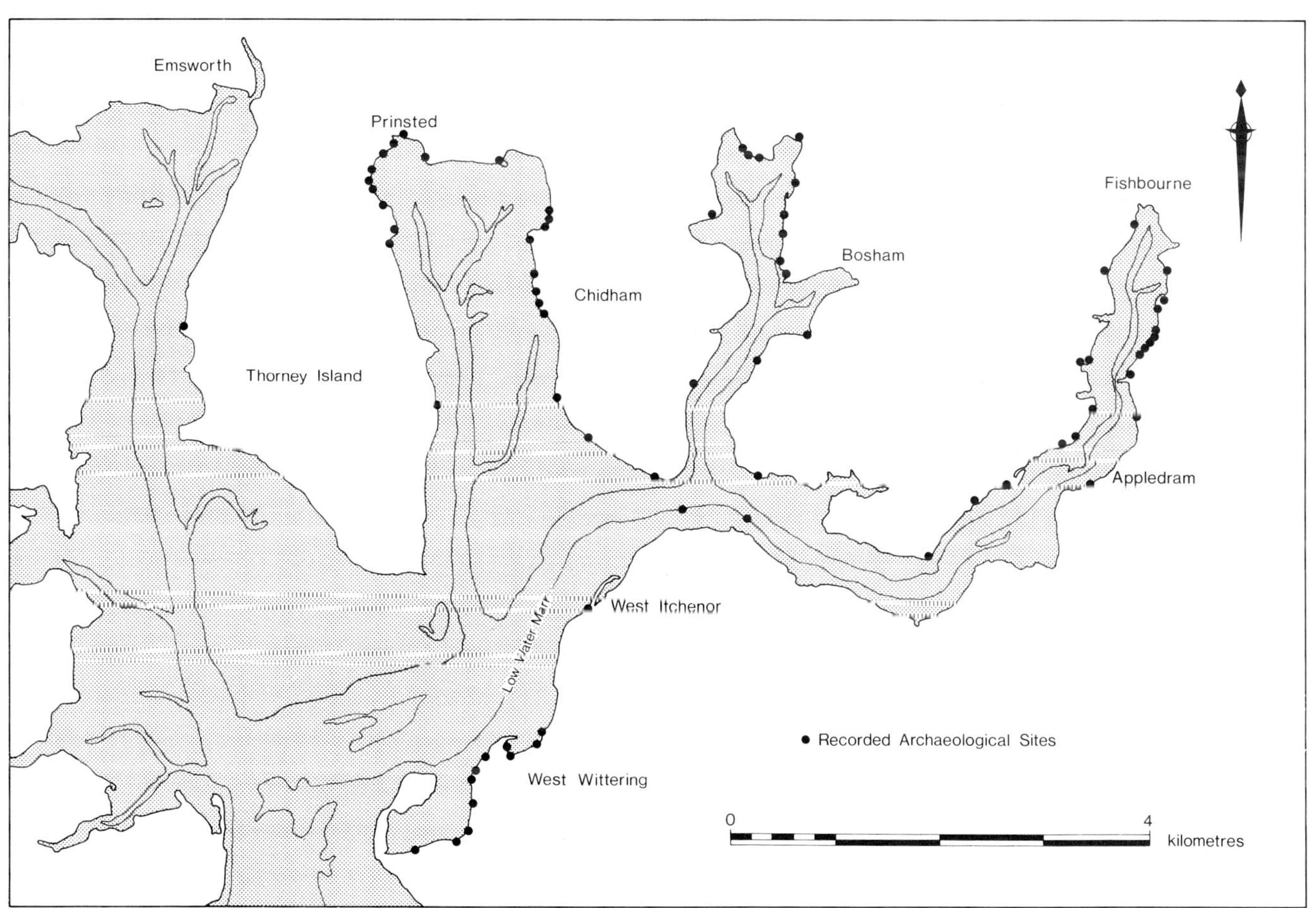

Figure 47   Plan of Chichester Harbour, showing the position of recorded sites after detailed field survey (after Cartwright 1984)

Figure 48   Roman signal station and medieval castle on the cliffs at Scarborough, North Yorkshire: nearly a quarter of the Roman signal station has been eroded away since it was in use during the fourth century

Today, the dominant land-use along the coastal frontage is extensive, and locally intensive, recreational and leisure activities of various sorts (Table 2). Improved sea defences and marshland reclamation schemes allow greater agricultural use of the coastlands than ever before. A little over 26% of the frontage is built up or given over to industrial uses.

Much of the coastal frontage is in public ownership, either by local authorities or by the National Trust which, through its Enterprise Neptune campaign, now owns, or has in covenant, some 512km of coastline in England.[37] Much, however, remains in private ownership, and most of this comprises relatively small blocks of land. Large stretches of coast, both public and private, are still relatively remote and isolated.

Given the ever-present natural forces and the diversity of land-use which now prevails, the coastlands face a wide range of threats which must be taken into account when seeking to manage the archaeological resource. The following may be considered in more detail.

Natural erosion

By far the most widespread and most damaging threat is the effect of natural erosion, especially cliff collapse, wave cutting, tidal movement, and blow-outs. Particularly at risk are coastlands dominated by soft rocks.

Wave cutting and the effects of storms and turbulent high tides are particularly notable on most types of coastline. At Brean Down, Somerset, it has been calculated that a strip of archaeological deposits nearly 1.5m wide, and along a frontage of about 100m at the back of the beach, has been lost each year for the last ten years at least.[38] In Sussex, cliff collapse at Belle Tout amounts to a loss of about 2m of land each year all along the cliff edge (Bradley 1970a). A similar story is clear at many other sites around the coast (Fig 48).

Tidal flow and the effects of currents are particularly visible along low-lying coasts, where archaeological deposits are widespread in the inter-tidal zone. Cyclical exposure of such deposits means that they have a fairly short life expectancy (Wilkinson and Murphy 1986).

Wind erosion not only has the effect of exposing sites, but also severely damages artefacts and structures by abrasion once they are exposed. At Tintagel, Cornwall, loss of surface vegetation through a ground fire resulted in extensive wind erosion of the very light sandy soils covering the buried archaeological features (Thomas and Fowler 1985).

Tourism and recreation

Increased recreational use of the coastlands puts archaeological sites at risk in a number of ways, although it should be emphasized that considerable variation exists in the intensity of visitor use along the coast, and that it tends to be only the most heavily-used areas that suffer.

Capital works, such as the construction of marinas, golf courses, car-parks, and approach roads, sometimes directly damage sites and also lead to changes in the natural pattern of erosion, which in turn threatens otherwise well-protected sites. Visitor activities, such as horseriding, motorbike scrambling, and fire lighting, can, on occasions, directly disturb archaeological deposits, but more often causes the ground surface to break up and expose deposits to other, more potent, agents of erosion. Coastal footpaths across unconsolidated ground frequently cut down into archaeological deposits, as for example near Trevosa, Cornwall (N Johnson and David 1982).

Beach works

Engineering works, such as resanding beaches to improve their appearance, groyne construction, mineral extraction (mostly sand and gravel), and cleaning-up operations after major pollution incidents, all have attendant direct or indirect effects on archaeological deposits. At Brean Down, Somerset, the construction of a sea wall along the back of the main beach has served to concentrate erosion at the northern end, where an extensive series of archaeological deposits lie.

Reclamation

Although coastal reclamation for agricultural and industrial land has been in progress for many centuries, the scale of works undertaken over the last few decades has increased dramatically. The effects on archaeological sites can sometimes be beneficial, for example where the forces of natural erosion are held back. More often, however, reclamation leads to desiccation of waterlogged deposits, and the scale of engineering works involved gives little chance for the unscathed survival of sites.

Table 3 Coastal frontage protected by special designation in England*

Designation	Frontage (km)	% of frontage
Areas of Outstanding Natural Beauty	922	29%
Sites of Special Scientific Interest	539	17%
National Parks	107	3%
Not designated	1660	51%
Total	3228	100%

* Data from Countryside Commission (1968)

Other

Less widespread, but no less important, threats to coastland archaeology are posed by oil drilling and exploration works, construction of oil and gas pipelines, and the dumping of colliery waste and other unwanted industrial materials. Rabbits and other burrowing animals cause disturbance to the stratigraphy of sand dunes.

No detailed evaluation of the effects of proposed barrages across various major river estuaries has yet been undertaken. The Channel Tunnel project will also have implications for coastland areas.

7.5 Management

Archaeological remains in the coastlands are especially vulnerable to both natural and human agencies. Many sites have already been lost, and special attention to the conservation and management of what remains is therefore essential.

Interest in the management and planning of development in coastal areas has a long history stretching back to the 1930s (Dougill 1936; Steers 1944), and, as a result, the coastlands are now among the more intensively managed sections of the English countryside. Much common ground exists between the aims of archaeological management and those of other interests, notably the National Trust, the National Park authorities, the Nature Conservancy Council, and the Countryside Commission.[39] Nearly 50% of the coastal frontage already lies within designated 'protected' areas of various sorts (Table 3).

In addition, the Countryside Commission has designated approximately 780km (24%) of the coastal frontage in England as Heritage Coast, and detailed management plans have been prepared, or are proposed, for these areas (Countryside Commission 1969; 1970a; 1970b; Cullen 1982). The National Trust owns, or has in covenant, about 16% of the English coastline (including much designated as Heritage Coast), and this too is the subject of area-specific management plans.[40]

In formulating management strategies for archaeological sites in coastal areas, two important factors have to be taken into account:

i   Environmental uncertainty: man's activities are relatively predictable and the effects can be minimized, but natural agencies are much less predictable, which brings into question the long-term value of some large-scale conservation projects.

ii   Cost of works: providing and maintaining protection for coastal sites, such as sea defences, coffer dykes, and stabilized ground, is very expensive, even for small areas.

Curatorial management

The main thrust of curatorial management must be directed towards preventing or minimizing natural erosion where this is practicable, and preventing desiccation and sub-surface damage where this might lead to a reduction in the quality of preserved evidence. Both coastally specific sites and coastally situated sites require attention, but it is important to distinguish clearly between sites where only natural processes are involved and sites where there is a need to control and manage man-induced pressures.

Approximately 140 sites within coastland areas are at present protected as Scheduled Monuments;[41] 19 monuments within coastland areas are in State Guardianship. Among the Scheduled Monuments are many classes of site, including settlements, middens, saltworks, fisheries, tide-mills, dockyards, ships, lighthouses, ferry crossings, sea walls, forts, signal stations, pill-boxes, gun emplacements, and anti-tank bollards. The whole of the island of Samson, Scilly, is scheduled because of its great wealth of surviving sites. Most of the Guardianship sites are medieval and post-medieval forts and defensive works.

Selecting coastland sites of national importance is especially difficult because so little evaluative survey work has been undertaken, and many sites only come to light when they are being destroyed. Moreover, in areas of very rapid erosion preservation may not be cost-effective or sufficiently assured.

In applying the criteria for the selection of sites for scheduling in coastal areas, priority must be given to sites which remain largely intact. Soil conditions likely to preserve a wide range of materials will be important in some areas. Coastally specific sites have to be assessed on the number of known examples in other coastal areas; types which are poorly represented must be given priority, but due consideration should be given to sites typical of the various types of coastline around the country. Coastally situated sites need to be assessed against their equivalents in other landscape environments.

Protecting some coastal sites is simply not cost effective, and attention must be given to sites where natural forces will assist rather than hinder management strategies. Sites which display a range of typical features within a restricted area, and which can be managed within a single coherent strategy, should be sought for preservation. Good documentation exists for many medieval and later defensive works, although for other classes of site documentation is often poor. Few previously excavated sites survive because the excavations were usually prompted by their destruction. Many classes of coastal site are either clustered in groups because of restrictions on their location, or, in the case of defensive works, are often part of a coherently planned chain of similar sites. Coastal sites sealed beneath sand dunes or salt marsh can rarely be seen in their entirety. If the protective coverings can be seen to be intact, then preservation beneath is likely to be good.

Few existing coastal management plans take full account of the archaeological evidence, although the stock of Scheduled Monuments is supplemented by sites protected through general conservation schemes within protected areas.

Figure 49 Palaeolithic settlement site under excavation at Hengistbury Head, Dorset: when occupied about 1200 bc, this site overlooked a river valley; now it faces Poole Harbour

Curatorial management works to safeguard coastal archaeological sites are far from straightforward. Little can be done to combat vigorous natural erosion without resort to large-scale works, such as the construction of sea defences. The most important tasks are therefore to prevent man-induced and natural erosion from getting a hold on sites. For this, rather simple measures such as planting marram grass over exposed dunes, routing footpaths away from archaeological sites, and preventing fire-lighting can be of considerable benefit. Eroding ground surfaces over known sites can be stabilized by carefully overlaying appropriate, more resilient, material. Rabbit populations need to be controlled near ancient monuments. Metal detectors, trial bike riding, and vehicle access should be restricted to specific, archaeologically sterile, areas.

Wherever curatorial management is undertaken, the consequences for other coastal areas must be examined. Coastlands are highly dynamic environments in which different areas are closely interrelated. The stopping of the erosion of material in one area, for example, will restrict the deposition of sediments in another, and in time erosion may start in place of deposition.

Recording

Since so many sites are only recognized when being eroded, local authority officers and workmen, wardens, landowners, and land-users should be alerted to the first signs of sites being eroded, and encouraged to report cases to appropriate organizations. In the longer term, the monitoring of sites under active erosion should be encouraged.

When sites are identified, recording often has to take place quickly. This may range from full-scale excavation to selective plotting of visible features. In general, where natural forces of erosion threaten a site, archaeological excavation is often more cost effective than a preservation scheme. In other landscape environments, the reverse is usually true.

Limitations on the execution of archaeological work in coastal areas are considerable, however, and both excavation and recording often have to be undertaken in difficult conditions (Fig 49). The health and safety implications of working on cliffs, or within the inter-tidal zone, are obvious, while the inaccessibility of many coastal areas may increase the

Figure 50 Roman shore-fort and medieval castle at Portchester, Hampshire: the square-shaped Roman fort was reused in medieval times as the site of a rather smaller castle; the site is now in the care of English Heritage and is a popular tourist attraction

cost of archaeological work. The practical problems of working in high wind with salt spray and airborne sand, which can back-fill excavations almost as quickly as deposits are dug out, can be especially trying. The short time available for excavation or recording on most beaches between high tides means that rapid techniques have to be developed to suit each situation.

Evaluation surveys can be carried out relatively quickly and at fairly low cost. Ground disturbance is widespread along the coastal frontage, but surveys need to be repeated regularly to monitor change and catch sites early, before erosion wrecks them. For the formulation of management plans, surveys need to pay particular attention to the extent of sites, the proportion exposed to erosion, the stability of any overburden offering protection to preserved deposits, and, most important, to the likely effects of long-term natural processes.

Exploitative management

The coastlands of England attract high levels of public attention. It has been estimated that a quarter of all the day-trips made in England are spent on the coast (ETB 1983, 28), and coastal resorts are also popular centres for longer holidays. English Heritage already has a considerable commitment to the provision of accessible sites, and, at present, there are 19 Guardianship monuments open to the public along the coast (Fig 50). These are mostly medieval and post-medieval forts and defensive works, which are among the most robust classes of monuments in the coastlands and can withstand large numbers of visitors. Most other classes of coastland site could not withstand such high pressure, and few could survive prolonged exposure.

Academic interest in the archaeology of the coastlands is high, because of the special kinds of site represented. Rescue excavation needs can usually be matched to the demands of academic work, because of the large number of sites faced with destruction.

8 Rivers, lakes, and alluvium spreads

8.1 Archaeological importance

The rivers, lakes, and alluvium deposits in England can be considered together as one landscape environment, because their origins, development, and management are intimately connected. Rivers are taken to include all natural inland watercourses, including canalized waterways, but excluding artificial cuts, such as canals and drainage works, which are considered in other chapters. Lakes comprise all naturally flooded areas of open water together with artificially drowned valleys (eg reservoirs), but excluding man-made lakes in old mineral workings.[42] Alluvium is here taken to mean fluvial and marine alluvium of Holocene date accumulated on river flood plains and in coastal areas.

Archaeologically, rivers, lakes, and alluvium-covered areas are important because of the types of site preserved, and the possibility of anaerobic conditions permitting the preservation of organic materials. This may be summarized under four headings:

i   Waterside sites: rivers and lakes are relatively stable features of the landscape and have always provided important natural resources, lines of communication, and, more recently, sources of energy to power machinery. Many classes of site situated in these areas are not found elsewhere in the countryside. Waterside sites are therefore important elements in the reconstruction of past settlement patterns.

ii   Preservation: because of high ground water levels and restricted drainage around rivers, lakes, and in washlands inundated by alluvium, the preservation of organic materials, such as wood, bone, and leather, is likely to be good. The exact range of material preserved will depend upon soil chemistry in the area. The fine sediments associated with most rivers and lakes also promote the preservation of inorganic remains, including many rare and remarkable objects. Where alluvium has been deposited, areas of ancient land surface may be sealed beneath layers of fine sediment, which effectively protects them from subsequent damage. Where sediment accumulation has taken place over a long period, several successive episodes of land-use may be preserved. This allows appraisal of the range of activities undertaken within a given area (the horizontal dimension) and over time (the vertical dimension).

iii   Environmental indicators: environmental evidence, such as pollen, mollusca, or diatoms, is often preserved in alluvium deposits or in sediments which accumulate on lake beds or in old river channels. Analysis of these allows sites to be set in the context of both their immediate surroundings and their local environment.

iv   Widespread occurrence: because rivers, lakes, and alluvium deposits are well distributed throughout England, they collectively provide a representative sample of life in earlier times over wide areas.

Rivers, lakes, and extensive alluvium spreads in England cover approximately 3478 square kilometres, about 2.6% of the total land area (Whitaker 1985). This is, however, a conservative estimate, since many smaller river valleys contain areas of alluvium not yet accurately mapped, but which account for a considerable area of land. Most of the larger rivers flow through lowland England, and it is here that the most extensive areas of alluvium are found (Fig 51).

Of all the landscape environments considered in this volume, rivers, lakes, and alluvium spreads are possibly the least well documented archaeologically, probably because, until disturbed, remains preserved in these areas are among the best protected in the country.

8.2 Origin and distribution

The formation of rivers, lakes, and alluvium deposits owes much to the relationship between water supply (springs and rainfall) and terrain. This in turn affects the kind of archaeological evidence likely to be preserved. The origin, development, and distribution of each may be considered separately.

Rivers

The basic drainage pattern represented by the rivers of England was established during the Pleistocene Ice Age, when many of the major river valleys were carved out by glaciers and shaped by very large amounts of melt water. It was in these high-energy situations that alluvial gravels and coarse sands were laid down as successive terrace deposits along many of the larger river valleys.[43]

Since Pleistocene times the amount of water carried by rivers has reduced dramatically, so that many water courses now only occupy part of their valleys, although seasonal fluctuations in level are common. Variations in rainfall over the millennia have not significantly affected the river pattern, and, in general, rivers have been one of the more constant features of the landscape through prehistoric and historic times. Minor variations in course (perhaps up to 2km) have taken place as a result of long-term fluvial processes, such as meandering, alluviation, and erosion (Sparks 1960, 120–6).

The sources of many rivers lie in upland areas, stimulated by high rainfall and rapid surface run-off. Naturally, the rate of flow and the size of a river change along its length, as does the sort of archaeological evidence that might be expected.

Since Roman times rivers have been controlled through canalization and the construction of artificial banks (levees). By the nineteenth century, river works had became very common because of the great reliance placed upon water transport. More recently, river works to control flow and drainage have taken over from the need to provide thoroughfares.

Lakes

Like rivers, most lakes owe their existence to terrain formed during or immediately after the Pleistocene Ice Age. Glacially-carved valleys blocked by morains, kettle holes, and glacial scour account for most of England's lakes. Artificial lakes are often created by dams across river valleys in much the same way as morains create restricted drainage.

Most English lakes lie in the formerly glaciated areas of the north and west. Shapes, sizes, and depths vary greatly. In cases where lakes formed after the area had been settled by man, as for example with many recent man-made lakes, a relict landscape will be present beneath the water.

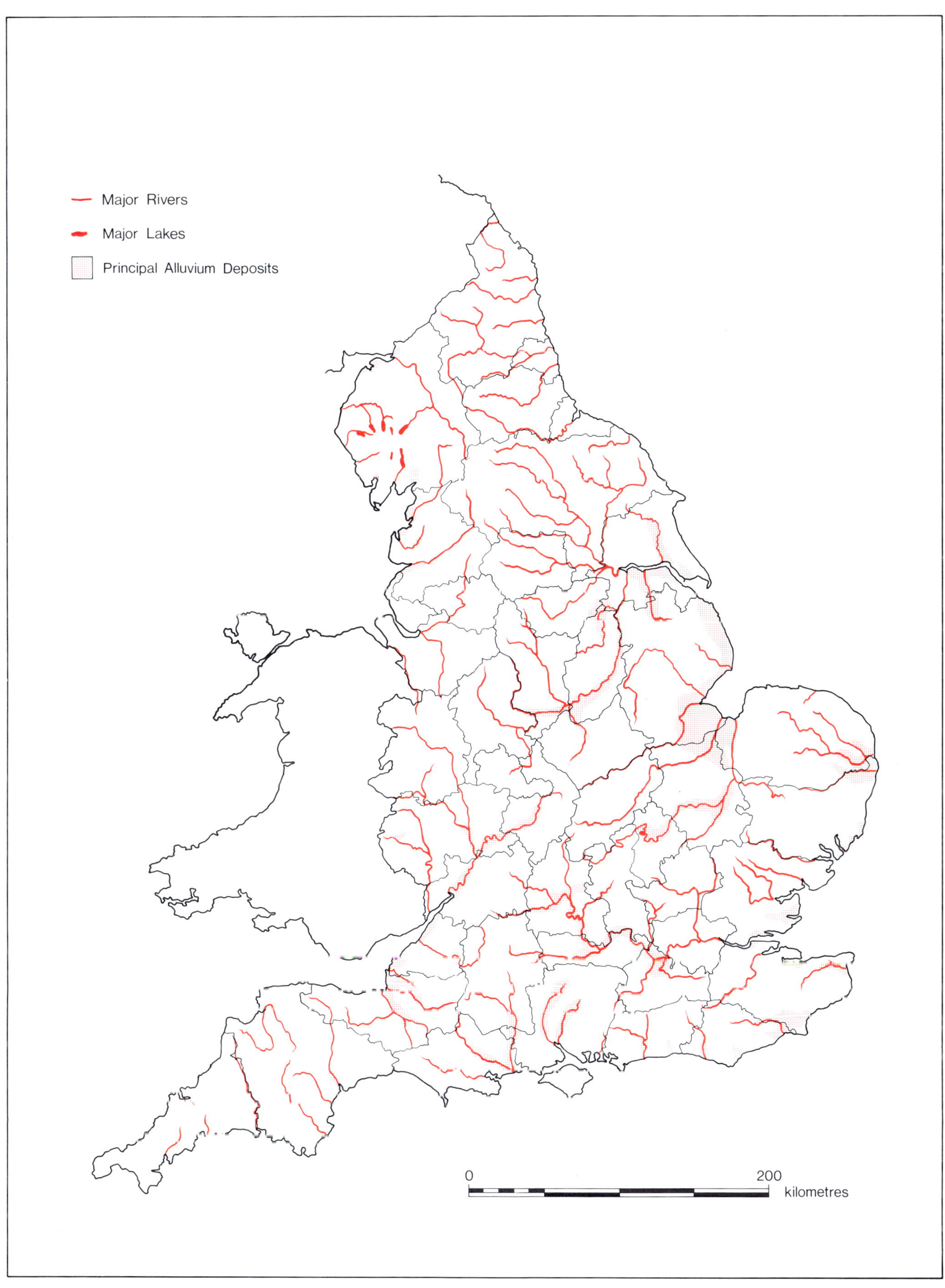

Figure 51   Major rivers, lakes, and alluvium spreads in England

Figure 52   Cleats and bars of boat 1 from the River Humber at North Ferriby, Humberside (scale totals 50cm)

The types of archaeological materials preserved will depend upon the acidity of the water and the nature of the lake sediments.

Alluvium

River alluvium forms wherever the flow of water is restricted and sediment held in suspension is deposited. This happens for a number of reasons, among them a reduction in velocity when a river meets the sea, the widening of the river bed, or because of obstacles in the channel. The most common cause of alluviation is flooding, when rivers burst their banks and inundate surrounding low-lying land. The reduction in velocity caused by this allows sediments to settle over the flooded land, leaving a thin deposit of silt, clay, or sand depending on the type of rock being carried by the river. After many successive floods, alluvium in river valleys may reach a thickness of 3m or more (Hazelden and Jarvis 1979; Robinson and Lambrick 1984).

Most alluviation takes place around the lower stretches of a river's course, simply because the amount of sediment carried in suspension is greater, and because flood plains tend to be wider. As a result, most substantial alluvium deposits lie in lowland England. Large rivers such as the Thames, Severn, Trent, and Ouse are flanked by alluvium spreads up to 5km wide. However, many smaller rivers also have associated alluvium spreads, in some cases up to about 1km wide.

Marine alluvium is deposited when land is flooded by the sea and is forced to deposit sediments held in suspension.[44] In contrast to river alluvium, these deposits are saline. Successive episodes of flooding can lead to the accumulation of several metres of alluvium.

Among the most extensive spreads of marine alluvium are the silt fens around the Wash in Lincolnshire, Cambridgeshire, and Norfolk, and around the Somerset Levels in Somerset and Avon. Attempts to prevent flooding, through the construction of sea defences and river levees, have successfully restricted alluviation in some areas. Among the earliest efforts in this direction so far recorded is the Carr Dyke in Cambridgeshire and Lincolnshire, which is of Roman date (B Simmons 1980a). Since then, the scale of engineering works connected with the prevention of alluviation has increased greatly.

The thickness, nature, and initiation of alluviation often relate to local land-use patterns. For example, Shotton (1978) has suggested that unconsolidated arable land adjacent to the Worcestershire Avon provided a ready supply of sediment for riverine transportation and subsequent deposition during Iron Age times. In Sussex, studies of sediments in the Upper Cuckmere Valley revealed that Neolithic and Bronze Age clearance of the vegetation cover resulted in the build-up of alluvium in the valley bottom (Scaife and Burrin 1985). Similar connections have been noted elsewhere (Kelly and Osborne 1964; J G Evans 1966; Bell 1982).

8.3   The archaeology of rivers, lakes, and alluvium spreads

Archaeological evidence from rivers, lakes, and alluvium spreads can be divided into four groups, according to where within a watercourse and its washland the evidence is found.

Figure 53   River finds: A (above) bronze helmet of late Iron Age date from the River Thames at Waterloo Bridge; B (right) bronze shield with three coral studs on the central boss, from the River Witham, Lincolnshire, of Iron Age date

These groups are: waterbound features and deposits; shoreline and bank features; deposits within and below alluvium; features on alluvium. Each of these may be considered separately.

Waterbound features and deposits

The majority of evidence from within rivers, old watercourses, and lakes comprises stray finds brought to light through dredging or riverworks. A great variety of objects is represented, and clearly relates to a wide range of different activities connected with the use of rivers and lakes. Unfortunately, because contextual information on these finds and their associations is often poor, such activities are hard to reconstruct in detail. Moreover, the river itself may have moved material downstream from where it was first deposited.

Rubbish of various sorts is the most common class of evidence from rivers and lakes, mostly broken pottery, animal bone, and other objects dumped into the water from nearby settlements. Accidental losses must also have contributed to these deposits. At North Ferriby, Humberside, for example, a collection of objects of Bronze Age date has been recovered from the River Humber. Among the items represented were the remains of three boats (Fig 52), various pieces of wood from other boats, broken wooden paddles, part of a possible winch, pottery, pieces of wickerwork, a bronze knife blade, and various pieces of stone (Wright and Wright 1947; Wright 1978).

Over 100 wooden boats of all periods, from the Bronze Age through to the Middle Ages, are known from English rivers (McGrail 1978; 1979). These range from simple logboats made from hollowed-out tree trunks to sophisticated craft of more recent times. Boats dating to before about AD 1650 are of special interest, since knowledge of boat building traditions before this date is poor and is based solely on archaeological evidence (Denford *et al* 1979). Boat finds have also been made in lakes, as for example at Giggleswick Tarn, North Yorkshire (McGrail and O'Connor 1979).

Some of the stray finds from rivers and lakes seem too good to be explained as rubbish deposits or accidental losses. Most of the finest late prehistoric metalwork known from England

Figure 54   Iron Age wooden causeway at Fiskerton, Lincolnshire (the upright scale totals 2m)

has been found in rivers and lakes. Among the best known pieces are the Witham shield from the River Witham, Lincolnshire (Fig 53A), the horned helmet from the Thames at Waterloo Bridge (Fig 53B), and the bronze cauldron of late Bronze Age date from the Thames at Battersea. Several thousand Bronze Age weapons including spears, swords, and rapiers have been recovered from English rivers and lakes over the last 150 years. Such objects are rarely, if ever, found on contemporary settlement sites, and this has led to the suggestion that during later prehistoric times fine metalwork was deliberately deposited in wet places, during some kind of water-related ritual or in connection with burial rites (Bradley 1979; Ehrenberg 1980).

Rivers, and sometimes lakes, often represent barriers to overland communications, with the result that ways of crossing the water have to be found. Bridge piers, both wood and stone, must be expected at suitable crossing points, and causeways or rough paving, stepping stones, or post bridges may be present at major fords. At Fiskerton, Lincolnshire, a wooden causeway of Iron Age date has been excavated (Fig 54; N Field nd). Concentrations of stray finds and rubbish may point to the former existence of crossing points.

Lake villages set within, or on the edge of, open water are well known on the Continent, but are less well documented in England.[45] The exploitation of natural resources is, however, represented, for example the wooden fish weirs of Anglo-Saxon and later date found in the River Trent at Colwick, Nottinghamshire (Fig 55; Salisbury 1981). Similar weirs and traps are still visible today on the Severn at Newnham, Gloucestershire, and were once numerous on many English rivers (A White 1984; Geraint Jenkins 1974, ch 2 and 3).

The preservation of artefacts within waterbound deposits is usually very good, the water itself providing anaerobic conditions for the preservation of organic materials, and the fine muds and silts providing a protective overburden. Locating archaeological features, except when they are being destroyed or damaged through exposure in some way, is, however, very difficult.

Bank and shoreline features

It is along river banks and lake shores that most of the evidence for the use and exploitation of rivers and lakes is found.

Settlements, often connected with ports or crossing places, are known from prehistoric times onwards. A recently excavated example beside the River Thames at Egham, Surrey, dates to the later Bronze Age and boasts the earliest recorded evidence for a wooden waterfront wall or quay (Longley 1980; Needham 1985). The usual range of burial sites and ritual monuments may be closely connected with prehistoric riverside settlements, for example at Roxton, Bedfordshire (Fig 56; A Taylor and Woodward 1985).

At Farmoor, Oxfordshire, an Iron Age and Romano-British riverside settlement has been extensively excavated to reveal a changing pattern of flood plain exploitation (Lambrick and Robinson 1979). Roman riverside settlements are known too, as at Littleport, Cambridgeshire (G Fowler 1950), but where there were suitable crossing points, many such sites later developed into small towns and villages.

In rural areas, medieval houses beside rivers were often moated to provide drainage, defence, and in some cases a supply of fresh fish (*see* papers in Aberg 1978). The example at Attleborough, Norfolk (Fig 57) has what may be a moated garden beside the house site.

Seasonal or temporary riverside and lakeside occupation sites date from the Mesolithic period onwards. Riverhead and riverside settlements were also common during early prehis-

Figure 55   Fish weirs and traps: A (top) eel traps in use at Caversham, Berkshire, probably around the turn of the century; B (bottom) Colwick, Nottinghamshire: remains of an Anglo-Saxon fish weir found in an old channel of the River Trent (the scales each total 1m)

Figure 56   Excavation of a Bronze Age ring-ditch burial monument at Roxton, Bedfordshire, on the banks of the River Ouse

toric times judging from the distribution of flint scatters (eg Bradley 1978b, 80 for study of Upper Wharfedale). Burnt mounds, probably cooking sites of Bronze Age or later date, and distinctive because of the build-up of fire-crazed stones, are often situated close to rivers or springs, for example in the New Forest (Passmore and Pallister 1967) and in the Midlands around Birmingham (L Barfield and Hodder 1981).

Bridges across rivers are most readily identified from traces of their abutments on the banks. Roman examples are known from Piercebridge, County Durham (Selkirk 1973), and Aldwincle, Northamptonshire (D Jackson and Ambrose 1976). At Chesters, Northumberland, a bridge was built to carry Hadrian's Wall over the North Tyne (Birley 1960, 31). Later bridges are also known from archaeological evidence, for example the Viking-age structure at Skerne, Humberside (Dent 1984). Stone bridges of considerable antiquity are common in the north and west of England. Unfortunately, many of the simple structures in rural areas, such as the clapper bridges of the south-west, are not easy to date (Wood 1972, 241–3 for summary of bridges). Parts of some medieval timber bridges still survive, for example at Bull Bridge, Wilton, Wiltshire (Eagles and Woodward 1984). During the transport revolution of the eighteenth and nineteenth centuries many new bridges were built, and a good number still survive.

Waterside religious sites of Roman and later date are widespread, especially on the upper reaches and springhead areas of rivers and streams (Ross 1967, 20–33).

Features associated with the use of waterways for communications and transportation abound on larger rivers with sufficient depth of water for barges and river boats. Trans-shipment quays and jetties, where goods were transferred from sea-going boats to river boats, are present near the mouth of many rivers, for example at Sharpness on the lower Severn, Gloucestershire. Wharfs and quays are sometimes associated with riverside storage facilities.

In order to promote waterborne transportation, short stretches of shallow or treacherous waterway were sometimes canalized to give greater draught; locks might occasionally be installed, as on the Bristol Avon and the Thames (Buchanan 1972, 292). Early riverworks to contain the flow of water, such as those documented along the Trent (Salisbury 1985), are also of archaeological interest.

Alongside many streams and rivers are traces of water mills often visible as ponds, leats, or even as the wheel site and mill structure itself. Early examples include the Roman mill built into the bridge abutment at Chesters, Northumberland, but most are medieval and post-medieval in date. The Domesday survey of 1086 records over 5600 mills in England at that time (Hodgen 1939; and cf Lennard 1959, 278), most of them corn mills. During the industrial revolution, water mills were used to provide power for many other activities including fulling, weaving, ore processing, and metalworking.

Riverside and shoreline features are often betrayed by distinctive earthworks or standing features, except where covered by alluvium or masked by levees and raised banks. Sites can be located by field survey and by checking exposed sections of bank. The preservation of artefacts is variable and depends upon the level of the water table, the height of the banks, and the chemistry of the soil.

Features in and below alluvium

Evidence for activities undertaken on the flood plains of rivers, or in coastal regions liable to periodic flooding, are likely to be preserved beneath alluvium. The date of alluviation varies greatly from one area to the next, as does the depth of overburden that accumulates. Early prehistoric finds from considerable depths in the more substantial alluvium deposits of southern England suggest that rather more areas of ancient landscape may be preserved in this way than is commonly realized.

Among the most extensively explored prehistoric landscapes beneath alluvium are those under the silt fens of East Anglia. At Haddenham, Cambridgeshire, the excavation of a causewayed camp has allowed insights into the internal organization of the site (C Evans and Hodder 1985). Another causewayed camp, at Etton, Cambridgeshire (Fig 58), sealed beneath about 1.3m of alluvium in the Nene Valley, also displays well-preserved internal features, and at this site the waterlogged ditches were found to contain well-preserved organic remains (Pryor and Kinnes 1982). Other early prehistoric settlements sealed by alluvium include Tattershall Thorpe, Lincolnshire (Chowne and Healy 1985).

Later prehistoric, Roman, and medieval landscapes are also represented below alluvium. At Ilchester, Somerset, for example, a late Iron Age site covering some 16ha and sealed beneath 0.5m of alluvium in the valley of the River Yeo has been investigated by excavation (Leach and Thew 1984). In the Somerset claylands, detailed field surveys coupled with limited excavation have revealed traces of intensive Roman occupation under up to 2.4m of alluvium (Leech 1981; McDonnell 1985, 12), which mostly accumulated in the late Roman period when the area was flooded by the sea. At one site, around Huntspill Level, a Roman landscape covering over 6 square kilometres is preserved.

Locating sites in and under alluvium depends very much on the depth of overburden. When sites are under relatively shallow deposits, aerial photography can be used to detect

Figure 57   Moated house (centre) and possible garden platform (top left) at Attleborough, Norfolk; drainage channels can be seen in the fields around the moats

Figure 58   Etton, Cambridgeshire: general view of part of the boundary ditch of a Neolithic causewayed enclosure after excavation, showing a causeway being planned; the site is sealed beneath up to 1m of alluvium

cropmarks, in conditions of extreme drought, and low earthworks where the undulating topography of buried sites is reflected as surface features (D Hall 1981, McDonnell 1979; Benson and Miles 1974; Lambrick 1981; 1983a). Buried evidence can also be identified where cropmarks are seen disappearing under alluvium deposits (Fig 59). In deeper alluvium deposits, ditch surveys and chance discoveries provide the only clues to the presence of buried sites (Fig 60).

Because alluvium forms in very wet conditions, preservation within and beneath it is often good, although the range of materials likely to survive in any given deposit largely depends on its soil chemistry.

Features on alluvium spreads

Where alluvium deposition has ceased or become retarded, perhaps through the control of flooding and inundation, sites

connected with the exploitation and occupation of alluviated areas will not become buried, and are therefore still present on the surface. The silt fens of East Anglia and parts of the clay moors around the Somerset Levels both represent extensive areas in which coastal defences and drainage works were constructed from Roman times onwards to prevent flooding and alluvium deposition. In these areas, evidence of Roman and medieval land-use abounds on the surface of the alluvium, including settlements, moated sites, canals, and field systems. Ancient coastlines within these alluvium spreads may be marked by abandoned salterns and other coastal sites now many kilometres from the sea (Leech 1981).

Water meadows are a common feature of the flood plains of many river valleys (Fig 61). These are mostly of medieval and post-medieval date, but some are still operational (Doherty and Pilkington 1984). Fish ponds, decoy ponds, and fishgarths were also built in riverside areas, often on alluvium, from the medieval period onwards (Aston forthcoming). The lay-out of the fields, hedges, and ditches in many river valleys has remained largely unchanged until the present century, when improved drainage schemes made these waterlogged areas available for other uses.

Sites on top of alluvium can be located through all the usual techniques of archaeological reconnaissance, especially field-walking, field survey, and aerial photography. Preservation of sites under pasture is generally good, and the survival of organic remains is high in some cases. Standing earthworks do not survive cultivation long, however, and in predominantly arable areas preservation tends to be poor.

8.4   Threats

As the land around rivers, lakes, and alluvium spreads tends to be rather wet, traditional land-use has focused on grazing or hay production. In recent decades, however, large-scale drainage works have been implemented in some areas, so that considerable variation in land-use now exists. The single most extensive area of alluvium, the silt fens of East Anglia, is now mostly under arable, although in smaller areas, like the Somerset Levels and Moors, pasture still predominates. High ground water levels and low soil permeability in most smaller river valleys have conspired to ensure that grazing remains the dominant land-use. In recent years, it has become fashionable to exploit open water for recreation, fishing, and water sports.

The following activities pose the greatest threats to the archaeological evidence.

Drainage

Although reclamation works and drainage have been taking place around rivers, lakes, and alluvium spreads for a long time, much of it was small-scale and piecemeal until the present century. This is now changing, as river boards and water authorities coordinate drainage schemes, and Government

Figure 59   North Muskham, Nottinghamshire: cropmarks visible on land beside the River Trent, but disappearing below spreads of alluvium marked by the dark bands

Figure 60   Freshly cleaned dyke section in the Norfolk Fens: the cross-section of an ancient pit or ditch sealed by alluvium is clearly visible next to the figure

grants are widely available for individual landowners to lay field drains (MAFF 1977).

Drainage presents two threats to archaeological remains: desiccation and shrinkage. Desiccation – even temporarily – effectively terminates anaerobic preservation of organic material. Shrinkage, which will vary in its effect according to the level of waterlogging, causes the conflation and disruption of archaeological deposits.

Problems connected with drainage are most acute in areas of alluvium, where naturally high ground water levels provide excellent conditions for the preservation of organic remains. In such areas, it is not only drainage for agriculture that presents a problem but also drainage for mineral extraction.

A study of fluctuating water levels at the Etton causewayed camp, Cambridgeshire, illustrates the impact of sustained drainage on waterlogged sites (French and Taylor 1985). Water levels were monitored in a series of boreholes across the site for two years, starting in 1982 (Fig 62). At that time, the lower fills of the causewayed ditches forming the enclosure were semi-waterlogged and preserved a plethora of organic remains.[46] Seasonal variations in water level were noted and, while these did not permit the waterlogged deposits to dry out completely, some deterioration in the quality of preserved remains was noted during very dry periods. In June 1983, pumps were installed in the adjacent field to facilitate gravel extraction, and from that time onwards the water levels on the enclosure site started to fall. The effect was dramatic and sustained, with water levels hovering about 1.0m below the level of the deepest archaeological deposits. The speed of this dewatering exacerbated the problems of desiccation and caused the Neolithic wood in the ditches to crack, splinter, and distort. It was estimated that within a relatively short period (a few years) most of the organic remains at the site would be beyond recovery, and a few years later still they would be completely gone.

Dredging

Although dredging is the principal means of discovering sites in rivers, its continued use causes the destruction of whatever archaeological remains survive. Also, by increasing the flow of water in a river, dredging may promote erosion of waterside sites.

Waterworks

River control works, and the construction of balancing ponds and artificial lakes, directly affects sites by exposing them and indirectly affects them by changing the flow of water, which in turn alters patterns of erosion and sediment deposition.

Mineral extraction

Many river valleys contain rich deposits of sand and gravel. Where these are covered by alluvium, it is a relatively simple matter to remove the overburden to get at the aggregates. Especially badly hit are the Thames Valley, Severn Valley, Trent Valley, and the Nene Valley (RCHME 1960). Gravel extraction in one area can also affect the surrounding fields by lowering the water table, which leads to the loss of valuable evidence from waterlogged deposits. An equally worrying problem is that the extraction of gravel from alluvium-covered landscapes involves the destruction of sites which may not be revealed by surface traces or aerial photography.

Agriculture

This threat is confined to sites on the top of alluvium or covered by only shallow deposits. In these cases, very well-preserved sites are at grave risk, because ploughing can level earthworks very quickly on soft damp soils (Fig 63).

Other

Other threats which might be briefly mentioned are riverside developments such as marinas or industrial operations, erosion by leisure activities, and natural erosion. All tend to be localized and relatively small-scale, however.

8.5   Management

Left alone, archaeological sites in rivers, lakes, and alluvium areas would survive well and provide a substantial reserve for future generations. However, given that these areas are under threat from a variety of sources, there is an urgent need to manage the archaeological resources more intensively than has been common hitherto.

There is much common ground between the aims of archaeological management schemes for rivers, lakes, and alluvium spreads and those of other countryside interests, notably the Countryside Commission, the Nature Conservancy Council, the British Waterways Board, and the regional Water Authorities.[47]

In formulating management strategies appropriate to these types of landscape, two important factors have to be taken into account:

Figure 61   *Water meadows: A (above) aerial view of the water meadows at Castle Acre, Norfolk; B (below) diagram showing the ideal arrangement of downers and drains in a water meadow system (after Doherty and Pilkington 1984, 9)*

i   Paucity of information: the level of information currently available about the nature of archaeological deposits in rivers, lakes, and alluvium areas is inadequate for the isolation of significant areas and the evaluation of sites in relation to one another.

ii   Extent of the areas involved: alluvium spreads cover large areas of ancient landscape, which need to be treated as single units as far as preservation and conservation are concerned.

Curatorial management

Maintaining high ground water levels and retaining alluvium deposits intact are the two most important aspects of curatorial management in this section of the landscape. The Water Act 1973[48] gives water authorities a duty to have regard to features of archaeological interest during all aspects of their work, but inadequate information about the types of evidence which might be expected, and insufficient guidance on methods of effective preservation, make such a task very difficult. Questions of ownership and management responsibility also arise when dealing with rivers and lakes.[49]

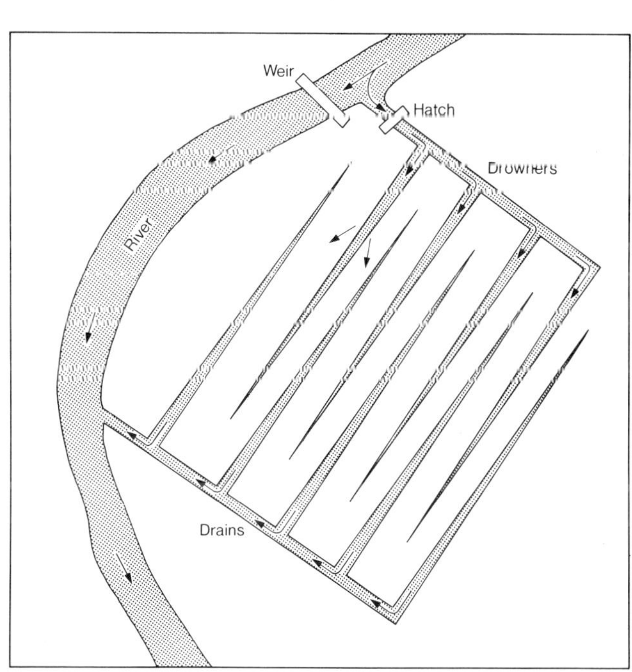

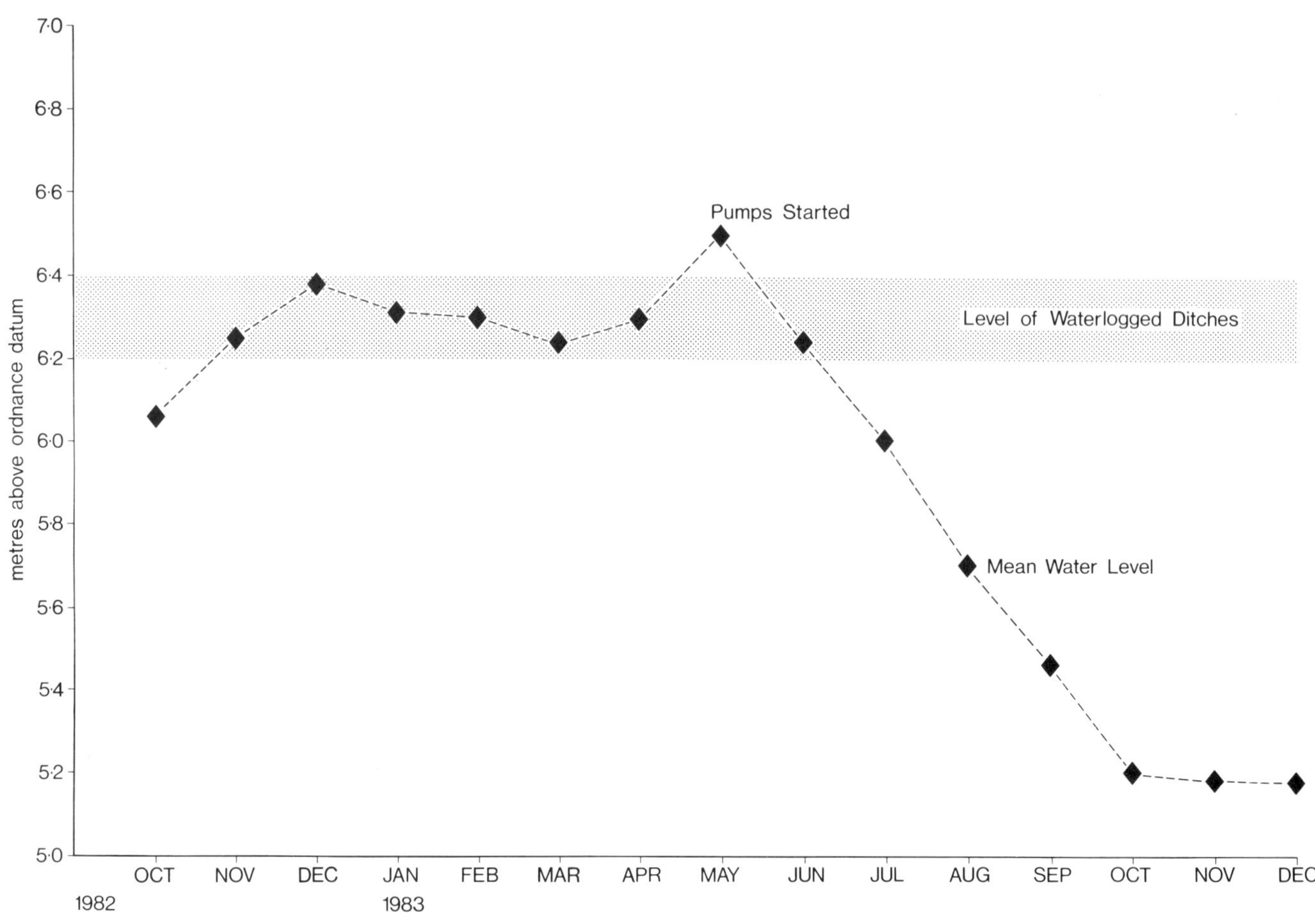

Figure 62   Graph showing water table changes relative to the waterlogged deposits within the Neolithic enclosure ditches at Etton, Cambridgeshire (data from French and Taylor 1985)

Approximately 1200 sites within this landscape type are currently protected as Scheduled Monuments.[50] A wide range of sites is included, among them an area of alluvium-covered landscape at Egham, Surrey, and a water meadow system in the Wey Valley, Hampshire. Eleven sites closely associated with rivers are in the care of English Heritage.

Selecting sites of national importance is especially difficult for rivers, lakes, and alluvium spreads, because waterbound sites and buried landscapes cannot be easily assessed or quantified using conventional archaeological techniques. There is thus a danger that only sites with surface traces or which are partially destroyed will be selected. Priority must, therefore, be given to areas of undisturbed alluvium, where the presence of a sealed landscape containing archaeological features can be demonstrated with reasonable certainty. Long-term waterlogging of deposits will also be important to ensure that a wide range of remains is preserved.

Sites specific to riverside and lakeside situations, and areas of landscape preserved beneath alluvium, are sufficiently rare to warrant special attention in future. The most fragile sites are those on the surface of alluvium and on exposed riverbanks, but the greatest diversity will be represented by the large areas of landscape sealed beneath alluvium, and heavily-used areas of riverbank and shoreline. Because of the permanence of rivers and lakes as landscape features, documentary records relating to their previous use are fairly numerous, especially for monuments such as mills and bridges. Concentrations of sites are not common according to present evidence, and therefore deserve special attention. In general, rivers, lakes, and alluvium spreads have great potential for exploration and preservation, but at present are among the most under-investigated sections of the landscape.

Supplementing the stock of Scheduled Monuments in Somerset are the Areas of High Archaeological Potential (AHAPs), defined by Somerset County Council (1983a; 1983b), in the Somerset Levels and Moors. In these areas, some of which include alluvium spreads and riverbanks, a voluntary notification scheme operates which alerts the county archaeological officer to operations such as earthmoving, new ploughing of old pasture, ditch clearance, and new drainage schemes. An assessment of the likely archaeological impact can then be made, and any necessary preliminary or concurrent action taken. Some riverside and lakeside areas are protected by designation as SSSIs or NNRs, and here management to conserve the natural environment is often sympathetic to the preservation of archaeological remains (Lambrick and McDonald 1985).

Locally, archaeological management for the well-being of sites in rivers, lakes, and alluvium spreads is straightforward. In rivers, clearance work should not cut deeper into the river bed than the existing channels, banks should be stabilized to prevent erosion, a buffer zone between the bank or shore and surrounding land established, and the hydrolic slope lessened to prevent over-scouring. Great care should be taken when repairing weirs and other river features, since they may be of considerable antiquity. Levees and artificial banks preserve old land surfaces which may be of interest. Riverside features can be preserved by maintaining pasture and minimizing activity

Figure 63   Hacconby Drove Roman settlement on the silt fens of Lincolnshire: A (top) earthworks, including tracks and house platforms, under pasture in 1952; B (bottom) site after ploughing with former upstanding remains showing as soil marks in 1970

Figure 64   Medieval clapper bridge at Postbridge, Dartmoor, Devon

when the ground is flooded. In areas of alluvium, plough depth should be kept above the base-level of the alluvium, and areas with surface earthworks should ideally be kept under pasture.

Special attention needs to be given to protecting river banks and lake shores, since it is here that maximum natural erosion and damage can take place, and also much of the most valuable evidence is found. The edges of alluvium spreads are also especially vulnerable, as deposits here are generally thinnest and the underlying ground surface most at risk.

Many of the demonstration farms contain rivers, lakes, and alluvium spreads, and include conservation of archaeological features in their management plans (Cobham 1984, 71–4).

Recording

Chance finds represent a large proportion of the evidence recovered from this part of the countryside, and landowners and land-users should be alert to the possibility of encountering archaeological remains during almost any works involving ground disturbance.

The excavation of sites within and beside rivers can present practical difficulties connected with the removal of ground water and the safety of personnel. Because waterlogged deposits may be present, the excavation of sites in this landscape category is usually relatively expensive.

In formulating management plans for rivers and lakes, it is important to determine the likely range of evidence preserved along the banks or in the water, and to balance this against the needs of clearance and water management. In alluvium areas it is important to establish the age, extent, character, depth, and degree of waterlogging present in any given area, together with an assessment of the likelihood that areas of ancient landscape will be preserved beneath.

Exploitative management

Public interest in riverside and lakeside areas for recreation is increasing (Fig 64) and, while much archaeological evidence is visible along public footpaths and in areas with public access, formally arranged sites are scarce. At present, there are eleven sites in State Guardianship, of which ten are bridges.

Academic interest in alluvium spreads in particular is increasing because of the prospect of examining large areas of well-preserved ancient landscape. There is an urgent need for more research-orientated excavation in these sorts of landscape to provide further detailed information on the range of archaeological and environmental evidence preserved under different circumstances, and on the ways in which sites can be recognized and assessed. Enough sites under threat of damage or destruction exist to cater for this research. Examination of sites which are partly waterlogged and partly desiccated provides useful insights into the nature of the remains encountered on dry-land sites.

Underwater archaeology has been relatively rarely applied to rivers and lakes in England, despite the obvious wealth of evidence preserved in these situations.

III   Archaeology in the countryside 2: Man-made landscapes

The following six chapters are concerned with the archaeology of man-made landscapes. In terms of their archaeology and management needs, these landscapes differ from those described in part II in two important respects. First, man-made landscapes are relatively recent creations, at least in the form we see them today, so that by implication such land was used in other ways, perhaps altogether different ways, in earlier times. Second, man-made landscapes depend upon the perpetuation of certain types of land-use for their continued existence. Thus, while the semi-natural landscapes such as the coast, major rivers, or areas of wetland would continue to be recognizable landscape categories if simply left alone, the same would not be true of man-made landscapes, because they would all ultimately revert to wild woodland if left unmaintained.

Five main themes are considered within each landscape category: its archaeological importance, its development as a landscape type, the nature of the archaeological resource represented, current threats facing the future well-being of the archaeological remains, and archaeologically appropriate management approaches.

9   Established grassland

9.1   Archaeological importance

The established grasslands of England comprise areas of permanent or long-term pasture which have not been improved mechanically in recent decades. Rotational grassland, which is subject to regular cultivation at less than five-year intervals, is not included here.[51] Archaeologically, established grassland is important because it represents a stable landscape environment ideal for the preservation of a great many types of ancient features. This may be considered under three headings:

i   Preservation of remains: minimal disturbance from root penetration and freedom from the effects of mechanical cultivators allow the survival of vulnerable remains such as walls, floors, banks, and other constructed features. Even where the build-up of deposits is very slight, clear stratification may survive. This provides the best possible evidence about the use and development of a monument.

ii   Landscape evidence: the formation of grassland often involves large areas of landscape, thus sealing and preserving extensive tracts under homogeneous conditions. This preserves information about the setting, extent, and interrelationships of sites.

iii Amenity value: monuments under established grassland can often be seen as surface features at ground level or from the air. They are therefore integral to local topography and make an important contribution to the visual impact of the landscape. In many cases an inspection of the visible traces provides a good impression of the structure and organization of the monument, which is especially useful for educational purposes and to aid the recognition of less well-preserved features elsewhere in the landscape.

Established grasslands cover approximately 31,706 square kilometres of England, about 24% of the total land area.[52] This is widely spread over central, western, and northern parts of England (Fig 65), but its archaeological value varies greatly. Grasslands which have been established for a century or more are the most important, but any grassland will preserve archaeological features more completely than land subject to a greater intensity of use. It should be emphasized that large areas of ancient grassland are rare, and mostly confined to steeply sloping ground.

The survival of environmental indicators on archaeological sites within areas of established grassland is less good than in some landscape environments. Calcareous soils militate against the survival of pollen, but do allow preservation of mollusca (J G Evans 1968; 1971). Particular problems arise when calcareous soils become decalcified subsequent to deposition, as little or no environmental material survives under such conditions (Dimbleby and Evans 1974).

Established grasslands do not require subdivision for archaeological purposes. Variation in soil type and acidity exists at a local level and this determines the range of archaeological evidence likely to be preserved. However, post-depositional changes in soil chemistry can upset all expectations, and this makes generalized subdivision impossible. Most established grasslands have a free draining structure (although wet flushes may be present) which makes their management broadly similar in different areas. The only exceptions are established riverside grasslands and meadow pasture on alluvium; these are dealt with in chapter 8 as the potential archaeological evidence and the management implications of such areas are specific to them.

9.2   History and distribution

All grasslands are artificial environments, the products of specialized and sustained land-use strategies (Ratcliffe 1977, 132). Archaeological evidence shows that tracts of grassland were first established and maintained in the early Neolithic period when woodland was cleared by early farming communities. On the chalk downs near Avebury, Wiltshire, for example, grassland had been established for several centuries before the construction of the long barrows at Beckhampton Road, Horslip, and South Street (Ashbee et al 1979). Cuttings through the bank at Avebury itself indicate that this huge monument was erected on ungrazed impoverished grassland about 2000 bc (J G Evans et al 1982). In later prehistoric times much more of the natural woodland was cleared, sometimes for pasture and at other times for some quite different purpose. Most areas probably experienced a succession of different land-use regimes during prehistory.

No areas of grassland can be proved to have survived untouched since prehistoric times, although some may exist. Most long-established grasslands known today have their origins in the later Middle Ages. From the mid-fourteenth century the abandonment of cultivated land in many regions and the subsequent conversion of much land to pasture prompted the spread of sheep farming (Postan 1975, 117). Monastic sheep farms played a particularly important role in this, especially those of the Cistercian order (J G Evans 1975, 178). By the beginning of the sixteenth century it is estimated that there were over 8 million sheep in England (Hoskins 1970, 137).

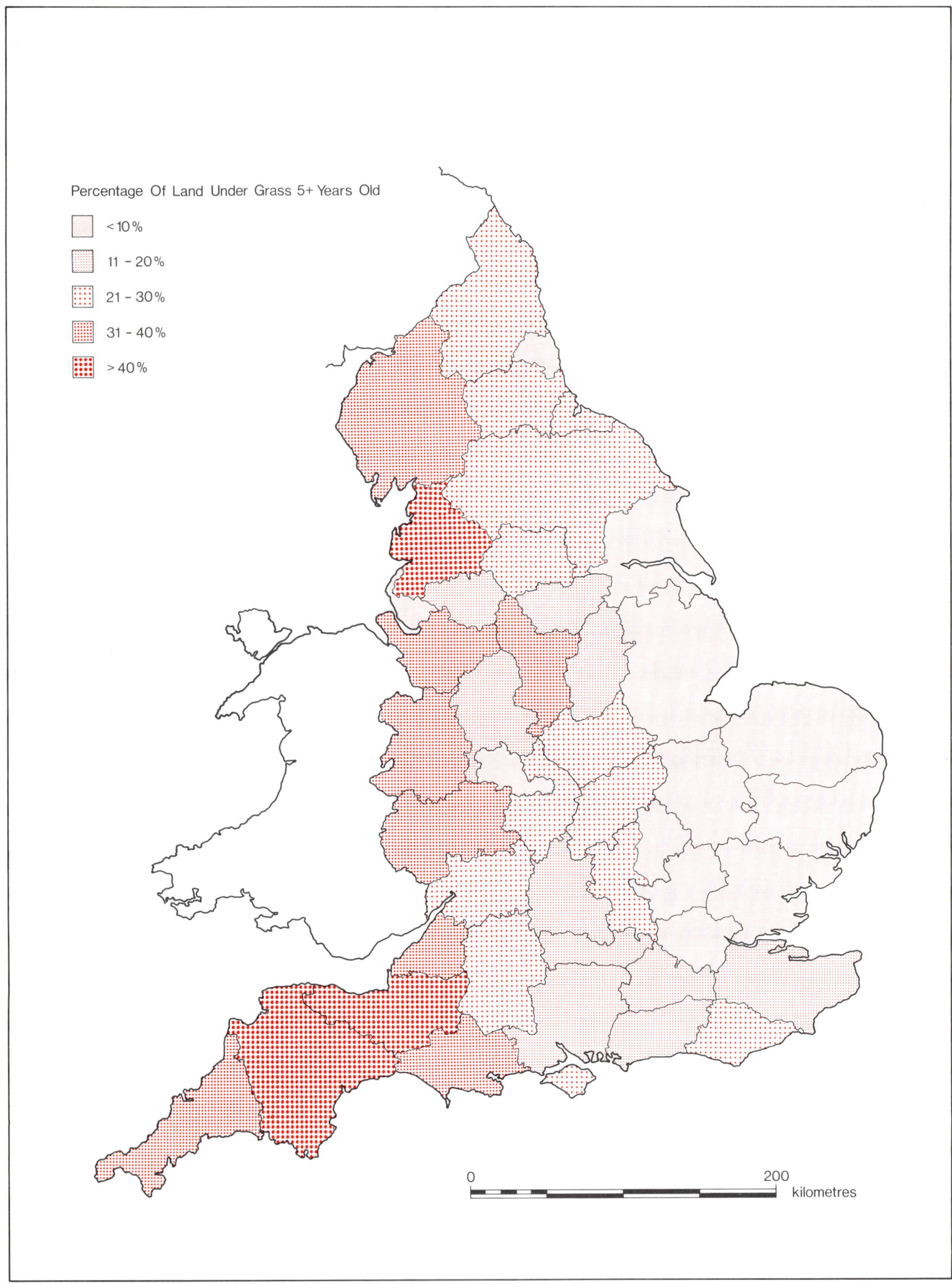

Figure 65   Map showing the distribution of land under established grassland in England (data from MAFF 1982)

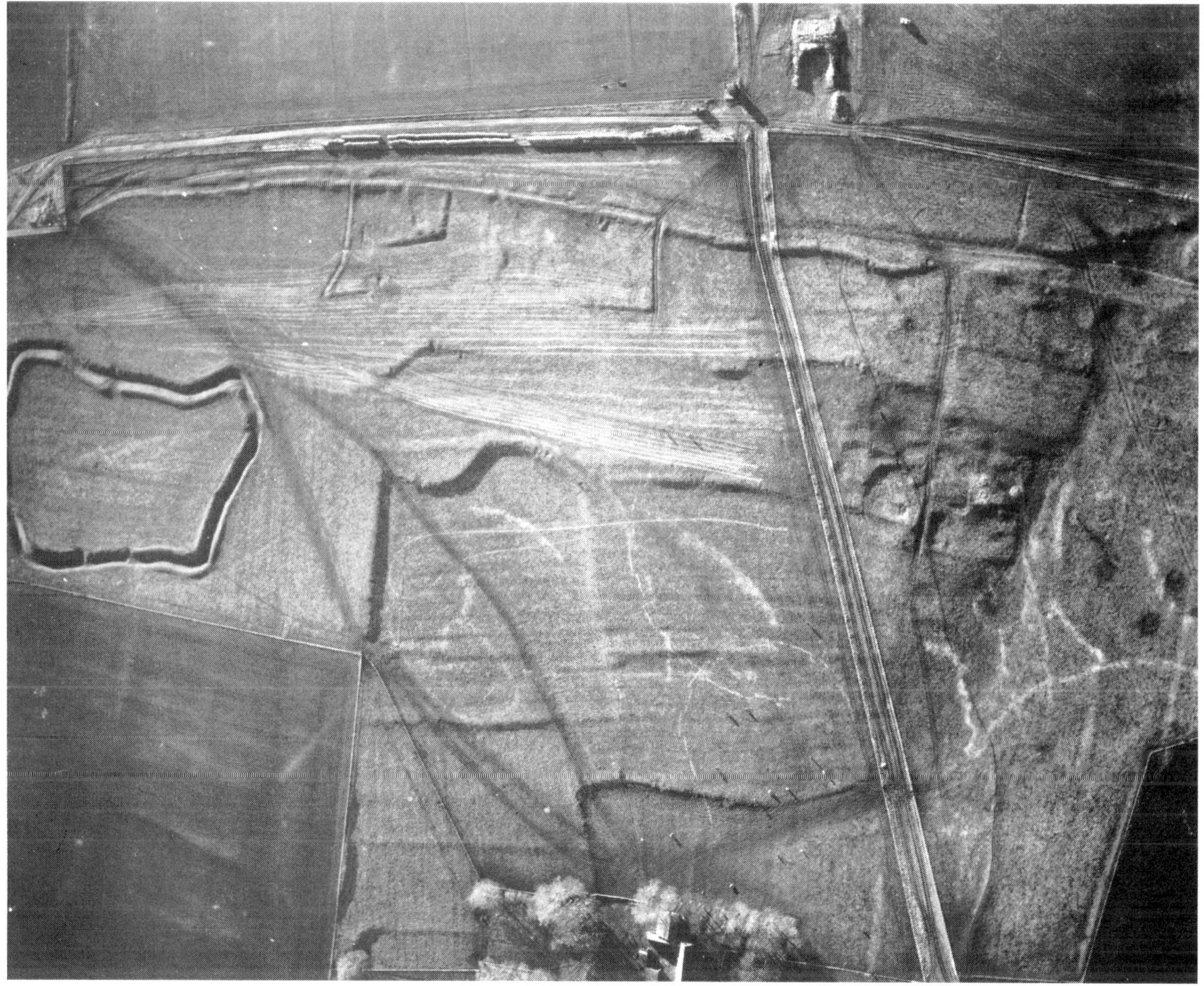

Figure 66   Quebec Farm, near Heytesbury, Wiltshire: Iron Age hillfort (left), Romano-British village (top right), and field system (centre and right) preserved under grassland on Salisbury Plain; the cultivated fields (bottom left and top left) once contained a continuation of these earthworks

Once established, most pasture lands remained under grass through the enclosure period of the seventeenth and eighteenth centuries, and it was not until demands for extra food production were established by the First and Second World Wars that substantial areas of grassland were brought back into cultivation. Between the wars and after the Second World War some areas reverted to pasture, but in the last few decades high cereal prices, government grants, and improved agricultural machinery have conspired to reverse this trend with the result that there is now less established grassland than for many centuries. Since the last war grassland has also been lost through scrub invasion brought about by the decline in rabbit populations during the 1950s. Rabbits were one of the main users of pasture, alongside sheep and cattle, and thus helped to keep it in healthy condition.

Old established grassland can be recognized by the diversity of plant species present, sometimes up to 45 per square metre (Ratcliffe 1977, 159). The range of species present in grassland varies with latitude from south to north and according to the chemistry of the underlying soil. Archaeologically, however, it does not matter greatly whether established grassland is maintained as multi-species sward or allowed to become dominated by a restricted range of species.

Much of the existing established grassland is found on the upland fringes of northern England, around the Cheviots, the Pennines, the Yorkshire Dales, the North York Moors, and the Peak District. Considerable tracts remain in the Midlands and on the Wolds of central southern England, especially the Cotswolds, Wessex Downs, and South Downs. In the south-west, grassland is again found around the periphery of the uplands.

Many surviving areas of established grassland are commons or public spaces (including golf courses etc), lands used by the Ministry of Defence for training, and steep slopes where cultivation is impractical.

Modern agriculture has tended to fragment grassland into small isolated blocks, so that few areas continuous grassland, such as once existed, now remain. Smaller areas, islands of grassland amid arable and mixed farming landscapes, are still, however, widespread, especially in midland and northern England. Most grassland is situated on land that falls within grades 2–4 of the Agricultural Land Classification (MAFF 1966).

Figure 67   Onley, Northamptonshire: medieval village set among its field system; the hollow-ways, croft boundaries, and house platforms of the village can be clearly seen, as can two types of cultivation; at the bottom left, narrow straight ridges are visible, while elsewhere rather wider curved ridges predominate; whether both types were in use at the same time, or represent different periods of land-use, is not known

9.3   Archaeological evidence

Areas of established grassland yield few stray finds to betray the existence of buried sites, and until surveyed in detail often represent voids in the distribution of recorded sites. However, detailed field surveys and aerial reconnaissance, at times of low-angle sunlight or after light snow falls, reveal a complexity of evidence commensurate with the excellent preservation offered by grassland environments.[53] Preferential plant growth can also reveal the presence of buried sites; for example nettles, buttercups, yarrow, hawkbit, daisies, and field woodrush have all proved valuable indicators of buried features or have highlighted earthworks (Selkirk 1985, 95).

Archaeological evidence under grassland largely relates to the time before the grassland itself was established. In many cases this involved relatively intensive land-use, perhaps agriculture or settlement. The important point is that preservation under grassland has minimized the natural and human agencies of decay and erosion and the evidence has often survived in good order. Obviously the age of the grassland will to some extent dictate the antiquity of the range of remains preserved beneath it.

Frequently, more than one episode of land-use is represented by archaeological evidence in grassland areas. At Overton Down, Wiltshire, for example, excavation and field survey have revealed a very long history of land-use. In late Neolithic times this particular piece of chalk downland was used as a cemetery.

It became the site of a settlement in the Iron Age and was incorporated within an extensive field system in later prehistoric and Roman times. It was abandoned in the sub-Roman period, cultivated again in the early medieval period, and was eventually put down to pasture in the late medieval period (P Fowler 1967). Similar changes in land-use represented by different types of superimposed earthworks can be seen at Grassington in North Yorkshire (Raistrick 1937), and in many other grassland areas.

It is characteristic of most archaeological sites in grassland areas that some surface traces survive, often as uneven ground or earthworks of some sort. Such features are of course only part of the site; much more lies beneath the surface than can be seen at ground level.

Given the diversity of sites present in grassland areas, it is perhaps useful to review the evidence available under a series of six headings.

Settlements

Settlement remains probably represent the most diverse and chronologically wide-ranging archaeological evidence in grassland areas. Very early prehistoric sites are represented by flint scatters and largely lie undetected except where the ground has been disturbed. The earliest earthworks associated with settlements are the causewayed enclosures of Neolithic date. One example under established grassland is Knap Hill, Wiltshire, where the ditch segments and banks can be clearly seen; later earthworks are also visible on the hilltop (Connah 1965).

Hillforts are among the most impressive earthwork sites of the later prehistoric period, and many are now situated in areas of established grassland (Fig 66). The defensive ramparts of most hillforts survive well in grassland conditions, and in favourable circumstances traces of internal features can also be seen (Forde-Johnson 1976). At Mam Tor, Derbyshire, for example, hut circles and platforms stand out clearly within the defended hilltop (Coombs 1976). Most hillforts lie on hilltops

with very thin soils so that the turf cover is often the only protection for any buried archaeological features such as houses, pits, or gullies.

Undefended settlements of later prehistoric and Roman date are well represented in the upland areas of established grassland where stone was the major building material, but in lowland areas such settlements often have very little surface trace, although they are present below ground level (C Taylor 1980).

Medieval settlements outside present-day built-up areas are often visible as substantial earthworks in grassland (Fig 67). The term 'deserted medieval village' covers a wide range of functionally distinct occupation sites including true villages, hamlets, farmsteads, and seasonal retreats. Such sites occur widely in both lowland and upland grassland areas (M Beresford and Hurst 1971). Some of the best examples are found in the Midlands, especially in Leicestershire and Northamptonshire, but many are also known on the Cotswolds, the Wiltshire downs, and the Yorkshire Wolds. Paradoxically, the swing to pastoral farming which has allowed the preservation of so many deserted villages was itself the direct result, if not the cause, of village abandonment and rural depopulation in the first place. In areas of low-lying grassland moated occupation sites of medieval date may be present. The moats offered defence, drainage, and a source of fresh fish (Emery 1962; and *see* papers in Aberg 1978).

Fields and agricultural features

Closely associated with many settlement sites in grassland areas are the remains of field systems (Bowen 1961) and agricultural facilities such as animal pens, droveways, barns, and ponds. Among the earliest are the 'Celtic' field systems of later prehistoric and Romano-British date (Fig 68). Among the best known are those on Overton Down and Fyfield Down, Wiltshire, which collectively cover over 80ha (Bowen and Fowler 1962). Excavations within the fields have revealed traces of later prehistoric or Romano-British ploughing where the top of the subsoil was scored by the passing of the plough

Figure 68   Chisledon, Wiltshire: Celtic fields under pasture overlaid by a later enclosure and field boundaries

Figure 69   Earthworks and rabbit warrens of various dates on Minchinhampton Common, Gloucestershire: the Bulwarks (bottom left) are probably of late Iron Age date and may be associated with the other lengths of rampart visible (left of centre and top right); the rectangular pillow mounds are very clear, and a cross-shaped vermin trap can be seen just to the right of the trackway leading to the house; anti-glider ditches overlie the medieval and post-medieval features; the area is now a golf course and four greens can be seen

tip (P Fowler 1967). Some of the field systems in Wessex may date back to Bronze Age times (Bradley 1978a).

Early field systems are well represented in most grassland areas in England, for example on the Cotswolds, the Peak District, and around Grassington in North Yorkshire. In Northumberland later prehistoric field systems under grassland can be seen beneath Roman military works such as around Housesteads on Hadrian's Wall (Frere and St Joseph 1983, 65). Strip lynchets and terraces are sometimes preserved on steep slopes (C Taylor 1966), demonstrating that animal traction and spade cultivation allowed crops to be grown almost anywhere.

Lowland grassland preserved large tracts of medieval field systems which effectively mask any traces of earlier patterns.[54] Particularly distinctive is the ridge-and-furrow cultivation practised in open fields, and easily recognized by the S-shaped curve to the plan of the furrows (Bowen 1961; D Hall 1982, 5–6). Headlands and meare stone are sometimes found associated with well-preserved areas of ridge-and-furrow, but in seeking to understand the preserved remains it should be borne in mind that several phases of cultivation may be present, each with a different amplitude and width of undulation.

Among the other archaeological evidence for farming activities which is commonly encountered on grassland, special mention may be made of rabbit warrens and vermin traps. Warrens, or pillow mounds as they are known in some areas, were used for rabbit farming in medieval times. Rectangular and circular types are known, and both contain rabbit runs and burrows (Crawford and Keiller 1928). Place-name evidence often allows the identification of former warrens. Associated with some warrens are vermin traps of different sorts. On Minchinhampton Common, Gloucestershire, aerial photography in 1964 (Fig 69) revealed a particularly fine set of rectangular warrens and cross-shaped traps which still survive under lightly-grazed grassland (Bowen 1975, 114–15).

Rubbing stones for animals, dew ponds in which to collect water when natural supplies are scarce, clearance cairns remaining from earlier periods of cultivation, animal shelters, and sheep dips are also characteristic features of established grassland areas (*see* Wood 1972 for general discussions of these features).

Boundaries

Boundaries are represented in many different forms, with marked regional variations reflecting local traditions and the availability of materials. The most common forms constructed

Figure 70   Wansdyke at Tan Hill, Wiltshire

in relatively recent times are stone walls, hedges, and banked hedges of different sorts. Some of these originated in medieval or earlier times and often support a wide variety of plant species. Hedges can sometimes be roughly dated by the number of species represented in a short stretch (Hooper 1975; Reece 1983).

Prehistoric boundaries of various sorts, including earthworks, so-called ranch boundaries (Bowen 1978), dykes, and cross-ridge dykes are fairly ephemeral structures and often only survive well under established grassland. On Hambledon Hill, Dorset, a linear boundary running between two spurs over 1km apart is known to be of middle Neolithic date and can still be traced on the ground today (Mercer 1980a, 19). Many upstanding boundary earthworks in Wessex can be shown to be of Bronze Age date, and similar features are known on the grasslands of the Welsh Marches (Guilbert 1975) and northern England (Higham 1978).

Large linear earthworks such as Wansdyke (Fig 70) and Offa's Dyke are best preserved in grassland areas (Crawford 1960, 107; M Gelling 1983). Smaller works include county and parish boundaries.

Associated with most boundary works are causeways and gates, and in more recent examples stiles, animal doors, and creep holes may be found, often constructed within distinctive regional traditions (Wood 1972, 203).

Tracks and roads

Droveways and green lanes are typical features of present-day and former grassland areas, sometimes still in use as thoroughfares but more often converted into fields. The antiquity of many such features is hard to determine, although old maps may provide clues to the line of truly ancient examples. In the case of long-distance routes such as the Berkshire Ridgeway, such thoroughfares are very wide as a result of their use as droving routes to take animals to market (Crawford 1960, 67–86).

Ritual monuments

Possibly the most numerous class of monuments found under grassland are ritual and ceremonial sites, especially those of prehistoric date such as long barrows, round barrows, henges, stone circles, standing stones, and cursus. Even in areas of arable farmland these monuments are often left as islands of grassland. At Arbor Low, Derbyshire (Fig 71), a henge monument under grassland contains the fallen or abandoned stones of a stone circle, while nearby is a large burial mound known as Gib Hill which still stands over 5m high (D Thompson 1963).

On Salisbury Plain, Wiltshire, quite large clusters of ritual monuments can be found, especially barrow cemeteries. At Winterbourne Monkton near Stonehenge, for example, one such cemetery comprises a single Neolithic long barrow and 35 round barrows, mostly under established grassland (see Fig 10; Grinsell nd). When excavated, barrows preserved under grassland yield a wealth of information about their construction and use. Especially important is evidence for the composition of the barrow mounds because even just a few episodes of ploughing will completely remove the outer layers of the monument. At Milton Lilbourne, near Pewsey, Wiltshire, excavations of barrow 4 in 1958 revealed a distinct weathered chalk envelope over a loam and soil core (Fig 72; Ashbee 1986). Barrows in grassland also allow studies of their form (Grinsell 1941).

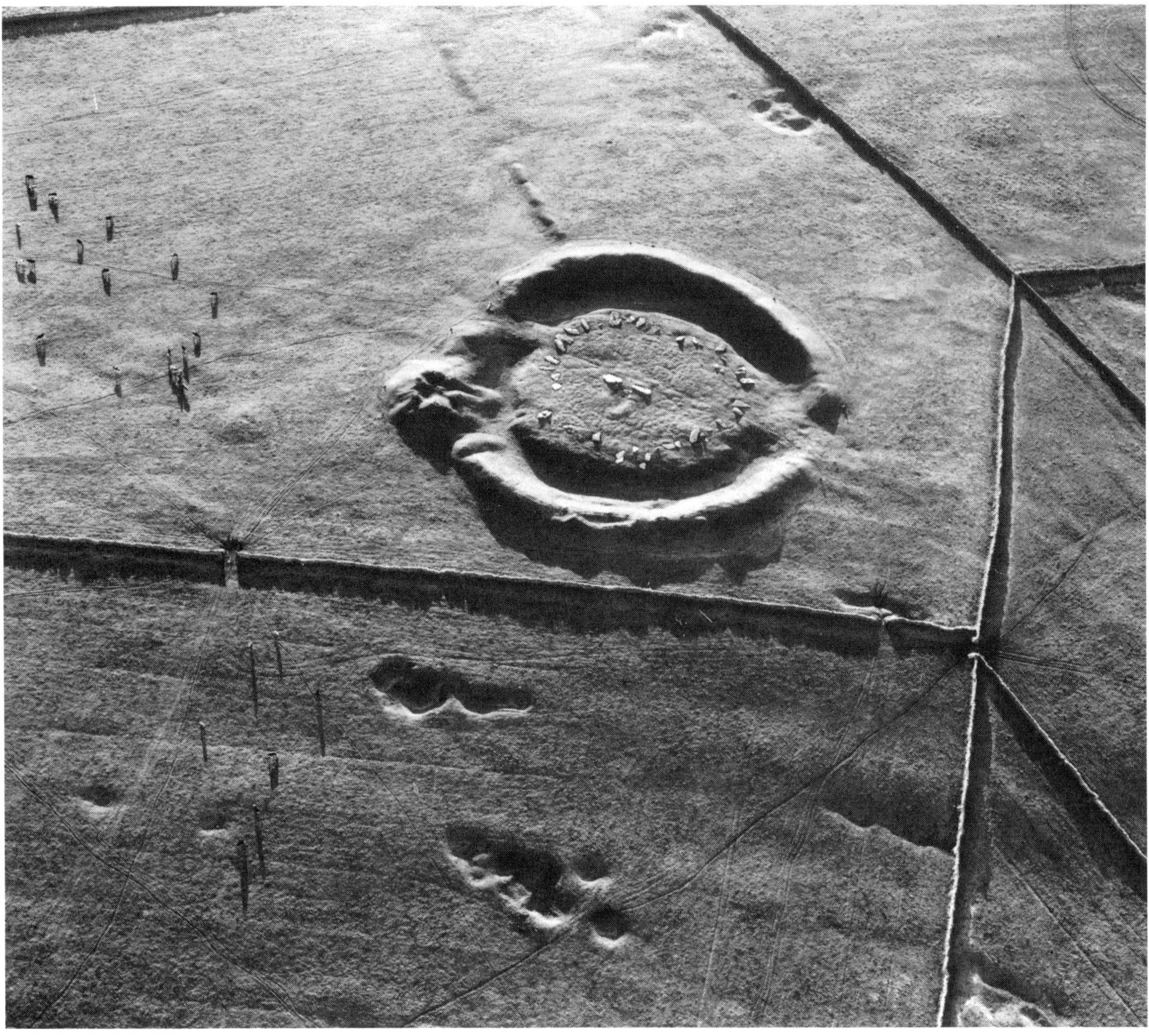

Figure 71   Arbor Low, Derbyshire: henge monument high in the Peak District, with remains of stone settings lying within the enclosed central area; a low bank projects from the henge, and traces of quarry pits can be seen in the foreground

In northern England similar burial monuments are known, but there are fewer large groups (Clack and Gosling 1976).

Industrial and miscellaneous features

Industrial features of many different types are found in grassland areas, usually as earthworks. Quarries of different sorts include prehistoric flint mines, recent marl pits, stone quarries, metal mines, and clay pits. Most show traces of the way in which the materials were extracted and are often associated with trackways for access. Spoil heaps may surround the workings. Dating is often difficult unless there are distinctive features or a stratigraphic relationship with a datable type of monument, as for example with the iron mines at Bentley Grange, West Yorkshire (Fig 73), which overlie ridge-and-furrow cultivation (Faull and Moorhouse 1981, 785–6). Leats and dams, mills of various sorts, and windmill mounds are all features commonly encountered in grassland areas.

Military works, including Roman forts, medieval castles, and temporary siege works, are often visible as earthworks under grassland. Second World War defensive works including anti-aircraft and anti-glider ditches, battery emplacements, decoys, and training sites, tend to be well preserved under grassland conditions.

On the chalklands of southern England the hill figures are particularly distinctive grassland features, among them the famous Uffington White Horse, Oxfordshire (see Fig 145), and the Long Man of Wilmington, Sussex. These figures were made by removing the turf to reveal the white bedrock beneath (Marples 1949). Most have been recut several times since they were first made, often with minor changes in design (Grinsell 1980).

Other features found on grassland include hunting butts, rifle ranges, and shooting butts of various sorts.

Sealed landscapes

In some grassland areas deposits of colluvium or head material

Figure 72   Milton Lilbourne, Dorset: excavation of barrow 4 in 1958; the section shows the augmented loam core and the weathered chalk envelope over the old ground surface (the scale totals 6 feet)

lie beneath the turf in dry valleys or at the foot of hill-slopes (Kerney *et al* 1964; Bell 1981). Most of this material accumulated during periods of arable cultivation, and can reach depths of 3m or more. The interest of these deposits is two-fold. First, the presence of an old ground surface sealed underneath may preserve features and traces of land-use. Second, there is the possibility of environmental evidence within the accumulation which may document changing conditions in the area during the time the deposit formed. At present much of the research on these deposits has been confined to southern England, but northern areas have equal potential.

9.4   Threats

Traditionally, established grassland was used for grazing sheep, cattle, and horses, for the production of hay, or for a combination of these. Established grasslands were run on a low-input/low-output basis, although the quality of output was often high.

Land-use in areas of established grassland today remains basically the same as in previous centuries, but the amount of such land has decreased dramatically over the last few decades, especially since the First World War. Modern farming practice does not favour long-term grassland and accordingly many areas of pasture are now managed as small islands within land given over to a variety of other uses. Enclosed grasslands tend to be exploited more intensively than open areas. Temporary pennings are normally used to control grazing within large enclosures.

Considerable regional variation exists in the amount of established grassland remaining. In Cumbria a recent survey suggested that as much as 82% of enclosed farmland was grassland, and that of this 11% was unimproved or semi-improved (NCC 1984, 103–4). In contrast, a survey carried out in Hampshire in 1980–2 revealed that only about 2% of the chalk downlands were under grass (Prescott 1983, 21). Perhaps the strongest reason for the variety in the use of established grassland lies in the variety of ownership. Many small enclosed areas are in private hands but a considerable portion of grassland is common land, in public ownership, or under the control of the Ministry of Defence.

Given this diversity of ownership arrangements there is a wide range of threats which must be taken into account when seeking to preserve archaeological remains. The following may be singled out for special mention.

Change of land-use

By far the greatest threat to remaining areas of established grassland is that posed by changes to existing land-use practices, especially a shift to arable, or rotational grassland, or forestry. This threat alone accounts for the loss of perhaps 95% of all grassland which has disappeared this century. Losses have been especially heavy in southern and midland counties. Dorset is probably fairly representative, and here the conversion of grassland to arable on the chalk downs between 1811 and 1972 has been particularly marked (Fig 74; C Jones 1973).

Most changes in land-use lie outside the control of planning authorities, unless protected sites are involved, and are largely dictated by changes in government grant structures and subsidies.

It has been estimated that in the Peak District it takes two ploughings to break the virgin sods and that after a third ploughing the shallow soils have been disturbed to bedrock depth, leaving little or no archaeological strata other than pits, ditches, or postholes cut into the secondary soils or natural rock (C R Hart 1981, 5). The same rapidity of destruction also applies to other areas of established grassland.

Pasture improvement

Sub-surface damage in grassland areas is caused by subsoiling and drainage works designed to improve pasture. Not only do these works cause irreparable damage along the actual cuts made in the ground, but they also cause ground fissuring and disturbance over a much wider area (Lambrick 1977, 7 on subsoiling).

Scrub invasion

If grassland is not properly maintained the natural succession of scrub growth followed by tree growth will begin, and this can be very damaging to buried archaeological features since they are often near the surface in grassland areas. Root penetration by scrub, trees, and bracken causes sub-surface ground disturbance.

Figure 73   Medieval iron-working pits dating to the thirteenth and fourteenth centuries at Bentley Grange, West Yorkshire; each pit is surrounded by a circular spoil-heap; slight traces of ridge-and-furrow cultivation can be seen between the pits suggesting that, before the area was mined, it was in arable cultivation

Over-grazing

Grassland used for high intensity grazing is especially susceptible to soil poaching. Again, because archaeological sites are often near the surface, serious damage can be caused by relatively minor disturbance of the overburden (Fig 75).

Removal of walls and boundaries

In many areas of established grassland the existing walls and hedges are often of considerable antiquity, or follow the line of ancient boundaries.

Other

Localized but no less serious threats to the archaeology of grassland areas are posed by treasure hunters using metal detectors, soil disturbance through footpath erosion, heavy use of the area by vehicles, and occasionally housing or industrial development.

9.5   Management

A well-maintained grassland cover is the best landscape environment for the preservation of archaeological remains. This is clearly demonstrated by the results obtained from observing the experimental earthwork constructed on Overton Down in 1960 (Jewell 1963).[55] After a short period of erosion and decay, both the bank and the ditch profiles stabilized and within 20 years had developed a mixed species grass cover which greatly reduced the rate of erosion.

Most important for the preservation of ancient monuments are those areas of pasture which have survived undisturbed for long periods. The management and conservation of these areas must be a priority, but the management of any grassland sites for their archaeological reserves often has a common objective with the needs of nature conservation. The converse is also true, as areas protected for their value as old grassland may also contain archaeological features (Ratcliffe 1977, 160). The main overlap here is with the Nature Conservancy Council and local naturalist trusts.[56]

In formulating management strategies for grassland monuments, two important factors must be taken into account:

i   Size of area: in many cases archaeological remains under grassland are spread over a considerable area, which ideally requires managing in a consistent way in order to provide equal preservation to the widest possible range of deposits.

ii   Low productivity: compared with the potential returns from intensive farming practices, long-term pasture has a relatively low yield which makes its retention therefore not always financially attractive. Such economics may be a short-term phenomenon, however. Well-maintained grassland provides a steady and sustainable output, albeit at a relatively low level.

Curatorial management

The main aim of curatorial management is to ensure that the ground surface is not broken and that a healthy grass cover is maintained. In grassland areas, archaeology begins immediately below the turf and so any disturbance which penetrates the turf must be avoided.

English Heritage, in conjunction with the National Trust, has recently undertaken a major programme of conservation work at Badbury Rings, Dorset (Thackray 1985). The site is an Iron Age hillfort in the heart of the chalk downlands and has suffered from widespread erosion, largely through visitor pressure along the ramparts. Areas of erosion were fenced, repaired, and reseeded with a mix of chalkland grass species to provide a stable grass cover to the earthworks. A similar programme of work has been initiated at Maiden Castle, also in Dorset, where comparable problems of soil poaching and erosion are present (Wainwright and Cunliffe 1985).

Management agreements established by English Heritage for monuments under other types of land-use often include arrangements for them to be put down to pasture in an effort

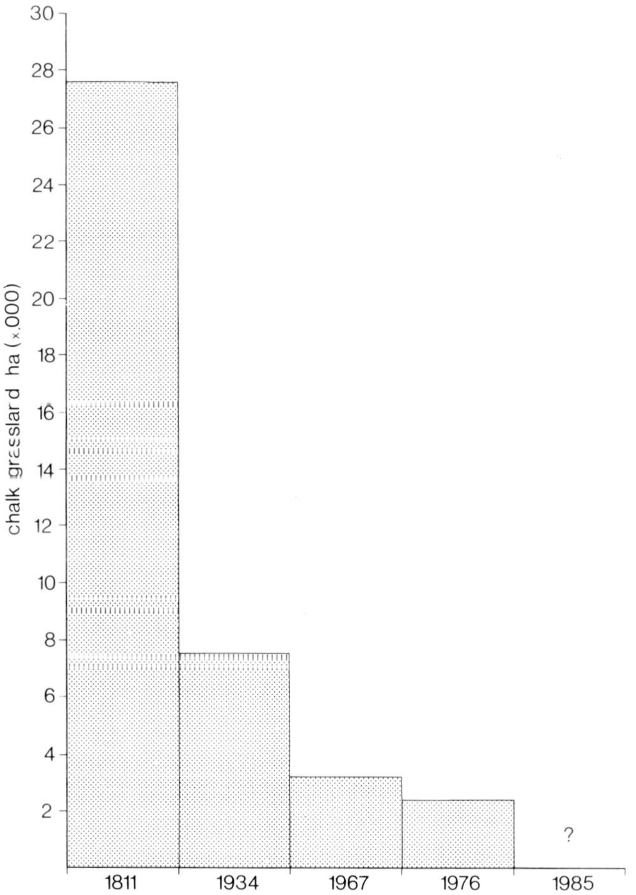

Figure 74   Histogram showing the reduction of grassland on the chalk downs of Dorset 1811–1976 (data from NCC 1984)

Figure 75   Poaching of grassland by cattle rubbing themselves on a marker post at Knook Castle, Wiltshire (see Fig 66 for aerial view of this site)

to reduce the effects of natural and human erosion on the buried remains.

At present there are approximately 4000 Scheduled Monuments under established grassland, including many sites which have been put down to pasture relatively recently through management agreements.[57] Most Guardianship sites in the countryside are maintained under grass, either grazed or mown, depending on the landscape category within which they happen to lie.

Selecting sites under pasture for designation as being of national importance is made difficult by the fact that when an area of grassland is surveyed the abundance of evidence recorded is overwhelming, and it is difficult to select the most representative sites or areas of landscape. When selection criteria are applied, sites should display clear evidence that they have not been disturbed by recent cultivation (ie they should have high plant-species counts) and clear indications of their form and extent. Large areas of grassland must be preferred to small isolated islands. The more ancient a piece of grassland the greater its importance if it has not been disturbed, although representative samples of grassland established at a number of different periods is desirable. Rare types of site which can be found in a grassland environment, and maintained under grassland conditions, must be accorded a high priority.

All grassland sites are fragile and need active positive management to ensure their preservation. Some areas of established grassland, however, contain ancient monuments of many periods and forms within a small area and these are especially important. Clusters of sites preserved under established grassland are likely to retain evidence of differences in their original structure and form, and this can often be detected on the surface.

Excavated sites in grassland areas are fairly common because, as upstanding monuments, such sites have attracted attention for generations. Generally, grassland areas are no better served by documentary evidence than any other sectors of the landscape, although features referred to in documents or place-names (eg rabbit warrens) may be easier to locate on the ground in grassland areas. The potential of grassland sites is relatively easy to determine in terms of size and structure, although details of sub-surface conditions, for example the survival of environmental remains, are much more difficult to assess.

Because of the fine preservation of sites in grassland areas selection often depends on choosing the best by giving some

Figure 76 Housesteads, Northumberland: aerial view of the fort and part of Hadrian's Wall, showing the layout of the buildings and the surrounding earthworks preserved under grassland

sort of relative value to a site. Experiments by Wiltshire County Council on the surviving monuments within the Salisbury Plain Military Training Area emphasize how difficult it is to decide where to draw the boundary lines between classes of site, for example between monuments of national importance and those of regional importance.[58]

The stock of Scheduled Monuments is supplemented by sites protected within SSSIs and NNRs. Among the most important of such areas is Overton Down, Wiltshire (P Fowler 1967). Commons also represent important areas where sites tend to be well preserved because of low intensity land-use.

The needs of archaeological conservation in areas of established grassland can easily be served by sympathetic management, bearing in mind the key principle that ground disturbance must be avoided. The best system for any individual site will depend on its location and exactly what is being preserved. Common themes can, however, be noted. Sheep grazing or a combination of sheep and cattle grazing are likely to be most effective in maintaining grassland in good condition. Chain harrowing and rolling to prevent matting and to flatten any mole-hills should present no problems for archaeological evidence, so long as the work is done when the ground is dry.

Pest control (especially of burrowing animals such as rabbits, badgers, and moles) may be necessary.

Large areas of grassland are generally easier to manage economically than small areas, and where sites are currently preserved as a series of adjacent islands of grassland it is preferable to join them together into a single grassland unit. Known sites under other land-use regimes near grassland monuments should be added to the permanent pasture wherever possible.

Special attention should be given to the siting of water troughs, making sure that they are well away from standing features, as they act as focal points for animals which causes poaching on the very areas that need most protection. Likewise, the siting of temporary penning and gateways must be carefully planned to avoid concentrating animal activity on earthworks and round upstanding features. Footpaths and tracks should be directed around upstanding features rather than over them.

It may be useful to mark sites with distinctive signs, as is presently done on Salisbury Plain. However, the signs should be positioned well away from the monument itself and should define a sensitive zone rather than the site boundary because the erection of the signs damages the monument and soil poaching may ensue as stock find them useful as rubbing posts (Fig 75).

Demonstration farms at Manor Farm, Wiltshire, and Ottercops and Raechester, Northumberland, contain substantial areas of grassland with known archaeological features managed in a way which will conserve them (Cobham 1984).

Recording

The opportunities for recording archaeological evidence in grassland landscapes are numerous and should be encouraged whenever possible. Field surveys and aerial surveys are particularly important and revealing.

In formulating management plans it is important to estimate or establish the date of grassland formation, the spatial limits of preserved remains, the minimum depth of overburden, the presence or absence of masking earthworks such as medieval ridge-and-furrow, and the likelihood of preserved old land surfaces beneath colluvium or head deposits within the grassland area. This information will allow an assessment of the range of agricultural techniques that can be used without disturbing the archaeological remains.

Exploitative management

Grassland sites with upstanding earthworks and visible features lend themselves particularly well to public display. Even without excavation much interpretation is possible. Grassland can withstand fairly high visitor levels, except when wet. The main attraction of grassland sites is their potential for explaining total landscapes rather than isolated features. Self-guided trails are widely used to control visitors at such monuments. The main difficulty in exploiting grassland sites is in balancing preservation with recreation (Bonsey 1970; Countryside Commission 1980c).

Among the monuments in State Guardianship which are maintained under pasture are the deserted medieval village at Wharram Percy, Yorkshire, the Iron Age hillfort at Maiden Castle, Dorset, and the Roman fort at Housesteads, Northumberland (Fig 76).

Academic interest in grassland sites is high because it is often possible to undertake extremely cost-effective excavations by carefully locating excavation trenches over parts of the site which are expected to yield most information. Minimal overburden cuts excavation costs, and the potential of colluvial sediments as environmental records makes these areas highly desirable.

10 Woodland

10.1 Archaeological importance

Woodlands are areas of landscape more or less densely covered in trees, either through semi-natural development or deliberate planting.[59] The variety of tree species varies greatly from one region to another according to altitude, soil conditions, latitude, and the influence of past and present woodland management. Woods are the oldest living things in the countryside and are enduring features of the landscape.[60]

Archaeologically, woodland is important for three main reasons:

i   Landscape specific sites: some woods are of great antiquity and represent archaeological features in their own right — living relics of past land-use. Around and within such woods there is often a range of archaeological features specific to its management, control, and exploitation.

ii   Preservation: any woodland established before about 1960 may contain well-preserved archaeological sites which have been spared damage from more intensive land-use practices such as agriculture and silviculture. In such cases, ancient monuments are often very well preserved, although root action will undoubtedly have caused some sub-surface disturbance. Post-1960 woodland also preserves sites either by chance or where they have been deliberately avoided during planting.

iii   Amenity value: woodland can easily be made accessible, with little risk to the trees, and therefore provides considerable scope for the interpretation and presentation of monuments.

Woodland covers approximately 9450 square kilometres of England (Forestry Commission 1985, tab 1), about 7.2% of the total land area (Fig 77). Of this, some 2410 square kilometres (25%) are owned by the Forestry Commission (Forestry Commission 1985, tab 1). Woodland is widely spread around the country on many different types of soil, but by European standards England is relatively lightly wooded; in France, for example, about 27% of the countryside is wooded, while in West Germany the coverage is nearly 30% (Forestry Commission 1985, tab 12).

As defined here, woodlands fall into five main types according to their structure: simple coppice woodlands, coppice with standards, high forest, wood pasture, and plantations. Archaeologically, these all provide slightly different preservational characteristics; for example open woodland, such as wood pasture and coppice, is more likely to allow better preservation of archaeological remains than dense closed woodland, such as can be found in many plantations. A more fundamental distinction may, however, be made between *primary woodland*, that is woodland that has never been cleared for other land-uses, and *secondary woodland*, which has regenerated or been deliberately planted on previously cleared land (Rackham 1976, 32; 1980). Ancient woodland, which may be primary or secondary, is woodland known to have been established before about AD 1700.

10.2 History and distribution

The history of English woodlands begins at the end of the Pleistocene Ice Age, after the retreat of the Devensian glaciation about 12,000 bc. As the climate became warmer and soils became more fertile, woodland began to develop and spread, until by about 4000 bc the greater part of the country was covered, up to altitudes of 450–600m, with various types of broad-leaved woodland in the south and extensive pine forests in the uplands (Pennington 1974; Birks *et al* 1975; Godwin 1975; Ratcliffe 1977).

Through archaeological evidence and the study of pollen profiles preserved in peat bogs or lake sediments, the vegetation and woodland history of much of England is well documented from late glacial times to the present day. Five phases in the development of the post-glacial vegetation can be recognized, each characterized by slightly different woodland composition, as climate and soil development affected the conditions under which the trees grew and as man began to affect the distribution and structure of the woodland (Table 4).

The early post-glacial woodlands have been termed the 'wildwoods' (Rackham 1976, 39), but few, if any, areas of woodland still extant can be shown to have descended directly from these wildwoods without at least some interference from

Table 4   Summary of the development of English woodland since the last Ice Age

Date	Vegetation zone	Characteristic woodland	Comments
	Sub-Atlantic	Oak and Alder	substantial clearances
500 bc			
	Sub-Boreal	Oak and Alder	first forest clearances
3000 bc			
	Atlantic	Oak, Alder, and Elm Pine, Hazel, and Elm	interference
5500 bc			
	Boreal	Pine and Hazel Birch, Pine, and Hazel	
7600 bc			
	Pre-Boreal	Birch, Pine, and Juniper	

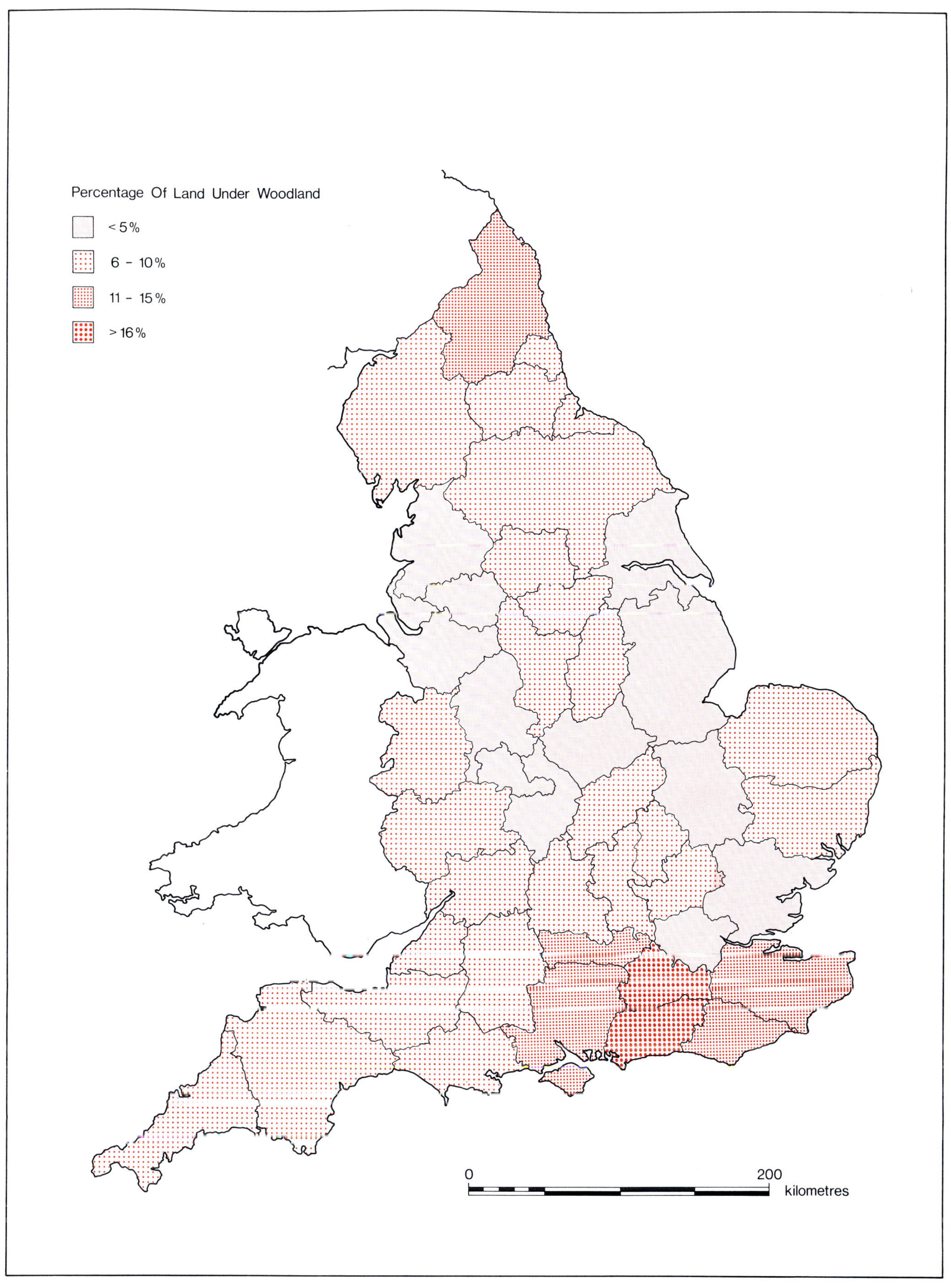

Figure 77   Map showing the percentage of woodland in England (data from Forestry Commission 1985)

man. The main reason for this is that, during prehistoric and later times, woodland was a valuable and heavily exploited resource. However, some woods occupy land which has been, as far as can be determined, woodland of one sort or another since early prehistoric times; this is truly primary woodland.

The first major episode of forest clearance in Britain began about 3000 bc, during the early part of the Neolithic period, when farming first became established in Britain (A Smith 1981). Before this, some relatively small-scale interference with the woodland cover might have taken place in upland areas to provide better grazing for animals, but the evidence is subject to more than one interpretation (Mellars 1976; I Simmons *et al* 1981, 103).

Neolithic farmers did not simply clear woodland, however. Evidence from the Somerset Levels and the Cambridgeshire Fens demonstrates that woodland management in the form of coppicing was also practiced, and by implication areas of woodland must have been enclosed to prevent the underwood being grazed (Rackham 1977; Pryor 1985b). The products of coppicing at this early date are known to have been used for hurdle-making among other things (Coles and Orme 1977).

Throughout later prehistoric and Roman times, woodland continued to be managed and heavily exploited. Timber was certainly used in large quantities for building works of various sorts, both domestic and ceremonial,[61] and must also have been consumed for fuel and many other purposes. Other woodland resources, such as nuts, berries, and bark, were also exploited. The overall area of woodland in Britain was reduced dramatically during later prehistoric and Roman times, partly because of the demand for woodland products, and partly because woodland occupied land which could profitably be brought into more productive use, for example cultivation. Place-names can sometimes help in the identification of early clearances (Rackham 1976, 55).

By the Domesday survey of 1086, the remaining areas of woodland occupied a fairly small percentage of the overall land area (Rackham 1976, 58; Darby 1973, 52–4; 1977, ch 6); in Hampshire, for example, only about 15% of the land was under woodland (Colebourn 1983, 8). During medieval times the great value of the remaining woodland was realized, and indeed woodlands were protected by law from the ninth century onwards (Colebourn 1983, 8; Rackham 1976, ch 4). Timber and wood remained the primary products and were essential for building houses and boats and for almost all other structural tasks for which iron or steel were later used. Wood was also used for making household utensils like plates, bowls, cups, barrels, and a wide range of containers. In addition, woodlands provided the setting for many industries reliant upon a ready source of fuel (eg potting, brickmaking, and lime-burning) and were also extensively used for charcoal making. Firewood was collected, and the pannage heavily exploited. Bark was saved for tanning, and honey was collected from wild and domestic bees. Acorns and hazelnuts were gathered. Hurdle-making, bowl-turning, and tool-making were also important woodland industries. The woods also provided important reserves for animals of the chase (Cox 1905). Woodland sports included cock shooting and trapping woodcock in nets strung across a re-entrant angle in a wood.

In order to support such heavy exploitation, the woods were actively managed on a grand scale, and were major centres of employment. Several different management strategies were used depending upon the structure and role of the wood. Custodians and stewards (woodwards) were appointed, and there were many lesser officers in charge of specific aspects of the woodland economy (Rackham 1976; Whitlock 1979).

The area of woodland in England continued to decline until, by the seventeenth century, insufficient remained to supply the home demand for timber and it began to be imported. Throughout the medieval and post-medieval period, timber was particularly important for ship-building.

Most woodlands lay on land that was unusable for much else; poorly drained ground, steep slopes, and in areas well away from the centres of population. The demand for timber remained high, however, and, from the middle of the seventeenth century, plantations began to be established, first as a gentleman's hobby, but later as a way of increasing the output of woodland products, principally timber and wood. These plantations did not follow traditional patterns of woodland management, and often contained species of tree which were not native to the area (Evelyn 1706).

After the First World War, woodland resources were in a very depleted state and there was considerable concern about the future of many woodland areas. In 1919 the Forestry Commission was created by Act of Parliament to make good this depletion, and more recently to act as forest authority and coordinator of forestry enterprise (Forestry Commission 1974; 1978). Plantations provided the obvious answer to increasing woodland reserves, and from 1920 onwards many were established, mostly in the uplands, where an abundance of land which appeared to be unsuitable for more intensive utilization was identified and exploited. Between 1946 and 1975, timber and wood output from English woodlands rose by 500% (Forestry Commission 1978, 15).

Traditional woodland management is now rare in England, although there are organizations such as the Woodland Trust which are trying to revive interest in such practices (Woodland Trust 1984). Most woodlands are operated under some form of silviculture, the propagation of trees from seed, followed by growth in plantations and harvesting by clear felling (Helliwell 1984). The range of products derived from woodland has also declined to the extent that forestry now focuses on three main products: sawn timber, pit timber, and pulp wood for making paper and particle board. Firewood output is now increasing. Alongside these changes in output, new uses for woodland have also developed, particularly multiple land-use involving water catchment and recreation (Watkins and Wheeler 1981; Carroll 1978; and cf Edlin 1949).

The distribution of woodland is highly variable over the country. Few large tracts remain outside core areas such as the Forest of Dean, The New Forest, the Breckland, Sherwood Forest, and Cheviot. Predominantly agricultural and built-up areas contain less than 5% of land area under woodland. Even heavily- wooded areas, such as Sussex and Berkshire or the uplands of Northumberland, can only boast a little over 15% of land under woodland. In general, most of today's woodland is fragmentary and is still found in marginal areas on the heaviest and poorest land or on steep slopes (Forestry Commission 1978; 1982). Government grants are available to encourage the planting of more trees, especially native hardwoods, and farmers are being enjoined to turn areas of agricultural land over to woodland, as a means of cutting production while retaining profitability.

At present it is not known exactly how much ancient woodland survives in the country as a whole, but in many counties some sort of vegetation survey is underway, which includes an assessment of the nature and extent of the woodland resource. Ancient woods, both primary and secondary, can generally be identified through the wide range of plant species present on the woodland floor, and through old maps and documentary evidence (Colebourn 1983, 30;

Figure 78   Wood bank at Felsham Hall Wood, Bradfield St George, Suffolk

Rackham 1976, 123). In Hampshire it has been estimated that nearly 50% of existing woodland is ancient (Colebourn 1983, 57), but elsewhere the figure is often much lower (T Barfield 1984; NCC 1984). Overall there appear to be few remaining areas of primary woodland over 20ha in extent, and most of what does survive lies in the south. Archaeologically all woodland is of some interest, but primary woods and very ancient secondary woods are of greatest value.[62]

10.3   The archaeology of woodland

Archaeological sites known within woodland naturally fall into two groups: woodland related features, and non-woodland features within woods.

Woodland related features

In both primary and secondary woodland, archaeological features connected with its management and exploitation may be found. Dating such features is often difficult, and some may be of much greater antiquity than is commonly assumed. As discussed in the last section, woodlands have been used in a variety of ways since early prehistoric times, and many have left their mark. In general, the older the wood the greater the quantity and variety of woodland related features that must be expected.

Woodland boundaries which were established before the nineteenth century are often substantial features, especially where woods were emparked as deer parks (*see* chapter 13). Earthworks comprising a bank and ditch are the most common (Fig 78). In some cases the ditch lies outside the bank, in others the bank is outside the ditch (Rackham 1976, 115; Crawford 1960, ch 18). Corner mounds were sometimes built from spare soil remaining after the construction of these earthworks, but great care must be taken when identifying them from surface traces alone, because they are easily confused with round barrows. Fences or hedges were in some cases set on top of the banks, with gaps left as deer leaps, or deer gates as they are known in some areas. Inside many woods, boundaries delimiting areas exploited in different ways are common; for example coppice and wood pasture may be separated by fences or earthworks. Drainage grips were established where necessary and sometimes survive as networks of small channels (Hendry *et al* 1984; Rackham 1976, 118).

Woodland crafts were numerous (10.3 above; Edlin 1949) and sometimes leave distinctive evidence (Fig 79). Charcoal-burning can sometimes be identified from piles of burnt soil

Figure 79 *Woodland crafts: A (above) Charcoal burning in Wyre Forest, near Bewdley, Hereford and Worcester, about 1936; B (below) nineteenth century saw-pit in use*

and charcoal associated with hollows, and perhaps traces of a hut or an encampment. More often traces of round 'pans', terraced into a hill-slope and covered in charcoal flecks, betray charcoal production sites. Temporary saw-pits for cutting timber occur in all shapes and sizes, although permanent pits are more likely to have been established near workshops rather than in the wood itself. Roads and tracks provided access to these craft areas, and also provide the arterial routeways for transporting products out of the wood (Aston 1985, 109 and 135). Some of these trackways can be very elaborate (Fig 80). Deep gullies running down moderate or steep slopes through a wood may be 'log runs', used to move quantities of timber to a loading bay or sawing area.

Industrial activities dependent upon a constant supply of wood for fuel often leave much evidence in the form of structures, and possibly quarries or mines. Roman pottery industries, such as those of the New Forest (Fulford 1975), Savernake Forest (Annable 1962), and Alice Holt (Lyne and Jefferies 1979), focused around extensive tracts of woodland, where suitable clays were also available. They are represented archaeologically by the remains of kiln structures and workshop areas. Similarly, the distribution of medieval pottery production centres shows a high correlation with remaining or once extant woodland, and much the same sort of remains survive, for example at Minety, Wiltshire (Musty 1973), and Laverstock, Dorset (Musty *et al* 1969). Brick and tile production followed similar lines (Drury 1981).

Figure 80   Walled trackway leading through Randwick Wood, Gloucestershire

In woodland near sources of iron ore, such as the Forest of Dean and the Weald of Kent and Sussex, traces of extraction, roasting, and smelting abound (Standing and Coates 1979; C Hart 1971; Cleere and Crossley 1985). Likewise, lime-burning combined localized sources of raw materials with the availability of fuel, as for example in the woodlands of Herefordshire (T Barfield 1984).

Quarries for stone or minerals were situated in woodland whenever possible, in order to minimize the loss of more productive land. When abandoned, workings in woodland were rarely backfilled and, although they have often since become overgrown, they provide some of the best examples of their class. A fine example of a mine producing micaceous haematite was found at Wray Cleave Wood in 1985 (Fig 81), during a survey of woodland in the Dartmoor area (McCrone 1985). Ochre pits and marl pits may also be found, where these materials outcrop.

The wide range of employment offered within woodland during medieval and earlier times means that traces of small settlements are widespread. Larger settlements would have been situated in clearances and are probably now in open countryside, but individual huts, cots, and houses are to be expected. The more humble examples were probably built of wood, but hunting lodges for the aristocracy were sometimes of stone. One, in Hazel Hanger Wood, Gloucestershire, was only visible as a mound until excavated, and had previously been misidentified as a barrow (G Harding 1978).

Non-woodland features

Many areas of secondary woodland conceal archaeological sites which were in open country during their use. In some cases, such sites lay within a large clearing in primary woodland which became reafforested after it was abandoned. In other cases, monuments became tree-covered during a programme of deliberate plantation or afforestation. Sometimes trees were deliberately planted on ancient monuments, because no other more productive use for the ground could be found, or because the addition of trees emphasized the site as a landscape feature. This practice is not, however, recommended.

The range of non-woodland sites found in woodland is extremely wide, as Sumner (1917) illustrates with examples from the New Forest. It is important, however, to realize that preservation of earthworks under woodland is especially good where modern heavy machinery has not been used. Some of the best prehistoric burial monuments lie under ancient woodland (Fig 82), among them the Bronze Age cemetery at Towthorpe, North Yorkshire (Mortimer 1905, 1–43). On the Cotswolds, the hillfort at Brakenbury Ditches, Gloucestershire, is probably the best preserved of over 30 such monuments of similar type and date in the area (RCHME 1976, 86–7), while at Danebury, Hampshire (Fig 83), a beech plantation established in the early nineteenth century preserves what has recently become one of the most thoroughly excavated hillforts in southern England (Cunliffe 1984).

Figure 81   *Wray Cleeve ore-dressing floor in woodland at Moretonhampstead, Devon*

A field survey in advance of the construction of the M3 motorway in Hampshire revealed that the only place where the earthworks of an Iron Age settlement remained upstanding was within Micheldever Wood (Fig 84; Fasham 1975b, 10). Everywhere else agriculture had completely removed any earthworks that once existed.

When in use, many of these prehistoric settlements and barrows may in fact have been situated within large woodland clearances.

Roman villas, deserted medieval villages, and many other traces of settlement have been found covered by secondary woodland (Fig 85). Many areas of secondary woodland contain traces of ridge-and-furrow cultivation, which serves to demonstrate that during the medieval period these woods were under active cultivation. Prehistoric field systems may also be found under woodland, as near South Lodge Camp, Cranborne Chase, Dorset.[63] Locating and recording of sites within woodland is not easy (cf Butler and Fasham 1975). Some techniques, such as aerial photography, cannot be used, and intensive systematic field survey is the only practical way of searching large areas. Usually such work has to be undertaken in the late winter (January–March), when vegetation is low and slight earthworks can be identified. The trees present additional problems during the preparation of accurate surveys, thus making such projects very time-consuming. Excavation too is hampered by the presence of roots, which favour the soft ground usually associated with sub-surface archaeological features such as ditches and pits. There are often numerous hollows resulting from trees being uprooted or the collapse of decayed stumps, and these tend to confuse the truly archaeological evidence and produce a background noise, which has to be filtered out when surveying monuments in woodland. Searches along drains and streams may reveal buried remains, and hollows left by fallen trees can sometimes turn up artefacts or evidence of structures.

10.4   Threats

By comparison with modern forestry, the traditional methods of managing and exploiting woodland were extremely complicated. A self-regenerating system was employed, so that wood and timber were indefinitely renewable, and crops of standards and underwood could be taken regularly. It was this system which perpetuated the longevity of many woodlands and, though causing minimal ground disturbance, promoted the survival of archaeological evidence.

Today, silviculture imposes rather different management practices upon woodlands. Although multiple land-use predominates, the overall range of uses is relatively small, and most of the threats to the future preservation of archaeological sites within woodlands result directly from forestry practice. It is characteristic of these threats that they have a high impact over short periods at key points in the cycle of woodland exploitation (Blatchford 1978): ground preparation and planting, thinning, and harvesting.

Ground preparation and planting

Whether for the afforestation of unwooded land or for reafforestation after clear felling, current forestry practice places great emphasis on ground preparation, ploughing, drainage, and the digging of planting furrows. This usually involves heavy and powerful machinery, for which archaeological sites

Figure 82   Bronze Age round barrow in Randwick Wood, Gloucestershire, one of the few barrows on the Cotswolds which has a visible ditch around the mound

pose little obstacle (cf G Taylor 1970). Small sites, such as cairns and burials, can be totally destroyed by one pass of such machines, while larger sites may survive in damaged form for two or at most three passes. Buried occupation layers, as well as upstanding monuments, are susceptible to this kind of threat (A Jackson 1978). The majority of recent plantation has been in upland areas (Fig 86). Since 1947, over 147,000ha have been taken into use as woodland in England (Forestry Commission 1982), and between 30% and 50% of ancient woodland extant in 1933 had by 1983 been lost through being cleared or taken into plantations (NCC 1984, 55).

Tree growth and thinning

Archaeological sites are under continuous threat during the time that the trees are growing. Root penetration causes floors to lift, walls to topple, and stratigraphy to become fragmented. Bedrock-cut features, such as pits and ditches, attract root systems because of their softer, often earthy, fills. Thinning usually involves little disturbance, unless young trees are pulled up rather than cut down.

Harvesting

The second major episode of disturbance comes at the time when woodland is felled.[64] Clear felling is the most damaging, for not only does much ground get disturbed by the hauling of trunks and the cutting of timber, but large machines, which churn up the ground and compress it, are now able to penetrate the woodland to reach areas not previously accessible.

Figure 83   Danebury, Hampshire: excavations inside the Iron Age hillfort, which was planted with trees in the early nineteenth century; storage pits and a roadway can be seen within the excavated area

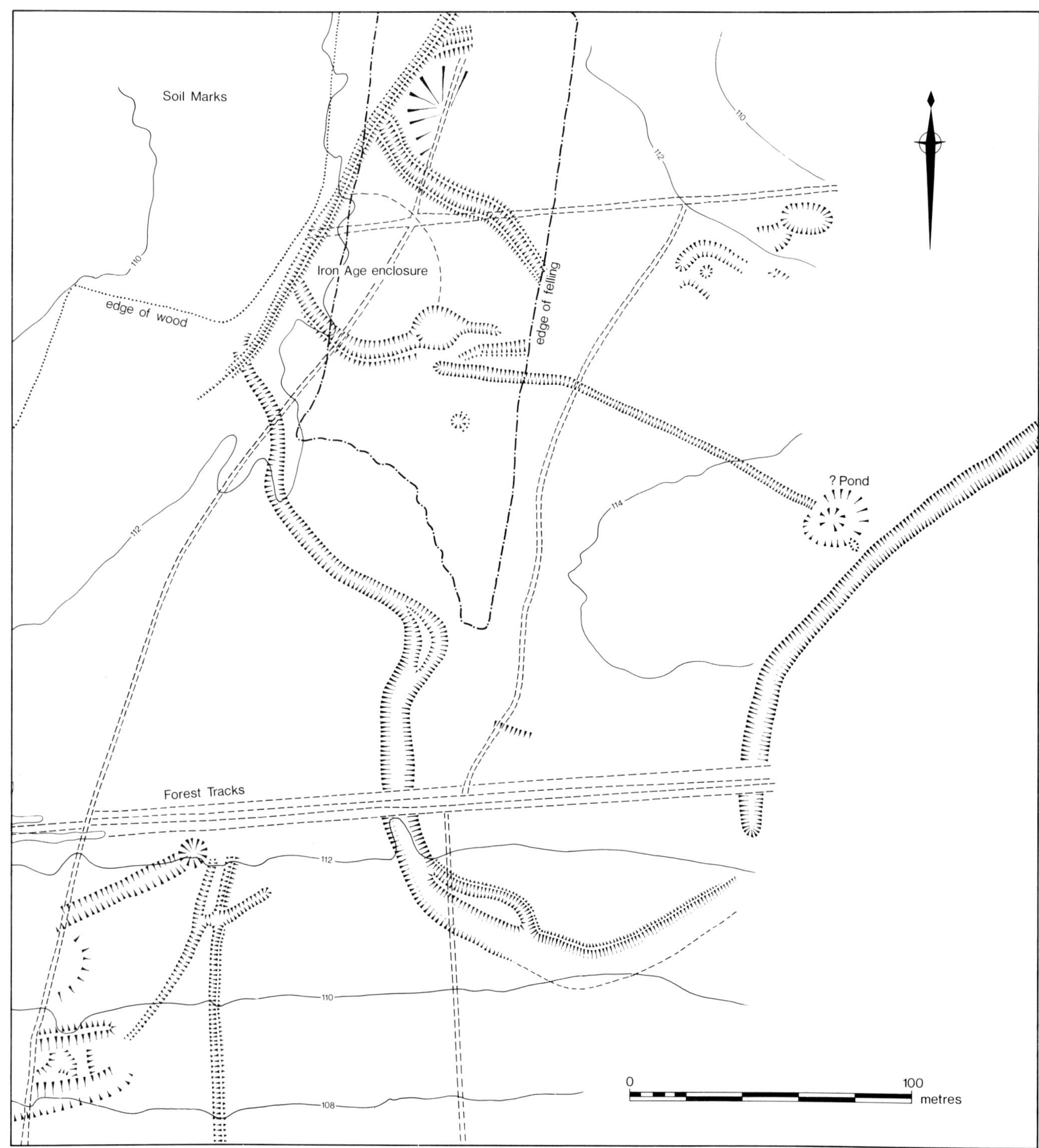

Figure 84   Plan of earthworks recorded in Micheldever Wood, Hampshire, cleared in advance of the construction of the M3 motorway (after Fasham 1975b, fig 2)

Figure 85   Stansted, Essex: the main eastern moat at Colchester Hall, cleared of trees (the ranging rods are at 10m intervals)

Other

Associated with modern forestry are various ancillary works which can pose a threat to archaeological sites. Most devastating is the provision of access roads and loading bays within woodland. Characteristically, the construction of these facilities involves clearing the topsoil and subsoil down to a firm foundation. The same applies to the provision of car-parks, which can be especially damaging to woodland boundary features where they exist.

Woodland soils are very fragile, and over archaeological sites are usually thin. Heavy pedestrian use of footpaths over monuments results in serious denudation and lays deposits open to attack by other forces, for example frost and water. Windthrow of trees on or near ancient monuments not only rips open the ground, exposing buried deposits to human and natural erosion, but also physically moves any portions of buried deposits caught in the stool.

10.5   Management

The thin soils and interpenetrating tree roots make archaeological sites under woodland especially fragile and vulnerable. Many areas of woodland containing archaeological sites have been lost to other land-uses over the past century or so, and many recently afforested areas have swallowed up sites in various states of preservation. If the distinctive assortment of sites known to exist within woodlands is to be retained for our own and future generations to enjoy, great attention must be given to the integration of archaeological needs with the management of all types of woodland.

The practicalities of appropriate conservation and management measures overlap considerably with the aims of other countryside interests, especially those of nature conservation aimed at preserving the great diversity of plant and animal species present in ancient woodland.[65] In recent years, the Forestry Commission have placed greater emphasis on conservation (Forestry Commission 1984d), and have instigated a number of schemes which improve the management of archaeological sites within woodland. A code of practice which covers the treatment of archaeological remains has been agreed by private forestry groups (Timber Growers UK 1985).

In formulating management strategies for woodland landscapes, the following two factors need to be taken into account:

i   Poor documentation: the problems associated with identifying and recording sites and monuments under woodland makes their inclusion in a plan of operations difficult, and ideally demands that a new survey is undertaken when such a plan is being drawn up.

ii   Inevitable damage: because root systems inevitably penetrate archaeological levels, maintaining sites under woodland cover is not cost-effective in terms of promoting the long-term survival of the site. Ideally, monuments should be preserved in clearings and glades within woodland. Wood pasture and coppiced woodland cause less damage than plantations or densely-stocked woodland.

Figure 86 Trewortha Marsh, Smallcombe, Cornwall: afforestation of an area of prehistoric and medieval settlement; earthworks forming boundaries and structures can be seen clearly in the non-wooded area, and also under the recently-planted areas

Curatorial management

Of all landscape categories, woodlands can claim the most ancient legislative concern for their protection. Laws restricting and controlling exploitation date back to Saxon times.[66] The Forestry Acts currently in force make little mention of the archaeological importance of woodlands, except to prevent the Forestry Commission from compulsorily purchasing Ancient Monuments for planting.[67] Archaeological considerations are not normally taken into account when conditional clauses are added to felling licenses issued by the Forestry Commission, nor are they included in conditions attached to grants for planting schemes.[68]

At present, there are approximately 2500 Scheduled Monuments in woodland.[69] Scheduled Monument Consent is required for reafforestation programmes affecting such sites, because replanting is not exempt under the class consent system (*see* chapter 5.3). Replanting monuments with trees is normally discouraged, and management agreements negotiated

by English Heritage provide for the removal of trees from monuments wherever possible, because of the damage caused by root action.

Selecting sites for scheduling is not easy, because of the limited amount of information currently available from surveys of woodland. Any monuments in good condition, regardless of period, lend themselves to protection through scheduling, especially where the survival of earthworks over a wide area can be demonstrated. Woods containing a wide diversity of sites are especially important, but so too are woods containing fragile and rare sites which need protection. Ancient woodland with good supporting documentary records is important, while the preservation of the setting and context of the monuments in large areas of woodland known to contain discrete clusters of related sites will be of special value.

In addition to the range of Scheduled Monuments, many areas of woodland designated as nature reserves or SSSIs contain archaeological sites, as do National Trust woodlands and many country parks and Forest Parks which should, at least

Figure 87   Forestry operations sympathetic to the archaeological monuments: A (top) aerial view of Bury Ditches, Shropshire, after clearance of the trees to help conserve the site; B (bottom left) Bury Ditches, Shropshire, showing an area of rampart cleared of trees with the stumps remaining in situ to rot away; C (bottom right) tractor with lifting arm being used to remove trunks from felling within Cawthorn Camp, North Yorkshire

in theory, all be managed in an exemplary way and make proper provision for archaeological sites.[70]

The basic requirements for the conservation of archaeological sites under woodland are simple and do little to diminish the potential return from well-managed woods. The key to success is to minimize ground disturbance. Traditional methods of self-regenerating woodland should ideally be adopted. Known sites should be left free of trees in clearings or glades. Simply creating islands of bare ground within woodland is not enough; the trees round the edge of the glade need to be thinned, and a light turf cover over the monument itself needs to be developed. If possible, shallow-rooted trees should be set in the vicinity of monuments to minimize the penetration of roots into archaeologically sensitive deposits. Rides or fire-breaks may provide useful treeless areas which can be adapted to the needs of conserving small sites, but care must be taken that such breaks in cover will not be exploited as thoroughfares by heavy vehicles. Large monuments such as hillforts are better cleared of trees completely wherever practical (Fig 87A), and it should be borne in mind that large sites need to be treated as a whole, so that good preservation is not confined to a limited, and perhaps unrepresentative, area.

The thinning and felling of trees on or near known sites requires great care. Stumps should be left in position and allowed to rot naturally (Fig 87B), because pulling them out means that any archaeological layers penetrated by the roots will be torn up as well. Vehicles with wide tyres which can lift tree trunks, rather than drag them, should be used to handle timber near archaeological sites in order to minimize ground disturbance (Fig 87C). Fires should only be lit well away from sites, so that charcoal and ash do not penetrate sub-surface layers and contaminate buried deposits.

Roads and access routes into and through woodland need to be planned so as to avoid known sites, particularly standing earthworks. The backfilling of hollows should be avoided, unless it has been determined that they are not archaeological features.

Special attention needs to be given to boundary earthworks when extending or reducing the size of a wood. Internal boundaries may be usefully retained as subdivisions within a wood.

Recording

Because archaeological features in woodland are relatively hard to identify, even during field survey, a careful watch for new features should be maintained by anyone working within a wood. The examination of windthrows and newly-cleared ground will usually reveal the presence of any sites.

A detailed management plan, or a plan of operations, ideally requires a comprehensive archaeological survey to provide sufficient information for specific proposals to be evaluated. It should be emphasized, however, that even a detailed survey is unlikely to identify all the sites in a large or dense area of woodland. When recording new sites, attention needs to be given to the extent, preservation, and previous history of the visible features, in particular to whether they are woodland features or of pre-woodland origin. Whenever an area of woodland has been cleared, for whatever reason, archaeological survey should be encouraged before replanting commences.

Pre-afforestation surveys provide the background information for developing a planting programme and plan of operations for countryside being taken into woodland management. Such surveys have been carried out very

successfully in the past, for example at Millstone Hill, Northumberland (Jobey 1981), and Wark Forest, Northumberland (T Hayes 1976).

As a last resort, excavation provides one way in which details of a site threatened with destruction by afforestation or reafforestation can be recorded.

Exploitation

Many woodland and forest areas already display ancient monuments as individual features, or as focal points of interest on forest trails.[71] Much potential for interpretation and presentation still exists, however, particularly as available statistics suggest a sustained increase in the number of visitors to woodland areas for informal recreation (Lloyd 1976; Orrom 1976; Forestry Commission 1984b). Archaeologically, the presentation of woodland-bound prehistoric sites is desirable, as the setting of such monuments is in many cases more authentic, and woodland can absorb high visitor numbers.

Academic interest in woodland sites is at present low because of the practical difficulties involved in field survey and excavation. However, well-preserved sites of types which are generally poorly preserved elsewhere are of special interest, and survey work can be very rewarding because thin soils allow detailed plotting of extant features (McCrone 1985).

11 Lowland heath

11.1 Archaeological importance

The lowland heaths of England comprise areas of open ground characterized by acidic podsolized soils which are low in nutrients and largely result from soil deterioration in prehistoric times. Today, lowland heaths carry a distinctive vegetation dominated by heathers and gorse.[72] They all lie below about 100m OD, and often represent land which has not been cultivated for millennia, if at all. In certain respects, these areas are lowland counterparts of upland moors, but there are important differences, notably the prevalence of mineral soils on lowland heaths and the fact that a more favourable climate on the lower ground has allowed a greater continuity of settlement. Most lowland heaths are defined as being of low agricultural potential, grade 5 in the Agricultural Land Classification, because of severe limitations on their use (MAFF 1966).

Archaeologically, lowland heaths are important for the range of monuments represented and the excellent state of preservation at most sites, because heathlands have not been subjected to intensive land-use in recent centuries. These factors may be discussed under four headings.

i   Preservation: monuments of earth, stone, or turf in heathland often survive in remarkably good condition, because the characteristic vegetation provides a complete surface cover, and traditional heathland management has prevented decay through ground disturbance or tree growth. This allows the survival of valuable information about the original form of monument types which are less well preserved elsewhere.

ii   Environmental indicators: heathlands often contain mires and bogs which preserve pollen profiles in close proximity to the archaeological evidence. Pollen may also be preserved in soils within archaeological sites themselves. This is all the more important because heathlands are scattered amongst other landscape types which do not preserve pollen at all well. Insights into both the local and regional environment are thus available.

iii   Landscape and stratigraphy: many areas of heathland preserve groups of interrelated sites within a small area, often representing components of an ancient landscape. Successive periods of use may be visible in the form of superimposed remains. This allows insights into the form and layout of individual landscapes at particular points in time and through time.

iv   Amenity value: most heathlands are accessible through a *de facto* right of access and provide much scope for the presentation and interpretation of the archaeological heritage in its landscape setting. This is particularly useful as an educational and amenity asset.

Lowland heaths cover approximately 2250 square kilometres[73] of the English countryside, about 1.72% of the total land area. All lie to the south-east of a notional line drawn between the Bristol Channel and York (Fig 88). Most heathlands exist as small fragmentary blocks, and there is some overlap between heathland and areas characterised here as wetland, woodland, and permanent pasture.

Heathlands are often divided into two main types: wet heaths and dry heaths. Although there are slight differences in vegetation cover and soil type between them, in archaeological terms they are very similar and present comparable problems of management. Except where mires (wetland) have formed (*see* chapter 6), wet heathland does not preserve organic materials because waterlogging is sporadic. Accordingly, heathlands are treated here as a single landscape category.

Heathlands are certainly among the most important landscape categories in terms of their preservation of archaeological remains, but there are two main limitations to the range of materials and sites represented. First, the acid soils characteristic of heathlands do not preserve calcareous materials, notably bone. Second, after their formation, heathlands have always represented highly specialized environments, and this has naturally conditioned the range of activities undertaken on such land.

11.2 History, distribution, and land-use

The formation and development of heathlands in England directly results from a number of complicated and interrelated processes, involving both natural agencies and human interference with the established vegetation (Dimbleby 1962; Pennington 1974, 111–13; Ratcliffe 1977, ch 6). Not all heathland in England was formed at the same time, nor in quite the same way, but there are sufficient similarities between the different areas to allow a general pattern to be discerned. Once established, however, heathland requires continuous management to maintain it, otherwise a natural succession of scrub growth and colonization by woodland will ensue.

Evidence from pollen profiles recovered from bogs and lake sediments, within and around what is now heathland, shows quite clearly that after the end of the last (Devensian) glaciation, these areas, like other sectors of the landscape, developed a woodland cover. At Hockham Mere, on the edge of Breckland in Norfolk, this woodland was dominated by oak and elm during the Mesolithic period (Bennett 1983). In the New Forest, at Church Moor, Hampshire, a mixed woodland of oak, pine, birch, hazel, elm, and willow prevailed at about the same time (Barber 1973). Where preserved beneath later earthworks, soils associated with this woodland were rich forest brown varieties which contained loess and cover sand (Dimbleby 1962; Limbrey 1975, 149–52).

Limited interference with the woodland cover during later Mesolithic and Neolithic times probably had little immediate effect on the soils of what are now heathlands (Limbrey 1975, 150), but may have opened the way for longer term processes of acidification. The wetter conditions of the Atlantic period may have triggered the onset of podsolization in some areas. On the Lizard, Cornwall, an early Bronze Age barrow at Caern Dhu appears to have been constructed in heathland dominated by heather (*Calluna*) (Bell 1984, 51), but to the north at the Iron Age settlement of Carn Euny in West Penwith, Cornwall, analysis of pollen from an old ground surface predating the settlement revealed a mixed woodland environment, suggesting that here the formation of heathland took place rather later (Dimbleby 1978).

Elsewhere also the picture is complicated. In south-east Dorset, some areas of heathland were probably developing during the middle of the second millennium bc, but it was not until the Iron Age that the more resilient clayey areas became

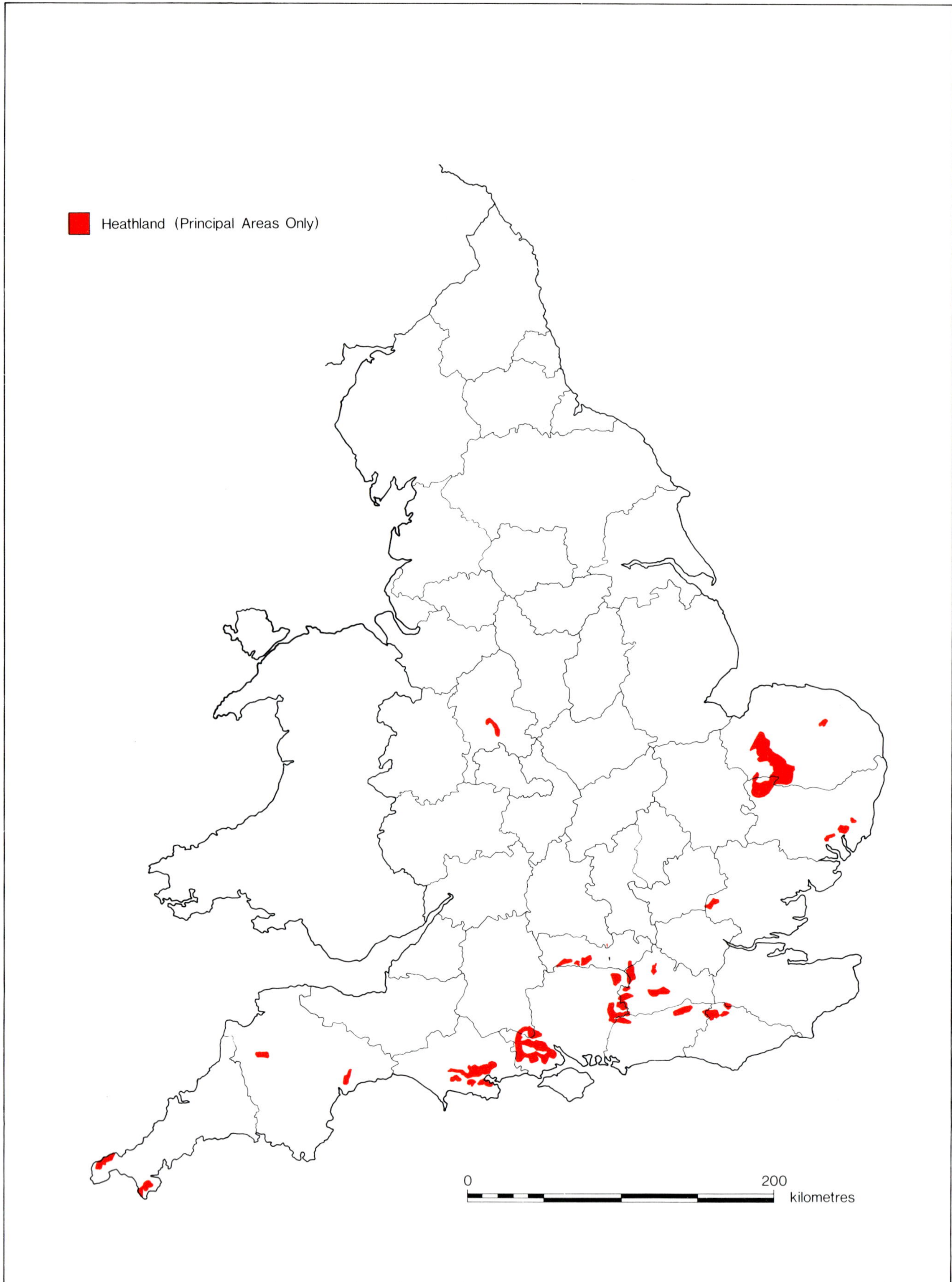

Figure 88   Map showing the main areas of heathland in England

Figure 89   Moor Green Barrow, West End, Hampshire: excavations in 1961; view of the north-east quadrant, showing the turf mound core and the sandy envelope derived from the ditch (scale totals 6ft)

podsolized to the extent that they supported typically heathland vegetation (Waton 1983). A similar development may be glimpsed in the New Forest, where analysis of the old ground surface sealed beneath a turf and soil barrow at Moor Green, Hampshire (Fig 89), showed that, although heather and bracken were present in the area, the local environment was dominated by birch woodland in the mid-second millennium bc (Ashbee and Dimbleby 1974). A similar pattern can be found on the Sussex/Surrey heaths (Dimbleby 1962), and again in the Breckland of East Anglia, where recent re-analysis of the Hockham Mere sequence suggests that there was not any significant increase in herb pollen in the area until about 550 bc, and amounts of heather remained low until after 500 bc (Murphy 1984a, 20–2; 1984b, 16).

The emerging pattern is that there were two major episodes of heathland formation. The first occurred during the Neolithic and early Bronze Age on fragile soils, where, perhaps because of excessive dryness in summer, it was never worth the manure or mineral fertilizers to replace nutrients lost by extraction and by leaching. These may be termed heathland nuclei and do indeed seem to form the focus of many heathland areas still extant today (Limbrey 1978, 25). Beyond these nuclei, heathland formation was rather delayed, for whatever reasons,

and the second episode probably resulted from the opening-up of the landscape during the later part of the first millennium bc (Tinsley 1981, 234–7). The proposed deterioration in climate after about 800 bc may have contributed to podsolization in some areas. Once heathland formation was set in motion, the spread of bracken, heather, and ling would accelerate the process of acidification.

Large areas of heathland certainly existed in Roman times, and from then onwards the limits of heathland were continually changing, according to economic circumstances and population changes within the communities living around them. Place-names in Anglo-Saxon charters suggest that heath was much more widespread than today, extending as far north as Northumberland (Rackham 1986, 287). No detailed records for heathland are contained in the Domesday survey, but by early medieval times patterns of heathland management had become established, and heathland was considered a valuable resource which was mostly held as common land (Rackham 1986, 291–3; Hazel 1983, 2–4).

In the medieval period, the main use of heathland was as low-intensity grazing land for sheep, cattle, and horses. Most heathland plants can be grazed, although bracken is poisonous, and widespread grazing had the effect of preventing scrub

108

Figure 90   Zennor, Cornwall: prehistoric field system, huts, and cairns under moorland

growth and the development of woodland, which would otherwise have overwhelmed the heathland vegetation. Burning was probably not an intentional part of heathland management during medieval times, although accidental fires certainly occurred. Furze and ling were cut for fuel, and ling was used as low-grade thatch. Bracken was cut for fuel, thatch, and litter for livestock. In the eighteenth and nineteenth centuries, bracken was burnt to produce potash for use in making glass, soap, and detergent. Peat cutting was also a feature of heathland management, where blanket bog or mire formed within heathland areas (Hazel 1983, 2–5; Rackham 1986, 295–6).

Another important use of heathland was for rabbit warrening, and indeed many heaths have since become known as warrens. Landowners, especially monastic owners, frequently increased their return from heathland by building warrens, simply because the breeding of rabbits was deemed not to infringe the rights of the commoners. The Breckland in particular witnessed the construction of a great many warrens.

Throughout medieval times, most heathland was the 'waste' beyond the focus of settlement. During periods of population growth, such as during the twelfth and thirteenth centuries, many assarts were driven into heathland to carve out new areas for cultivation or improved grazing. In other areas, land was turned into heath through overgrazing of wood pasture. Dedham Heath, Essex, is an example of this process (Rackham 1986, 291–2).

Another factor which preserved much heathland through the medieval period was its inclusion within Royal Forests (Rackham 1986, 293). In these areas, Forest Law restricted the range of activities possible, although it has been argued that in the case of the New Forest, Hampshire, it was the poor enforcement of the Forest Laws by the local Crown officials (regards, agisters, etc) that promoted the survival of heathland (Hazel 1983, 4).

During the agricultural revolution of the eighteenth and nineteenth centuries, the first major reductions in heathland area came about, and attitudes towards the value of heaths changed.[74] Innovations in farming technology made it practical to cultivate all but the most difficult soils, and much heathland in private ownership was enclosed and converted to farmland. Bracken and ling ceased to be regarded as crops, and rabbits

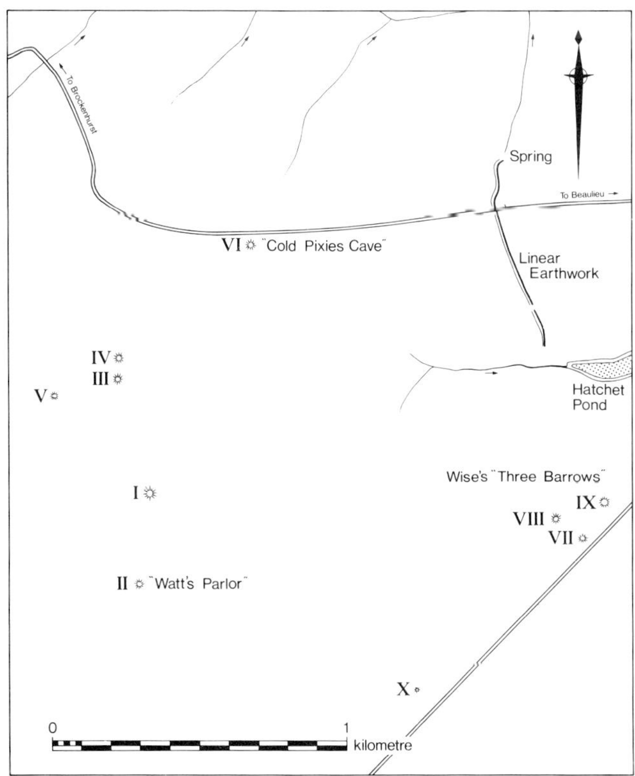

Figure 91 Beaulieu Heath, Hampshire: plan of barrows and earthworks recorded on the heath (after C M Piggott 1943)

declined in importance as a source of food. Together these factors effectively reduced the usefulness of most heaths to local communities.

Further reductions in heathland occurred during the early years of the twentieth century, again largely through reclamation for afforestation and conversion to more intensively utilized farmland. The heathland which survives today mostly comprises small fragmentary patches, representing the remains of formerly much larger expanses. Heathland is almost wholly confined to areas of tertiary sands and gravels or the greensands of southern and eastern England, and is found in Dorset, Hampshire, Sussex, Surrey, Essex, Norfolk, and Staffordshire. The largest areas are those in the New Forest, around Purbright, Surrey, and the Breckland of East Anglia. One rather anomalous area of heathland is on the granitic rocks of western Cornwall on the Lizard and in West Penwith (Hopkins 1983). In many respects, these areas could be considered extensions of upland moorland, but their favourable climate, low altitude, heathland vegetation cover, and long history of intensive land-use allies them closely with lowland heaths elsewhere in England.

Today, most areas of lowland heath are used for low intensity grazing, military training, and recreation. Demand for heathland products is almost non-existent, and, as a landscape category, heathland is in great danger of extinction. Common ownership of some remaining areas is the principal factor which is preserving them, although the fact that many are designated as AONBs, NNRs, or SSSIs also no doubt plays a part, and is significant in planning their future.

Figure 92 West Heath, Sussex: general view of one of the barrows under excavation, showing the ditches which surrounded the mound and the central grave pit

Figure 93   Bawsey, Norfolk: A (top) barrow being surveyed prior to excavation; B (bottom) central portion of the barrow, showing turf lines in the section and the outline of the coffin containing the central burial in the bottom of the excavation (the scale totals 50cm)

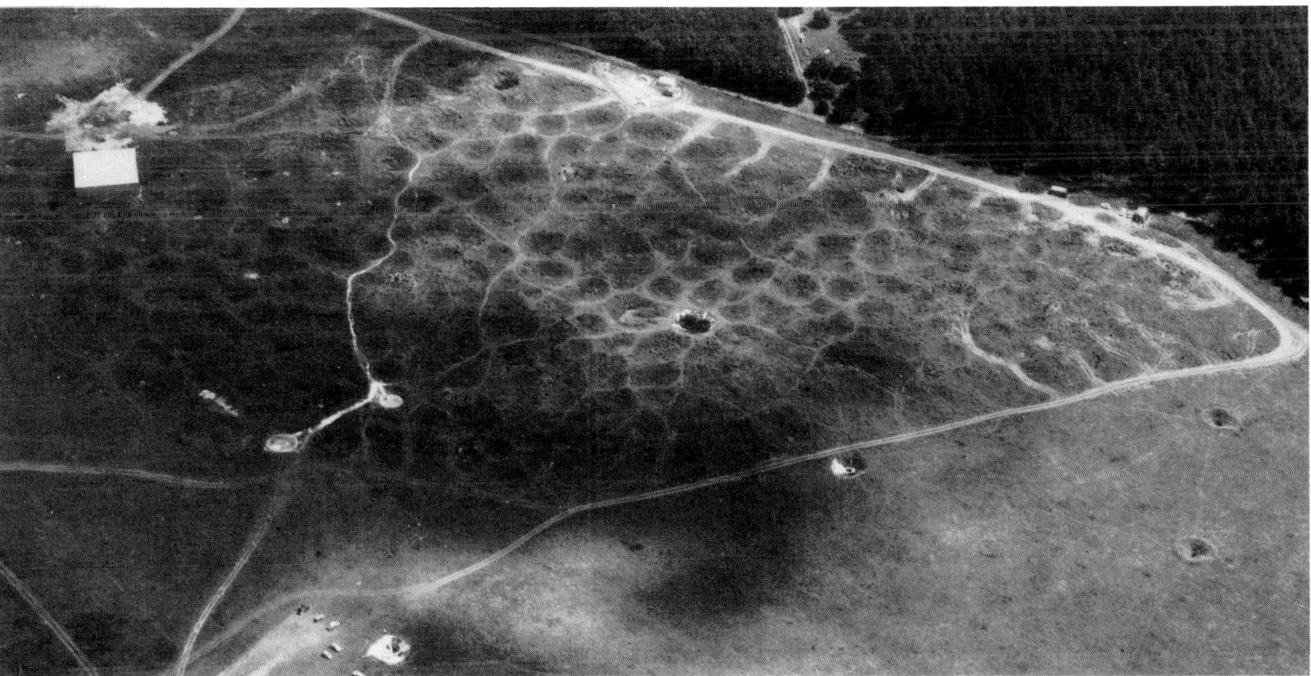

Figure 94   Grimes Graves, Norfolk: Neolithic flint mines on the edge of Breckland, East Anglia; the numerous quarry pits now appear as depressions surrounded by spoil heaps and flint-knapping debris

11.3   The archaeology of heathlands

The archaeology of heathland areas is less well studied than that of many other landscape categories. Only a few areas have been surveyed in any detail, and, generally speaking, the evidence can be divided into two groups: first, that relating to the periods before heathlands formed, and second, that relating to the exploitation of heathland itself. This division in fact represents a broadly chronological partitioning of the evidence either side of the later Iron Age.

Pre-heathland archaeology

Mesolithic sites are particularly well represented in heathland areas in Hampshire, Surrey, Dorset, East Anglia, and Staffordshire (Jacobi 1978a). Among the most fully investigated is Oakhanger on the Surrey-Hampshire border. Here, pits and hearths were located at several discrete occupation areas. Most appear to be of late Mesolithic date (Rankine and Dimbleby 1960).

Early farming communities do not seem to have favoured the light, well-drained forest soils known to precede today's heathland. No early–middle Neolithic enclosures or tombs are known in heathland areas, and the only firm evidence for their use at this time is scattered evidence for small settlements, usually comprising little more than a pit and a scatter of pottery and flintwork. One excavated example at Poldowrian, Cornwall, was dated to about 3000 bc (G Smith and Harris 1982). Gabbroic clays from the Lizard were used in the manufacture of pottery in the early Neolithic (Peacock 1969), but the working-sites have not yet been identified. Igneous and metamorphic rocks were also exploited for tool-making.

Late Neolithic and Bronze Age settlement on areas now under heathland is well represented. At Bosiliack, West Penwith, survey work has revealed the existence of an extensive field system, defined by low stone banks, among which there are stone hut foundations and a small chambered cairn of entrance grave type. Excavations in 1984 showed that the fields had been cultivated in prehistoric times (Thomas and Ratcliffe 1984). Similar field systems are known around Lanyon and Zennor (Fig 90), and elsewhere in West Penwith too, but to what extent they occur elsewhere is at present unknown (N Johnson and Rose 1983). Ritual and ceremonial monuments, such as stone circles and standing stones, also occur in south-western England, but apparently only rarely elsewhere on heathland.

Bronze Age barrows represent the most easily identified features of heathlands in Dorset, Hampshire, Sussex, Surrey, and East Anglia. At Beaulieu Heath in the New Forest, excavation of a group of ten barrows (Fig 91) showed that they had been constructed over a long period of time during the early second millennium bc. All were well preserved and stood to a height of about 1.75m. They were constructed from turf and soil, and during excavation it was possible to see the outline of individual turves (C M Piggott 1943). At West Heath, Sussex, excavations revealed a similar cemetery, which may have been used for 500 years or more between the late Neolithic and the middle Bronze Age (Fig 92; Drewett 1976; 1985). When excavated, barrows on heathland often preserve minute details of the mound construction and grave. At Bawsey, Norfolk, the outline of the wooden coffin in the central grave pit, and the turves used in constructing the mound, could be clearly seen as dark staining in the sandy soil (Fig 93).

Evidence of occupation sites to set alongside what is known of the barrows is rather scant. Boundary earthworks and enclosures of various sorts can be traced in the vicinity of barrow groups in the New Forest, but their date and purpose is unclear (C M Piggott 1943, figs 1 and 2). Burnt mounds are also known, and these may represent cooking sites of some sort (Passmore and Pallister 1967). One possible explanation

Figure 95 Sutton Hoo, Suffolk: Saxon barrow cemetery in which the famous ship burial was discovered in 1939; the linear ditches are anti-glider ditches dug during the Second World War

for the paucity of settlement evidence is that the barrows were placed in peripheral areas used for grazing, so that minimum inconvenience was caused to agricultural land near the settlements.

The exploitation of natural resources in heathland areas continued through prehistoric times. In Cornwall, stone axes were manufactured during the later Neolithic, and in Norfolk the Grimes Graves flint mines, which until the early twentieth century AD were set amid grassland heath on the fringes of the Breckland (Fig 94), came into operation shortly before 2000 bc (Mercer 1981a).

Iron Age settlement is scarce on heathland, probably because during this period podsolization was accelerating. Exceptions can, however, be found, for example on the Breckland margins at Barnham, Suffolk, where a double-ditched enclosure has been excavated (Murphy 1984b, 16), and in West Penwith, where a number of Iron Age settlements have been recorded, including the well-known clusters of courtyard-houses at Carn Euny and Chysauster (Christie 1978). Field systems are associated with these last mentioned sites.

Heathland archaeology

What little evidence is available for Roman use of heathlands suggests low intensity activities. Pottery production was certainly a feature of the exploitation of the south-east Dorset heaths, where black-burnished wares were produced for export all over Britain (D Williams 1977, 185), while in the New Forest a major local industry developed a wide range of products during the later Roman period (Fulford 1975). Otherwise, settlement evidence is very sparse. At Gallow's Hill near Thetford, the excavation of what was thought to be a Bronze Age round barrow turned out to be a burial monument used in the fourth century AD. Evidence that wind erosion of soils was taking place in the area at the time that the barrow was built came from the analysis of the old ground surface sealed beneath the barrow mound (Murphy 1984b, 16).

Post-Roman use of heathlands followed earlier patterns, again perhaps because these areas were peripheral to settlement. A small patch of heathland at Sutton Hoo, Suffolk, however, preserves a cemetery of 14 burial mounds (Fig 95), of which the largest, first excavated immediately before the Second World War, contained the well-known Saxon ship burial – possibly the richest burial ever discovered in Britain (Bruce-Mitford 1975).

The use of heathlands in medieval and post-medieval times has left behind abundant traces. Boundary works of various sorts defining grazing areas and the limits of land holdings can be seen on most heathlands, and there may also be evidence of abandoned assarts and short-lived cultivation in the form of ridge-and-furrow. Turf-cutting areas result from use of the heaths as sources of fuel, and there may well be turf-drying platforms associated with these works. One such drying platform excavated at Goonhilly on the Lizard, Cornwall, was dated to the thirteenth–fifteenth centuries AD (G Smith 1984). Some platforms may have been used for burning turf and peat to make charcoal.

Pillow mounds, or rabbit warrens, occur on many heathlands, often clustered into small groups. They are usually rectangular earthen mounds flanked by slight ditches to provide drainage. At Thetford Warren, Norfolk, rabbit enclosures were surrounded by turf banks up to 1.25m high. The rabbits were trapped in 'tripes', which comprised pitfalls up to 2.25m deep, lined with flints and closed by a trapdoor (Wood 1972, 236).

In West Penwith, evidence for agricultural use of the heathland is supplemented by widespread evidence for the mining of copper and tin. Mines, shafts, waste heaps, and the remains of ore crushing mills stand alongside the familiar engine houses. Pits dug by tinners to investigate the local geology while prospecting for new veins of ore riddle the landscape and often cut into earlier features (N Johnson and Rose 1983). Military works from the Second World War and earlier can be seen on some heathlands, among the most conspicuous being anti-glider ditches, several of which cut across the burial mounds at Sutton Hoo (Fig 95).

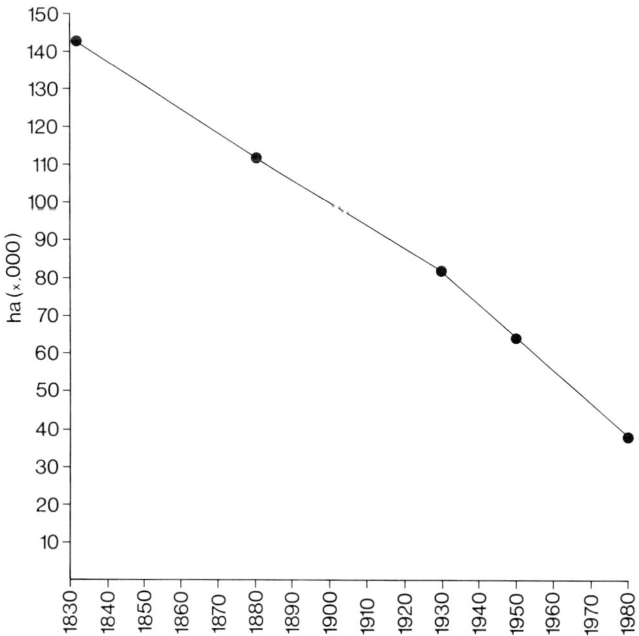

Figure 96 Histogram showing the loss of heathland 1830–1980 (data from NCC 1984)

Locating and recording sites on heathland follow broadly similar principles to those used on upland moors. Field survey coupled with aerial photography allows most features with surface evidence to be located.[75]

Vegetation, especially bracken, provides the biggest obstacle to this work, and experience shows that the ideal conditions are when accidental fires have cleared the bracken and gorse to leave a relatively clear ground surface.

11.4 Threats

Over the last few centuries, heathlands have been exploited at a relatively low intensity for grazing and the supply of natural resources in a way that has favoured the survival of archaeological sites. The scale of exploitation was generally small and, in some areas, seasonal. These traditional ways of managing and exploiting heathland are now under considerable pressure. Grazing has been reduced and, in many areas, only rabbits and human intervention prevent the regeneration of woodland. Moreover, heathland can now be used for other purposes which produce a greater return, with the result that small blocks of heathland surrounded by more intensively-used land are particularly at risk. Given this situation, there is a wide range of threats currently facing the archaeological evidence which must be taken into account when seeking to preserve sites. The following activities can be singled out for special attention.

Heathland conversion

Conversion simply involves transforming heathland to other uses, mostly improved pasture, forestry, or cultivation. This usually involves clearing stones from the land and bulldozing flat any upstanding features. Ploughing for arable or reseeding may follow.

The rate of heathland conversion has been rapid over the last 100 years or so. In West Penwith, records suggest that in

1840 there were some 7882ha of heathland, but by 1980 only about 4217ha remained (N Johnson and Rose 1983, 8–10). In south-east Dorset, there were some 40,000ha in 1750, but by 1983 this had fallen to only 6100ha (Waton 1983). In England as a whole, the NCC has estimated a 40% loss of lowland heath between 1950 and 1984 (Fig 96; NCC 1984, 52–3).

Many ancient monuments have been lost as a result of heathland conversion, most of them totally unrecorded. Examples from West Penwith include the area around Chysauster Iron Age village, which involved the destruction of much of the associated field system (N Johnson and Rose 1983, 11), and at Boslow nearby, where a prehistoric settlement, comprising several enclosures with internal features visible on the ground, was cleared and ploughed up between 1980 and 1985 (N Johnson and Rose 1983, 11–12). In Norfolk, the magnitude of barrow loss through heathland conversion can be gauged from the fact that when the area was first recorded some 220 barrows stood on heathland, but by 1980 only 54 of these remained in the same landscape category (Lawson 1981, 34). One effect of heathland conversion is to fragment remaining areas, and this greatly reduces its value for preserving groups of related sites within a specific area (Fig 97).

Animal and natural erosion

Overstocking and prolonged use by animals cause soil poaching and structural damage to buried archaeological features, as well as disturbance of upstanding remains such as walls, mounds, and banks. Breaking the surface vegetation cover encourages natural erosion to take hold.

Colonization by bracken is archaeologically undesirable because the roots penetrate deep into the subsoil and disturb sub-surface deposits. Bracken also obscures monuments.

Visitor erosion

Heathland provides an important amenity resource for leisure and recreation, and, given that these activities are predominantly extensive, can support a certain amount of use without harmful side-effects to archaeological monuments. Where visitor use becomes intensive, however, damage to fragile sites may result. Motor-bike scrambling is common on heathland areas, and as a result vegetation is quickly broken, the soil exposed, and erosion soon follows. Severe heathland fires can have much the same effect.

Mining and quarrying

This threat tends to be restricted in its distribution, but potentially highly damaging where it occurs. In West Penwith, extraction of china clay, together with associated dumping of waste from washing and refining processes, affects some areas, while elsewhere the reworking of old spoil heaps from mines and quarries represents a relatively new threat (N Johnson and Rose 1983). On other heathlands, the extraction of sand and gravel, either on a large scale or for local needs, constitutes the main problem. At Simons Ground, Dorset, excavations in advance of sand quarrying at various times between 1950 and 1969 revealed an extensive cemetery containing seven barrows, in and around which were over 300 burials in pottery urns, dating to between 1200 and 600 bc (D White 1982).

Figure 97   Aerial view of Carn Gaze enclosure on an isolated block of heathland in West Penwith, Cornwall

11.5   Management

The archaeological remains found in heathland areas are generally fragile and vulnerable, and present special problems of management. Many areas of heathland have been lost over the last century or so, and much of what remains is fragmentary and represents only the last vestiges of what were once quite large tracts of land. Special attention to the conservation and management of remaining heathland is therefore essential, if even a sample of the unique archaeological evidence in this type of landscape is to be preserved.

In addition to their archaeological value, heathlands also support unique ranges of wildlife and flora which are of European significance (NCC 1981). The aims of conserving and managing heathland with reference to the archaeological remains are very similar to those connected with sustaining the natural heathland environment, and there is therefore much common ground between archaeology and nature conservation.[76]

In formulating management strategies for heathland areas, the following two factors must be taken into account:

i   Potential for conversion: the potential of heathland for the preservation and conversion of ancient monuments is high and can be achieved very much more economically than in some other landscape categories.

ii   Present understanding: at present our understanding of the archaeology of heathlands is based on inadequate information. More surveys are urgently needed to establish the range of monuments represented on the different areas of heathland.

Curatorial management

Preventing ground disturbance of any sort and maintaining a healthy vegetation cover are the key factors in preserving monuments on heathland. Where soil and gravel alone were used in construction, monuments are especially vulnerable. Despite the fact that much heathland lies within designated AONBs, for example West Penwith, the Lizard, Dorset, East Hampshire, and Cannock Chase, the rate at which heathland is being lost is still considerable.

At present, there are approximately 2500 Scheduled Monuments in heathland areas,[77] the majority of them standing earthworks, particularly barrows and Bronze Age funerary monuments. Other types of scheduled site include engine houses, enclosures, linear boundaries, and warrens.

Selecting sites on heathland for scheduling is particularly difficult because of the lack of information from detailed surveys. However, in the light of the results of work in West Penwith and elsewhere, it is now clear that a much greater range of sites exists in these areas than was previously thought. In applying the selection criteria, special attention must be given to protecting the more fragile sites which preserve the greatest range of evidence. Sites which survive more or less intact, and which have not been disturbed by turf cutting, merit special attention. Groups of related sites are fairly common on heathland, and so those with substantial areas of heathland surviving round about, which might preserve less visible contemporary features, will probably be the most important. Documentation tends to be poor for heathland sites, so those for which records survive also merit attention. Finding a diversity of monuments within a small area is not always easy, because of the geographically discrete distribution of some classes of site.

In Hampshire and Cornwall, the stock of statutorily protected sites is supplemented by monuments designated as being of county importance (N Johnson and Rose 1983; Hampshire County Council 1984). In Cornwall, all the heathland in West Penwith is designated as an area of Great Historic Value by the County Council, and represents a step towards preserving the integrity of the heathland landscape in this area.

Managing heathland landscapes in a way which is sympathetic to the archaeological evidence can be cheap and simple, especially in a low input/low output agricultural regime. A combination of controlled grazing, heather cutting, and, where necessary, controlled burning of small areas to build up a mosaic of plant communities of different ages is ideal. This will have the effect of maintaining a healthy vegetation cover and minimizing disturbance of the soil. If burning can be avoided, so much the better for archaeological sites. Bracken needs to be controlled, and around archaeological monuments this should be done mechanically or with chemicals. If trees develop in sufficient numbers to threaten the heathland, they should be cut down and the stumps poisoned rather than pulled out of the ground.

Recording

For the early prehistoric periods, chance finds represent one of the most important ways of discovering the existence of sites, and therefore a special watch needs to be maintained where ground disturbance occurs for any reason. Opportunities for intensive field survey, such as when vegetation is low or has been burnt off, need to be exploited. Aerial photography, for example, is almost pointless on heathland infested with bracken.

In formulating management plans, it is important to know the age and extent of sites, what is likely to be represented below the ground in the vicinity of standing monuments, the nature and robustness of the building materials used, and the type of vegetation covering the site. This will allow some assessment of the range of activities able to be carried out in

Figure 98   Chysauster, Cornwall: State Guardianship monument on heathland

the area without detrimentally affecting the ancient monuments.

Rescue excavations on heathland are usually in response to specific threats, such as quarrying, mineral-working, or industrial development. Techniques for excavating in heathland landscapes are relatively undeveloped, although research into soil stablization, recording methods, and geophysical surveying are currently being undertaken at Sutton Hoo, Suffolk (Carver 1986).

Exploitative management

Public display of monuments in heathland areas is practical, provided that careful visitor management prevents the over-use of any individual sites. Heathlands provide a valuable amenity resource, and recreation represents one of the expanding land-uses for these areas. Archaeological sites could play a major part in this, through the development of self-guided trails and guided walks.

Among existing visitor attractions in heathland areas are the Carn Euny and Chysauster Iron Age villages in West Penwith which are in State Guardianship (Fig 98).

Academic interest in heathland areas has largely been eclipsed by studies of upland moors, and this may account for the relative paucity of survey evidence and excavated sites. Heathland sites do, however, have considerable potential for research, because of the kinds of evidence preserved and the possibilities of examining landscape dynamics and landscape organization at different times.

12   Arable land

12.1   Archaeological importance

The arable lands of England comprise those areas regularly cultivated for the production of cereals, fodder, and vegetable crops. Areas of short fallow are included in this.

Arable landscapes are totally man-made and, while they represent the largest single landscape category in England, they are also among the most unstable environments discussed in this volume; unless regularly cultivated, they will revert to a wild state through a natural succession of grassland, scrubland, and ultimately woodland.

Arable lands are of very great archaeological importance, because they occur mostly in areas which have attracted human settlement over and over again, and because they cover such a large proportion of the English countryside. Their importance may be discussed under three headings.

i   Diachronic value: because many arable areas have been the focus of settlement for long periods, the archaeological evidence preserved in them provides a very clear picture of the changing pattern of land-use and settlement within a specific region. Whereas some landscape categories were only heavily used episodically, arable lands tend to preserve evidence of continually changing land-use.

ii   Diversity and variety: the range of different types of site represented in arable areas exceeds that in almost any other landscape category. This is partly because of the large area under arable, and partly because rich arable lands have attracted more or less continuous occupation and intensive land-use of various sorts for many millennia. This has led to the frequent superimposition of many phases of archaeological remains.

iii   Landscape value: in some arable areas, relict landscapes exist in various states of articulation and preservation, including, for example, settlements, fields, industrial sites, and burial areas. Population has always concentrated on the most productive land, and it is just as crucial to know something of lifestyles in these areas as it is to know about life in the uplands or in marginal areas.

Arable areas cover approximately 62,346 square kilometres of the English countryside, or some 39% of the total land area (MAFF 1982). They tend to be concentrated where there is the greatest summer warmth and sunshine, the lowest rainfall and windspeed, and low elevation, flat relief, and fertile soils (Fig 99). There is some overlap between arable lands and other landscape categories, for example wetlands and river valleys (see chapters 6 and 8).

Many different cultivation techniques are used on arable land, according to the soil type and the crops being grown(Lambrick 1977). Most mean that the topsoil is heavily and regularly disturbed to provide a suitable seedbed and good conditions for the germination and growth of each successive crop. During cultivation there is often disturbance to the subsoil, and, where soils are thin, the top of the natural bedrock too. Naturally, such conditions militate against the preservation of archaeological remains, and it is true to say that, archaeologically, arable lands represent the least hospitable of all landscape categories (Hinchliffe and Schadla-Hall 1980). Nevertheless, it is surprising how much has survived in these areas and how, by sympathetic management, the rate of loss can be slowed down and sites preserved *in situ*.

12.2   History and distribution

Arable areas have only been a feature of the English countryside for the last 5000 years or so, ever since the beginning of the Neolithic period, when farming became the main source of food (C Taylor 1975; P Fowler 1983). Naturally, the extent and distribution of arable lands has changed since that time, and it is only in the last few centuries that cultivated sections of the landscape have taken on the appearance which is so familiar today. Over the course of time, the extent of cultivation fluctuates in harmony with changes to soil fertility and the local economy. As a result there are few, if any, pieces of land which can be said to have been in continuous cultivation for more than a few centuries, although there have probably been arable areas somewhere or other within every parish for millennia.

Former areas of arable can be recognized in many different ways, and these give clues to the methods and extent of cultivation at different times.[78] The clearest evidence is that of relict arable plots and cultivation marks. These are sometimes preserved as abandoned features which now lie in other sorts of landscape, but they more commonly occur within areas still used for arable. Some of the most distinctive pieces of evidence result from local changes in topography caused by cultivation. Ploughing promotes soil creep and down-slope movement, which often leads to the build-up of lynchets where some obstacle blocks the movement of soil, for example a fence line or wall. In other cases, particular patterns of cultivation will result in the formation of ridge-and-furrow patterns.

On a wider scale, environmental evidence from pollen profiles in bogs or lakes provides information on the amount of woodland clearance in the vicinity and, through the types of pollen represented, the species of the crops grown. Sediments in alluvium or colluvium often provide tell-tale records of soil erosion from cultivated land (Shotton 1978; Bell 1983). Also important is the distribution of cultivation tools, such as hoes, ards, sickles, and plough shares. Together, these different lines of evidence allow the build-up of a fairly detailed picture of the development of arable land.

The earliest well attested episode of arable cultivation so far recorded in England is represented by a series of ard marks below the South Street long barrow in Wiltshire. Here, careful excavation of the old ground surface beneath the mound revealed criss-cross grooves cut into the natural subsoil (Ashbee *et al* 1979). These marks were probably made by a light ard during one or more episodes of cultivation, the particular technique used being cross ploughing. Radiocarbon dates suggest that cultivation here took place before about 2810 ± 130 bc (BM 356). This example only survived because a large burial monument was built over the previously cultivated soil, thus sealing it and protecting it. Paradoxically, the site was excavated in 1966–7 because modern cultivation threatened to obliterate the mound and what lay beneath. Other pieces of Neolithic land surface sealed beneath barrows and other monuments also display evidence of cultivation, for example the Kilham long barrow, Humberside (Manby 1976).

The crook-ard remained the dominant tool used for cultivation, at least in southern England, throughout much of prehistory (P Fowler 1971). Spade cultivation was, however,

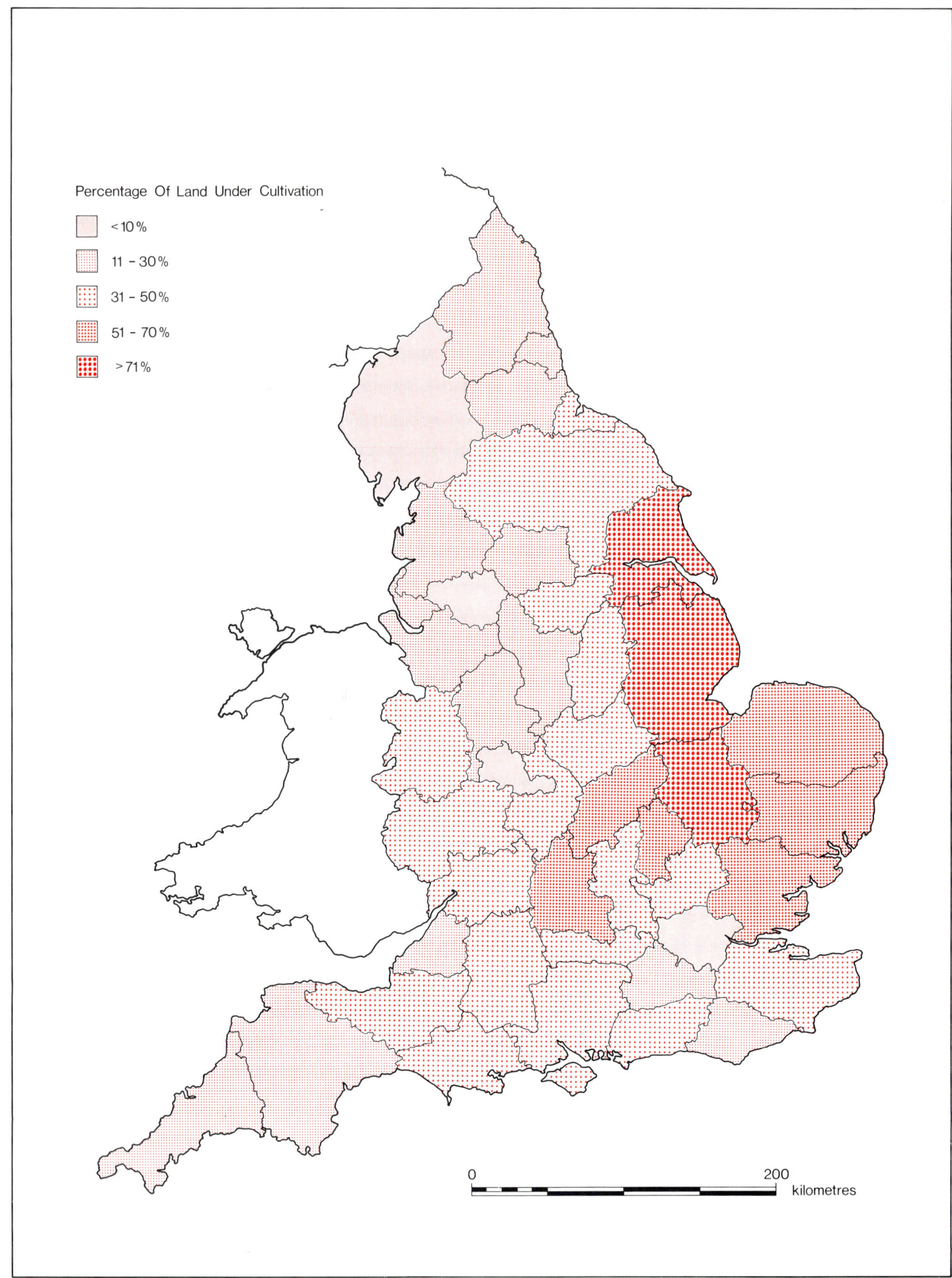

Figure 99   Distribution of arable land in England (data from MAFF 1982)

Figure 100 Early cultivation marks preserved in sand dunes at Gwithian, Cornwall: A (top) plough marks of Neolithic or early Bronze Age date; B (bottom) Bronze Age spade/shovel marks

Figure 101   Gravelly Guy, Oxfordshire: aerial view of the site under excavation, showing the abundant Iron Age storage pits between field boundaries

also practised, and again traces have been found where old land surfaces have been preserved, and where digging penetrated through the topsoil to leave scoops in the subsoil. One of the most notable examples of this is at Gwithian, Cornwall, where sand dune inundations preserved a small Bronze Age field (Fig 100; Thomas 1970).

Early prehistoric cultivation plots were generally small, and during the Neolithic period were probably quite restricted in extent. The principal crops were wheat (*Triticum dicoccum*), barley (*Hordeum vulgare*), and perhaps small quantities of flax and beans (*Vicia faba*) (A Smith 1981). Clearance of the post-glacial forest during periods of expanding population had the cumulative effect of opening up more of the countryside for cultivation. Pollen diagrams illustrate this very clearly, and, in northern and western England, clearance cairns of stones removed from field surfaces preparatory to cultivation are common.

By about 1300 bc, field systems comprising agglomerations of numerous cultivation plots and enclosed pasture plots were widespread, even in upland areas such as Dartmoor and the Pennines (Fleming 1978; 1983b). Wessex is particularly rich in the remains of these fields, some of which are called 'celtic' fields (Holleyman 1935). Many different patterns of development can be identified. Some were clearly set out to a single design, often along a common axis. Others appear to have developed in a more organic fashion, odd plots being added to a core area one at a time (Bradley 1978a; Bowen 1961).

During the Iron Age, arable lands were more widespread than ever before. The ratio of arable to pasture is impossible to gauge, and anyway must have varied both regionally and through time. It is, however, clear that much of the downland of southern England, most of the major river valleys throughout the country, and much of the available fertile land were under some form of cultivation, whether continuously or in rotation. Where large-scale excavations and aerial photographic surveys have revealed the plan of individuals farmsteads or pieces of landscape, it is clear that the countryside was well organized with enclosed fields and trackways linking settlements to agricultural areas (*see*, for example, C Smith 1979; and Fig 11).

Grain storage areas made up of pit groups were constructed in major cereal-producing regions, for example in the upper Thames Valley (Fig 101), presumably as field stores for seed corn. The basic range of crops expanded to include rye (*S. cereale*), oats (*Avena sp.*), new strains of wheat (*Triticum dicoccum, Tr. spelta, Tr. compactum*, and *Tr. aestivum*) and barley (*Hordeum distichum* and *H. hexastichum*), and a range of legumes, including celtic beans (*Vicia faba minor*), peas (*Pisum sativum*), fat hen (*Chenopodium album*), flax (*Linum usitatissimum*), and Gold of Pleasure (*Camelina sativa*) (Reynolds 1985). By the end of the Iron Age, corn was one of Britain's exports to the Mediterranean world, which implies surplus production.

Arable cultivation was a major feature of the Roman economy (Frere 1967, ch 13; C Taylor 1975). The existing arrangements seem to have been adapted and developed, to the extent that output probably increased. New agricultural implements included more sophisticated iron tools, for example scythes; and a reaping machine, which separated the heads of cereals from the straw, was used, although how widely is not known. Manuring was certainly a widespread practice, as indeed it probably had been for millennia. Heavier ploughs came into use (Manning 1964). These were not wheeled ploughs, but they did have a coulter and mould board, which turned the soil and allowed the cultivation of much heavier soils than had previously been possible. Traction was still, of course, by animal power. Spade cultivation undoubtedly continued too. Crop processing facilities increased at farmstead sites, for example barns and corn drying/malting ovens. Landholding arrangements probably changed to reflect a more market-orientated agricultural system. Some villa estates covered over 800ha, and there is the suggestion that some medieval parishes were based on Roman estate units (Finberg 1955; Reece 1983). Land reclamation for arable cultivation took place around the Fens and in the Somerset Levels (*see* chapter 6).

During late Saxon and medieval times, arable cultivation took on a rather different aspect with individual landholdings playing a major part in the way that land was cultivated, although exactly how and when this change came about is not clear.[79] Plough teams were valued assets to a community and were often shared (Darby 1973, 47–9).

Regionally distinct systems emerged. In the midlands and over much of southern and eastern England, the well-known open field system developed. This was based on two or three large common fields, which were unenclosed and unhedged. They were farmed jointly with all the farmers agreeing on cropping and rotations. Land was divided into strips or lands, which were in turn grouped into fields or furlongs. Many of these became fossilized in the distinctive ridge-and-furrow, which can still be seen all over the midlands, in central southern England, and also in many parts of northern England. The processes leading to the formation of ridge-and-furrow are complicated and by no means fully understood. Since the most deeply incised furrows are found on heavy wet land, drainage was probably one factor in its development, but the way the strips were ploughed was probably also important.[80] This kind of ridge-and-furrow is typified by long, wide, high-backed ridges which have a reversed S-shaped plan.

In western and northern areas, arable plots were generally smaller and more scattered. The open field system was rare, and instead various infield–outfield systems predominated (Gray 1915; C Taylor 1975, 68–9; D Hall 1982). These systems were based on the farm rather than the village, so that areas were usually small, up to perhaps 200ha. Near the farmstead would be an area known as the infield (about one-fifth of the total area), which was continuously cultivated using a three- or four-fold rotation. There was no fallow, as fertility was maintained by manuring. The remainder of the holding was the outfield and received no manure. It was ploughed for perhaps five successive years and then put down to grass for a long time. Cultivation in the infield often included strip cultivation, but here the pattern of ridges, known as run-rig, is altogether different, being generally narrow, low, and parallel in plan.

The modern pattern of arable cultivation first developed in the late medieval and post-medieval period with the enclosure of much cultivated land and the development of many new techniques and pieces of equipment, and new strains of domesticated plants (Chambers and Mingay 1966; Tate 1967). This period has retrospectively become known as the agricultural revolution. Output was increased through greater management of the land, through increased capital investment in drainage, fencing, and equipment, and through the use of

Figure 102   Hazleton, Gloucestershire: a Neolithic long barrow cleared of topsoil to reveal the stone structure of the cairn; quarries may be seen on either side of the mound (the scales each total 2m)

Figure 103   Iron Age enclosures: A (top) aerial view of the circular Iron Age enclosed settlement at Gussage All Saints, Dorset during excavation; B (bottom) reconstruction drawing of Thorpe Thewles, Cleveland, based on the excavated evidence

Figure 104   Aerial view of cropmarks of a Roman villa at Lidgate, Suffolk: the main villa buildings and an adjacent out-building (?barn) can be clearly seen as cropmarks

the new strains of crops, which were better suited to the range of environments across the country. Methods of improving soil fertility and crop rotation systems also became more widespread, although in some cases they were probably simply developments of earlier practices. Arable farming underwent many episodes of prosperity and decline during the nineteenth and twentieth centuries. Mechanization since the First World War has been a key development, allowing much greater flexibility in preferred cultivation techniques. Today's arable areas support a very wide range of crops. Wheat and barley remain dominant, but oats and rye are also grown, along with oilseed rape, sugar beet, clover, grass for fodder, and a variety of vegetables. Techniques of cultivation have also diversified. Chemical fertilizers and pesticides are widely used and allow areas which were formally marginal to be brought into cultivation. In some parts of eastern England, arable monoculture has become the norm in recent years, but elsewhere rotation systems still prevail.

The traditional practice of ploughing followed by harrowing, drilling, and rolling is still favoured for its versatility and reliability, but in some areas minimum cultivation or direct drilling hold advantages of cost and, in favourable circumstances, increased productivity. Climate and topography still largely determine the distribution of arable areas, the focus of arable land being in eastern England, in Lincolnshire, Cambridgeshire, Humberside, and East Anglia, with a broad belt of only slightly less heavily cultivated land stretching from Dorset north-eastwards up to Yorkshire. In England as a whole, arable agriculture has become very successful in terms of productivity and quality of output.

12.3   The archaeology of arable land

As arable lands now cover a large part of the countryside, a very great variety of archaeology is represented, including sites which were in quite different environments during their use.

The survival of ancient monuments under arable is highly variable. Sometimes sites exist as islands of uncultivated land in the midst of ploughed ground, the main reason for this being that the site itself is too stony to plough. In other cases, farmers have quite deliberately ploughed round a site out of respect for it. However, the majority of sites in arable have been flattened by repeated ploughings and so are difficult to detect on the surface. In such cases, archaeological deposits may lie within and below the ploughsoil, and there are numerous instances where crops are today being grown amid the disintegrating bones of an ancient burial ground, in the chambers of a denuded tomb (Fig 102), or on the kitchen midden of some long-abandoned settlement.

Familiar types of monument can look quite different when ploughed flat, and sometimes are even called by different names. Thus, for example, round barrows which have lost their mounds and survive under arable simply as circular rock-cut ditches with central burial pits are called ring ditches, and causewayed enclosures, recognized only as ploughed-out ditches on aerial photographs, are called interrupted-ditch systems (D K Wilson 1975b).

Settlements

The most numerous archaeological remains from arable areas are settlements of various sorts. These range in date from early prehistoric hunter-gatherer sites, through early farming community settlements, such as causewayed enclosures, and on to later prehistoric, Roman, and medieval farms and villages.

The earliest sites tend to be fairly small, perhaps less than 0.1ha, but causewayed enclosures may be up to 10ha or more in area. At Hambledon Hill, Dorset, a whole hilltop about 1km

Figure 105   Silchester, Hampshire: aerial view of the walled area of the Roman city which now lies under fields, except for one farm and the church which can be seen centre right; cropmarks of the street pattern are particularly clear, and many individual buildings can be picked out; the town walls are not ploughed, but can be clearly seen as a line of trees and hedges

long by 0.5km wide has recently been investigated and found to include enclosures, ramparts, flint mines, and burial areas, all dating to between 3000 and 2400 bc and now largely under cultivation (Mercer 1980a; 1980b).

Perhaps the most widespread types of prehistoric settlement known in arable areas are the enclosures of Iron Age date. These are variously round, square, polygonal, or rectangular and may be connected to field systems or isolated features. When excavated, most turn out to be small farmsteads, as at Gussage All Saints, Dorset (Wainwright 1979; Fig 103a), and Thorpe Thewles, Cleveland (Heslop 1987; Fig 103b)

Roman villas are particularly numerous in arable areas, probably because of the superior quality of the land which has over and over again been used for arable down the centuries. They are often recognized from aerial photographs (Fig 104; D R Wilson 1974).

Roman and medieval towns and villages may be found in arable areas today virtually deserted, and with little or no surface traces. Perhaps the largest such Roman town is Silchester, Hampshire, covering some 95ha and complete with its walls, streets, buildings, houses, and temples (Fig 105). Much of the interior of this site and most of its immediate surroundings have been ploughed in recent years (Boon 1974). A comparable site, again largely under arable, is Wroxeter, Shropshire, which covers about 75ha (D R Wilson 1984). Numerous smaller towns could be mentioned, among them Wycomb, Gloucestershire, Mildenhall, Wiltshire, and Irchester, Northamptonshire (*see* Frere and St Joseph 1983 for examples). Medieval deserted and shrunken villages are legion, especially in the midlands (M Beresford and Hurst 1971).

Field systems and agricultural facilities

Closely connected with many settlements are fields and agricultural facilities, but most of those which survive are of later prehistoric, Roman, or medieval date.

Regional variations in the type of field systems present can be discerned (*see* 12.2). On slopes, lynchets are often the most distinctive remaining traces, while elsewhere boundary earthworks, drainage ditches, hedge banks, and walls may be found. Trackways between fields are also common. Features relating to pastoral farming must also be expected, for example dykes and boundaries of various sorts. In the east Midlands, these are especially well represented (*see* essays in Bowen and Fowler 1978). Rather more enigmatic are the pit alignments recorded in arable areas in southern and eastern England (D R Wilson 1978).

Industrial monuments

Industrial sites can also be found under plough. Among the earliest are the flint-working sites of the Sussex Downs, for example at Blackpatch (R Holgate, pers comm). Flint knapping sites also abound and, in some cases, represent the only remaining elements of a settlement pattern. Stone quarries, marl pits, clay pits, pottery workshops, brickyards, tile works, pipe factories, and many other industries are represented by sites under cultivation.

Ritual and ceremonial monuments

A wide variety of ritual and ceremonial sites is known in arable areas. In eastern England, where large stones suitable for monument building are rare, such structures have left little or no upstanding evidence because wood was used instead of stone and has now rotted away, leaving only postholes and beam slots in the subsoil. Thus, henge monuments, such as the one at Arminghall, Norfolk, would once have been much more impressive than when they were excavated (J D G Clark 1936). Even in stone-rich areas, it is often the stones which survive while the earthworks have been levelled. At Rollright, for example, on the Oxfordshire Cotswolds, the stone circle and standing stone are well known, but recent survey work has shown that once there were three or four burial cairns beside the upstanding monuments (Lambrick 1983b). Other ritual sites include cursus, barrows, and avenues of prehistoric date. It has sometimes been claimed that certain types of prehistoric burial monuments, for example long barrows, were not built in lowland river valleys, because none have survived there in the form that occurs elsewhere. It is now clear, however, that in some heavily cultivated areas long barrows do survive, but only as levelled monuments (Erith 1971).

In Roman times, rural temples, shrines, and mausolea were very common, and many survive under arable fields today (Fig 106). One such site at Uley, Gloucestershire, was discovered while a pipeline was being laid along the road from Stroud to Dursley. Excavation later showed that this temple was dedicated to Mercury and had a long history from late Iron Age times through into the early sub-Roman period (Ellison 1980). Priories, abbeys, and friaries of medieval date also survive partially or wholly under arable.

Fortified sites

Some of the most impressive monuments in arable areas are the fortified structures. Many motte and bailey castles, for example, have large mottes which are ploughed around because they are an obstacle to cultivation. Earlier forts, Iron Age hillforts for example, are also under plough in many areas. In some cases, the ramparts are left unploughed, while the flat interior is cultivated.

Hillwash sites

Cultivation inevitably leaves soil exposed and open to erosion.

Figure 106   Bancroft, Buckinghamshire: Roman mausoleum under excavation with the central burial area fully cleared to reveal the surviving floor (the scale totals 2m)

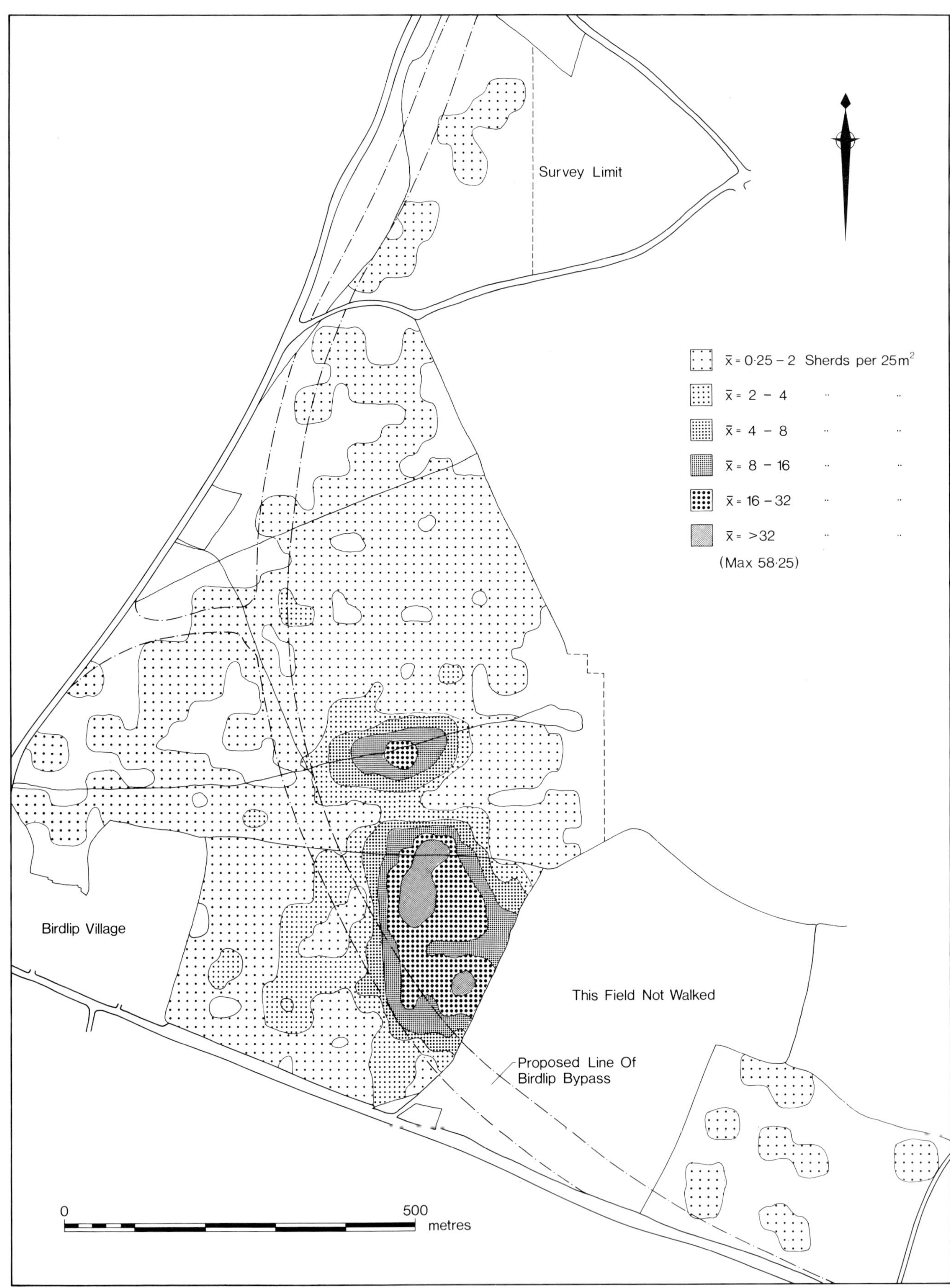

Figure 107   Birdlip, Gloucestershire: plot of Roman pottery recovered during fieldwalking in 1984; the three distinct clusters indicate the position and extent of former buildings (after Darvill 1984a, fig 25)

Figure 108   Thornborough, North Yorkshire: one of three henge monuments in the vicinity, of which the bank on this example is left unploughed as an island; the aerial photograph reveals that ploughing is disturbing the ditches and other features; the parallel ditches visible top left represent the edges of a cursus which underlies the henge

In some circumstances, downslope movements of soil can cause a build-up of hillwash in valley bottoms. Both alluvial and colluvial processes may contribute to the formation of such deposits, and sometimes they can seal ancient land surfaces to depths of 1.5 to 2.0m or more. The number and extent of these hillwash-covered sites is only just beginning to be realized, but they represent a valuable archaeological resource, which is protected from cultivation by the depth of overburden (Bell 1982; 1983; Darvill and Timby 1985). Moreover, the hillwash deposits themselves can preserve environmental evidence, such as pollen or snail shells, which can be used to reconstruct the landscape at the time that the hillwash was forming.

Field archaeology in arable areas

Locating and recording sites in arable landscapes draws on almost all the techniques available to field archaeology (chapter 2.3). Field survey can reveal much, even when sites are heavily eroded by ploughing, but the two most powerful techniques are fieldwalking and aerial photography. Paradoxically, both really only work well when agricultural practices are, in effect, eroding a site. Thus, many of the most fully recorded sites are probably those in their final stages of destruction.

Fieldwalking can lead to the discovery of many different types of site where material is being brought to the surface by the plough (Shennan 1985; Hayfield 1980; Darvill 1984a). Roman and later settlements are especially easy to identify, because large quantities of pottery, building materials, and sometimes small objects, such as coins or brooches, come to the surface. Careful systematic collection can lead to the identification of individual building plots within a settlement or occupation area (Fig 107). Earlier sites less easy to spot because the evidence is usually very fragile, and more often than not the only indication of their presence will be a scatter of stone tools. Thus there are biases in the types of sites able to be identified by fieldwalking. Burials and many types of ritual site are unlikely to be found in this way. Research is in progress to establish the relationships between the recovered material and the kinds of features which lie beneath the soil, but it seems clear that ploughing does not move finds far from where they originate below the ploughsoil.

Aerial photography has wide application in arable areas. Cropmarks often betray the existence of buried structures where little or no surface trace can be seen. In the spring, crop growth is appreciably more rapid in areas of rich soil, perhaps over ancient middens or above humic ditch fills. Later in the year, growth differential may reveal the presence of buried walls as parched marks caused by thin soils and limited root penetration. In the late summer, differential ripening of crops

Figure 109   Wootton, near Ombury, Shropshire: enclosure showing as a cropmark in a small portion of the field in the centre of the picture; the remainder of the field appears to be covered in hillwash which is masking and protecting any other features in the vicinity

over ditches, pits, and walls may be seen (Fig 108). Studies of the major river valleys, especially the Thames, Severn, and Trent, have revealed many square kilometres of cropmark sites (Leech 1977; Benson and Miles 1974; RCHME 1960; Webster and Hobley 1964; Riley 1980).

Field-names can also make a contribution to the discovery of long-vanished sites. Names such as 'barrow ground' or 'windmill field' are obvious cases, where some existing or well-remembered feature has been used to identify a particular piece of ground (J Field 1972; M Gelling 1978; C Taylor 1974, 87).

The hardest types of site to find under arable are those masked by hillwash. Cropmarks will probably not develop, because the depth of overburden is too great (Fig 109), and since the plough is not disturbing the lower levels, no finds will come to the surface for collection during fieldwalking. Often, hillwash sites are only discovered when drainage ditches are dug or the ground is disturbed to a considerable depth in some other way.

12.4   Threats

Of all the landscape categories described in this book, the archaeology of arable lands is probably the most extensively and most intensively threatened. This in itself, however, is not new (Bonney 1980). The very process of cultivation is disruptive to archaeological deposits, and prehistoric, Roman, and medieval farmers have, in their turn, all contributed to the destruction of monuments built by their ancestors. Early cultivation was destructive by virtue of the long time-span over which attrition took place, often measured in centuries. Ards and light ploughs pulled by animal traction tended to ride up over buried features, such as cairns or walls, and there were severe limitations on the steepness of slope that could be tackled. Ridge-and-furrow cultivation also caused much damage, but at the same time preserved some archaeological deposits, for while the furrows tended to cut down into any underlying strata, the accumulating ridges of soil served to protect features very well.

This has changed as more powerful traction units have become available, so that now it is possible to work on much steeper slopes and cut straight through obstacles rather than ride over them (Lambrick 1977). Thus it is a change in the scale and intensity of cultivation which is putting archaeological sites in arable land under acute threat. The main problems may be summarized as follows.

Ploughing

Numerous surveys in many different parts of England have demonstrated the widespread and destructive power of ploughing on archaeological sites (Hinchliffe and Schadla-Hall 1980). The extensive use of steam ploughs during the inter-war years marked the first acceleration of this destruction, but it has continued as increasingly powerful tractors, which can do as much damage in one pass as primitive cultivation would have done in perhaps 50 years, become widely used.

Ploughing causes damage in three ways. First, the passage of the plough itself causes abrasion and attrition of underlying deposits by vibration and drag, when the soil is turned. This is especially noticeable where soil loss through erosion is taking place because, at a consistent plough depth, subsoil or archaeological deposits are continually brought into the ploughzone to maintain topsoil depth. This leads not only to the erosion of sites, but also to the lowering of the bedrock surface. Second, ploughing opens up the soil structure, allowing the elements to penetrate further into buried deposits than they otherwise would; frost and water are especially harmful. This in turn leads to the breakdown of archaeological deposits, making them doubly vulnerable to attrition at the next pass of the plough. Third, the way in which the soil is lifted and turned by the plough tears any loosened archaeological material from its context of origin – a phenomenon known as plucking.

Ploughing does not cause damage evenly over cultivated land. Areas where soil is accumulating through downslope movement are less at risk, since the lower limit of ploughing will rise commensurately given a consistent plough depth. Most vulnerable are slopes, where soils tend to be thinner and where the plough tends to dig deeper, especially if the ploughman uses the shares of the plough as an anchor to brake the speed of a tractor as it runs downhill. Also vulnerable are pits and ditches with a fill that is softer than the surrounding area, because here the plough tends to dip down into the fill. Deep ploughing, that is periodic ploughing to a greater than normal depth, simply exacerbates these problems.

Both standing earthworks and buried features are at risk from ploughing. The rate of destruction varies greatly according to bedrock type, soil conditions, slope, and the exact method of cultivation used. On the Sussex Downs, ploughing of a late Bronze Age cross-ridge dyke for a period of 35 years between 1939 and 1974 just about halved its original height, which works out at an average loss of about 0.02m per year. Also in Sussex, ploughing of a Neolithic enclosure earthwork for 16 years resulted in an average annual loss of about 0.04m of bank (Drewett 1980). Even if monuments stabilize at a certain point, the effect of ploughing is to produce a peneplain surface with the consequent truncation of the archaeological deposits beneath. Three stages in the way that a site is damaged by ploughing have been identified by Hinchliffe (1980, 13):

i   Survival of contemporary levels – minimum disturbance, after which floors, surfaces, rubbish accumulations, middens, and evidence of superstructure still survive

Figure 110   Sezincote, Gloucestershire: Bronze Age round barrow which survived as an island within arable after being ploughed over in 1976 (the scales each total 2m)

ii Survival of structural evidence only – significant disturbance, after which only subsoil-cut features, such as pits, postholes, and beam slots, and robust remains, such as wall foundations, survive

iii Survival of deep features only – heavy disturbance, after which only features such as pits, ditches, wells, etc survive because they have been cut deep into the underlying bedrock. The upper levels of these will of course be disturbed.

Naturally, the survival of different types of site will to some extent depend on the types of features present. Thus, hunter-gatherer settlements, with few if any bedrock-cut features, will never be recognizable beyond stage i, whereas a flint mine cut perhaps 10–15m into the chalk will survive much longer, at least as a rock-cut feature. The important point here, however, is that the quantity, quality, and range of evidence represented at a site decreases through each successive stage. Sites thus gradually lose their archaeological value, and the potential yield of information is reduced.

Pan busting, subsoiling, and drainage work

These techniques are closely connected with arable cultivation and have special roles in improving drainage and soil structure.[81] Pan busting and subsoiling frequently use special implements which can penetrate up to 1m or so in depth, and the damage caused to archaeological sites in the process can be considerable. The soil is not inverted, as in ploughing, but the ground is loosened over a wide area through fissuring. This increases the effects of subsequent ploughing.

Drainage works vary greatly in their effects on archaeological sites. Generalization is difficult because of the widely differing soil types on which the work is undertaken. Mole drainage has a similar effect to subsoiling. Laying ceramic or plastic field drains can be much more devastating, not just along the lines of the actual trenches dug to lay the drains, but in the loosening of the ground round about. Criss-crossing a site with drains of whatever type effectively severs the crucial relationships between one area and the next.

Field boundary and hedge removal

The strips of land under field boundaries and hedges, together with the relatively uncultivated headlands on either side, may represent the best-preserved portions of a site which is under cultivation. Many boundaries were originally set out with obstacles such as barrows or banks actually on the boundary itself, where they would not interfere with farming practices. Strange alignments or kinks in field boundaries often result from having to cultivate round an existing feature like an upstanding archaeological monument and, even when the site has gone, the strange line of the boundary may be perpetuated. Hedges and fences also provide a barrier to downslope movement of soil (even on very slight slopes) and so are frequently edged on their upslope side by a greater depth of soil, which in turn provides a good context for the preservation of sites. One such site was at Street House, Loftus, Cleveland. Here, the site was first recognized as a Bronze Age barrow surviving in a hedgeline. Upon excavation it proved to be well preserved on the upslope side, where a greater soil depth covered it, but poorly preserved on the downslope side, where the plough had bitten into the cairn structure. In this particular case, a Neolithic burial mound pre-dated the round barrow, so in fact there were two burial monuments, one above the other, preserved in this boundary (Vyner 1984).

Encroachment

Sites which exist as islands of uncultivated ground in an arable field lend themselves to gradual denudation by the encroachment of the plough an extra furrow or two at a time, until eventually the site is ploughed right over (Fig 110). This problem was found to be common on the Cotswolds during a survey of known sites carried out in 1979 (Saville 1980). It is also widespread in other areas, and is especially worrying because most upstanding earthworks in arable represent only the visible portion of what is actually a much more extensive site below ground level. Thus, at the very least, encroachment acts to sever the links between the upstanding remains and the rest of the site.

Chemicals and burning

This is an area which has yet to be fully researched, but there is much very real concern over the effects on archaeological deposits of chemicals (including weedkillers, fertilizers, and nitrates) applied to arable land, especially on less fertile soils which require liberal additions of fertilizers to maintain yields. Archaeological artefacts have often been buried in the soil for thousands of years and have, in terms of their chemistry, reached an equilibrium with the surrounding soil. Changing the chemical composition or the acidity of the soil will upset this balance and may cause the deterioration of material such as bone and metalwork.

Stubble burning and bonfires create considerable quantities of mobile carbon (charcoal) which, through worm action and the activities of burrowing animals, can easily find its way to depths of 0.4–0.5m or more, effectively contaminating archaeological layers with modern carbon. This could have particularly deleterious effects on samples submitted for radiocarbon dating.

Expansion and preparation works

The effects of arable expansion into other landscape categories are discussed elsewhere in this book. Particularly damaging, however, are the bulldozing of ground to flatten it or to remove stone scatters in order to make cultivation easier. Often, such operations take place without the farmer knowing that a mound or bump is of archaeological interest, and the damage caused is usually quite unintentional. In some cases, a halt is called to works when it is discovered that something of interest is being disturbed, as at Sale's Lot, Withington, Gloucestershire. Here, an unrecorded Neolithic long barrow was encountered during field clearance, but through the quick thinking of the workmen and the landowner the site is now preserved (O'Neil 1966).

Indiscriminate surface collection

Intensive collection of artefacts from the ploughsoil above known sites has two effects. First, it makes the site less recognizable for what it is, and second, it destroys any patterning in the distribution of objects over a site which might give clues to its layout, date, and function. The finds in the topsoil of a heavily-ploughed site derive from all the layers which have been cut away by the plough, and, in the case of an intensively cultivated site with no bedrock-cut features, all evidence for it may now be in the ploughsoil. For this reason, detailed records must be made whenever artefacts are removed from the ploughsoil. Treasure hunting, metal detecting, and unstructured fieldwalking are simply diminishing the amount of information about a site which is preserved in the ground.

12.5   Management

The integration of heritage management with the demands of farming is not easy, but the fact that monuments are so threatened by cultivation means that positive action is very necessary. There is little overlap between the aims of heritage management and those of other countryside interests, because arable lands tend to be written off from the point of view of nature conservation. More common ground may develop in future.

In formulating management strategies for archaeological monuments in arable areas, the following two factors must be taken into account:

i   Conflicts of interest: very real conflicts of interest exist between normal agricultural uses of arable areas and the preservation and exploitation of ancient monuments. These need to be reconciled before a particular approach is developed.

ii   The extent of arable land: at present, arable land represents the single most widespread landscape category and on a national scale probably contains the greatest diversity of archaeological remains.

Curatorial management

Preventing, or at least minimizing, ground disturbance is the most important factor in preserving sites in arable. Ideally, sites need to be taken out of cultivation altogether, but this is often difficult and may be quite impractical on farms which have no livestock and which rely solely on crop production. Unfortunately, archaeological sites tend to comprise land units which are uneconomical to manage as separate units under a different regime from the rest of the farm.

Some progress can be made on small sites by creating uncultivated islands. There are problems with this, however, not least that, if left unattended, such sites revert to scrub and ultimately woodland, and also provide a haven for pests which damage the surrounding crops. Some sort of mechanical or chemical control is therefore essential.

Where sites cannot be taken out of cultivation, some form of minimum cultivation may be appropriate (Milne 1977; R Hughes 1980; Whitaker 1980). Direct drilling is one such technique, but would have to be undertaken without resort to periodic episodes of subsoiling, as this would reverse in one action much of the success achieved by not disturbing the soil to any significant degree during the intervening seasons. Light cultivation with a chisel plough set high, a disc harrow, a spring tine cultivator, or a power rotary cultivator may also provide a useful compromise.

At present there are approximately 4500 Scheduled Monuments in arable areas,[82] including examples of most, if not all, of the known types of sites represented in the sort of countryside given over to arable. Many of the management agreements concluded by English Heritage relate to sites under arable, mostly providing for the maintenance of monuments taken out of cultivation. No Guardianship sites lie under arable, because they will have been taken out of cultivation as part of the Guardianship processes. The selection of sites of national importance in arable is most difficult, because surface indications which give an indication of their exact nature are in most cases few. Cropmarks cannot be used as a reliable guide, because many of the clearest sets of marks are produced by sites which are heavily eroded, perhaps in late stage ii or stage iii of the sequence of decay outlined above. Cropmarks may, however, indicate the presence of rich deposits nearby, where deeper soil, hillwash, or different cultivation practices have preserved an ancient landscape rather better.

In applying the non-statutory selection criteria, special attention for preservation must focus on sites where disturbance has been minimal, and where part or all of the monument remains in relatively good condition. Sites of all periods are represented in arable lands and can be given equal treatment, but some classes of site are rare on a national scale, and these need to be identified. All sites under arable are fragile and vulnerable, but some will be in situations where their future management, with a view to preservation, is more practicable than others.

In areas of intensive occupation the diversity of sites in a small area may be great; at the same time, however, there is a need to consider sites which represent a single type, uncluttered by later activity. Documentary evidence providing details of the history of a site and of former excavations can be found for many sites in rich arable areas, as they have often attracted the attention of antiquaries and historians. Those sites which preserve several components of relict landscape, for example settlements, field systems, burials, and ceremonial areas in close proximity, are of special importance to set alongside contemporary monuments in other landscape categories. Perhaps most important in the arable situation are those sites which include areas sealed by hillwash or alluvium, and which have associated waterlogged deposits which might extend the range of information potentially recoverable.

Only a fraction of sites under arable will ever be scheduled or subject to management agreements. Much, however, can be achieved in preserving sites through individual initiatives. The removal of hedges, fences, and headlands which cross cultivated sites — these areas will almost certainly contain the most completely preserved part of the site — should be avoided, together with the lighting of fires on cultivated sites, and the use of deep cultivation and subsoiling. Drainage works should be routed round sites wherever possible.

On a more positive note, the planning of new boundary lines round fields may usefully take monuments into the boundary zone, and broad headlands may be left along one side of a field so that monuments can be included in this space where they will not interfere with cultivation. When costing new techniques, the application of minimum cultivation to fields containing monuments might be considered. Whenever sites are ploughed, it is worth double-checking that the plough depth is not exceeding the previous maximum, and that the plough is only turning the topsoil, rather than bringing up material from lower down. Priority should be given to this where a site constitutes a sufficiently large area to merit management in a more sympathetic way. In the case of large sites such as hillforts, it is much better if the whole monument can be treated as a single unit, and preferably all of it taken into pasture.

Special attention needs to be given to the edges of sites, as these are often at greatest risk. Uncultivated buffer zones, or safety zones round a site, offer one cheap solution. This works best when the farmer is doing the ploughing himself, but is less likely to be successful when contractors are employed. Marking the boundary of the monument may, however, help to solve this. A ring of posts is the simplest method and, while not providing an obstacle to the plough, serves as a reminder, especially if painted with fluorescent paint. Posts are cheap, easy to put in, replaceable when necessary and, if circumstances change, easily removed. They are unlikely to cause much serious archaeological damage and could be set up by the farmer, perhaps with a little archaeological help. It helps to

Figure 111   Raunds, Stanwick, Northamptonshire: view of building with mosaic floors under excavation; note the plough scores where cultivation has hit the archaeological levels

monitor them on a regular basis, and on Scheduled Monuments this can be done by a Field Monument Warden. If livestock are likely to graze the field, it is a good idea to cut the posts down in height so that they do not form an erosion focus by acting as rubbing posts. An alternative to posts are concrete bollards, but, while these have their uses on some sites, they are generally inconvenient, difficult, costly to erect, and complicated to remove. One final form of delineation is by a fence. This is relatively expensive and tends to isolate the monument with the result that the natural succession of scrub and tree growth will begin, unless carefully controlled.

There is much scope for looking into new ways of protecting monuments in arable areas. One solution might be to raise the base of the ploughsoil above the top of preserved deposits by covering the site with an additional layer of soil. This is not only costly but also raises questions about where any new soil would come from; this may contain its own archaeological material and potentially sow further confusion on and around the site.

Recording

Since finds from cultivated fields represent one of the main ways of identifying the presence and extent of buried sites, particularly those with no surface traces, a special watch should be kept for artefacts coming to the surface in areas where nothing has previously been recorded. Exceptional pieces may be recovered, noting its findspot as accurately as possible, but where a considerable quantity of material has been turned up, it should as far as possible be left in place with only a few representative pieces taken for specialist identification, usually to the county archaeological officer or a local museum. A special watch should be maintained during drainage works in areas devoid of known sites to see whether there are buried surfaces below hillwash or colluvium.

In formulating management plans for monuments in arable areas, it is important to determine the age and extent of remains, their character in terms of the sort of features which might be expected, and their vulnerability to different cultivation practices. It is also important to establish the maximum depth of former ploughing, so that future works can be coordinated to penetrate less deeply. The presence of deep soil areas and patches of hillwash or alluvium, and the possibility of waterlogged deposits, should also be recorded.

Trial trenching, in order to determine management requirements, is probably more desirable on arable land than in most other landscape categories, and can be done at minimal cost.[83] In the case of Coneybury Henge on the chalk downlands of central Wiltshire, excavations demonstrated that ploughing was not damaging to the old ground surface inside the monument, and that there was no reason to change existing practices (Morgan Evans 1986, 11). One of the most difficult problems connected with sites under arable is deciding when preservation becomes impracticable and when rescue excavation becomes desirable (Fig 111). Large areas are often involved, and excavations can be very costly. The resources are simply not available for the excavation of plough-threatened sites in any number.

Exploitative management

Many sites under arable do not lend themselves well to display. Flat sites are of little visual interest, and access to sites in the midst of cultivated ground is frequently difficult. Nonetheless, barrows, earthworks, hillforts, and deserted villages, for example, do represent visually interesting monuments and may be exploited, either as single monuments or as part of farm trails or similar attractions. Again, taking monuments into field edges or unploughed headlands allows greater flexibility in the use of monuments as tourist attractions.

Academic interest in monuments under arable is high, because the structure and layout of the sites can sometimes be appreciated in advance of excavation through fieldwalking and aerial photography. In this way, trenches can be positioned for maximum return of information, and some indication of the size of the site, and of other contemporary sites in the vicinity, may be glimpsed. Large areas of the site under study can be made available in the time between harvest and sowing, and topsoil can be quickly and easily removed and replaced. There is the added value that excavating sites which are under plough means that details which may be lost through further ploughing can at least be recorded on paper. The main problem with ploughed sites is that the upper layers, if not the whole stratigraphic sequence above bedrock level, may be disturbed. As a resource for investigating the kinds of deposits contained in rock-cut features, arable sites are unrivalled for their potential.

13 Parkland and ornamental gardens

13.1 Archaeological importance

The parklands of the English countryside are wholly artificial landscapes, comprising enclosed areas of land within which an ornamental environment has been created, usually to some sort of coherent design, to provide an imposing, 'natural', picturesque, romantic, or rustic aspect.[84] Over the past 500 years, the form and function of parks have undergone almost continuous change, with the result that their history and development are quite complicated and bound up with changes in other landscape categories and with the changing popularity of pleasure gardens.

Today, the characteristic vegetation of most parkland is dominated by mixed species grassland with a low density tree cover, forming either part of a landscape scheme or wood pasture. Small areas may be given over to horticulture, and a feature of many parks is the presence of a formal garden of some kind. In a few cases, the garden occupies the entire enclosed area. Parkland is found on many different types of soils, usually within areas dominated by grades 2 and 3 agricultural land.[85]

Archaeologically parkland is a valuable resource, not only because parks themselves are works of man, and so of great interest, but also because many preserve monuments dating to the time before the park was established. These may be reviewed under three headings.

i   Parks as monuments: parklands, and the gardens and other works associated with them, are themselves archaeological monuments, in the sense that they represent man-made features, albeit on a large scale. They were deliberately built for specific recreational, leisure, and ornamental purposes, and often represent very substantial investments of time and money.

ii Preservation: once established, parkland was usually managed intensively to maintain and preserve its character and its main features. Aesthetic rather than financial gain was often the rationale behind management, so intensive land-use, which would have been detrimental to the artificial environment within the park, was generally excluded. This promoted the preservation of both parkland and pre-park features. Parkland found in areas of countryside extensively given over to arable cultivation and other intensive land-uses provides an important reserve of less disturbed ground, within which the survival of earthworks is generally good. Thus, parkland provides almost ideal conditions for the survival of field monuments.[86]

iii Historical context: because parks were mostly created by members of the aristocracy, or wealthy institutions such as monasteries or colleges, records detailing various aspects of their foundation and management often exist in the form of accounts, maps, designs, and letters. In some cases, the landscape architect is known, along with the dates of the initial emparkment and subsequent improvements. During the medieval period, for example, Royal licences were required to empark woodland, and many of these survive. Thus, parklands provide an example of a landscape type within which changes may be very well documented.

Parklands cover approximately 1340 square kilometres of the countryside, about 1% of the total land area in England.[87] Individual parks are generally small land units of between a quarter and three-quarters of a square kilometre. Larger parks are, however, fairly common: Woodstock Park, Oxfordshire, for example, covers four square kilometres (Bond 1986, 153). The majority of parkland lies in the south and east of England (Fig 112).

Several different types of parkland can be identified on the basis of the dates of foundation, the whims of patrons, and the skills of the landscape architect who created them. At one extreme are highly organized formal gardens, while at the other there are extensive tracts of wood pasture browsed by deer, horses, or sheep. The implications of these differences for the archaeological importance and management of parklands are negligible, and accordingly all types are considered here as a single category.

There are, of course, certain limitations to the archaeological evidence found in parkland. First, parks themselves relate to the activities and aspirations of a specific section of medieval and post-medieval society – the aristocracy. Second, the distribution of parkland in England means that only archaeological monuments in a restricted range of lowland environments will incidentally be preserved as the result of emparking.

13.2 The history, development, and distribution of parkland

The origins of parkland in Britain have been traced back to the early medieval period, and particularly to the Norman interest in deer husbandry (Rackham 1986, 122–3). One possible pre-conquest park is known at Ongar, Essex, as it was referred to in a will dated AD 1045 (Whitelock 1930, no xiii), but the majority were probably founded after the Norman conquest.[88] The Domesday Book of 1086 records 35 parks in those areas of England surveyed (Rackham 1986, 123).

These early parks were rather different from those of today (Fig 113). They were wooded, and their primary purpose was the supply of meat, especially venison, and to a lesser extent wood and timber. The boundary, or park pale, was usually a strong wooden fence made from oak stakes individually set in the ground and nailed to a rail. Sometimes the pale was set on a bank with an adjacent ditch, variously placed inside or out (Rackham 1976, ch 8; 1986, 123; Shirley 1867).

During the twelfth and thirteenth centuries, the number of parks in England rose dramatically, probably because of the introduction of fallow deer which were easier to manage within a confined space than the native red and roe deer. In the thirteenth century systematic records of emparking began, when Royal licences were required to establish or enlarge a park. These grants are recorded in the Pipe Rolls and the Close Rolls,[89] and it has been estimated that, by about 1300, there were some 3200 parks in England (Rackham 1980, 191). Many were established on marginal land, waste, or woodland, where competition from other more demanding types of land-use was minimal, but some occupied prime agricultural land.

The average size of these medieval parks was about 100ha, and they were especially numerous in Hertfordshire, Worcestershire, Staffordshire, Warwickshire, and Berkshire.[90] Anyone who could afford to create a park did so, and most earls, bishops, and monasteries had several. Parks were mainly status symbols, and accordingly some nunneries, minor gentry, and colleges had them too.

Hunting occasionally took place in the larger parks, and there

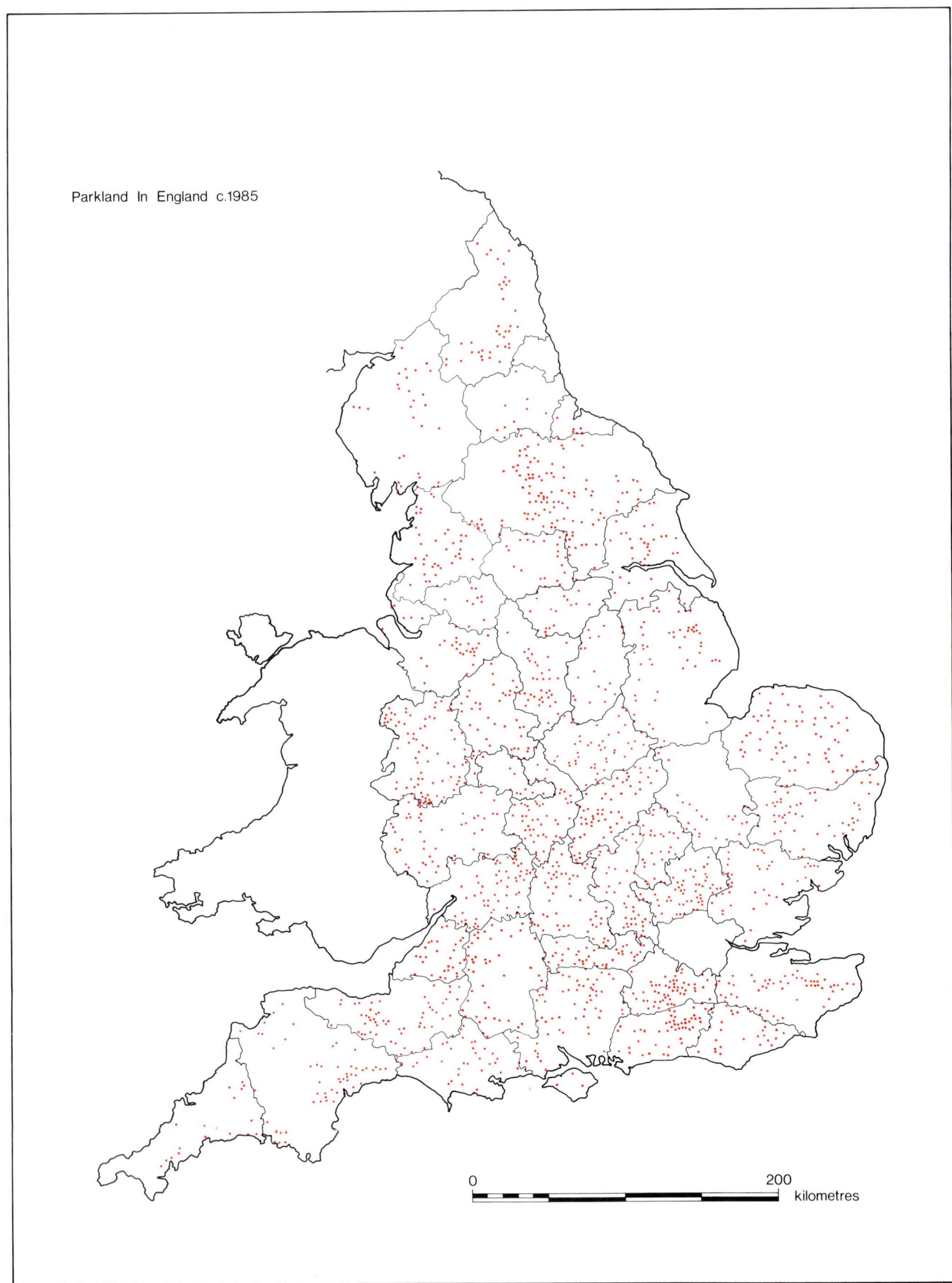

Figure 112   The distribution of parklands and ornamental gardens in England (excluding urban areas)

Figure 113   Medieval deer park at Buckenham, Norfolk: the park boundary can be clearly seen, also the central pond

is the well-known record of Henry III giving permission for the Abbess of Barking to chase fox in Havering Park, Essex, in 1221 (Rackham 1986, 125). On the whole, however, medieval parks retained their earlier roles as sources of meat, timber, and wood. Deer remained the most common animal kept in parks, but swine, cattle, and rabbits are recorded too.

Parks were managed by appointed officers (parkers) from a park lodge, which was usually set in the middle of the enclosure, perhaps on a piece of high ground to give a good view over the whole park. At this time it was rare for the owner to live in, or even adjacent to, the park.

The main expense incurred in making a park was the construction of the boundary. Early parks tend to be rounded or sub-rectangular in outline with rounded corners. Parish boundaries often make a detour round them. Later examples tend to be more irregular in outline and frequently follow the line of existing parish boundaries, where they are situated on the edge of a parish. Some parks were internally uncompartmented and were available for browsing all the time. Other parks, perhaps as many as 50% of them, were compartmented into areas for grazing and areas for woodland. Banks and fences within the park were used to demarcate the different areas, which could be numerous.

In the later medieval period, particularly in the sixteenth and seventeenth centuries, the use of parks declined. Few new parks were established, and many reverted to woodland or, in the case of those which had been overgrazed in the preceding centuries, were given over to arable cultivation or pasture. New roles began to be found for those that remained, most notably as recreational and ornamental landscapes. Mansions began for the first time to be built in or near parks.

One early instance of a park being used for recreational purposes occurred in 1528. In that year the monks of Butley, Suffolk, apparently took the Queen of France for a picnic with fun and games under the oaks in Staverton Park (Dickens 1951).

This transitional period in the history of parklands is well summarized on a national scale by Rackham (1976, 148; 1986, 126–9) and C Taylor (1983b), and, on a more localized scale, for Hampshire by Bilikowski (1983) and Oxfordshire by Bond (1981).

The Dissolution of the monasteries in 1534–7 made available many large houses which could be adapted to domestic functions, the surrounding land often being emparked and the gardens enlarged.

Gardens had been a feature of important houses since at least Roman times, if not earlier (Cunliffe 1971, 120–40; C Taylor

Figure 114   Engraving by Hollar (1660) of Boscobel House, White Ladies Priory, and surrounding park (now in West Midlands)

1983b), but in the Tudor period gardens became larger and more numerous (Steane 1977; Maclean 1981; Harvey 1981). Like many fashions in medieval England, the inspiration for formal gardens and their integration with the recreational use of parks began at the topmost level of society. Prototypes include Henry I's palace at Woodstock, Oxfordshire (Woodward 1982), and Henry III's palace at Clarendon (Colvin 1963, 912). A particularly vivid example of the way in which the recreational use of parks and gardens could come about is provided by the case of Elvetham Park, Hampshire, the summer residence of the Seymour family. In 1591, in order to regain the favour of Queen Elizabeth I, Edward Seymour organized a masque which was to be staged during a visit by the Queen. In preparation for this, 300 workmen were employed to enlarge the house in order to accommodate the court. As an open air setting for the presentation of the masque, Edward Seymour ordered the construction of a pond 'cut in the perfect figure of a half moon'. In the pond were three islands, one shaped like a ship, one shaped like a fort, and the other a 'Snaykl Mount', rising to four circles of 'greene privie' hedge 6m high and 12m broad at the bottom. The entertainment on this occasion lasted for four days (J Wilson 1980; Hatchards nd).

Much of the history of parklands through late medieval and post-medieval times is dominated by the part played by ornamental gardens in their layout and use (Thacker 1979; Hadfield 1979; Prince 1967). From the middle of the sixteenth century to the beginning of the eighteenth, gardens were mostly formal. Recurring features were terraces, mounts, ponds,

and canals, and in the design of these there was a continuous interplay between social aspirations, artistic aims, changing fashions, wealth, and status. Many new ideas for both the design of gardens and the plants and trees included in them came from abroad. Some of the great mansions built at this time such as Hampton Court were surrounded by formal gardens, and beyond these was less formal parkland. By the early eighteenth century, French and Dutch influences were strong. The Le Notre style was highly formal and largely based on the use of water in canals, pools, cascades, and fountains, on broad controlled vistas, and on the planting of woods through which carefully placed paths were cut. Rigid symmetry was favoured. Groves of trees, follies, and grottoes became features of the larger gardens (Thacker 1979; Hadfield 1979; Hussey 1967). Straight lines and rides were included in large wooded parks, so that deer could be seen when they broke cover during a hunt. Some understanding of the quality and size of these parks and gardens can be glimpsed from contemporary drawings (Fig 114).

By the mid-eighteenth century, a reaction against the formal gardens was in full swing, and the landscape park became fashionable, marking the full integration of the large garden and the recreational/ornamental park. A renewed phase of emparking began around those mansions not already situated in parks. The earlier practice of taking parkland from marginal areas was abandoned, and areas were selected for their landscape beauty and setting. This often meant uprooting whole communities, diverting long-established roads and

Figure 115   A ha-ha ditch at West Wycombe, Buckinghamshire

footpaths, and taking over arable fields and grazing land. In the case of Milton Abbas, Dorset, a small town was moved between 1770 and 1790, during the time that Joseph Damer, later Viscount Milton, laid out his great park around the main house which had formerly been a monastery (C Taylor 1983b; RCHME 1970, 182–200). At Wimpole, Cambridgeshire, the old village stood in the way of eighteenth century improvements and was rebuilt as a model village, outside the gates of the park (Phibbs 1980).

The fashion which promoted the development of landscape parks, and really set the seal on their survival down to the present day, was the idea of a 'naturalized' landscape which swept right up to the walls of the mansion. Achieving this was often a feat of considerable engineering skill, involving not just the creation of a new landscape but the selection and accentuation of the best existing features. Patrons wanted 'instant' parklands, so although new trees were planted and features left to blend in with the surroundings, the skill lay in utilizing what already existed, whether it was ancient woodland, field boundaries, or an occasional mature oak.

Before about the 1750s, landscaping tended to be undertaken on a small scale, and some of it was rather formal. After about 1760, much larger areas were landscaped, and the previously popular formal elements were abandoned. This general period was the era of famous landscape gardeners such as William Kent (1648–1748), Charles Bridgeman (? to 1738), Lancelot 'Capability' Brown (1716–1783) (Stroud 1957), and Humphry Repton (1752–1818) (Stroud 1962; Repton 1980), to mention

just a few. All made their reputation through their cunning designs.[91]

The construction of landscape parks often involved the levelling or grassing-over of the formal gardens built by earlier generations, as for example at Watford, Northamptonshire, described by C Taylor (1983b, 62; and *see* Fig 118). The ha-ha ditch, apparently invented by Charles Bridgeman, and comprising a ditch with a wall in the bottom, provided a suitable boundary to prevent livestock from getting too close to the house without spoiling the view (Fig 115).

Lakes or ponds often provided the centrepiece of a park, sometimes because they already existed and would have been difficult to drain effectively. Streams were rerouted and widened, and, where appropriate, lakes were created. In all these works, the aim was to make things look natural. An appreciation of the work involved in achieving this can, however, be gauged from the work of Capability Brown at Fawsley, Northamptonshire. From the house, the lake appears as a single sheet of water, which starts near the house and stretches the full length of the park. In fact, it is not one lake but two. A single lake would have been impossible to construct and unsightly, so Brown set one lake slightly below the other, so that, when viewed from the top, the dam separating the two was almost invisible (C Taylor 1983b, 60; RCHME 1981, 88–91).

As part of the attempt to make things look natural, ruins were incorporated into the landscape; in some cases these were genuine antiquities (Daniel 1959; Thacker 1979, 215). At Toddington Manor, Gloucestershire, for example, the remains of the old manor (Fig 116) stand isolated within the park of the new mansion constructed by the Tracy family in about 1820 (Sudeley 1969). More unusual is the monument at Park Place, Remenham, Berkshire, which comprises a Neolithic chambered tomb brought from Jersey in the Channel Islands and re-erected within the park in 1778 (Crawford 1930).

Temples and pavilions were also built, but these often had a functional value as retreats or summer houses. Sometimes works were undertaken outside the park proper, perhaps by adding clumps of trees or a folly to a distant hilltop, visible from the park or house, to make it more interesting. At Studley Royal, North Yorkshire, Fountains Abbey provided the romantic ruins on a grand scale, while one of the main avenues through the park was aligned on the tower of Ripon Cathedral about 5km away (Beard 1961).

The construction of parks around new and rebuilt country houses continued right through the nineteenth century, and some impression of the scale of emparkment can be gained by comparing early Ordnance Survey maps with their modern counterparts. Even quite modest houses, such as vicarages, sometimes had small areas of parkland or landscaped garden round about. In Victorian times, it again became traditional to construct gardens around the houses themselves, and these are often characterized by balustraded terraces and flower beds. Ornamental gardens were also commonly associated with urban fringe villas (T Slater 1978).

The parks which survive today include some of great antiquity, which have passed through all the different stages of medieval and post-medieval change, and some which are really quite recent creations, dating back to the era of landscape emparkment in the nineteenth century. Up until the Second World War many parks were privately owned, but since that time the costs of maintaining and managing parkland and the houses that go with it have risen sharply, with the result that many have been taken into institutional ownership as schools, colleges, and offices, or into public ownership. A considerable

Figure 116   Ruins of a medieval manor house in parkland at Toddington, Gloucestershire; the ruin was used as an ornamental feature within the park attached to the mansion built in about 1820

number of parks are now owned by the National Trust or by local authorities. The recreational aspect of parkland has, over the last 20 years, taken two new dimensions, which in their way clearly illustrate the continuing evolution of the countryside. First, there are now many areas of parkland open to the public, either as gardens or as fun-fairs, safari parks, or theme parks. Second, country parks have been created by local authorities as recreation areas and picnic sites. Some of these are in areas of ancient park, others are in effect new parks, taken into local authority ownership for the benefit of the community.[92]

13.3   The archaeology of parklands

Archaeological evidence in parkland naturally falls into two main classes, relating to the period before emparking, and to the construction, use, and development of the park itself. These two groups may be considered separately.

Pre-parkland sites

Archaeological monuments which existed on a piece of land prior to emparkment frequently became incorporated into its layout. In the case of buried sites, or sites with only slight surface traces, this was pure accident, but some of the larger and more obvious monuments were often deliberately incorporated into the design of the park. The date of emparkment to some extent determines the range of evidence likely to be preserved, because once a park was established, earlier modes of land-use would be curtailed or caused to cease altogether. Thus, in looking at these pre-parkland sites, it is always

important to bear in mind that when in use they lay within quite different environments.

Early prehistoric sites are rare in parkland, largely because the opportunities for their discovery have been few and there is little or no surface evidence for them. That they exist, however, is beyond doubt, and a number have come to light during the excavation of later, more visible, monuments.[93] From the Neolithic period onwards much more survives to be seen in parkland, notably barrows and earthwork sites. It has long been recognized that the most completely preserved Neolithic chambered tomb on the Cotswolds is the example in Lodge Park, Gloucestershire, which appears to be unopened and still stands over 2m high (Crawford 1925, 6). The massive earthen mound in the grounds of Marlborough College, Wiltshire, is probably of prehistoric origin and in some respects compares with the more well-known monument at Silbury Hill nearby (Burl 1979, 133–4).

One of the most completely recorded prehistoric landscapes in parkland is at Rushmore Park, Dorset. This estate was owned by General Pitt Rivers, and between 1880 and 1893 he excavated a number of sites inside the park, including a cemetery of six Bronze Age barrows and the well-known Bronze Age enclosure at South Lodge (M Thompson 1977). Renewed interest in the archaeology of Rushmore Park has increased still further the number and variety of monuments recorded, and it is now clear that in addition to the barrows and camps there are field systems, enclosures, and boundaries (Barrett *et al* 1983).

Roman villas are a feature of many parks, perhaps because, as Hoskins (1970, 167) points out, similar situations were favoured by the designers and occupants of grand houses in both Roman and medieval times. Among the most fully investigated is Barnsley Park, Gloucestershire (Webster 1981; Webster *et al* 1985). Here, excavations and field survey have revealed not just the villa itself but an associated field system and a network of tracks and roads linking the villa to the surrounding countryside (Fig 117). Another villa excavation in parkland, at Littlecote Park, Wiltshire, revealed an extremely well appointed structure with an associated temple (Selkirk 1981). Other Roman features known in parkland include forts, roads, and farms. Excavations by Sir Mortimer Wheeler in Lydney Park, Gloucestershire, revealed a temple complex dedicated to the god Nodens set within an Iron Age hillfort (Wheeler and Wheeler 1932). At Badminton Park, Avon, an extensive Iron Age or Romano-British field system has been recorded (RCHME 1976, 6).

Perhaps the most plentiful evidence preserved in parkland relates to medieval settlement and land-use, particularly in landscape parks established from the eighteenth century onwards. In addition to such features as former farmsteads, mills, and mottes, there are abundant traces of deserted villages. Some of these were abandoned in the fourteenth and fifteenth centuries and they tend to survive as earthworks, as at Watford Court, Northamptonshire (Fig 118), which was emparked early in the eighteenth century (RCHME 1981, 188–93).

Many villages were destroyed to make way for the construction of parks, and in these cases any standing earthworks were often flattened during emparkment. Where the approximate date of abandonment is known, these deserted villages provide excellent examples of settlements fossilized in the course of their development. At Holdenby, Northamptonshire, a sixteenth century emparkment involved the clearance of the village, leaving only the church (M Beresford and St Joseph 1979, 57–9; RCHME 1981, 103–9). Similar patterns can be seen elsewhere, and a lone church inside a park often indicates the site of a substantial pre-park settlement.

The forerunners of many large late medieval and post-medieval mansions were often moated manors or other forms of large medieval house. These can sometimes be found in parklands set apart from the more recent houses. There are many reasons for this. At Toddington, Gloucestershire, for example, documents record that the medieval moated manor house was abandoned in favour of the mansion built by Charles Hanbury-Tracy in 1820, because the old moated manor house was deemed damp (Sudeley 1969).

Most lowland parks created over arable land preserve areas of medieval ridge-and-furrow cultivation. Often these field systems are fairly complete and, like the deserted villages, have been fossilized as working systems rather than as sites which suffered a long period of decline before eventual abandonment (*see* chapter 12).

Former roads and tracks related to medieval settlements can be located in parklands. A survey of the park at Hardington, Somerset, revealed many other types of earthwork which could be interpreted as hollow-ways, a village, a moated site, and lynchets (Aston 1978).

Remains of monasteries and ecclesiastical houses, together with associated buildings and estate features, occur within many parks, principally because they were created as a result of land grants made by the king after the dissolution of the monasteries. Often monastic buildings were used as sources of stone for a new house and then left in ruins, while elsewhere the original buildings were converted for domestic use. One of the most spectacular cases is Fountains Abbey, North Yorkshire (Fig 119). Here Stephen Proctor, son of one of the early ironmasters, constructed Fountains Hall with stone from the abbey in 1611. Later, both the hall and the abbey were incorporated within the ornamental gardens of Studley Royal, which were begun about 1716. The surroundings of the abbey were landscaped and picturesque additions built on (Gilyard-Beer 1970).

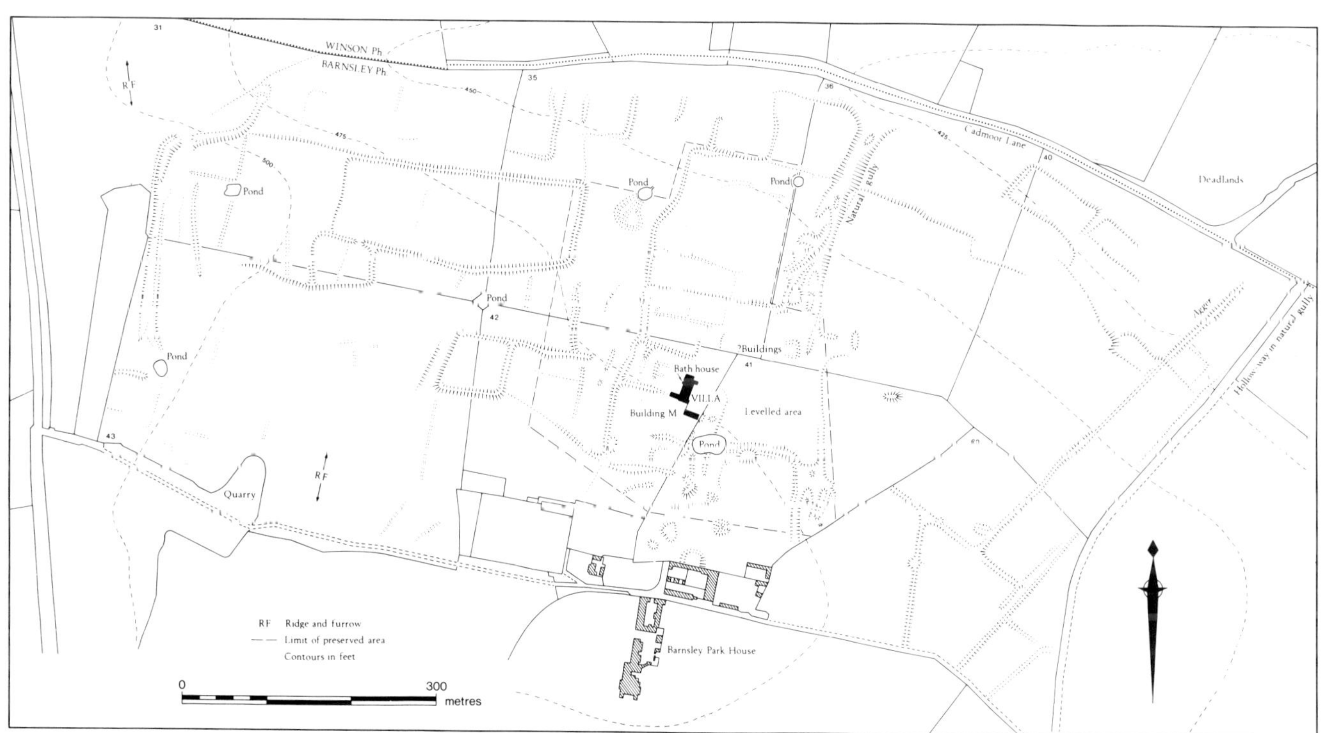

Figure 117   Plan of a Romano-British field system and associated features recorded in Barnsley Park, Gloucestershire (after Webster et al 1985, fig 3)

Figure 118   Watford Court, Northamptonshire: in the foreground are the remains of house sites, gardens, and plough ridges of part of the medieval village of Watford, and in the background are other garden plots; all were incorporated into the park when it was laid out in the early eighteenth century. At that time the park had a rigidly formal appearance with a sunken tree-lined drive across it, now the hollow-way, and a group of rectangular ponds; in the mid nineteenth century the park was made less formal

Figure 119   Fountains Abbey and Studley Royal, North Yorkshire: general view, showing the main house (lower left), the ruins of the abbey (centre), and the landscaped park (top) within which can be seen portions of the ornamental lakes, St Mary's Church, and one of the follies

Few cases of industrial remains have been recorded in parkland, probably because former industrial landscapes were not the sort of places in which parks were established. Among the exceptions, however, is Sutton Coldfield Park, West Midlands, where a former reservoir formed the basis for an ornamental pond, and Attingham Park, Shropshire, where there are traces of ironworking and part of an unfinished canal designed by Thomas Telford (Rackham 1976, 149). No doubt detailed surveys would reveal the presence of other industrial activities in areas later taken over by parkland.

Parkland features

The variety of features connected with the construction and use of parkland is considerable. Leaving aside the houses and mansions, which fall outside the scope of this volume, there are many different types of buildings and structures, as well as earthworks.

Evidence of early medieval parks, mostly deer parks, can be found through the remains of the park pale. This may include a bank and ditch boundary or a wall, as at Barnsdale Park, Leicestershire, which is recorded in 1269 (Rackham 1976, 144). Wooden pales from medieval parks will have rotted away, but postholes and beam slots may survive. Close examination of park boundaries may reveal evidence for enlargements to the initial area. Internal boundaries sometimes survive as earthworks, and lodges, fishponds, and rabbit warrens may also be present.[94] Chapter 10 describes the sort of evidence that will be found within sections of parks given over to woodland.

Formal gardens can be found as earthworks in many parks which were later given over to less formal arrangements, as at Lyveden, Northamptonshire (A Brown and Taylor 1972), Alderton, Northamptonshire (Fig 120), and Hardington and Low Ham, Somerset (Aston 1978). One well-recorded example is at Boughton House, Weekley, Northamptonshire, which was laid out under the orders of Ralph Montagu in the French style between 1685 and 1709 (RCHME 1979, 152–3; C Taylor 1983b, 48–9). Examples of what these formal gardens looked like can still be seen at some sites, for example Kirby Hall, Northamptonshire (RCHME 1979, 59–61), and Bramshill, Hampshire (Bilikowski 1983, 12). Engravings such as those by Johannes Kip (1652–1727) and others show the appearance of these gardens when new (*see* Fig 114). Terraces, ponds, canals, avenues, bowling greens, and stairways were characteristic features of formal gardens, and all can often be detected as archaeological evidence. Vistas created through openings in the garden or park boundary are more difficult to find unless they survive more or less intact. Very noticeable, however, are the

Figure 120   Fields, ponds, and garden features at Alderton, Northamptonshire: in the centre of the picture stands a large circular mound, originally a prospect mount overlooking the terraced gardens to the right; the original house, built in 1582, stood below the terraces and to the left of the road, in the area occupied by farm buildings and stockyards in this picture

mounts or conical-shaped mounds from which the garden could be viewed to appreciate its form and symmetry. These are usually earthen and may preserve the path used to climb up them. On the top, there would have been some kind of shelter or ornamental feature. At Packwood House, Warwickshire, the mount is crowned by a great yew tree (Hadfield 1973, 229), while at Marlborough College, Wiltshire, there was a summer house on the top (Burl 1979, 134).

Avenues formed approaches to formal gardens and parks, and many survive as lines of trees, often set on slight banks to accentuate the perspective (Fig 121). Rides and groves in woodland, either within or adjacent to the park, were also common. Follies were erected, and amazing ingenuity was displayed in their design (Fig 122; B Jones 1953). Classical temples were probably the favourite theme, but a more unusual example is the pyramid recorded at Poulton Park, Hampshire (Bilikowski 1983, 17); the ruined prehistoric monuments already discussed (13.3) were in many cases incorporated as landscape features. These romantic landscapes also included ruins, urns, obelisks, towers, and statuary. Care has to be taken when interpreting these monuments because some may be ruins from pre-parkland times, while others were deliberate fakes.

Typical garden features introduced into parkland in the eighteenth and nineteenth centuries include grottoes, belvederes, gazebos, pavilions, sundials, mazes, and ornamental bridges (B Jones 1953; Matthews 1922). Small woodland plantations were also made as part of the general landscaping,[95] and care has to be taken that the tree-holes and protecting banks associated with these plantations are not mistaken for much earlier features, such as late Neolithic timber circles (Bradley and Mead 1985).

Among the most unusual archaeological evidence connected with parks and gardens are the recorded remains of the masque at Elvetham, Hampshire (*see* 13.2). Aerial photography has revealed the lake, the associated dam, and traces of buildings around the hall (J Wilson and D Wilson 1982).

Archaeological evidence relating to the landscape parks of the eighteenth, nineteenth, and early twentieth centuries mostly comprises traces of the engineering works involved in their construction. These may include dams, lakes, new stream courses, cuttings, terraces, and embankments. Natural-looking features were frequently incorporated into these designs, and again great care must be taken in separating the genuine from the artificial. Ha-ha walls and the park boundary work are

Figure 121   Tree-lined ride at Tynley Hall, Hampshire

additional archaeological features to be noted.

Most parks were managed as complete units, and there may be evidence for horticultural and industrial activities connected with the running of the park and provision of food for the house. Walled kitchen gardens are often present, sometimes with heated greenhouses, and orchards may also be found, sometimes surrounded by characteristic crinkle-crankle walling. Greenhouses and arboreta provided the plants for the gardens and parks, and ice houses and dovecotes (Yorke 1955; Cooke 1920) were associated with the domestic side of estate management. Shooting may have contributed to the range of recreations offered and may leave traces in the form of game coverts and shooting butts. Small areas of woodland may be managed to provide timber for use in the park (for fencing etc), and perhaps for sale to provide a little extra income.

Another commonplace industry closely connected with large parks which leaves abundant archaeological traces is brick-making. This was often undertaken on a seasonal basis. A good example is Ashburnham Park, Sussex (Leslie 1971). Here, records suggest that production began on a small scale about 1840, mainly to provide bricks for the rebuilding of Ashburnham House. Later, bricks were sold to outside buyers, but during periods of repair and extension to buildings within the park itself, outside sales were minimal. After 1928 the brickworks expanded production to commercial sales, which continued down to 1968 when the works were closed down. Another but rather earlier example is the pottery industry which started before the fourteenth century on the edge of Clarendon Park, Laverstock, Wiltshire (Musty *et al* 1969).

Locating and recording archaeological features within parkland rely heavily on field survey, and such work in Dorset, Cambridgeshire, Northamptonshire, and Gloucestershire by RCHME has brought to light much interesting detail about sites preserved in parkland. Aerial photography can be useful, especially with oblique sunlight to throw low earthworks into relief.

The significance of old maps and documents must not be underestimated. Maps may show the landscape before emparkment, or before medieval changes had taken effect, and field names and place-names can help identify former parkland features. Engravings and pictures may show details of gardens, parks, and the surrounding landscape which only survive today as archaeological features.

13.4   Threats

As a landscape category, parklands have probably fared rather well amidst the various changes in the use of the countryside over the last few decades. A number have been lost to urban development or been brought under the plough, but the scale of loss has not been great. Traditional land-uses, involving low intensity grazing and recreation, have continued to dominate the management of parklands, whether they are privately owned or in the public sector. There appears to be a considerable demand for recreation in parklands, very much along the lines for which they were designed 200 years or more ago. Some have expanded the range of recreations offered by including fun-fairs, safari parks, and a bewildering range of amusement facilities, and, while something of the former tranquil atmosphere of these parks has undoubtedly been lost, the principles behind their creation in the first place have been perpetuated.

Parklands are by no means immune to threats, however. There are many demands and pressures facing their continued well being, which affect their archaeological value and which must therefore be taken into account when planning for the future. The following may be singled out for attention.

Fragmentation

Large parks are extremely valuable pieces of estate, but this value is effectively tied up in the land itself. When capital

Figure 122   Gothic Tent folly at Painshill, Surrey

Figure 123   Earthworks, tracks, and modern quarry in Okehampton Park, Devon

transfer tax payments have to be made, for example, the only way to pay is often to divide the park or sell off portions of it in order to pay duty on the remainder.[96] Obviously this diminishes the landscape integrity of the area and also its archaeological value. Fragmentation is particularly damaging if the portions which are sold off are then given over to some more intensive land-use, such as agriculture or housing (Fig 123).

A survey of parks and gardens in Hampshire revealed that at least half of the sites visited (excluding those owned by the National Trust or Government Departments) were shared between two or more different owners. One effect of this is that different portions of the same park are being managed in different ways (Bilikowski 1983, 28).

Agriculture

Normal agricultural practices, designed to enable owners to pay their way without destroying the parkland as they see it, are sometimes imposed on grassland and wood pasture within parks. All the obvious features, such as the lakes, trees, and architectural details, are preserved and maintained as they should be, but when the old grassland is ploughed up for cultivation or reseeding, the result is devastating to earthworks.

Lack of maintenance

The costs of maintaining parkland, particularly the buildings and gardens therein, are very high and generally show little financial return on investment. Many parks are now reaching a mature stage of development and require major programmes of renovation and restoration to give them a new lease of life (Strong *et al* 1974). Since the 1960s, routine maintenance work has been neglected in many parks because of high labour costs. Once features such as watercourses, lakes, and standing buildings fall into disrepair, the cost of putting them back in good order is very high indeed. Some idea of the scale of works needed can be gauged from the fact that in 1983 the National Trust launched an appeal for £1 million to carry out essential work on the garden and parkland at Fountains Abbey, North Yorkshire (National Trust 1983).

Over-exploitation

Most parkland was created for pleasure and can take a certain amount of visitor attention without adverse effect. Heavy visitor use can, however, be detrimental to the park as a complete entity. From the archaeological point of view, the ideal circumstances for the preservation of earthworks and garden features offered by parkland take on a rather qualified nature when the ground is constantly being disturbed to build new roads, car-parks, visitor facilities, or fun-fairs, and when soil poaching takes place because the surface vegetation has been broken by the passage of many feet.

Other

Many archaeological features in parkland are destroyed or damaged through ignorance of what survives. This is especially true of pre-parkland features, for while day-to-day management may respect the structure of the park itself, other features might not be recognised or given the same respect.

Pasture improvement by ploughing and reseeding sometimes takes place within parkland in order to increase the stocking level. Ground disturbance of this sort may seriously damage parkland features and earlier earthworks too.

13.5 Management

Parklands and gardens require a highly specialized form of countryside management for their upkeep, which is often labour-intensive and involves combining the skills of gardener, livestock manager, and builder. However, over the last two centuries this form of management has saved many archaeological sites and in so doing has created its own distinctive archaeological features. If this important reserve of both parkland and pre-parkland sites is to be maintained, then conservation and parkland management must continue at the same sort of level as has been the case for several centuries.

The management of parkland with a view to the conservation of archaeological features is wholly compatible with the maintenance of gardens and the preservation of the amenity and recreational value inherent in parkland. In this there is much overlap of interest between archaeological organizations and the appropriate departments of the National Trust and the Countryside Commission.[97] Moreover, parklands provide sanctuaries for wildlife and flora, and here there will be common ground with the aims of the Nature Conservancy Council.

In formulating management strategies for archaeological monuments in parkland, two important factors need to be taken into account:

i   Landscape integrity: the various ways in which the archaeological and historic importance of parks and gardens are protected are at present orientated towards specific features rather than whole parks. Preservation and conservation ideally need to be applied evenly across the whole land unit.

ii   High maintenance cost for low return: the labour-intensive requirements of maintaining parkland, and the low input/low output agricultural regimes compatible with preserving the character of parks and gardens, make running costs high with the result that, without additional (usually non-agricultural) income, parkland is not a viable economic proposition.

Figure 124   Blenheim Palace, Woodstock, Oxfordshire: general view of the palace and part of the associated park which shows landscaping on a very large scale

Curatorial management

Minimizing ground disturbance and keeping up regular maintenance works are crucial to preserving archaeological sites within parkland. As wholly artificial environments, parks and gardens need a great deal of regular maintenance, and, because their value lies in their landscape integrity, it is important that management covers the whole area rather than simply one aspect of it; the park pale is just as important as the formal garden near the main house.

Ancient monuments within parks can be scheduled, whether they relate to the park itself or are remains from pre-park landscapes. At present there are approximately 1400 Scheduled Monuments within parkland environments,[98] including deserted villages, barrows, Roman villas, and park features such as park pales, dovecots, mounts, and bridges.

Selecting monuments for scheduling is made difficult by the fact that few detailed surveys focusing on the archaeological aspects of parkland have been undertaken. The survival of monuments is one important factor, and here comparison must be made between sites in parkland and those in the general area round about. Rarity will also be important, because every park or garden tends to be unique in one respect or another. In large parks, group value may play a part, and in some later emparkments monuments of many different periods may be represented. Because parks have a long history, it is clearly important to include examples from different periods of emparkment. Parkland tends to be well documented, and this often includes something on the history of monuments within the park, or at least their treatment over the last few centuries. Famous people, or events of national significance, are associated with some parks.

In addition to scheduling, the buildings and structures within parks and gardens may be 'listed' as historic buildings. There are also some areas of parkland designated as NNRs and SSSIs, but, like listing and scheduling, these methods of protection tend to cover only parts of parks or gardens and fail to provide for the complete units.[99]

The main methods of protecting whole parks are through State Guardianship or direct ownership by a local authority or the National Trust. At present there are some 17 gardens and parks in Guardianship, and the National Trust owns many more. In a few counties Conservation Areas include parkland, and this too provides some control over changes which might affect landscape integrity (Jenkins 1984).

An important recent initiative by English Heritage is the compilation of a national register of parks and gardens of special historic interest.[100] Only parks or gardens with historic features dating from 1939 or before are included on the register. The first stage of cataloguing, when complete in 1987, will have listed about 1200 parks and gardens in England as a whole, but it is expected that, when the second phase of work is completed, somewhere in the region of 5000 sites will fulfil the requirements and be included on the register. Each park or garden on the register is allocated a grade according to the qualities it displays:

Grade I – Parks or gardens which by reason of their historic layout, features, and architectural ornaments considered together are of exceptional interest.

Grade II* – Parks and gardens which by reason of their historic layout, features, and architectural ornaments considered together are, if not of exceptional interest, nevertheless of great quality.

Grade II – Parks and gardens which by reason of their historic layout, features, and architectural ornaments considered together are of special interest.

No special controls apply to gardens or parks on the register, nor are any existing planning or Listed Building controls affected in any way. A number of local authorities have, however, used the register as the basis for selecting sites to be given additional protection through planning controls at county level.

The basic elements of traditional management of parkland are well known and need not be reiterated here. Small areas of parkland are just as important for their archaeological remains as large tracts, although it is realized that such areas are often uneconomical to manage along traditional lines. Special care must be taken not to overgraze pasture in parklands, as this may lead to soil poaching and expose the ground to erosion. Broadly speaking, the same practical measures as were outlined for permanent pasture (*see* chapter 9) apply also to parkland. Some care needs to be exercised when dealing with trees, and it is archaeologically more acceptable to reduce tree cover if possible, and to remove tree stumps by poisoning or letting them rot naturally (*see* chapter 10).

Recording

As many archaeological sites in parkland are hidden from view, either below ground or by later superimposed features, it is always worth keeping a special watch for stray finds or buried deposits when ground disturbance takes place within an area of parkland. Careful scrutiny of old maps and documents may help to pinpoint ancient features, and it is important that staff working in parklands are aware of the importance of the features present, and of the potential for discovering new features during the course of everyday activities.

In preparing management plans, attention needs to be given both to the archaeological aspects of the park itself and to any pre-parkland features which are known or suspected.[101] The age, extent, and nature of such features need to be known, so that they can be conserved, or, in the case of garden features, treated appropriately within the overall design.

Exploitative management

Parklands are among the most extensively exploited landscape categories, and much experience in arranging and displaying parks and gardens has been gained in recent years. In many cases, the historical value of the park or garden is often exploited alongside its aesthetic value, but little is made of the archaeological features. The time-depth perspective to the development of the site is rarely explained, and it is not often made clear to visitors that some of the monuments and ruins to which attention is directed (for example abbeys and castles) relate to a time well before the parkland itself was established.

At present, there are some 17 areas of parkland in State Guardianship, but there are many more exploited as tourist attractions and opened to the public by the National Trust and private owners (Fig 124). Various charities make use of private parklands opened to the public for perhaps one or two days a year to raise funds.

There is much potential for the reconstruction and interpretation of monuments in parkland situations; indeed one of the earliest pieces of conscious archaeological reconstruction work ever attempted was the rebuilding by General Pitt Rivers of South Lodge Camp in his park at Rushmore, Dorset (M Thompson 1977; Barrett *et al* 1983). Archaeological sites within the now fashionable, and numerous, country parks run by local authorities could often benefit from a little more attention to their interpretation and display.[102]

Academic interest in parklands, as archaeological features in their own right, is a developing field of interest closely connected with studies of garden history. In the past, however, parklands have often provided the ideal setting for research excavations, where good quality of preservation is desirable and pressure to get the job finished is minimal. It may also be said that the owners of many parklands appreciate the historic value of their estates and are often interested to know something of their history and the sites within their bounds. Several excavation projects within parklands have been undertaken, with a long-term view to developing both the excavation and the site itself as tourist attractions within a more broadly-based recreation and leisure plan for the park.

14 Upland moor

14.1 Archaeological importance

The upland moors of England comprise areas of uncultivated hill-land, generally high altitude open country with characteristic short rough vegetation and thin peaty soils with localized areas of exposed bedrock. They are generally classified as being of low agricultural potential, usually grade 5 in the Agricultural Land Classification, because of the severe limitations on their use (MAFF 1966; ADAS 1980). No firm altitudinal limits can be placed on the designation of upland moors, but they mostly lie above about 200m OD. On the north-west side of upland massifs, where climate is generally more harsh, moorland may be found at lower altitudes.

Archaeologically, upland moors are especially important because a wide range of monuments are exceptionally well preserved as a result of the fact that, in recent decades, these areas have remained relatively isolated and have not been subjected to the intensity of land-use prevalent elsewhere.[103] The implications of this may be discussed under four headings.

i Upstanding remains: upland moors are probably best known for the wide range of upstanding monuments, which appear today much as they did shortly after their abandonment centuries or even millennia ago. Stone was one of the main building materials used by upland communities, and because of this sites have a robustness and resilience to natural and man-induced decay which are rare in other areas. Lack of intensive land-use also means that even ephemeral traces of wooden structures may be preserved as postholes and soil marks beneath the surface. Overall, sites in the uplands tend to be better preserved than their counterparts elsewhere.

ii Landscape and stratigraphy: it is not just single sites which have fared well in the uplands. Extensive tracts of landscape have experienced similar land-use conditions, and accordingly, relatively complete patterns of ancient activity can be traced, including, for example, settlements and ritual monuments alongside their contemporary fields, paddocks, grazing areas, and land boundaries. Perhaps most important, the formation of the archaeological record in upland areas has been such that many sites, after being abandoned, were neglected and so became stabilized, before the onset of another phase of activity in the area. This makes the superimposed periods of occupation easier to disentangle and allows insights into both the organization of the landscape at different times and the way the landscape changed through time. Many upland moors contain groups of monuments which can truly be described as relict landscapes.

iii Environmental indicators: most upland moors contain areas of wetland, mire, and blanket bog (chapter 6) which provide sources of environmental evidence to set alongside the archaeological record. Also, the acidic peaty soil of many uplands allows the preservation of pollen, insect remains, and sometimes even wood within archaeological sites. This provides insights into the environment of the site itself before, during, and after its use.

iv Amenity value: relatively good access to upland moors, the fact that much of what survives is visible, and the fact that most upland monuments can take a certain amount of visitor attention without adverse effect together mean that the display and interpretative value of sites in these areas is very high. Being relatively undisturbed, sites on upland moors provide a guide to what monuments may have looked like in the past.

Upland moors cover approximately 12,950 square kilometres of England, about 9.9% of the total land area.[104] They are mostly confined to the north and west of England, and generally comprise large contiguous units (Fig 125). There is a slight overlap with wetland landscapes, permanent pasture, and forest, but on a national scale this is minimal.

The upland moors cannot easily be divided into types. There are great variations of topography, geology, soil-type, and climate between different areas, but, in terms of the potential for human settlement, the main factor is the gradual change in environment with latitude. Thus, the northern uplands are somewhat less hospitable than those of the south-west peninsula, with lower average temperatures and a shorter growing season (J A Taylor 1976; Darvill 1986a, ch 1).

Although upland moors may appear to provide ideal circumstances for the preservation of archaeological remains, there are three important limitations. First, because the uplands have always represented an extreme environment, only certain classes of site are represented. Second, intensive settlement and land-use in the uplands have only been possible at specific times so that only a few periods are well represented. Third, upland sites tend to be poor in artefacts, partly because the sorts of contexts likely to preserve objects are scarce, and partly because communities living in upland areas seem to have survived with a more limited material culture than communities elsewhere.

14.2 History and distribution

The upland moors are often regarded as natural landscapes, remote wildernesses. But this is not so. As we see them today, the upland moors of England are the result of a long and complicated series of changes, caused by a combination of the effects of human interference with the natural landscape and changing climatic conditions over the last 10,000 years. At times, upland moors were heavily settled and intensively exploited. Indeed, it can be argued that today's upland moors are largely a product of over-exploitation in prehistoric times (Rackham 1986, 306).

Pollen sequences derived from peat bogs and lake sediments within upland areas indicate that after the end of the last (Devensian) Ice Age woodland developed on the higher ground up to altitudes of about 600m OD. At first, this woodland was dominated by pine and birch, but by about 5500 bc this had given way to a mixed oak forest, containing oak, alder, lime, elm, and hazel. Naturally, there were regional variations in species composition and density, but all except the highest peaks seem to have been clothed in woodland. The remains of some of the trees of this woodland have been preserved in high altitude wetland contexts.

Changes in the natural woodland began during the Mesolithic period, when the uplands were exploited by hunter-gatherer groups. Layers of charcoal, preserved in peat deposits and frequently associated with decreases in arboreal pollen levels, suggest episodes of forest clearance by burning

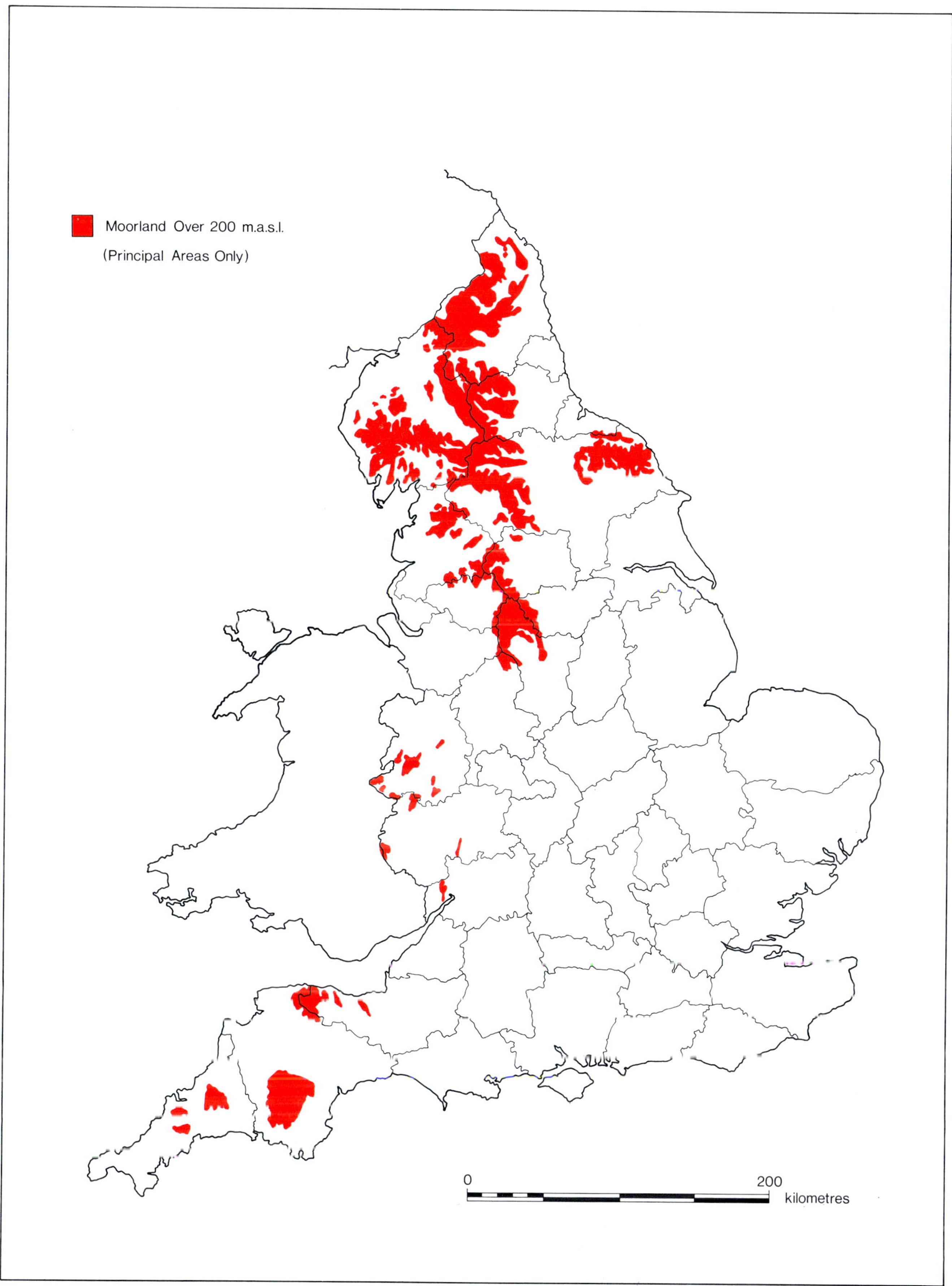

Figure 125   Distribution of upland moorland in England

(Mellars 1976; C Williams 1985; I Simmons *et al* 1981, 103). It is not known whether these were accidental fires (eg the result of lightning strikes) or deliberate acts by hunter-gatherer communities to improve the browsing and so attract more animals to clearings. Whichever, these small-scale clearings marked the beginning of moorland formation. Hazel scrub and herbaceous plant communities become more common and, in the Pennines, pollen sequences from sites in the vicinity of known Mesolithic occupation display evidence for the spread of heather. In a few areas, for example central Dartmoor and the high Pennines, blanket bog may have begun to form at this time (Staines 1979; Tinsley 1981, 215).

Small-scale clearances continued to be made through the Neolithic period. Early farming communities settled round the fringes of the uplands, but apparently made little use of the high ground, except where the presence of fine stone for tool-making attracted them. After about 2000 bc this began to change, and major clearances of upland areas began. The Fountains Earth pollen diagram, from a topogenous bog at 365m OD in the Pennines of North Yorkshire, allows the first major onslaught in this area to be dated to 1930 ± 100 bc (GaK-2934; Tinsley 1981, 240), whereas further south at Leash Fen, Derbyshire, clearances began a little later at about 1500 ± 110 bc (GaK-2287; Hicks 1971). On Dartmoor, clearance probably began about 2500 bc if not earlier (Staines 1979). In many areas, this opening up of the higher ground was accompanied by the spread of arable cultivation into upland areas, and during the later prehistoric climatic optimum, between about 1500 and 800 bc, many such areas were heavily settled, with highly organized and well-planned agricultural landscapes (Spratt and Burgess 1985; Fleming 1978; 1983a; 1983b).

The postulated climatic deterioration in the centuries after 800 bc may have been partly or wholly responsible for a widespread retreat of settlement from the uplands (J Turner 1981, 256; Barber 1982). Fields and settlements were abandoned, and on Dartmoor in particular there is evidence that blanket bog developed over some of these former settlement areas. Closely connected with this episode of cultivation followed by abandonment was the podsolization and gleying of soils (Limbrey 1975, 154–60; Curtis *et al* 1976, 54–69). The upland fringes continued to be used, and there was some occupation on the higher ground during the Iron Age, albeit at a much reduced level compared with earlier times. Soil erosion became a problem in the early first millennium bc, and some of what are now regarded as typical upland features, such as tors and limestone pavements, were exposed.

By the beginning of the Roman period the upland moors had probably taken on the characteristics still seen today, and during the Roman period occupation remained at a low intensity. Northern areas especially were heavily used for military training, and as frontier zones. Minerals were extracted wherever possible. All of these activities contributed much to the archaeological wealth of the uplands, but the landscape itself was altered very little (Todd 1986). Post-Roman times represent the nadir of settlement on the upland moors (Mytum 1986).

From the ninth century AD, a slight improvement in climate promoted greater use of upland moors, and for perhaps 300–400 years settlement increased in density, reaching a peak in the twelfth and thirteenth centuries. At Farnacre on Bodmin Moor, a settlement was established at nearly 305m OD.[105] Place-names and charters often use the term 'moor' to describe settlements in the uplands, for example Moretonhampstead on the eastern edge of Dartmoor, confirming that such landscapes were well established by the medieval period. Royal hunting forests were created on the upland moors, as the open landscapes provided ideal conditions for the chase. About one-third of all Royal Forests were established on moorland, mostly at altitudes of between 300 and 600m OD. Dartmoor Forest, which covered 20,000ha, was one of the most extensive and was far larger than any wooded forest. Monastic exploitation of upland moors for grazing was extensive (Rackham 1986, 308–9).

In later medieval and post-medieval times, the intensity of occupation in upland areas declined. The grazing of cattle and, more recently, of sheep took over as the most usual farming practice, sometimes on a seasonal basis as a small-scale transhumance system based on the surrounding lowlands (Moorhouse 1986). The agricultural revolution had little effect on the high moorland, although substantial areas of moorland fringe were enclosed and improved to the extent that present-day farmed landscapes in upland areas largely result from this period. The exploitation of minerals continued and in some areas, such as Dartmoor and the Pennines, supported substantial communities which left behind a wealth of industrial monuments. Metal ores and stone were the chief resources exploited (Linsley and Falconer 1986).

Today, most upland moors are experiencing another episode of intensifying exploitation (Allaby 1983; Countryside Commission 1978a). Many traditional forms of land-use are being pursued on a hitherto unprecedented scale, while new demands are also being placed upon these isolated areas. Perhaps the most remarkable change in land-use is the emergence of multiple uses for the same land. Thus, moorland used for grazing and recreation might also serve as a water-catchment area or perhaps as a military training ground for part of the year. Mineral exploitation has tended to become more nucleated, but the range of minerals sought has expanded to include lead, silver, zinc, coal, stone, slate, clays, tin, copper, gold, fluorspar, barytes, and iron.

The upland moors have also been recognized for their recreational and amenity value. All of the seven National Parks in England contain substantial areas of upland moor. The population remains thinly scattered in upland areas, and the moorlands themselves are virtually unoccupied (Countryside Commission 1984).

Upland moors are often owned as common land, but substantial tracts are in private hands while other areas are owned by water authorities or the Crown.

14.3   The archaeology of upland moors

The wealth and diversity of archaeological evidence on upland moors has been highlighted by recent surveys, such as those covering Bodmin Moor, parts of Dartmoor, the Cheviots, Exmoor, and parts of the Lake District, and also by excavations, particularly those on Dartmoor and Cheviot (Darvill 1986a, ch 3). All show that archaeological sites on these moors have a number of distinctive characteristics. First, those which are built of stone usually survive as standing monuments. Second, most sites have a very thin soil cover, in some cases little more than matted vegetation. Third, features such as pits and ditches are very rare, largely because the bedrock is so hard. However, this does not mean that upland sites are stratigraphically more simple than their lowland counterparts.

No useful divisions of the evidence can be made on the basis of the location or occurrence of sites, and the following review is therefore arranged as a series of themes, reflecting the main

Figure 126 Prehistoric settlements on upland moorland: A (top) round house on Craddock Moor, Bodmin, Cornwall; B (bottom) enclosure under excavation at Shaugh Moor, Dartmoor

Figure 127 Crosby Ravensworth West, Cumbria: late prehistoric and Romano-British farmstead/hamlet comprising buildings, yards, enclosures, and paddocks with larger enclosures beyond

classes of site represented. It is important to re-emphasize that settlement on most upland moorland has been episodic, in the sense that during certain periods these areas were intensively utilized and at other times were hardly used at all. The cause of this largely lies in the changing environment and in the economic and social pressures brought to bear by communities living in the more populous lowlands around about. The effect of these fluctuations in archaeological terms is that there are, as it were, a series of tide-lines of cultural evidence, representing the limits of occupation at different times. The most frequently exploited areas lie within what are now the moorland fringes; the least often used are the higher and more remote areas.

Settlements

Settlements are probably the most numerous type of site in upland areas, and they are known in many different forms. From early prehistoric times mention may be made of the hunter-gatherer sites, often represented by little more than scatters of worked flints, dominated by broken weapons and tools used in making and mending weapons. These were probably temporary encampments, perhaps in seasonal hunting grounds. In the Pennines, most upland camps of Mesolithic date lie in the altitude range 350 to 500m OD, probably because here the tree cover was slightly thinner (Jacobi 1978b). Caves, where present, were used for shelter and also for burial throughout prehistoric times.

Settlements of the early farming communities on the uplands appear to be very few; one enclosure has been identified at Helman Tor, Bodmin Moor, Cornwall (Mercer 1981b, 91), and elsewhere there are a few stray finds of flints, stone tools, and pottery which hint at small-scale settlements. By the later Neolithic, more widespread settlement is known, and from the Bronze Age, evidence is abundant. Circular houses with timber or stone foundations became the norm right across England, some upland examples being up to 10m in diameter, giving them a floor area greater than most small houses built today (Fig 126). The arrangement and situation of the houses varies enormously from area to area, and probably through time as well. Three general patterns can be discerned. First, there are dispersed structures occurring as single buildings, often scattered amongst fields and paddocks. Second, there are clusters of anything up to 20 structures set in a line along the contour of a hillside or nucleated on a piece of flat ground. Third, there are enclosed groups of anything up to 60 buildings set within a palisaded or stone-walled enclosure. Not all of these structures were used as houses, however: some were animal shelters and storage buildings. Hilltop enclosures and hillforts of Bronze Age and Iron Age date are known, for example at Stowes Pound on Bodmin Moor,[106] Shoulsbury on Exmoor, Mam Tor on the Pennines in Derbyshire, and literally hundreds of examples on the Cheviots of Northumberland (Gates 1983). Some of the structures loosely termed hillforts in northern England are, however, little more than defended farmsteads.

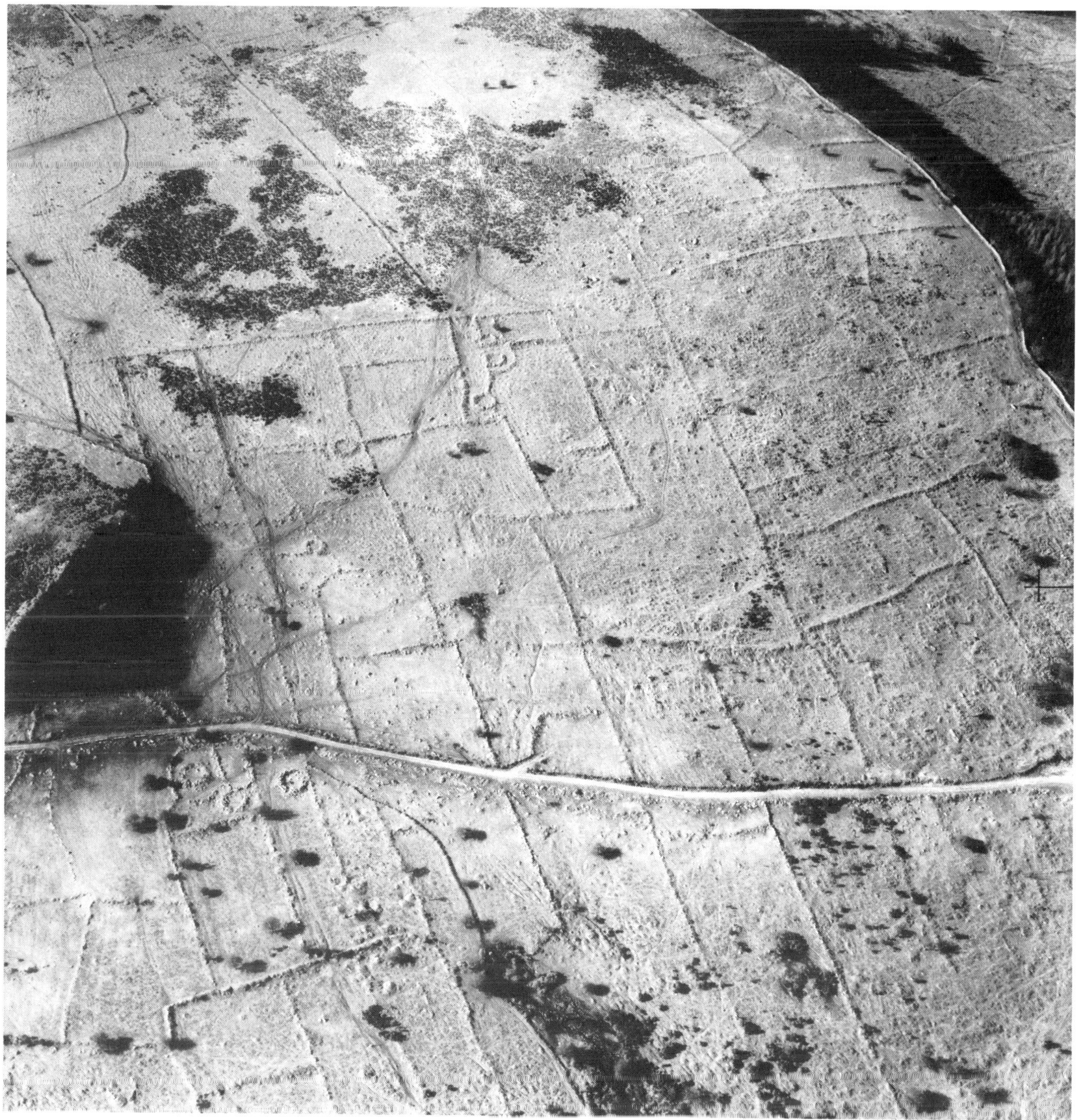

Figure 128 Aerial view of Horridge Common, Dartmoor, showing the well-preserved prehistoric field system with circular buildings scattered widely within it; the rectilinear form of the layout can be clearly seen

Figure 129   Bronze Age reave under excavation at Shaugh Moor, Dartmoor: this cross-section through the reave shows its construction from soil and stone and the old ground surface (dark line) preserved beneath it

Figure 130   Rabbit warrens and old field boundaries at Ditsworthy Warren, Dartmoor: rectangular ditched rabbit warrens can be seen spread widely across the hillslope; an earthwork runs across the bottom right-hand corner of the picture

Where Romano-British settlements have been recorded, as for example at Crosby Ravensworth, Cumbria (Fig 127), round-houses predominate, and clustered, or enclosed, sites seem to have been usual (*see* papers in Clack and Haselgrove 1982). By the medieval period, when the intensity of land-use in many upland areas again increased, the house styles had changed somewhat and long-houses appear to have been universal (Fleming and Ralph 1982; Pearce 1985 on Dartmoor). There are many variations in the design of these long-houses, some consisting of little more than living quarters, while others included byres and barns on either side of the living area. Villages and hamlets can be identified, often still preserved in very good order. At Hound Tor, Dartmoor, excavations revealed that occupation began in the eleventh century and continued through to about the fourteenth century (G Beresford 1979). In contrast, at Simy Folds in Upper Teesdale, settlement began rather earlier in the eighth century. The inhabitants of this farmstead were also involved in ironworking (Coggins *et al* 1983).

Settlements of late medieval and post-medieval date are scarce on upland moors, except where a few workers' houses cluster round some industrial site, or where a seasonal residence was established as part of a transhumance system.

Field systems and agricultural facilities

Close to many settlements are traces of field systems and sites connected with food production. Among the earliest and most spectacular are the field systems on Dartmoor which were laid out about 1500 bc, probably as part of a carefully planned reorganization of the landscape and of the definition of landholdings (Fig 128). The main archaeological evidence for these divisions is a complicated series of low stone banks or reaves (Fig 129), which not only divided areas of high open moorland from more intensively-used land, but also defined fields, paddocks, and grazing areas (Fleming 1982; 1983b; 1985). Survey suggests that over 1000ha were enclosed by reave systems, and so far over 250km of reaves have been located. Despite much searching, nothing quite comparable has been found elsewhere, although on a more limited scale stone boundary banks marking out fields and grazing areas have been found around settlements in most moorland areas which show traces of occupation, notably in the Peak District of Derbyshire, on the North York Moors, and on Bodmin Moor (*see* papers in Spratt and Burgess 1985; Spratt 1982).

Medieval field systems tend to be smaller than prehistoric examples, with more emphasis on enclosed 'infields', within which may be traces of rig-and-furrow (or run-rig), and less elaborate boundaries for outfields and grazing areas (Feachem 1973; Pearce 1985). In some cases, medieval fields simply reused or modified existing prehistoric boundaries, and indeed on moorland fringes it is often possible to see that prehistoric alignments preserved in moorland continue into enclosed land as modern boundaries.

Scattered widely across areas of upland moor which at some time in the past have been used for cultivation there are clearance cairns, comprising piles of stones collected during field clearance. They can sometimes be confused with burial cairns, and indeed the functions of these two types of structure were sometimes interchangable; burial monuments proved suitable places to pile stones during clearance, while a convenient clearance cairn often provided a ready-made burial monument. A survey of Danby Rigg, North Yorkshire, recorded over 600 clearance cairns within an area of only 1 square kilometre (A Harding 1984). Dating the construction of such cairns is most difficult.

Post-medieval use of upland moors for grazing has produced its own distinctive archaeology, including sheep folds, pens, shelters, sheep creeps through walls on semi-enclosed moorland, and shielings and summer residences for seasonal use. Rabbit warrens or pillow mounds are known to have been built from the twelfth century onwards, and a particularly fine group is known at Ditsworthy Warren, Dartmoor (Fig 130;

Figure 131   Chew Green, Northumberland: a series of six forts of different sizes beside Dere Street (right) running northwards across the Cheviots

Figure 132   Hardknott Fort, Cumbria: aerial view of the fort and associated bath house, situated overlooking Hard Knott Pass which provides a major east–west route through the Lake District

Lineham 1966). Vermin traps of characteristic cross-shaped design are often associated with these warrens (Hansford Worth 1967). Hunting is represented by shooting butts and hunting stands of various sorts.

Military monuments

Another aspect of the upland settlement pattern is the military use of what are now upland moors. This was most intensive during Roman times. Hadrian's Wall, defining the northern boundary of the Roman province of Britannia, runs across the northern upland moors of the Whin Sill in Northumberland (Breeze and Dobson 1976). In addition there are numerous forts, fortlets, camps, and signal stations. The group at Chew Green, Northumberland (Fig 131), is particularly impressive, as there are no fewer than six overlapping but superimposed forts of different sizes (Frere and St Joseph 1983, 140–2). Some military establishments were temporary and short-lived, but among the more permanent was Hardknott Fort, built high in

the Lake District (Fig 132) to control movements across the high ground. Later fortifications are not common on upland moors but, along the Scottish border country, bastles, tower houses, and peel towers are occasionally found on the high ground and represent defended farmsteads (Ramm *et al* 1970).

Ritual and ceremonial monuments

Ritual and ceremonial sites on upland moors are perhaps the best known and certainly among the most diverse types of evidence in this landscape category. Neolithic chambered cairns, although rare, are widespread and may hint at more extensive upland occupation at this time than is often imagined. Fine examples are known on Bodmin Moor at Bearah[107] and on the Pennines at Bradley Moor (Feather and Manby 1970). It is with the expansion of settlement during the second millennium bc, however, that most ritual and ceremonial sites on upland moors are associated. There is often clear evidence for the distinction between ritual sites and settlements and

Figure 133   Bronze Age round cairn under excavation at Shaugh Moor, Dartmoor

fields, perhaps because ritual sites were set in less intensively-used grazing zones which were peripheral to occupation areas, or perhaps because communities set aside portions of the landscape as ritual/ceremonial retreats. Burial mounds, either singly or as groups in small cemeteries, are characteristic of all areas (Fig 133) and were often situated on hilltops or prominent places. Over 250 such cairns are now known on Bodmin Moor as a result of a survey carried out between 1982 and 1985. Many different shapes and sizes can be distinguished, some of them very elaborate and complicated in form. Ring cairns, platform cairns, and embanked circles are further variations in the range of burial monuments represented in the uplands (cf Lynch 1972).

Stone circles (Fig 134), stone rows, stone avenues, and standing stones are also widespread and sometimes occur in spectacular groupings, such as the Hurlers on Bodmin Moor, Merrivale on Dartmoor, and Burn Moor in the Lake District.[108] The exact function of these sites is far from clear, although a ceremonial role seems likely. During Roman times there were a few temples and shrines associated with military installations, for example the temple of Mithras at Carrawburgh, just to the south of Hadrian's Wall. During the post-Roman and early medieval periods, carved stone crosses and inscribed stones were erected, but the settlements in upland areas were too small to contain established churches, and while monastic land-holdings in the uplands were extensive, the focus of these estates was invariably on lower ground.

Industrial monuments

Industrial sites are common on almost every area of upland moor, because a tremendous range of natural resources was

Figure 134   Bronze Age stone circle at Divock Cockpit, Cumbria

Figure 135   Great Langdale, Cumbria: A (left) scree slope comprising debris from Neolithic quarrying and stone-working; B (right) Neolithic flaking floor (scale totals 1m)

exploited. Among the earliest are the Neolithic stone quarries, such as those round Great Langdale in the Lake District (Fig 135), which today comprise extensive scree deposits, resulting from the quarrying and flaking of stone for the production of axes and other implements (Houlder 1979; Bradley *et al* 1985; Quartermaine and Claris 1986). The demand for metals — copper, tin, and lead — during the Bronze Age may have been one factor in the expansion of settlement into upland areas, and almost certainly underlies the wealth of archaeology represented on Dartmoor and Bodmin Moor. Unfortunately, much of the evidence for prehistoric exploitation of metal ores has disappeared in the course of more recent exploitation, which has been on a much larger scale. Tin streaming is, however, known on Dartmoor to date to before Roman times, and continued to be widespread in the south-west through the medieval and post-medieval periods. The distinctive braided channels of streaming works, together with leats, dams, and reservoirs associated with water control, are still prominent features of the landscape (Greeves 1985; Crossley 1981).

With the introduction of water-powered, and later steam-powered, machinery, the scale of operations at mines and quarries increased greatly. Much evidence of these workings still survives, especially engine and wheel houses, waste tips, leats, crushing mills, and blowing houses. Even prospecting for resources has left its traces as trial pits and investigatory shafts. Much of this evidence is of course restricted in its distribution, because of the limited outcrops of the particular materials being exploited; the wealth and variety of evidence results from the great range of materials exploited.

In addition to metal ore, coal, stone, and minerals were also worked. Lime burning was a major industry in the central Pennines (Fig 136), and, on the upland fringes, fulling mills and water-powered processing plants sprang up from late medieval times onwards. Peat digging, evidenced by turbaries and peat drying platforms of various sorts, was widespread and provided a major source of fuel.

Trackways and roads

Communications within and across upland areas have always been a problem because of the difficult terrain. Long-distance tracks of prehistoric date are not known with certainty, but on a more localized scale droveways and tracks are well represented, linking settlements and joining occupation areas with their fields. Roman roads across upland areas are among the most spectacular examples in the country. Some, like Dere Street, Northumberland, leading north from Hadrian's Wall across the Cheviots, were essentially military roads, but others were probably built to facilitate the movement of materials from upland extraction sites.

In medieval and post-medieval times drove roads led down from the uplands to market towns round about, and transhumance tracks can sometimes be traced. After the industrial revolution, tramways often brought materials from quarries and mines down to the railheads and canals which criss-crossed the uplands and provided the means of transporting raw materials to factories and workshops elsewhere.

Boundaries

Boundary works, except those connected with field systems, are relatively rare on upland moors. Marker stones were sometimes placed along parish or county boundaries in post-medieval times, but often large blocks of moorland fell within single administrative units, and so boundaries rarely run across them (Pearce 1985 for Dartmoor evidence).

Field archaeology on upland moors

The location and recording of sites on upland moorland is perhaps easier than for any other landscape category, once the basic skills of recognizing, interpreting, and plotting the field evidence have been acquired. Two methods are commonly used, both involving the application of aerial photography and field survey. In the first, information from all available aerial photographs is plotted onto base maps, which are then taken into the field and checked on the ground in detail. Features which did not show on the photographs are added, and any which prove to be natural removed. In the second, fieldwork provides the primary stage, the evidence later being compared with available aerial cover, preparatory to a further phase of field survey to check results and clear up any outstanding ambiguities. Whichever course is followed, field survey is an important part of the work, but one accompanied by special problems in the uplands (Mercer 1980c; 1982). Field survey is really only practical in the late winter and early spring, which of course coincides with the most inhospitable weather. However, when undertaken thoroughly, field survey can often reveal evidence of relationships between features; on occasion, therefore, the relative dates of monuments can be determined. Phosphate surveys, and to a lesser extent geophysical surveys, also have a useful role to play in recording sites on upland moors (Balaam and Porter 1982).

It is noticeable that much of what is currently known of the archaeology on upland moors relates to stone monuments. This of course represents the upstanding archaeology and is the easiest to record. Where extensive excavation has taken place, however, it is clear that stone structures were often preceded by wooden ones, now represented by buried postholes, slots, and soilmarks. The first phase of some of the reaves on Dartmoor, for example, was wooden fences, and the first phase of many buildings which have been excavated is also a timber one (Fleming 1985). One important question is that of the number of sites which were built only in timber and never in stone, and which are therefore now invisible on the surface. Wood was widely available during the earlier prehistoric period, and some of the gaps in existing knowledge of settlement during the Mesolithic and Neolithic may simply result from the use of rather different construction techniques and materials during these periods.

14.4 Threats

Upland moors have been used for many different purposes over the centuries, often quite intensively but mostly episodically. Over the last two decades, a new phase of intensive exploitation has been gaining momentum. Many traditional land-uses remain, for example grazing, military training, and mineral extraction, but are now pursued on an unprecedented scale (Darvill 1986a, ch 5; 1986b). New demands are being made on upland moors, for example recreation and water catchment, and, perhaps most worrying of all, more productive uses are being found for what is essentially low grade land as technology and capital become available to make such projects viable.[109]

The following activities can be singled out for comment as they pose significant threats to the archaeological heritage of upland moors.

Moorland conversion

The practice of taking moorland into more intensive use is widespread. The most common changes involve conversion to improved pasture through ploughing, drainage, and reseeding, or afforestation. In either case ground clearance works, usually involving stone clearance and ploughing of some sort, are a crucial part of the scheme. Large areas of landscape are usually involved. In northern England forestry is the biggest problem (Fig 137) while in the south west the improvement of grazing is the major cause for concern (Fig 138).

Moorland conversion takes place in a piecemeal and insidious fashion. Most at risk are moorland fringes, which in

Figure 136   Post-medieval furnace at Grassington, North Yorkshire

Figure 137   Ploughing in advance of afforestation on the Cheviots, Northumberland

archaeological terms are highly sensitive because it is here that the most diverse range of sites is found. Bodmin Moor illustrates the process of encroachment very clearly (N Johnson 1983). Land improvements along the main river valleys dissecting the uplands fragmented the moorland. As more land was improved, so the total length of moorland edge increased and this in turn put more areas at risk. Also vulnerable are pockets of moorland surrounded by improved land, since modern technology makes their incorporation both possible and economically desirable (Darvill 1986a, 5.3).

In addition to improving the land itself, moorland conversion often involves the creation of new access roads and tracks. This in itself can cause damage to monuments unless routes are carefully selected. Perhaps of greater importance, however, is the fact that it allows machinery and equipment access to land which was previously beyond reach.

Mineral extraction and quarrying

The extraction of minerals affects archaeological sites not just in terms of the holes dug to acquire the reserves but also through the dumping of waste and the construction of plant and ancillary buildings. One of the most dramatic cases in recent years concerned china clay workings on Dartmoor. Excavations of very well-preserved Bronze Age field systems, settlements, and ritual monuments at Shaugh Moor were made necessary by the expansion of waste tips (Balaam *et al* 1982). Similar problems have also been posed at Crown Hill Down, Devon, where waste from tungsten mines threatens to smother

a large portion of landscape preserving some outstanding Bronze Age features.[110]

Possibly because of their characteristic hilltop position, hillforts seem to be especially at risk from quarrying. Meg Dyke, West Yorkshire (Faull and Moorhouse 1981), for example, has had its interior virtually quarried away, leaving only the ramparts. At West Whelpington, Northumberland (Fig 139), a deserted medieval village is being progressively destroyed as the hill on which it stands is quarried away for whinstone (M Beresford and St Joseph 1979, 129–32).

Natural erosion

Localized, but nonetheless serious, damage to sites can result from natural erosion such as soil movement and peat decay, which may or may not be triggered by human agency. At Blackstone Edge, Greater Manchester, for example, water draining down the hill-slope is washing away parts of the exposed ancient road surface, causing pitting, deposition of silt, and the loosening of the metalling (*see* chapter 6.4; Walker 1984). Over a longer period, the despoliation which led to the creation of limestone pavements in Cumbria has effectively sterilized a number of archaeological sites by leaving only the stone outlines of once-impressive huts and field boundaries.[111] Wind erosion was contributory to the displacement of Mesolithic material from the surface of Stanage Barrows in the Pennines (Henderson 1979). Acid rain may also be taking its toll on the peat overburden which covers many sites on upland moors (chapter 6.4).

Visitor erosion and vandalism

Tourists, farm animals, motor-cross riders, and horse riders are individually or collectively responsible for considerable erosion on archaeological sites on upland moors. This is especially true in areas close to large centres of population, where footpaths and bridleways cut deep into underlying soil

The problems encountered along Hadrian's Wall have prompted a thorough review of visitor management (HWCC 1984). Comparable cases on a slightly smaller scale can be cited at Grimspound, Dartmoor, and Altarnun Nine Stones, Bodmin Moor (Darvill 1986a, 5.2f). Visitor erosion can also lead to the acceleration of natural erosion. The large-scale removal of Neolithic axe-working debris from scree slopes at Great Langdale in the Lake District is a particular cause for concern.

Vandalism tends to be confined to sites in the vicinity of areas of high population, for example in the Pennines. Because moorlands are easy of access, respect for property seems to be reduced.

Industrial monuments suffer especially badly from graffiti, stone robbing, and, sometimes, illicit dumping of rubbish. Caves are vulnerable to damage, often quite unintentional, from cavers digging out floor deposits to gain access to deeper chambers or to enlarge passages. Such deposits may contain archaeological layers.

Public utilities

The impact upon archaeology of road widening, car-park construction, waste disposal, and the building of pipelines and reservoirs should not be underestimated. The Colliford Reservoir on Bodmin Moor involved the drowning of over 3.7 square kilometres of land rich in archaeological remains, which ranged in date from the Mesolithic through to the post-medieval period (Griffiths 1984). Water erosion round the edges of large reservoirs through fluctuating water levels is a constant source of damage.

While there are few new reservoirs planned which will affect moorland, hydroelectric schemes and other new types of public utility look set to have an effect in due course.

14.5 Management

Upland moors are probably the least intensively managed parts of the English countryside and have been for centuries. This factor, coupled with the conservatism of many landowners and the relative isolation of most upland moors, has largely been responsible for the survival, in good condition, of such a wealth of archaeological evidence. But, although archaeological sites on upland moors are often made of robust materials, structurally they are very fragile: walls can easily be toppled, banks broken down, and cairns dispersed. As the demands placed upon moorland increase, so too does the need for active management, even if it is only active in the sense of resistance to change.[112]

In addition to being of immense archaeological importance, upland moors are also valued for their wildlife, game reserves, rich flora, and their general landscape interest (Ratcliffe 1977, 288–93). Because of this, there is often a good deal of common ground between the aims of archaeological management schemes and those of other countryside interests, particularly the Nature Conservancy Council (1983d), the National Park Authorities (CNP 1984b), and the Countryside Commission (1984). There is also much interest among the general public in maintaining upland landscapes much as they are today (MacEwen and Sinclair 1983).

In formulating management strategies for archaeological monuments on upland moors, the following two factors must be taken into account:

Figure 138   Aerial view of land improvements and the enclosure of improved grazing at Widecombe-in-the-Moor, Devon

Figure 139   Whelpington, Northumberland: deserted medieval village with exceptionally clear croft boundaries; the site was abandoned before the mid eighteenth century, but is now under threat from stone quarrying, which will eventually mean its total destruction

i   Size of sites: many monuments cover substantial areas and comprise a series of related or potentially related components. Such areas should ideally be managed as a single unit, although this can be difficult when more than one landowner is involved.

ii   Diversity of evidence: the circumstances of preservation at different types of sites within a small area can vary greatly, for example masonry structures which are upstanding, earthworks which are covered in vegetation, and earth and stone features which are uncovered. Each may require slightly different treatment within the overall strategy.

Curatorial management

Minimizing disturbance to archaeological sites is the key to preserving monuments on upland moors. Soil cover is usually thin, which means that there is a very fine balance between preserving a site and exposing it to decay.

At present, there are about 700 Scheduled Monuments in moorland areas,[113] including a wide range of monument types. Recent surveys have, however, emphasized the fact that much more survives in these areas than had previously been realized, and that in due course an even greater range of monuments must be taken into the schedule to make it representative.

The selection of sites on upland moors for scheduling is made difficult by the fact that so many sites are still in good condition; questions of survival often have to be combined with those of group value and diversity in order to pick out areas of landscape which display a range of contemporary, and therefore presumably interrelated, monuments. Since some periods and types of monument are apparently poorly represented, at least by upstanding evidence, special attention has to be given to preserving those sites in order to maintain a balanced picture of the evidence. Few sites on upland moors are well documented, but those which are deserve special attention. The potential for understanding how communities lived and worked when virtually their entire landscape is available for study is clearly immense.

Moorland as a landscape category is subject to a number of controls and constraints when it lies within a National Park, and this indirectly serves to help preserve the archaeological remains in these areas. National Park Authorities are obliged to compile maps showing areas of moor or heath where, in the opinion of the authority, the conservation of natural beauty is particularly important.[114] These maps in turn provide the basis for assessing the impact of planning applications. In addition, a notification procedure operates on moorland conversions, and National Park Authorities can use their powers to block potentially damaging agricultural works.

The wealth and abundance of archaeological remains on upland moors means that the survival of this resource still rests largely in the hands of landowners and land-users. Most forms of traditional management are largely compatible with preserving sites, which is how they have survived up until now.

Stocking levels need to be carefully monitored to prevent overgrazing. Some sort of vegetation cover needs to be maintained wherever possible, and accordingly the rotational burning of heather moors in patches or strips prevents large areas being exposed to soil loss. Bracken needs to be controlled, ideally by spraying rather than by mechanical means, since tractors and machines can cause much damage to upstanding

Figure 140 Party visiting an engine house at Minions, Bodmin Moor, Cornwall

monuments. Stone clearance, or the use of ancient cairns as a ready source of stones for building, must be avoided at all costs.

Generally speaking, areas given over to multiple land-use are less at risk than areas with a single use. Likewise, moors in communal ownership are on the whole less at risk than areas under private ownership, where the incentive and capacity to undertake improvement schemes is greater. In all cases, the most vulnerable areas are moorland fringes, and here great care to protect monuments is needed.

Recording

Upstanding evidence constitutes the largest part of what is known from upland moors. Large monuments can be easily seen, but only experience at recognizing more subtle features will allow identification of smaller monuments. Vegetation and lighting conditions often play an important part in seeing significant evidence, and it must be expected that even detailed survey will bring to light only about 80% of what is actually present (N Johnson 1983). Completely buried sites do from time to time come to light, and landowners and land-users should be alert to the implications of ground disturbance works. They should also be encouraged to report any finds so that they can be properly recorded and if necessary conserved.

Survey work on upland moors is rather different from survey work in other types of landscape. The safety of personnel has to be given special attention and proper provision made for emergencies. Access is often difficult and usually necessitates four-wheel-drive vehicles and equipment which can be carried easily over rough terrain. The practicalities of surveying and systematically searching a landscape in which there are few references points must also be considered (Mercer 1980c).

Rescue excavation is subject to much the same constraints as survey work. When they arise, threats tend to involve large areas of upland landscape, so that excavation often has to be selective. Fortunately, where detailed survey and excavation can be combined, high cost-effectiveness is possible since only key points need to be examined in detail.

In formulating management plans, it is important to determine the extent and character of the sites, the degree to which monuments may be interrelated and therefore worth treating as a single unit, and the conditions of soil and vegetation cover.[115] Voids in the distribution of sites do occur, especially on very high moorland, and these may be identified and, if other circumstances are favourable, recommended for uses which are incompatible with preserving archaeological remains.

Exploitative management

Many areas of upland moor provide excellent opportunities for the interpretation and display of monuments. Easy access is relatively widespread through *de facto* rights, and most monuments can withstand a certain degree of visitor attention without any adverse effects (Fig 140). Management of visitors at more popular sites is, however, necessary.

At present, there are seven sites in State Guardianship on upland moors, among them the stone circles at the Hurlers, Bodmin Moor, the Merrivale ceremonial complex and the Hound Tor deserted medieval village on Dartmoor, Hardknott Roman fort in the Lake District, and much of Hadrian's Wall in Northumberland. Many other monuments lie within National Trust holdings on upland moors.

Recreation and leisure use of upland moorland tends to be informal, and so self-guided trails and guided walks provide a less intensive form of exploiting the potential of sites (Darvill 1986a, appendix C; Countryside Commission 1978b; 1980a; 1980b).

Upland sites also have a good educational value, because relatively complete landscapes can be examined and the relationships between sites clearly seen. Moreover, because monuments are well preserved, the evidence is easier to see and explain. Archaeological sites have much potential as components within a more broadly-based tourist economy, which can stimulate jobs and income for upland areas. Several National Park Authorities are promoting the tourist potential of selected archaeological monuments on upland moorland.

Academic interest in upland areas is high. Many university departments use upland areas for training and for research. Again, the main appeal lies in the quality of preservation and the completeness of the evidence (Darvill 1986a, ch 8).

IV   Looking forward

In this final chapter, two important questions are addressed. Why are the ancient monuments of the countryside worth bothering with at all? And where do we go from here? The answer to the second of these questions is not intended as a rigid policy statement in itself; the purpose is rather to touch upon a number of points from which a rolling programme of action can be developed.

15   Ancient monuments in the countryside today and tomorrow

15.1   The importance of the past

The ancient monuments of the English countryside provide a direct link with our past – a link with our ancestors who built and used these sites anything up to a quarter of a million years ago. Archaeology is the study of those now vanished societies through the remains they left behind, but the value of the remains themselves lies not only in what they can tell us about the past, but also in what they can offer to society as a whole today.[116]

In looking towards the future of ancient monuments in the countryside, it is perhaps helpful to review first some of the different ways in which the archaeological heritage contributes to our everyday lives and to the quality of life in general. This can be considered under five headings.

Landscape and environment

In the broadest terms, the English landscape which we cherish today is an archaeological artefact, modified and changed by man for many thousands of years. Very little of what can be seen today is actually 'natural': there are not only the obvious remains of man's activities, but also the characteristics of the whole landscapes which have been shaped by human occupation and use at some period, as described in chapters 6–14. Archaeological monuments in their day represented key points in the lives of their makers and, over the course of time, became integral components of the countryside. Barrows, standing stones, Roman camps, deserted villages, and hillforts, to name but a few types of site, are just as much a part of the landscape as open moors, rounded hills, leafy valleys, and twisting lanes (Fig 141). To remove archaeological monuments is to alter the appearance of the landscape and to deprive the countryside of its chronological depth.

As a discipline, archaeology helps to provide an understanding of the landscape and the environment: it is an aid to the appreciation of evolution in the past and to the prediction of the consequences of change in the future.

Educational and academic value

The study of mankind is of paramount importance to the understanding of modern society, and archaeology, the essential focus of which is the study of man and human societies through the ages, is an indispensable foundation to our understanding of history.

The only source of information for the history of England during most of its past is archaeological evidence. Even for recent periods, archaeology provides information about the conditions of life that documentary sources hardly ever record. Therefore, the sites and monuments in the countryside provide a key component of the academic data bank relating to our past.

Archaeological research and the information contained in archaeological sites also make a valuable contribution to other academic disciplines, notably geography, biology, botany, palynology, anthropology, and sociology. Such contributions include details of the spread of animal and plant species, the history and incidence of disease among past human and animal communities, the development of social organization, and the history of our natural vegetation.

In practical terms, archaeological monuments offer valuable teaching resources for schools. The remains, being three-dimensional, can readily stimulate the imagination of children. In addition, they are predictable: their visible existence will not be affected by the season or the weather (Fig 142).

At university level and in adult education, archaeological studies bridge the gap between the human and the natural sciences and provide important contributions to environmental studies of many kinds. Extra-mural departments cater for thousands of adult archaeology students each year, many of whom see it as a way of getting to know more about the landscape in which they live and the way in which their predecessors lived. Archaeological programmes are broadcast on both television and radio.

Leisure and recreation

Arguably the single largest growth area within archaeology is the use of sites for their value as leisure and recreation amenities (Fig 143A). Studies by the Countryside Commission show that visiting archaeological sites and places of historic interest is among the top ten of the most popular tourist activities in most areas (Countryside Commission 1985). Over 650,000 visitors were recorded at Stonehenge, Wiltshire, in 1986, and nationally it is estimated that over four million visits were made to the monuments in the care of English Heritage in 1986/87. The development of this side of archaeological management is of course closely linked to the expansion of tourism and recreation generally, but it has met with so much success principally because archaeological remains have a number of fundamental advantages for their use in this way.

One important feature of archaeological sites and monuments is that they can be exploited in many different ways. At one level, the fact that a proportion of sites, such as barrows, hillforts, and deserted villages, are marked on Ordnance Survey outdoor leisure maps means that they provide points of interest for walkers, hikers, and pony trekkers. For the more dedicated, walking may be incidental to the visiting of sites, perhaps for sheer enjoyment or to use them as subjects and inspiration for photography, painting, drawing, or writing. Self-guided trails represent the next level of exploitation, in which sites along a suitable route are selected and described. With the aid of such trails, the sense of discovery and exploration, which provides such an important component of visits to sites, is retained, and in many areas, such as the uplands of England, there is every likelihood that once a visitor arrives at a site described in the guidebook, there will be other things to see in the immediate vicinity. At the most intensive level of exploitation are the

Figure 141   The British Camp on the Malvern Hills, Hereford and Worcester: a hilltop sculptured by man as a hillfort and later as a castle

Figure 142   School party at North Leigh Roman villa, Oxfordshire, during a special education day organized by English Heritage

Figure 143   Tourism and archaeology: A (above) one of the white-on-brown tourist information signs introduced in 1986, in this case directing visitors to Neolithic tombs in Kent; B (below) signboarding and viewing platform at Crickley Hill Iron Age hillfort, Gloucestershire

fully-presented sites, given over specifically to visitor interests with carefully-planned displays and visitor facilities (Fig 143B). Each of these three levels has a role to play in both formal and informal recreation.

When integrated with other aspects of countryside-based recreation, archaeological sites have a particularly important role to play. Monuments can be visited at almost any time of the year and thus serve to extend the visitor season. Farmhouse breaks, theme holidays, and adventure weekends particularly benefit from this extended season and also from the fact that visible monuments are guaranteed and are not dependent on the vagaries of the weather or the lateness of the season.

Economic value

Much of the value of archaeological resources cannot easily be reduced to figures on a balance sheet, but this does not mean that there are no direct economic attractions.

Income from visitor interest in monuments is not inconsiderable. Direct revenue from entrance fees, car-parking charges, and the sale of merchandise and souvenirs accrue to the owners and managers of ancient monuments.

Less direct income for the owners of monuments, and for local communities in areas where monuments attract tourists and public interest, results from providing services, especially accommodation and food. Public houses, hotels, and guest houses near monuments have often done very well, and there has recently been an increase in the number of farm-based schemes in which the archaeological heritage plays a greater or lesser part. Such schemes minimize the leakage of income from tourist exploitation, as spending is maintained within local economies.

The creation of jobs related to monument management and care entirely depends on how attitudes and policies develop over the next few years. English Heritage itself employs around 150 custodians and a labour force of about 450 skilled

craftsmen and women for the maintenance of properties in care, and there are many more posts in local authorities, archaeological trusts, units, and Manpower Services Commission schemes. As management of the archaeological resource increases, so will opportunities for employment, ranging from seasonal guides through to full-time maintenance contractors.

Aesthetic and psychological value

The past means different things to different people, and many consider the presence of the past as somehow improving the quality of life. Beneath this general concept, however, there is a rather more fundamental trait of human nature which attracts people to ancient monuments.

Understanding, exploring, and conquering the mystery of the past, and seeking answers to the questions posed by ancient monuments, such as stone circles and burial mounds, is something inbuilt in human nature. For many people, the remains of the past provide a sense of security and continuity in an uncertain world, a thread of timelessness running through a rapidly changing environment.

15.2 Foundations for the future

The primary objectives of archaeological resource management are to ensure that the national archaeological heritage of sites, monuments, and ancient buildings remains as large and diverse as possible, and to attempt to relieve conflicts of interest where they occur. Within this framework the objectives of English Heritage can be simply stated. They are to seek the preservation of monuments through the scheduling of those of national importance; to offer grants and management agreements; and to discourage unauthorized work and damage to monuments through advice to, and education of, the public. The first aim is preservation, and the key to that is the identification, protection, and management of the most important monuments.

Much has been learned about the heritage and its management over the last ten years or so, as is illustrated by the chapters in parts II and III of this review. Three main considerations which are crucial to the development of a forward-looking approach to the future management of ancient monuments in the countryside can be identified: the scale of the resource, the practicalities of management, and public interest.

The scale of the resource

A rapid assessment of available records in 1982 revealed that some 650,000 sites had been recorded in England up to that time (HBMC 1984b). This figure is in itself an underestimate of what must actually exist, and of course makes no distinction between the many different types and sizes of monument loosely called sites. It was for the most part based on a trawl through existing records of variable quality. Where areas of landscape have been subject to rigorous and systematic field survey, for example the Cheviots, Salisbury Plain military training areas, and West Penwith, the number of sites known has increased by a factor of perhaps three or four. To this figure also must be added all the 'hidden' sites sealed beneath hillwash, alluvium, and deep soil cover, which have yet to be located and characterized.

The practicalities of management

In the past, many ancient monuments in the countryside have survived by default — often through neglect or by being on

Figure 144   County archaeologist for Wiltshire discussing damage to an ancient monument on Salisbury Plain with representatives from the Army and Property Services Agency

Figure 145   Uffington Castle and White Horse on the Berkshire Ridgeway in Oxfordshire

land which was not extensively used. This has changed with increasing land values and extra incentives to increase output. However, much can be achieved to safeguard monuments in a positive and practical way, by forward planning and by resolving conflicts of interest at an early stage through an appreciation of landscape dynamics and multi-option management strategies in which, quite properly, the needs of the landowner or tenant are worked into an integrated approach to the monuments' well-being (Fig 144).

Public interest

Public interest in archaeology is now at a high level. Membership of local archaeological societies has on the whole been rising over the past decade or so, and membership of English Heritage, which was only launched in 1984, stands at over 86,000 at the time of writing. Attendances at many museums offering traditional types of static display are down, but the more innovative displays can boast increased visitor figures over the last few years.

15.3   The way forward

This book is not intended to answer all questions about archaeology in the countryside, nor to offer management prescriptions to fit every site. The message is essentially that management of archaeological sites can and should be tailored to fit the needs not only of the site but also of the owner. While, in a limited number of cases, the best interests of important monuments may be served by removing them from the mainstream of farming or other countryside activities, in general the well-being of ancient monuments, as of other features in the countryside, depends on a healthy rural economy and an integrated approach to land management.

The future of our monuments in the countryside depends heavily on the initiatives of bodies such as the Countryside Commission, the Nature Conservancy Council, the National Parks, and the local authorities, with whose interests English

Heritage has much in common. It depends even more on the understanding and sympathy of all those landowners and land-users in whose care 95% of archaeological sites will continue to rest. English Heritage, as the statutory body chiefly responsible for the protection and conservation of monuments, must have the main duty of developing a broad framework and objectives for the better protection and enjoyment of our archaeological heritage. Implementation will, however, depend on close liaison with all the other interests involved, and on the development of greater public understanding of the importance of this heritage and the means of preserving it.

At national level, the main task must be to identify those sites which are of such importance that they should be afforded statutory protection by scheduling. It has been estimated that only some 2% of known archaeological sites are currently so protected. On criteria already established, the percentage which ought to be protected is perhaps as much as 10% of the 650,000 or so known sites. English Heritage has already over the last few years been helping counties to improve their records in order to establish a firmer data base for surveying the nation's stock of monuments. A programme to sift out sites which ought not now to be on the Schedule, and to add those which have been omitted, began in 1987 and is expected to continue for some ten years, depending upon the availability of resources.

Scheduling by itself cannot guarantee the future well-being of sites, although it should enable proper consideration to be given to any proposal to carry out work to them. As set out in the preceding chapters, the key to preservation must be plans for management. Proposals to schedule any further sites will therefore be preceded by discussion with the owners and users on the importance of each site and the kind of regime which might be adopted or continued to its benefit. In some cases formal management agreements may be appropriate, but this will depend very much on the pattern of land-use on protected sites and on other factors which may affect the owner's agreement. Regular visits by Field Monument Wardens will also continue to ensure that advice is locally available to farmers and other landowners, and that the state of protected monuments is kept under review.

It is not only Scheduled Monuments that need care and management. Even when the monument survey is complete, some 90% of sites of some importance will be in need of some provision for their future well-being, although it is recognized that not all of these will be capable of long-term preservation. English Heritage will continue to look to other national bodies and local authorities to take account of these sites and to incorporate their needs in development and general management strategies. Schemes such as those adopted in Hampshire and Somerset for the positive management of sensitive areas are very much to be encouraged, and many local authorities, particularly at county level, have the expertise to develop plans on their own initiative. English Heritage remains ready to help and advise, where local expertise is absent.

There remain significant gaps in our understanding of the reserve of archaeological sites and the best way to manage them. It is English Heritage policy to channel funds for rescue excavation and survey work into those areas where, by consensus of the experts both in and out of government, more information is most urgently needed. English Heritage is by no means the only funder of excavations: the Manpower Services Commission and developers have each contributed as much in recent years, in addition to funding from local authorities and other sources. Many of the major and most complex projects are, however, funded very largely by English Heritage, and it must be an objective of these and other projects to bring work to publication stage at the earliest opportunity, so that information can be widely shared.

Survey work directed towards revising and monitoring the reserve of sites is an important component not only of finding out about the past, but also of providing the basic information with which to manage the resource. In addition to purely archaeological surveys, there may be scope for the study of agricultural and other practices which may have a bearing on practical management problems; such studies would have to be undertaken in close cooperation with other countryside interests.

Educational initiatives also need greater emphasis. At the end of the day, the resources available for the preservation of the heritage will depend on public support for that cause. While there is already a good deal of specialized enthusiasm for archaeology around the country, much more needs to be done to increase awareness at every level of society of the remains which exist and their long-term value to the nation.

15.4   The strength of conviction

This volume provides part of the much needed background to ancient monuments in the English countryside, and presents a framework which will allow the quality, quantity, value, and potential of the evidence to be recognized. Traces of man's past use of the countryside provide an important but finite national resource for our own and future generations to draw upon for a wide variety of purposes (Fig 145). The greatest concern now is for the future of the resource. Indeed, it is one of the marks of a civilized society that care is devoted to the management of change, so that resources are not squandered or unthinkingly disposed of for short-term gain.

The way forward undoubtedly lies in balancing demands placed upon the resource against both long-term and short-term value. Most decisions relating to the countryside, whether concerned with the day-to-day running of a farm or with the construction of some new public work, have an environmental dimension to them, and part of that relates to the impact on the archaeological resource. Forward projections of current rates of loss are not acceptable, if anything is to survive into the next century. Effective management, through the careful documentation of the nature and scale of the resource to be managed, the assessment of the management implications of different types of monuments, forward planning, and cooperation with other interests, provides the sensible way forward. Doing nothing is not a sensible management option. Action is needed on a wide front, and taking a pride in the ancient monuments of our countryside is the surest way of providing our past with a secure future.

Appendix A
Names and addresses of archaeological organizations in England

1 Historic Buildings and Monuments Commission for England

For all matters relating to Scheduled Monuments, management agreements, Scheduled Monument Consent, and rescue archaeology, contact staff in Ancient Monuments Division of English Heritage. This Division is arranged, for administrative purposes, into three regional sections, as follows:

Northern

Cheshire, Cleveland, Cumbria, Durham, Greater Manchester, Humberside, Lancashire, Merseyside, Northumberland, North Yorkshire, South Yorkshire, Tyne and Wear, and West Yorkshire.

Midland

Bedfordshire, Buckinghamshire, Cambridgeshire, Derbyshire, Essex, Hereford and Worcester, Hertfortshire, Leicestershire, Lincolnshire, Norfolk, Northamptonshire, Nottinghamshire, Shropshire, Staffordshire, Suffolk, Warwickshire, and West Midlands.

Southern

Avon, Berkshire, Cornwall and Scilly, Devon, Dorset, East Sussex, Gloucestershire, Hampshire, Isle of Wight, Kent, Oxfordshire, Somerset, Surrey, West Sussex, and Wiltshire.

The address for all three regions is:
Ancient Monuments Division, English Heritage, HBMC, Fortress House, 23 Savile Row, London W1X 2HE. Tel: (01) 734 6010

For enquiries about Guardianship sites and properties in care, contact the Properties in Care Group of HBMC. This department is divided, for administrative purposes, into four regional sections, as follows:

Northern

Cheshire, Cleveland, Cumbria, Durham, Greater Manchester, Humberside, Lancashire, North Yorkshire, Northumberland, South Yorkshire, Tyne and Wear, and West Yorkshire.

Midland

Bedfordshire, Cambridgeshire, Derbyshire, Essex, Hereford and Worcester, Hertfordshire, Leicestershire, Lincolnshire, Norfolk, Northamptonshire, Nottinghamshire, Shropshire, Staffordshire, Suffolk, Warwickshire, and West Midlands.

Thames

Berkshire, Buckinghamshire, Oxfordshire, Greater London; Essex, Hertfordshire, Kent, and Surrey adjoining London.

Southern

Avon, Cornwall and Scilly, Devon, Dorset, East Sussex, Gloucestershire, Hampshire, Isle of Wight, Kent, Somerset, Surrey, West Sussex, and Wiltshire.

The address for all four regions is:
Properties in Care Group, English Heritage, HBMC, Fortress House, 23 Savile Row, London W1X 2HE. Tel: (01) 734 6010

2 Archaeological advice by county

For enquiries about the formulation of management plans, access to the local Sites and Monuments Record, and advice on the archaeological implications of planning matters contact your county archaeological officer.

Avon

County Archaeological Officer, Planning Department, Avon County Council, Avon House North, St James Barton, Bristol BS99 7EJ. Tel: (0272) 290777 ext 530

Bedfordshire

Principal Conservation Officer, Planning Department, Bedfordshire County Council, County Hall, Bedford MK42 9AP. Tel: (0234) 63222 ext 2071

Berkshire

Archaeological Officer, Department of Highways and Planning, Berkshire County Council, Shire Hall, Shinfield Park, Reading RG2 9XG. Tel: (0734) 875444 ext 4938

Buckinghamshire

County Archaeologist, County Museum, Buckinghamshire County Council, Church Street, Aylesbury HP20 2QP. Tel: (0296) 82158

Cambridgeshire

County Archaeologist, Department of Lands and Buildings, Cambridgeshire County Council, Shire Hall, Castle Hill, Cambridge CB3 0AP. Tel: (0223) 317111 ext 3312

Cheshire

Principal Archaeologist, Planning Department, Cheshire County Council, Commerce House, Hunter Street, Chester CH1 1SN. Tel: (0244) 603160

Cleveland

County Archaeologist, Cleveland Archaeology, PO Box 41, Southlands Centre, Ormesby Road, Middlesbrough TS3 0YZ. Tel: (0642) 327583 ext 223

Cornwall and Scilly

County Archaeological Officer, Cornwall Committee for Archaeology, Room 4, Old County Hall, Station Road, Truro TR1 3EX. Tel: (0872) 74282 ext 3602

Cumbria

County Archaeological Officer, Planning Department, Cumbria County Council, County Offices, Kendal LA9 4RQ. Tel: (0539) 21000 ext 378

Derbyshire

Sites and Monuments Officer, Peak District National Park (see 3 below).

Devon

Archaeology Officer, Property Department, Devon County Council, County Hall, Exeter EX2 4QQ. Tel: (0392) 77977 ext 2266

Dorset

County Archaeological Officer, Planning Department, Dorset County Council, County Hall, Dorchester DT1 1XJ. Tel: (0305) 251000 ext 4277

Durham

County Archaeological Officer, Bowes Castle Museum, Barnard Castle. Tel: (0833) 37139

East Sussex

Archaeological Adviser, Planning Department, East Sussex County Council, Southover House, Southover Road, Lewes BN7 1YA. Tel: (0273) 475400 ext 727

Essex

County Archaeologist, Planning Department, Essex County Council, Globe House, New Street, Chelmsford CM1 1LF. Tel: (0245) 492211

Gloucestershire

County Archaeological Officer, Planning Department, Gloucestershire County Council, Shire Hall, Gloucester GL1 2TN. Tel: (0452) 425683

Greater London

Archaeological Officer, London Division, HBMC, Chesham House, 30 Warwick Street, London W1R 6AB. Tel: (01) 734 8144 ext 6

Greater Manchester

Greater Manchester Archaeological Unit, Department of Archaeology, University of Manchester, Oxford Road, Manchester M13 9PD. Tel: (061) 273 3333 ext 3704

Hampshire

Archaeological Officer, Planning Department, Hampshire County Council, The Castle, Winchester SO23 8UE. Tel: (0962) 54411 ext 641

Hereford and Worcester

County Archaeological Officer, Archaeology Department, County Council of Hereford and Worcester, Tetbury Drive, Warndon, Worcester WR4 9LS. Tel: (0905) 58608

Hertfordshire

County Archaeologist, Planning Department, Hertfordshire County Council, County Hall, Hertford SG13 8N. Tel: (0992) 555244

Humberside

County Archaeologist, County Architect's Department, Humberside County Council, County Hall, Lairgate, Beverley HU17 9BA. Tel: (0482) 867131 ext 3701

Isle of Wight

County Archaeological Officer, Archaeology Unit, Isle of Wight County Council, Clatterford School, 61 Clatterford Road, Carisbrooke, Newport PO30 1NZ. Tel: (0983) 529963

Lancashire

County Archaeologist, Cumbria and Lancashire Archaeological Unit, University of Lancaster, Physics Building, Bailrigg, Lancaster LA1 4YB. Tel: (0524) 65201 ext 308

Leicestershire

County Archaeological Officer, County Museum Service, Jewry Wall Museum, St Nicholas Circle, Leicester LE1 7BY. Tel: (0533) 554100 ext 218

Lincolnshire

County Archaeological Officer, Lincolnshire Museums, Aquis House, Clasketgate, Lincoln LN2 1NG. Tel: (0522) 30401

Merseyside

County Archaeological Officer, Archaeological Survey of Merseyside, Merseyside County Museum, William Brown Street, Liverpool L3 8EN. Tel: (051) 207 0001 ext 14

Norfolk

County Archaeologist, Norfolk Archaeological Unit, Union House, Gressenhall, Dereham NR20 4DR. Tel: (0362) 860528

Northampton

County Archaeologist, County Secretary's Department, Northamptonshire County Council, County Hall, Northampton NN1 1DN. Tel: (0604) 256885

Northumberland

County Archaeological Officer, Planning Department, Northumberland County Council, County Hall, Morpeth NE61 2EF. Tel: (0670) 514343 ext 3507

North Yorkshire

County Archaeologist, Planning Department, North Yorkshire County Council, County Hall, Northallerton DL7 8AQ. Tel: (0609) 780780 ext 2330

Nottinghamshire

County Archaeologist, Planning and Transportation, Nottinghamshire County Council, Trent Bridge House, Fox Road, West Bridgford, Nottingham NG2 6BJ. Tel: (0602) 824824 ext 395

Oxfordshire

County Archaeological Officer, Department of Museum Services, County Museum, Fletcher's House, Woodstock OX7 1SN. Tel: (0993) 811456

Shropshire

County Archaeological Officer, Planning Department, Shropshire County Council, Shire Hall, Abbey Foregate, Shrewsbury. Tel: (0743) 252563

Somerset

Field Archaeologist, Planning Department, Somerset County Council, County Hall, Taunton TA1 4DY. Tel: (0823) 333451 ext 5426

South Yorkshire

County Archaeologist, Archaeology Section, South Yorkshire County Council, Cultural Activities Centre, Ellin Street, Sheffield S1 4PL. Tel: (0742) 29191 ext 31

Staffordshire

County Archaeological Officer, Planning Department, Staffordshire County Council, Martin Street, Stafford ST16 2LE. Tel: (0785) 223121 ext 7280

Suffolk

County Archaeologist, Archaeology Unit, Suffolk County Council, Shire Hall, Bury St Edmunds. Tel: (0284) 63141 ext 2023

Surrey

County Archaeologist, Planning Department, Surrey County Council, County Hall, Kingston on Thames KT1 2DT. Tel: (01) 546 1050 ext 3665

Tyne and Wear

County Archaeological Officer, Planning Department, Tyne and Wear County Council, Sandyford House, Archbold Terrace, Newcastle-upon-Tyne NE2 1ED. Tel: (0632) 816144

Warwickshire

Field Archaeologist, County Museum, Warwickshire County Council, Market Hall, Warwick CV34 4SA. Tel: (0926) 493431 ext 2276

West Midlands

County Archaeological Officer, Department of Planning and Architecture, Dudley Metropolitan Borough Council, 3 St James Road, Dudley. Tel: (0384) 55433 ext 5655

West Sussex

Archaeological Officer, Planning Department, West Sussex County Council, County Hall, Tower Street, Chichester PO19 1RL. Tel: (0243) 777625

West Yorkshire

West Yorkshire Archaeology Service,, 14 St John's North, Wakefield WF1 3QA. Tel: (0924) 367111 ext 4763

Wiltshire

County Archaeological Officer, Library and Museum Service, Wiltshire County Council, County Hall, Bythesea Road, Trowbridge BA14 8BS. Tel: (022) 14 3641 ext 2743

3　National Parks

Two National Park authorities in England have archaeological officers.

Dartmoor

Archaeological Officer, Parke, Haytor Road, Bovey Tracey TQ13 9JQ. Tel: (0626) 832093

Peak District

Archaeological Officer, Aldern House, Baslow Road, Bakewell DE4 1AE. Tel: (062) 981 4321 ext 206

4 Other useful addresses

Council for British Archaeology

Council for British Archaeology, 112 Kennington Road, London SE11 6RE. Tel: (01) 582 0494

Countryside Commission

Countryside Commission, John Dower House, Cresent Place, Cheltenham GL50 3RA. Tel: (0242) 521381

Farming and Wildlife Advisory Group

Farming and Wildlife Advisory Group, The Lodge, Sandy SG19 2DL. Tel: (0767) 80551

Forestry Commission

Forestry Commission, 231 Corstorphine Road, Edinburgh EH12 7AT Tel: (031) 334 0303

Institute of Field Archaeologists

Institute of Field Archaeologists, Minerals Engineering Building, University of Birmingham, PO Box 363, Birmingham B15 2TT. Tel: (021) 471 2788

Ministry of Agriculture, Fisheries and Food

Ministry of Agriculture, Fisheries and Food, Whitehall Place, London SW1A 2HH. Tel: (01) 233 3000

National Farmers Union

National Farmers Union, Agriculture House, 25–31 Knightsbridge, London SW1X 7NJ. Tel: (01) 235 5077

National Monuments Record

National Monuments Record, Royal Commission on the Historical Monuments of England, Fortress House, 23 Savile Row, London W1X 2HE. Tel: (01) 734 6010

National Trust

Archaeological Adviser, The National Trust, Spitalgate Lane, Cirencester GL7 2DE. Tel: (0285) 61818

Nature Conservancy Council

Nature Conservancy Council (Headquarters), Northminster House, Peterborough PE1 1UA. Tel: (0733) 40345

Royal Commission on the Historical Monuments of England

Royal Commission on the Historical Monuments of England, Fortress House, 23 Savile Row, London W1X 2HE. Tel: (01) 734 6010

Appendix B
Ancient Monuments and related legislation

1 Ancient Monuments legislation

The following list includes all current and previous Ancient Monuments and related Acts in chronological order:

A Ancient Monuments Protection Act 1882 (1882 c. 73) (Totally repealed)
B Ancient Monuments Consolidation and Amendment Act 1913 (1913 c. 32) (Totally repealed)
C Ancient Monuments Act 1931 (1931 c. 16) (Totally repealed)
D Historic Buildings and Ancient Monuments Act 1953 (1953 c. 49) (ss. 1, 2 (2), 3 (2), 7, 10–20 and 22 (2), and Schedule repealed by later Acts. Other sections variously amended by later Acts. The remaining parts relate only to listed buildings.)
E Field Monument Act 1972 (1972 c. 43) (Totally repealed)
F Ancient Monuments and Archaeological Areas Act 1979 (1979 c, 46) (Amended by 1983 Act)
G National Heritage Act 1980 (1980 c.17)
H National Heritage Act 1983 (1983 c.47)

2 Legislation containing sections relevant to ancient monuments in the countryside

A *General – countryside, planning, and recreation*

The National Parks and Access to the Countryside Act 1949 (1949 c. 97)

Countryside Act 1968 (1968 c. 41) (esp Section 12)

Town and Country Planning Act 1971 (1971 c. 78) (esp Sections 52* and 277), with later amendments

Wildlife and Countryside Act 1981 (1981 c. 69) (esp ss. 39, 42, 43 and 48), as amended by the Wildlife and Countryside (Amendment) Act 1985 (1985 c. 31)

Agriculture Act 1986 (1986 c. 49) (esp ss. 17 and 18)

B *Finance*

General Rate Act 1967 (1967 c. 9) (esp Schedule 1.1*)

Capital Transfer Tax Act 1984 (1984 c. 51) (esp ss. 26, 27, 30 and Schedules 3 and 4), with slight amendments in Finance Act 1985

C *Acts dealing with specific potential threats to archaeological sites*

Electricity (Supply) Act 1926 (1926 c. 51) (s. 44(3)*)
The Secretary of State for the Environment has to be consulted, if representations are made over the placing of any electric line above ground which might prejudicially affect an Ancient Monument.

174

Coastal Protection Act 1949 (1949 c. 74) (s. 47(d)*)
During the construction of coastal defences, for which special powers are given to Local Authorities under this Act, proper procedure relating to ancient monuments must be followed.

Coal Mining Subsidence Act 1957 (1957 c. 59) (s. 9(1)*)
The National Coal Board is given a special duty to restore to its former state any Scheduled Monument damaged because of subsidence due to coal mining.

Land Powers Defence Act 1958 (1958 c. 30) (s. 6(4)b*)
During the use of private land for defence training, for which special powers are given under section 6 of this Act, nothing shall authorize any person to injure or deface any Scheduled Monument.

Mines (Working Facilities and Support) Act 1966 (1966 c. 4) (s. 7(8)*)
Applications for the support of Ancient Monuments, either lateral or vertical, may be considered in planning restrictions placed on mines and mineral workings in cases where the preservation of monuments is threatened by inadequate support, as a result of mining or mineral working. In these cases, application has to be made by the Secretary of State for the Environment or the appropriate Local Authority, if the monument is in their ownership or Guardianship (s. 7(8)).

Forestry Act 1967 (1967 c. 10) (s. 40(2))
The Forestry Commission may not compulsorily purchase land, which is the site of an Ancient Monument or other object of archaeological interest.

Water Act 1973 (1973 c. 37) (s. 22(1)) amended by Wildlife and Countryside Act 1971.
In formulating or considering any proposals relating to the discharge of any of the functions of water authorities, those authorities and the appropriate Minister or Ministers shall have regard to the desirability of protecting buildings or other objects of archaeological, architectural, or historical interest.

Land Drainage Act 1976 (1976 c. 70) (s. 111)
Nothing in this Act authorizes any person to execute any works or do anything in contravention of the provisions of the Ancient Monuments legislation.

D Other

Coroners Act 1887 (1887 c. 71) (s. 36)

National Trust Act 1907 (Local and Private 1907, cxxxvi) Additions and amendments in Local and Private Acts 1919, lxxxiv and 1937, lvii

Protection of Military Remains Act 1986 (1986 c. 35)

*Note: consequential amendments in Ancient Monuments and Archaeological Areas Act 1979 (Schedule 4).

Appendix C
Code of practice for mineral operators

The following code of practice for mineral operators has been established under the sponsorship of the Confederation of British Industry, with the cooperation of the Council for British Archaeology, HBMC, and the Department of the Environment. The Code sets down the normal practice of most operators.

1 The operator will notify the relevant Archaeological Body* as early as practicable of his intention to extend existing operations or to apply for planning permission for new development. Wherever possible he will give or procure rights of access for reconnaissance.

2 The Operator will use his best endeavour to restrict access for the purpose of searching for and excavating archaeological objects, to personnel approved by the Archaeological Body. Other groups and individuals (whether or not metal detector users) will be discouraged from the site and referred to the Archaeological Body.

3 The Archaeological Body will carry out reconnaissance as soon as practicable and inform the Operator whether it would be interested in carrying out further investigation or not.

4 In the case of new development the Operator will consult as necessary with the Archaeological Body concerned over such matters as the timetable of works, methods of topsoil stripping, safety and legal requirements, access arrangements before and during works, emergency procedures for dealing with unexpected discoveries, and deposition of finds. The Operator will send the Archaeological Body details of the application for planning permission when submitted.

5 If the Archaeological Body is reasonably satisfied that the application proposes adequate provision for the archaeological needs, it should so advise the planning authority.

6 In all cases where further archaeological investigation is desired the Operator will, before operations begin, consult the Archaeological Body and agree a programme of investigation which may be modified in the light of subsequent developments or discoveries.

7 In any case of difficulty advice may be sought from HBMC.

8 The Operator will allow the Archaeological Body reasonable access for monitoring throughout the whole period of investigation.

9 The Archaeological Body will require its members or agents on the Operators site to comply with the Operator's reasonable requirements, and to have insurance cover adequate to meet any claims that may arise from their acts or omissions.

*Usually a county or regional archaeological unit/trust or the relevant county council archaeology department.

Notes

1   English Heritage is the popular name of the Historic Buildings and Monuments Commission for England and is used to refer to the Commission throughout this volume except in chapter 5, which deals with legislation and which therefore reflects the terminology of the Acts of Parliament.

2   General accounts of the range of field monuments in Britain are provided by: Allcroft 1908; Crawford 1960; Ordnance Survey 1973; Wood 1972.

3   For general accounts of field archaeology *see*: Coles 1972, C Taylor 1975, Aston and Rowley 1974, and Aston 1985.

4   The literature on this aspect of archaeological work is very extensive. Papers in the volume edited by P Phillips (1985) cover many of the main themes and provide abundant earlier references. *See also* Tite 1972 on the methods of physical examination, and Gillespie 1984 on radiocarbon dating.

5   Environmental archaeology is a major field of study in its own right. Butzer (1972), J G Evans (1978), and Shackley (1985) provide useful introductions to the subject. I Simmons and Tooley (1981) present a series of papers reviewing aspects of the environment during prehistoric times (including flora, fauna, soils, climate, and sea level), and regional surveys of work to 1984 have been published by HBMC (Keeley 1984; 1987).

6   Great care has to be exercised when using dates derived from objects or materials found within structures or features. In some cases, such material may be residual from earlier periods of use and may thus predate a feature, while in other cases a feature may be in existence for many years before artefacts become associated with it.

7   The main period terms for prehistory are still widely used: *see* Glossary for general definitions. It should be emphasized, however, that no firm dividing line can ever be established between each successive period, and that, as absolute dates become more widely available, the use of these terms will diminish.

8   Emotively summarized by Shoard (1980), Mabey (1980), Body (1982), and O'Riordan (1982); *see also* the overview of the changing countryside, edited by Blunden and Curry (1985), for a more objective appraisal.

9   Much has been written on the need for heritage management in Britain (eg: P Fowler 1977; J Hunter 1977; Addyman 1979; Millman 1979; Brandon and Millman 1981; Tittensor 1985; C Hall 1985; M Hughes and Rowley 1986), but as a field within the discipline of archaeology it has remained relatively undeveloped, despite the influence of work in America and elsewhere (*see* Schiffer and Gumerman 1977; Sneed 1980; D Fowler 1982; Cleere 1984). The present interest in archaeological resource management in Britain stems largely from the development of concern over the allocation of funds, and the scale of destruction in the countryside, which was voiced at a number of conferences and symposia in the mid–late 1970s (*see* for example: Rowley and Breakall 1977; Darvill *et al* 1978; Hinchliffe and Schadla-Hall 1980).

10   The following are exempt from definition as monuments: (1) any ecclesiastical building, for the time being used for ecclesiastical purposes, and (2) a site comprising, or comprising the remains of, any vessel which is protected by an order under section 1 of the Protection of Wrecks Act 1973, designating an area round the site as a restricted area. The term 'remains' is taken to include any trace or sign of the previous existence of the thing in question.

11   In order to preserve the terminology of the legislation, in this chapter only, English Heritage is referred to by its full title of the Historic Buildings and Monuments Commission for England, or HBMC.

12   The CBA (1977) produced notes on the use of structure plans and local plans in archaeology.

13   Because the emphasis of this volume is on the countryside, scant attention is paid here to listed building regulations; scheduled buildings are, however, included.

14   Monuments within UK territorial waters can be scheduled and can be taken into Guardianship, but the definition of the term 'monument' cannot be extended to sites protected by an order under section 1 of the Protection of Wrecks Act 1973 (*see* note 10), and such powers do not apply to these sites.

15   Statutory Instruments 1981 no 1302 and 1984 no 222.

16   A person who without lawful excuse destroys or damages any protected monument, whether a Scheduled Monument or any monument under the Guardianship or ownership of the Secretary of State, HBMC, or a local authority, knowing that it is a protected monument, and intending to destroy or damage the monument, or being reckless as to whether the monument would be destroyed or damaged, shall be guilty of a criminal offence.

17   Section 52 of the Town and Country Planning Act 1971, Section 17 of the Ancient Monuments and Archaeological Areas Act 1979, or Section 39 of the Wildlife and Countryside Act 1971. *See* Feist (1978) for a general (but now rather outdated) study of management agreements, and Ancient Monuments Secretariat (1982) for applications in National Parks.

18   Existing arrangements for funding rescue excavations are complex and highly variable because, in addition to grants from HBMC, there is a substantial input from the Manpower Services Commission through job creation and retraining schemes (*c* £5 million per annum to archaeology), and also money from private developers.

19   In normal circumstances the owner and/or occupier is contacted in advance.

20   In such cases, the power of the Coroner is limited. He cannot make any statement as to title to the property. The landowner may, however, sue for trespass in the case of a finder claiming Treasure Trove, who was without the landowner's permission to be on the land in the first place. The Theft Act 1968 abolished the old criminal offence of concealment of Treasure Trove. The obligation to surrender a find is a general one derived, by implication, from the fact that one person (the finder) has come into the possession of the property of another person.

21   If a person uses a metal detector in a protected place (a Scheduled Monument or a monument in the ownership or Guardianship of the Secretary of State, HBMC, or a local authority) without the written permission of HBMC, he shall be guilty of a criminal offence and liable on summary conviction to a fine not exceeding £200. If a person without written consent removes any object of archaeological or historical interest, which he has discovered by the use of a metal detector in a protected place, he shall be guilty of an offence and liable on summary conviction to a fine not exceeding the statutory maximum or on conviction on indictment to a fine.

22   Examples of this patterning can be seen in the results of general surveys. Chowne (1980) describes Bronze Age settlement in south Lincolnshire, essays in the volume edited by C Phillips (1970) provide an overview of the Fens in Roman times, and Darby (1940), using historical geography strictly more than archaeology, describes the medieval Fenlands.

23   Following Ratcliffe (1977, 249), the term *mire* is used here

as a general term to cover bogs, swamps, fens, and marshes, which each have rather specific (but often confused) meanings.

24 Dates from the lower peat/clay interface include 3340 ± 80 bc (HAR-1857) from below the Sweet Track, and 3700 ± 70 bc (HAR-1831) from below the Rowland's Track (Coles and Orme 1985, 85 with earlier refs).

25 Information from R Turner and D Ramsay, Cheshire County Council.

26 Some islands remained unaffected by peat growth and are therefore no different from dry-land sites, except that perhaps deeper features may be waterlogged. Islands inundated by peat subsequent to settlement will probably be better preserved than their dry-land equivalents.

27 For example, used at Flag Fen, Cambridgeshire, to determine extent of the site – information from F Pryor.

28 The water content of peat is about 50% by volume and 95% by weight. With this removed, deposits collapse and compact, shrink, and decay through biochemical oxidation (see Coles 1984, 26).

29 Figures from Somerset County Council (1983a). It is estimated that by the year 2011 some 2384ha of peatland in Somerset will have been totally exhausted of peat (see Curtis et al 1976). It should, however, be noted that peat cutting has been taking place for over 800 years, and that very large quantities have been lost without record.

30 Several guides to conservation practices in wetland landscapes have been published by the NCC (1977; 1982a; 1983f; 1983g), and see also the paper by McDonald (1982).

31 Water Act 1973, Section 22, amended by the Wildlife and Countryside Act 1971, Section 48.

32 The number of Scheduled Monuments given here for wetland areas is an estimate based on a study of the situation of approximately one-half of all Scheduled Monuments.

33 Considerable regional variation exists in the effects of these processes; see essays in F Thompson (1980).

34 For example, the Bronze Age burial mounds at Low Hauxley, Northumberland (see Proc Prehist Soc, **50**, 398 for summary), and the Iron Age cemetery at Harlyn Bay, Cornwall (Whimster 1977).

35 See Wood (1972, 179) for a summary of defensive works.

36 See Muckelroy (1978) for a review of some coastal shipwrecks. Information on Minehead boat from Dr I Burrow, Somerset County Council.

37 Information from R Harland, National Trust.

38 Information from Dr M Bell, St David's University College, Lampeter, Dyfed.

39 A number of general studies and guides to conservation in coastal and estuarine areas have been published by the Countryside Commission (1968; 1969; 1970a; 1970b), the NCC (1982b; 1982c; 1982d; 1983a), and Hampshire County Council (Colebourn 1984).

40 See note 37.

41 The number of Scheduled Monuments given here for coastland areas is an estimate based on a study of the situation of approximately one-half of all Scheduled Monuments.

42 Lakes in old mineral workings (usually gravel pits) are archaeologically sterile, because all deposits will have been removed during mineral extraction. The lake shores and unworked islands may, however, be of interest.

43 Intermixed within many alluvial gravels is archaeological evidence for Palaeolithic occupation (Wymer 1968; Roe 1981).

44 The major areas of marine alluvium occur in close association with river alluvium, as coastal inundation usually drowns low-lying river valleys. Where marine and riverine alluvium meet, the stratigraphy can be very complex.

45 So-called lake villages at Glastonbury and Meare, Somerset, were in fact marsh settlements. Pile dwellings are known on the Thames near Southchurch and Brentford, and in Yorkshire along the marshy edge of what was Lake Pickering, now Ryedale, at Costa Beck, and at Ulrome in Holderness (Wood 1972, 105).

46 Conditions at the start of the project were not 'natural', since the Maxey Cut – a main fenland drain – was already maintaining the water table at an artificially low level.

47 In recent years, there has been an upsurge in conservation interest in waterways; many management schemes for recreation and water control have been developed, and many booklets and leaflets deal with the conservation of riverside and lakeside areas (eg Brook 1981; Wessex Water Authority nd; Thames Water Authority 1979; NCC nd; 1983b; 1983c).

48 Section 22, amended by the Wildlife and Countryside Act 1981, Section 48.

49 Water authorities are responsible for rivers and streams designated as 'main rivers'.

50 The number of Scheduled Monuments given here for rivers, lakes, and alluvium spreads is an estimate based on a study of the situation of approximately one-half of all Scheduled Monuments.

51 This broadly follows the definition of established grassland used by MAFF (1982). See Sheail and Wells (1970) for general discussion of old grassland and its archaeological importance.

52 Estimating the area of grassland extant today is most difficult, and the figures cited derive from MAFF (1982), but include all grassland which has not been cultivated for at least five years.

53 Early aerial photographs, for example the wartime RAF surveys, provide a very valuable record of archaeological features under grassland because so much more grassland was extant at that time.

54 Preservation of archaeological remains beneath medieval cultivation varies considerably. In general, survival is good beneath the ridges, but stratigraphy is usually truncated by the furrows.

55 Regular reports on the experimental earthworks appear in the CBA's annual publication Archaeology in Britain.

56 A number of publications deal with the conservation of grassland and the preservation of archaeological monuments under grassland, including: Sheail and Wells 1970; P Fowler 1970; NCC 1982g; Lambrick and McDonald 1985; Lewis and Miles 1985.

57 The number of Scheduled Monuments given here for grassland areas is an estimate based on a study of the situation of approximately one-half of all Scheduled Monuments.

58 Information from R Canham, Wiltshire County Council.

59 The term forest is often generally equated with woodland, but actually has a rather different meaning, since it includes areas of pasture and open treeless ground as well as woodland. Royal Forests were areas of land, of which some was woodland, subject to the jurisdiction of Forest Law and controlled by the Crown. Hunting rights in these areas were very strictly controlled.

60 For general works on the history and archaeology of woodland see Rackham 1976; 1980, Colebourn 1983, Whitlock 1979, and the papers in Bell and Limbrey 1982.

61 It has been estimated, for example, that 3.5ha of woodland would have been needed to supply the timber necessary for the construction of just one of the round buildings found within the henge monument at Durrington Walls, Wiltshire (Wainwright and Longworth 1971, 223)

62   A number of archaeological studies of woodland areas have been published, for example: Caiger 1964, Butler and Fasham 1975, Rackham 1975, T Barfield 1984, Hendry *et al* 1984, McCrone 1985.

63   R Bradley, University of Reading, pers comm.

64   Harvesting accounts for 50–90% of the costs of production in modern forestry systems, so cost cutting at this stage is always being sought (Helliwell 1984).

65   Much has been written about the conservation of woodland. The following cover the main arguments presented: Peterkin 1981, BTCV 1982, Savage 1983, NCC 1982f; 1982g, Kirby 1984, Forestry Commission 1984a; 1984b; 1984c; 1984d.

66   The earliest forest laws were the Laws of Ine, King of the West Saxons from AD 688, which made it an offence to destroy woodland (Colebourn 1983, 8; Forestry Commission 1974).

67   Forestry Act 1967 (amended 1981), Section 40.

68   The Forestry Commission recommends that: 'Owners are advised, before they commence planting, that if there is any likelihood of an area being a site requiring protection they should ask the Inspector of Ancient Monuments to inspect the ground or give his clearance before planting commences' (Blatchford 1978, 129).

69   The number of Scheduled Monuments given here for woodland areas is an estimate based on a study of the situation of approximately one-half of all Scheduled Monuments.

70   In 1976, 30 National Nature Reserves included woodland totalling 1955ha, and 5 Forest Nature Reserves contained a total of 136ha of woodland (Steele 1976).

71   The Forestry Commission currently manages a total of 290 walks and trails in England (Forestry Commission 1985, Tab 10).

72   For general discussions of heathlands *see* Dimbleby 1962; 1976, Underhill 1971, and, for Hampshire, Hazel 1983.

73   Area based on Ordnance Survey Land Classification Maps, with some modifications in the light of recent surveys.

74   The later history of heathlands is well described by Rackham (1986, 291–302).

75   Recent experiments at Sutton Hoo (Carver 1984) include the use of high-powered floodlights at night to help pick out low-relief features.

76   A number of publications relevant to heathland management and conservation are available, including: Underhill 1971, Gimingham 1972; NCC 1981, Daniels 1983, Hazel 1983 (esp 21), Farrell 1983.

77   The number of Scheduled Monuments given here for lowland heath areas is an estimate based on a study of the situation of approximately one-half of all Scheduled Monuments.

78   For general accounts of ancient fields, *see* Gray 1915, Bowen 1961, C Taylor 1975, Mercer 1981c, D Hall 1982, and P Fowler 1983.

79   *See* A Baker and Butlin 1973, Ault 1969, C Taylor 1975, D Hall 1982, and Aston 1985, ch 10.

80   The earliest ridge-and-furrow is certainly pre-eleventh century (Aston 1985, 121).

81   *See* Lambrick 1977 and Spoor 1980. Often these tools are used as part of the normal agricultural practice, and their damaging effect is not realized. Moreover, their use is undetectable from the surface after one subsequent ploughing.

82   The number of Scheduled Monuments given here for arable areas is an estimate based on a study of the situation of approximately one-half of all Scheduled Monuments.

83   Such an excavation need not involve the removal of all archaeological deposits, but it does necessitate sampling the complete sequence to check the depth of cut features.

84   For general discussions of parkland *see*: Rackham 1976, ch 8; 1986, ch 6, C Taylor 1983b, 60, Bilikowski 1983.

85   A new generation of parkland in the wider sense comprises the many country parks established and run by local authorities. The management and the archaeological content of these is very similar to earlier types of parkland.

86   The quality of preservation offered can be judged on a sliding scale, where the best preservation is provided by parks which have undergone minimum landscaping, the worst by parks in which the former landscape has been radically changed.

87   Based on the areas of parklands and ornamental garden depicted on the 1:50,000 Ordnance Survey Sheets, Landranger Series.

88   Other early parks include Woodstock (now Blenheim), Oxfordshire, which may have been founded before AD 1000 (Hoskins 1970, 169). There may well be other early parks, and the possibility of Roman and earlier parks cannot be ruled out.

89   But *see* Bond (1986, 153) for an appraisal of the value of these records.

90   Medieval deer parks have been catalogued for many areas: *see*, for example, Rackham 1986, 123, Prince 1967, Cantor 1962; 1971; 1983, J D Wilson 1974, Hatherly and Cantor 1979–1980, Bond 1981, and Bilikowski 1983.

91   Some insight into the changes wrought by these landscape gardeners can be glimpsed from the 'before' and 'after' sketches made by Repton and others.

92   In 1983, some 158 country parks in England were recognized by the Countryside Commission (Countryside Commission 1983b).

93   Excavations at Barnsley Park, Gloucestershire, for example, brought to light a large quantity of Mesolithic, Neolithic, and Bronze Age flintwork (Webster 1981).

94   Some lodges may have been moated buildings (for protection against livestock?). The moated sites which survive in Barley Park, Mapledurham, and Cokethorpe Home Wood, all in Oxfordshire, probably represent park lodges (Bond 1986, 153).

95   During the course of barrow surveys, Leslie Grinsell has noted a number of hilltop barrows, planted with trees and sometimes enclosed by a ditch. He suggests (*in litt* 23/6/1986) that such plantations may sometimes have been made to commemorate specific events, as with Easton 1, Wiltshire, planted in 1762, possibly to mark the coronation of George III.

96   Capital Transfer Tax exemption is possible, when management provisions for parkland of historic importance are agreed – *see* chapter 5.

97   For general conservation issues relating to parks and gardens, *see* Gruffydd 1977, Binney 1978, and Garden History Society 1984.

98   The number of Scheduled Monuments given here for parkland and ornamental gardens is an estimate based on a study of the situation of approximately one-half of all Scheduled Monuments.

99   In addition, Tree Preservation Orders may be used to protect trees.

100   The register is published as fascicules, as each county is surveyed. Entries are copied to the owner and/or occupier, as well as the relevant local authority and the Secretary of State for the Environment (*see* National Heritage Act 1983, Sched 4, para 10). An index of parks and gardens is also being compiled by the Centre for the Conservation of Historic Parks and Gardens at York.

101   For general guidance on researching the history of gardens, *see Documenting a Garden's History*, published by the

Centre for the Conservation of Historic Parks and Gardens, York.

102   One example of such a display is at the Queen Elizabeth Country Park, Hampshire, where the Butser Hill Iron Age Farm runs a display area (Reynolds 1979). Many country parks contain ancient monuments.

103   For general works covering the archaeology of the uplands *see*: Darvill 1986a; 1986b, J G Evans *et al* 1975, Spratt and Burgess 1985. The Countryside Commission has recently completed a wide-ranging investigation of changing land-use and social conditions in the uplands (Allaby 1983; Countryside Commission 1984; nd; Sinclair and Bell 1983). They defined the uplands as being areas of land mostly above 240m above sea level (Countryside Commission 1984, 9).

104   Based on extent of upland moorland shown on Ordnance Survey Land Utilization maps, with minor adjustments in the light of recent survey work.

105   Information from N Johnson, Cornwall Archaeology Unit.

106   Information from N Johnson and P Rose, Cornwall Archaeology Unit.

107   Information from N Johnson, Cornwall Archaeology Unit, in advance of publication.

108   For circles *see* Burl 1976, and for stone rows *see* Emmett 1979.

109   Changing land-use in the uplands has been well documented by the Countryside Commission. *See* Countryside Commission 1978a, Allaby 1983, Woods 1984.

110   Information from CBA Regional Group 13.

111   Information for Cumbria from T Clare, Cumbria County Council.

112   General works dealing with management and conservation in the uplands include: Curtis and Walker 1980, Countryside Commission 1976; 1984; nd, NCC 1982e; 1982d, P Fowler and Ellison 1977, ADAS 1984, Wager 1981, Haynes 1983, Darvill 1986a ch 9.

113   The number of Scheduled Monuments given here for upland moors is an estimate based on a study of the situation of approximately one-half of all Scheduled Monuments.

114   These maps are prepared under section 42 of the Wildlife and Countryside Act 1981; and *see* chapter 5.

115   *See*, for example, Bransdale Moor and Levisham Moor management plans, which integrate archaeology and nature conservation (Statham 1982; R Hayes 1983).

116   For more wide-ranging discussion of the value of the past, *see* Lowenthal and Binney 1981; Gold and Burgess 1982.

Acknowledgements

The Ancient Monuments in the Countryside Project, from which this volume resulted, was directed by a steering committee comprising Geoffrey Wainwright, Bill Startin, and Dai Morgan Evans, who individually and collectively contributed much to the content, form, and style of the report. Within the Ancient Monuments Division of English Heritage Bob Bewley, Graham Fairclough, David Fraser, Paul Gosling, Michael Parker Pearson, Bob Smith, Roger Thomas, and Philip Walker provided valuable information on current projects and commented on early drafts of the text. Many other members of the staff of English Heritage directly or indirectly contributed to the volume through answering questions, providing illustrations, and commenting on sections of draft text. All are gratefully thanked for their help. Thanks are also due to the staff of the Publications Section, Chief Inspector's Division, for the considerable work involved in the preparation of the text for publication: Stephen Johnson, Val Horsler, and Robin Taylor.

Special thanks go to the following individuals for their assistance in various ways during the preparation of this volume: G Andrews, P Ashbee, M Aston, M Bell, T Betts, D Bonney, I Burrow, R Burton, R Canham, J Coles, E Dennison, L Grinsell, D Hall, R Harland, N Johnson, R Mercer, F Oldfield, E Price, F Pryor, D Ramsay, B Roberts, P Rose, A Saville, C Taylor, J Taylor, C Thacker, D Thackray, R Turner, B Vyner, R Whimster, D R Wilson.

The following individuals and organizations are thanked for permission to reproduce photographs: P Ashbee (Figs 72, 89); Ashmolean Museum, Oxford (Figs 68, 145); N Barton (Fig 49); Bedfordshire County Council (Fig 56); M Bell (Fig 41); British Museum (Figs 33, 53A, 53B); Cambridge University Committee for Aerial Photography (front cover and Figs 3, 9, 10, 13, 14, 15A, 15B, 45, 48, 50, 59, 61, 63A, 63B, 67, 69, 70, 71, 73, 94, 95, 104, 105, 108, 109, 113, 118, 119, 120, 124, 127, 128, 130, 131, 132, 138, 139); T Clark (Fig 5A); Central Excavation Unit of English Heritage (Figs 20A, 111, 126A, 129, 133); T Clare (Fig 134); Cleveland County Council Archaeological Unit (Fig 103); Clwyd Powys Archaeological Trust (Fig 87A); Cornwall Archaeological Unit (Fig 42); Cumbria and Lancashire Archaeological Unit (Fig 135); B Cunliffe (Fig 83); Dartmoor National Park (Figs 26, 81); T Darvill (Figs 2, 16D, 19, 22, 64, 75, 80, 82, 87B, 116, 126A, 136, 140, 141, 143A, 143B); English Heritage Photographic Department (Figs 7A, 7C, 98, 114, 142); Essex County Council Planning Department (Figs 39A, 39B, 85); Devon County Council (Figs 20B, 123); T Gates (Fig 137); Hazleton Excavation Project, Cheltenham (Fig 102); Humberside County Council (Fig 20C); Institute of Archaeology Field Unit (Fig 92); Trust for Lincolnshire Archaeology (Fig 54); T Manby (Fig 8); M Millett (Fig 32); Milton Keynes Archaeological Unit (Fig 12, 106); Museum of English Rural Life, Reading (Figs 16A, 16B, 16C, 55A, 79A, 79B); National Maritime Museum (Fig 52); National Trust (Fig 18B); Norfolk Archaeological Unit (Figs 57, 60, 93A, 93B); North York Moors National Park (Fig 87C); Oxford Archaeological Unit (Fig 101); F Pryor (Figs 29, 58); O Rackham (Fig 78); Royal Commission on the Historical Monuments of England (Figs 1, 76, 86, 90, 97); C Salisbury (Fig 55B); A Saville (Fig 110); R Scaife (Fig 7B); Somerset County Council Planning Department (Figs 36, 44); Somerset Levels Project (Figs 31, 37); C Thacker (Figs 115, 121, 122); C Thomas (Figs 100A, 100B); J Wilkinson (Fig 144); H Wills (Fig 43); Wiltshire County Council (Figs 18A, 66). Figures 14, 15A, 45, 61A, 63A, 73, 113 are Crown Copyright. The colour print of the Rollright Stones on the back cover is reproduced by permission of Charles Collin from a Christmas card made by him. The maps and line drawings throughout this report were prepared by Andy McLaren.

List of abbreviations used in the text

AAI   Areas of Archaeological Importance
AHAP   Areas of High Archaeological Potential
AD   *Anno Domini*
ADAS   Agricultural Development Advisory Service
AONB   Area of Outstanding Natural Beauty
BC/bc   Before Christ (uncalibrated radiocarbon dates used throughout this report; *see* Glossary under Radiocarbon dating)
CAP   Common Agricultural Policy
CBA   Council for British Archaeology
DoE   Department of the Environment
EEC   European Economic Community
HBMC   Historic Buildings and Monuments Commission for England (English Heritage)
km   kilometre(s)
LFA   Less Favoured Area
m   metre(s)
MAFF   Ministry of Agriculture, Fisheries and Food
NCC   Nature Conservancy Council
NFU   National Farmers Union
NMR   National Monuments Record
NNR   National Nature Reserve
OD   Ordnance Datum (= height above sea level)
RCHME   Royal Commission on the Historical Monuments of England
SMC   Scheduled Monument Consent
SMR   Sites and Monuments Record
SSSI   Site of Special Scientific Interest

Glossary

Archaeological resource management: Making proper and appropriate use of archaeological sites and monuments for common benefit through the control of their destiny.

Artefact: A product of human workmanship, including tools, weapons, ornaments, utensils, etc.

Assemblage: An associated set of artefacts.

Blowing house: A furnace used for smelting tin in the south-west of England.

Bronze Age: Period of prehistory traditionally characterized by the extensive use of bronze for tools; *c* 2000–650 bc

Clearance cairn: A pile of stones built up from clearing fields or grazing areas.

Curatorial management: The maintenance of ancient monuments with the intention of preserving them for as long as possible.

Dendrochronology: A technique of dating pieces of timber by counting the number of annual rings developed during growth.

Exchange: Transfer of goods, services, or information between individuals or groups of individuals. Such transfers may not necessarily involve payments or reciprocation with equivalence. The term is often used by prehistorians wishing to avoid the modern connotations of the word 'trade'.

Exploitative management: The controlled use of archaeological sites or monuments for some specific purpose, for example as tourist attractions, leisure facilities, or for the advancement of knowledge about the past (academic or research excavation).

Iron Age: Period of prehistory traditionally defined by the common use of iron; *c* 650 bc to AD 43. The Romans arrived in AD 43, but in some upland zones Iron Age lifestyles continued unchanged well into the first millennium AD.

Management option: A preferred course of action or policy selected as appropriate for a given situation.

Marginal (land): Land on the edge of intensively-used areas, the quality of which is not compatible with intensive use under the prevailing circumstances. The limits of this type of land change over time, so that what might be regarded as marginal now was not always so.

Material culture: The sum total of artefacts made, used, or owned by a given society. Used to refer to physical possessions, rather than the spiritual or ideological side of a culture.

Mesolithic: Period of prehistory after the last Ice Age and before the introduction of farming; *c* 8000–3500 bc.

Millennium: A period of 1000 years.

Multi-option (or multi-purpose) management strategy: Two or more management options taken together, in series or in parallel, to provide a coherent and unified approach to an area of land, a proposition, or the solving of a problem. The options selected to be part of the strategy will probably relate to a wide range of different activities, for example archaeological resource management, nature conservation, forestry, water management, agriculture, and so on.

Neolithic: Period of prehistory characterized by early farming economies, before the use of metal; *c* 3500–2000 bc.

Palaeolithic: Earliest period of prehistory extending back through the last Ice Age. During this time, man evolved from early hominid species to modern man. Before *c* 8000 bc.

Palaeo-: Prefix meaning old or ancient; thus palaeoenvironment (ancient environment), palaeoeconomy (ancient economy), etc.

Petrology: Study of the origin and structure of rocks. Used in archaeology to characterize stone and determine its source.

Pillow mounds: Low oblong mounds of earth and stones, often with a shallow ditch round them, constructed as rabbit warrens in the Middle Ages.

Radiocarbon dating: All living things contain carbon, some of it in the form of the radioactive isotope ^{14}C and some in the form of ordinary carbon ^{12}C. While they are alive, the level of radioactive carbon remains constant, but once animals, humans, trees, or plants die and are no longer exposed to the sun's radiation, the radioactive carbon they contain decays at a steady rate. Thus by measuring the amount of radioactive carbon left within a sample of ancient preserved organic matter, and by comparing this with the amounts of ordinary carbon present, its date of death or burial can be calculated. Dates produced in this way do not accurately correspond with calendar years; fluctuations in the amount of ^{14}C in the atmosphere and other factors mean that radiocarbon dates have to be 'calibrated' in order to correspond more precisely with actual years BC. In this report, all the dates BC are based on radiocarbon evidence and are expressed as uncalibrated dates, for which the conventional designation is 'bc'.

Rescue excavation: The investigation of a site, by excavation, in advance of its destruction. In this sense, the site is being 'rescued' from destruction by being recorded.

Settlement pattern: The distribution of archaeological sites within a particular geographical area.

Shieling: Northern term for a seasonal hut for shepherds or herdsmen. Sometimes with enclosures for stock.

Social change: A variation in the structuring or execution of activities within a society. Such variations do not necessarily represent a 'development' in the sense of change for the better.

Stone row: Upright stones set either in a single line or in two or more parallel lines. Purpose unknown, but presumed to be some sort of ceremonial or ritual monument. Mostly late Neolithic or Bronze Age in date.

Stratification: Superimposition of one deposit over an earlier one.

Subsistence: Having to do with the provision of basic human requirements, principally food supplies.

Transhumance: Seasonal moving of livestock (and section of the population) to take advantage of short-lived grazing away from the home farmstead.

Bibliography

Aberg, A (ed), 1978 *Medieval moated sites*, CBA Res Rep, **17**, London

ADAS, 1980 *The classification of land in the hills and uplands of England and Wales*, Agricultural Development Advisory Service, London

——, 1984 *Farming and conservation in the uplands*, Agricultural Development Advisory Service, London and Cardiff

——, 1985 *Soil erosion by wind*, Agricultural Development Advisory Service, Alnwick

——, 1986 *The living farm – Advice on conservation from ADAS*, Agricultural Development Advisory Service, London

——, nd *Farming and the countryside*, Agricultural Development Advisory Service, London

Addyman, P V, 1979 Protecting past from present: a new charter for Britain's archaeological remains, *Country Life*, **166**, 830–2

Allaby, M, 1983 *The changing uplands*, Cheltenham

Allcroft, A H, 1908 *Earthwork of England*, London

Allen, G W G, 1984 Discovery from the air, *Aerial Archaeol*, **10**, 1–97

Ancient Monuments Secretariat, 1982 *The 1979 Ancient Monuments Act and National Parks*, London

Annable, F K, 1962 A Romano-British pottery in Savernake Forest, kilns 1–2, *Wiltshire Archaeol Natur Hist Mag*, **58**, 142–55

ApSimon, A M, 1968 The Bronze Age pottery from Ash Hole, Brixham, Devon, *Proc Devon Archaeol Soc*, **26**, 21–30

ApSimon, A M, Donovan, D T, and Taylor, M B, 1961 The stratigraphy and archaeology of the late glacial and post-glacial deposits at Brean Down, Somerset, *Proc Univ Bristol Spelaeol Soc*, **9**, 67–136

Arnold, C J, 1984 *Roman Britain to Saxon England*, London

Ashbee, P, 1972 Field archaeology: its origins and development, in *Archaeology and the landscape* (ed P J Fowler), 38–74, London

——, 1984 *The earthen long barrow in Britain*, 2 edn, Norwich

——, 1986 The excavation of Milton Lilbourne Barrows 1–5, *Wiltshire Archaeol Natur Hist Mag*, **80**, 23–96

Ashbee, P, and Dimbleby, G W, 1974 The Moor Green Barrow, West End, Hampshire, excavations, 1961, *Proc Hampshire Fld Club Archaeol Soc*, **31**, 5–18

Ashbee, P, Smith, I F, and Evans, J G, 1979 Excavation of three long barrows near Avebury, Wiltshire, *Proc Prehist Soc*, **45**, 207–300

Ashton, T S, 1948 *The Industrial Revolution 1760–1830*, Oxford

Aston, M, 1978 Gardens and earthworks at Hardington and Low Ham, *Proc Somerset Archaeol Natur Hist Soc*, **122**, 11–28

——, 1985 *Interpreting the landscape*, London

——(ed), forthcoming *Medieval fish, fisheries and fishponds* BAR, Oxford

Aston, M, and Rowley, T, 1974 *Landscape archaeology*, London

Ault, W O, 1969 *Open field farming in medieval England*, London

Baker, A R H, and Butlin, R A (eds), 1973 *Studies of field systems in the British Isles*, Cambridge

Baker, W A, 1975 Infra-red techniques, in D R Wilson 1975, 46–51

Balaam, N D, and Porter, H M, 1982 The phosphate surveys, in Balaam *et al* 1982, 215–19

Balaam, N D, Smith, K, and Wainwright, G J, 1982 The Shaugh Moor project: fourth report – environment, context and conclusion, *Proc Prehist Soc*, **48**, 203–78

Barber, D, 1985 The shape of things to come – the CAP and the landscape, *Country Life*, **177**, 1800–2

Barber, K, 1973 Vegetational history of the New Forest: a preliminary note, *Proc Hampshire Fld Club Archaeol Soc*, **30**, 5–8

——, 1982 Peat stratigraphy as a proxy climate record, in A Harding 1982, 103–113

Barfield, L, and Hodder, M, 1981 Birmingham's Bronze Age, *Curr Archaeol*, **7**, 198–200

Barfield, T, 1984 *A Herefordshire woodland survey*, Hereford

Barker, P, 1977 *Techniques of archaeological excavation*, London

——, 1986 *Understanding archaeological excavation*, London

Barrett, J, and Bradley, R (eds), 1980 *Settlement and society in the British later Bronze Age*, BAR, **83**, Oxford

Barrett, J, Bradley, R, Bowden, M, and Mead, B, 1983 South Lodge after Pitt Rivers, *Antiquity*, **47**, 193–204

Barton, N, and James, P, 1983 Hengistbury Head, *Curr Archaeol*, **8**, 172–4

Beales, P W, 1980 The late Devensian and Flandrian vegetational history of Crose Mere, Shropshire, *New Phytol*, **85**, 133–61

Beard, G, 1961 Studley Royal, Yorkshire, *Country Life*, **130**, 284–7

Beazley, E, 1971 *The countryside on view*, London

Bedwin, O, 1980 Neolithic and Iron Age material from a coastal site at Chidham, West Sussex, 1978, *Sussex Archaeol Collect*, **118**, 163–70

Bedwin, O, Rudling, D, and Roberts, M, 1985 Rescue archaeology in Sussex 1983: a tenth progress report on the Sussex Archaeological Field Unit, *Bull Inst Archaeol Univ London*, **21/22**, 31–48

Beeson, E B, and Masterman, M C H, 1979 *Archaeological survey of enclosed land in Widecombe-in-the-Moor parish*, Devon Archaeol Soc Occas Pap, **7**, Exeter

Bell, M, 1981 Valley sediments and environmental change, in *The environment of man: the Iron Age to the Anglo-Saxon period* (eds M Jones and G W Dimbleby), BAR, **87**, 75–91, Oxford

——, 1982 The effects of land-use and climate on valley sedimentation, in A Harding 1982, 127–142

——, 1983 Valley sediments as evidence of prehistoric land-use on the South Downs, *Proc Prehist Soc*, **49**, 119–150

——, 1984 Environmental archaeology in south-west England, in Keeley 1984, 43–133

——, 1985 *Brean Down 1985*, Lampeter

Bell, M, and Limbrey, S (eds), 1982 *Archaeological aspects of woodland ecology*, BAR, **S146**, Oxford

Bennett, K D, 1983 Devensian, late glacial, and flandrian vegetation history at Hockham Mere, Norfolk, England: I. Pollen percentages and conclusions, *New Phytol*, **95**, 457–487

Benson, D, and Miles, D, 1974 *The upper Thames Valley – an archaeological survey of the river gravels*, Oxford Archaeol Unit Survey, **2**, Oxford

Beresford, G, 1979 Three deserted medieval settlements on Dartmoor: a report on the late E Marie Minter's excavations, *Medieval Archaeol*, **23**, 98–158

Beresford, M W, and Hurst, J G (eds), 1971 *Deserted medieval villages*, London

Beresford, M W, and St Joseph, J K S, 1979 *Medieval England: an aerial survey*, 2 edn, Cambridge

Bewley, B, 1986 The smallest wetland in Europe?, *Newswarp*, **1**, 18–19

Bilikowski, K, 1983 *Hampshire's countryside heritage 5: historic parks and gardens*, Winchester

Binney, M, 1978 Protecting historic gardens, *Country Life*, **164**, 822–4

Bird, A, 1986 The work of the River Wey Trust, in Hughes and Rowley 1986, 127–32

Birks, H J B, Deacon, J, and Pegler, S, 1975 Pollen maps for the British Isles 5000 years ago, *Proc Roy Soc London (B)*, **189**, 87–105

Birley, E, 1960 *Chesters Roman Fort, Northumberland*, London

Blacksell, M, and Gilg, A, 1981 *Countryside planning and change*, London

Blatchford, O N, 1978 Forestry practice, *Forestry Commission Bull*, **14**, London

Blunden, J, and Curry, N (eds), 1985 *The changing countryside*, London

Body, R, 1982 *Agriculture: the triumph and the shame*, London

Bond, C J, 1981 Woodstock Park under the Plantagenet kings: the exploitation and use of wood and timber in a medieval deer park, *Arboricultural J*, **5**, 201–213

——, 1986 The Oxford region in the Middle Ages, in *The archaeology of the Oxford region* (eds G Briggs, J Cook, and T Rowley), 135–59, Oxford

Bonney, D J, 1980 Damage by medieval and later cultivation, in Hinchliffe and Schadla-Hall 1980, 41–8

Bonsall, C, Sutherland, D G, Tipping, R M, and Cherry, J, forthcoming The Eskmeals project: Late Mesolithic settlement and environment in north-west England, in *The Mesolithic in Europe: Proceedings of the third International Symposium, Edinburgh, 1985* (ed C Bonsall)

Bonsey, C, 1970 The problems of recreation on sites of archaeological and ecological interest, in Sheail and Wells 1970, 73–9

Boon, G, 1974 *Silchester: the Roman town of Calleva*, Newton Abbot

Bowen, H C, 1961 *Ancient fields*, London

——, 1975 Air photography and the development of the landscape in central parts of southern England, in D R Wilson 1975, 103–17

——, 1978 Celtic fields and ranch boundaries in Wessex, in Limbrey and Evans 1978, 115–23

Bowen, H C, and Fowler, P J, 1962 The archaeology of Fyfield and Overton Down, Wiltshire, *Wiltshire Archaeol Natur Hist Mag*, **58**, 98–115

—— and ——(eds), 1978 *Early land allotment*, BAR, **48**, Oxford

Bradley, R, 1970a Where have all the houses gone?, *Curr Archaeol*, **2**, 264–6

——, 1970b The excavation of a beaker settlement at Belle Tout, East Sussex, England, *Proc Prehist Soc*, **36**, 312–79

——, 1975 Salt and settlement in the Hampshire-Sussex borderland, in de Brisay and Evans 1975, 20–4

——, 1978a Prehistoric field systems in Britain and north-west Europe – a review of some recent evidence, *World Archaeol*, **9**, 265–80

——, 1978b *The prehistoric settlement of Britain*, London

——, 1979 The interpretation of later Bronze Age metalwork from British rivers, *Int J Naut Archaeol Underwater Explor*, **8**, 3–6

——, 1984 *The social foundations of prehistoric Britain*, London

Bradley, R, Edmonds, M, Entwistle, R, and Ford, S, 1985 Fieldwork at Great Langdale, Cumbria, 1985 – interim report, *Lithics*, **6**, 10–14

Bradley, R, and Hooper, B, 1973 Recent discoveries from Portsmouth and Langstone Harbours: Mesolithic to Iron Age, *Proc Hampshire Fld Club Archaeol Soc*, **30**, 17–27

Bradley, R, and Mead, B, 1985 The Woodhenge and the trees, *Antiquity*, **49**, 44–5

Brandon, P F, and Millman, R N L, 1981 *The threat to the historic rural landscape*, London

Breeze, D J, and Dobson, B, 1976 *Hadrian's Wall*, London

Britnell, R H, 1981 The proliferation of markets in England 1200–1349, *Econ Hist Rev*, 2 ser, **34**, 209–21

Brook, A, 1981 *Waterways and wetlands: a practical conservation handbook*, Wallingford

Brothwell, D, and Dimbleby, G (eds), 1981 *Environmental aspects of coasts and islands*, BAR, **S94**, Oxford

Brown, A E, and Taylor, C C, 1972 The gardens at Lyveden, Northamptonshire, *Archaeol J*, **129**, 154–60

Brown, R A, 1976 *English castles*, London

Bruce-Mitford, R, 1975 *The Sutton Hoo ship burial I: excavations, background, the ship, dating and inventory*, London

BTCV, 1982 *Woodlands: a practical conservation handbook*, British Trust for Conservation Volunteers, Wallingford

Buchanan, R A, 1972 *Industrial archaeology in Britain*, Harmondsworth

Buckley, F, 1925 The microlithic industries of Northumberland, *Archaeol Aeliana*, 4 ser, **1**, 42–7

Burchell, J P T, 1957 The Upchurch Marshes, Kent, *Archaeol Newsletter*, **6**, 89–91

Burchell, J P T, and Piggott, S, 1939 Decorated prehistoric pottery from the bed of the Ebbsfleet, Northfleet, Kent, *Antiq J*, **14**, 405–20

Burgess, C, 1980 *The age of Stonehenge*, London

Burgess, C, Coombs, D, and Gareth-Davies, D, 1972 The Broadward complex and barbed spearheads, in *Prehistoric man in Wales and the west* (eds F Lynch and C Burgess), 211–84, Bath

Burl, A, 1976 *The stone circles of the British Isles*, London and New Haven

——, 1979 *Prehistoric Avebury*, London and New Haven

Burrow, I, 1981 *Hillfort and hilltop settlement in Somerset in the first millennium AD*, BAR, **91**, Oxford

——(ed), 1985 *County archaeological records and progress and potential*, Taunton

Burton, R G O, and Robson, J D, 1985 Current work of the soil survey of England and Wales in the Fenland, *Fenland Res*, **2**, 41–4

Butcher, S A, 1978 Excavations at Nornour, Isles of Scilly, 1969–73: the pre-Roman settlement, *Cornish Archaeol*, **17**, 29–112

Butler, C, and Fasham, P, 1975 Earthworks in Micheldever Wood, in Fasham 1975, 6–9

Butzer, K W, 1972 *Environment and archaeology*, London

Caiger, J E L, 1964 Dareth Wood: its earthworks and antiquities, *Archaeol Cantiana*, **79**, 77–94

Campbell, J B, 1977 *The upper Palaeolithic of Britain: a study of man and nature in the late Ice Age*, Oxford

Cantor, L M, 1962 The medieval parks of south Staffordshire, *Trans Birmingham Warwickshire Archaeol Soc*, **80**, 1–9

——, 1971 The medieval deer parks of Leicestershire, *Trans Leicestershire Archaeol Hist Soc*, **46**, 9–24

——, 1983 *The medieval parks of England: a gazetteer*, Loughborough

Cantor, L M (ed), 1982 *The English medieval landscape*, London

Carroll, M R, 1978 *Multiple use of woodlands*, Univ Cambridge Dep Land Economy Occas Pap, **10**, Cambridge

Cartwright, C R, 1984 Field survey of Chichester harbour 1982, *Sussex Archaeol Collect*, **122**, 23–7

Carver, M, 1984 Techniques: throwing light upon the past, *Fld Archaeol*, **2**, 19

——, 1986 Evaluation, *Bull Sutton Hoo Res Comm*, **4**, 7–41

CBA, 1948 *A survey and policy of field research in the archaeology of Great Britain*, London

——, 1977 *Archaeology in structure and local plans*, London

Chambers, J D, and Mingay, G E, 1966 *The agricultural revolution 1750–1880*, London

Chowne, P, 1980 Bronze Age settlement in south Lincolnshire, in Barrett and Bradley 1980, 295–305

Chowne, P, and Healy, F, 1983 Artefacts from a prehistoric cemetery and settlement in Anwick Fen, Lincolnshire, *Lincolnshire Hist Archaeol*, **18**, 37–46

—— and ——, 1985 A Neolithic settlement at Tattershall Thorpe, Lincolnshire, *Fenland Res*, **2**, 25–31

Christie, P M L, 1978 The excavation of an Iron Age souterrain and settlement at Carn Euny, Sancreed, Cornwall, *Proc Prehist Soc*, **44**, 309–434

Churchill, D M, 1965 The kitchen midden site at Westward Ho!, Devon, England: ecology, age and relation to changes in land and sea levels, *Proc Prehist Soc*, **31**, 74–84

Clack, P A G, and Gosling, P F (eds), 1976 *Archaeology in the north*, Durham

Clack, P A G, and Haselgrove, C (eds), 1982 *Rural settlement in the Roman north*, Durham

Clark, A J, 1975 Archaeological prospecting: a progress report, *J Archaeol Sci*, **2**, 297–314

Clarke, H, 1984 *The archaeology of medieval England*, London

Clark, J D G, 1936 The timber monument at Arminghall and its affinities, *Proc Prehist Soc*, **2**, 1–51

——, 1954 *Excavations at Star Carr*, Cambridge

——, 1963 Neolithic bows from Somerset, England, and the prehistory of archery in north-west Europe, *Proc Prehist Soc*, **29**, 50–98

Clark, J D G, and Godwin, H, 1962 The Neolithic of the Cambridgeshire Fens, *Antiquity*, **37**, 10–23

Cleere, H (ed), 1984 *Approaches to the archaeological heritage*, Cambridge

Cleere, H, and Crossley, D, 1985 *The iron industry of the Weald*, Leicester

CNP, 1984a *Know your national parks*, London, Council for National Parks

——, 1984b *Response by the Council for National Parks to the Countryside Commission's report 'A better future for the uplands'*, London

Cobham, R, 1984 *Agricultural landscapes demonstration farms*, Cheltenham

Coggins, D, Fairless, K J, and Batey, C E, 1983 Simy Folds: an early medieval settlement in upper Teesdale, *Medieval Archaeol*, **27**, 1–26

Colebourn, P, 1983 *Hampshire's countryside heritage 2: ancient woodlands*, Winchester

——, 1984 *Hampshire's countryside heritage 7: the coast*, Winchester

Coles, B, and Coles, J, 1986 *Sweet track to Glastonbury*, London

Coles, J M, 1972 *Field archaeology in Britain*, London

——, 1984 *The archaeology of wetlands*, Edinburgh

Coles, J M, Heal, S V E, and Orme, B J, 1978 The use and character of wood in prehistoric Britain and Ireland, *Proc Prehist Soc*, **44**, 1–46

Coles, J M, and Hibbert, F A, 1972 A Neolithic wooden mallet from the Somerset Levels, *Antiquity*, **46**, 52–4

Coles, J M, and Lawson, A J, 1986 *European wetlands in prehistory*, Oxford

Coles, J M, and Orme, B, 1977 Neolithic hurdles from Walton Heath, Somerset, *Somerset Levels Pap*, **3**, 6–29

—— and ——, 1980 *Prehistory of the Somerset Levels*, Cambridge and Exeter

—— and ——, 1983a The Sedgemoor Survey 1982, *Somerset Levels Pap*, **9**, 6–8

—— and ——, 1983b Archaeology in the Somerset Levels 1982, *Somerset Levels Pap*, **9**, 5–6

—— and ——, 1985 Radiocarbon dates: fifth list, *Somerset Levels Pap*, **11**, 85

Collins, E J T, 1978 *The economy of upland Britain 1750–1950: an illustrated review*, Centre for Agricultural Strategy Pap, **4**, Reading

Colvin, H M, 1963 *History of the Kings Works*, **2**, London

Connah, G, 1965 Excavations at Knap Hill, Alton Priors, 1961, *Wiltshire Archaeol Natur Hist Mag*, **60**, 1–23

Conway, V M, 1954 Stratigraphy and pollen analysis of southern Pennine blanket peats, *J Ecol*, **42**, 117–47

Cooke, A O, 1920 *A book of dovecotes*, London

Coombs, D G, 1976 Excavations at Mam Tor, Derbyshire, 1965–1969, in *Hillforts: later prehistoric earthworks in Britain and Ireland* (ed D W Harding), 147–52, London

Countryside Commission, 1968 *The coasts of England and Wales: measurements of use, protection and development*, London

——, 1969 *Nature conservation at the coast*, Coastal Preservation and Development Project Special Study Rep, **2**, London

——, 1970a *The coastal heritage*, London

——, 1970b *The planning of the coastline: a report on a study of coastal preservation and development in England and Wales*, London

——, 1976 *The Lake District upland management experiment*, Cheltenham

——, 1978a *Upland land use*, Cheltenham

——, 1978b *Guided walks*, Advisory Ser, **4**, Cheltenham

——, 1980a *Self-guided trails*, Advisory Ser, **9**, Cheltenham

——, 1980b *Countryside conservation handbook*, Cheltenham

——, 1980c *Grassland establishment for countryside recreation*, Advisory Ser, **13**, Cheltenham

——, 1983a *Areas of Outstanding Natural Beauty: policy statement 1983*, Cheltenham

——, 1983b *Country parks*, Cheltenham

——, 1984 *A better future for the uplands*, Cheltenham

——, 1985 *National countryside recreation survey 1984*, Cheltenham

——, 1986 *Heritage landscapes management plans*, Cheltenham

——, nd *What future for the uplands?*, Cheltenham

Cox, J C, 1905 *The Royal Forests of England*, London

Craddock, P T, Gurney, D, Pryor, F, and Hughes, M J, 1985 The application of phosphate analysis to the location and interpretation of archaeological sites, *Archaeol J*, **142**, 361–76

Crawford, O G S, 1925 *The long barrows of the Cotswolds*, Gloucester

——, 1930 The unknown megalith, *Antiquity*, **4**, 364 and 493

——, 1960 *Archaeology in the field*, London

Crawford, O G S, and Keiller, A, 1928 *Wessex from the air*, Oxford

Croad, S J, and Fowler, P J, 1984 RCHM's first 75 years: an outline history, 1908–83, *RCHME Annu Rev*, 1983–4, 8–13

Crossley, D W (ed), 1981 *Medieval industry*, CBA Res Rep, **40**, London

Crummy, P, Hillan, J, and Crossan, C, 1982 Mersea Island: the Anglo-Saxon causeway, *Essex Archaeol Hist*, **14**, 77–86

Cullen, P, 1982 *An evaluation of the Heritage Coast programme in England and Wales*, Cheltenham

Cunliffe, B, 1971 *Excavations at Fishbourne 1961–1969*, Rep Res Comm Soc Antiq London, **26**, London

——, 1978a *Iron Age communities in Britain*, 2 edn, London

——, 1978b *Hengistbury Head*, London

——, 1980 The evolution of Romney Marsh: a preliminary statement, in F H Thompson 1980, 37–55

——, 1984 *Danebury – an Iron Age hillfort in Hampshire*, CBA Res Rep, **52**, London

Cunliffe, B, and Miles, D (eds), 1984 *Aspects of the Iron Age in central southern Britain*, Univ Oxford Comm Archaeol Monogr, **2**, Oxford

Cunliffe, B, and Rowley, T (eds), 1976 *Oppida in barbarian Europe*, BAR, **S11**, Oxford

Curtis, L F, Courtney, F M, and Trudgill, S, 1976 *Soils in the British Isles*, London

Curtis, L F, and Walker, A J, 1980 Exmoor: a problem of landscape planning and management, *J Landscape Design*, **130**, 7–13

Daniel, G E, 1950 *The prehistoric chamber tombs of England and Wales*, Cambridge

——, 1959 Some megalithic follies, *Antiquity*, **33**, 282–4

——, 1967 *The origins and growth of archaeology*, Harmondsworth

——, 1975 *A hundred and fifty years of archaeology*, London

——, 1981 *A short history of archaeology*, London

Daniels, J L (ed), 1983 *Heathland management in amenity areas*, Cheltenham

Darbishire, R D, 1874 Notes on discoveries in Ehenside Tarn, Cumberland, *Archaeologia*, **44**, 273–92

Darby, H C, 1940 *The medieval Fenland*, Cambridge

——, 1956 *The draining of the Fens*, 2 edn, Cambridge

——, 1973 *A new historical geography of England*, Cambridge

——, 1977 *Domesday England*, Cambridge

Darvill, T C, 1982 *The megalithic chambered tombs of the Cotswold-Severn region*, Vorda Res Ser, **5**, Highworth

——, 1984a *Birdlip bypass project – first report: field survey and archaeological assessment*, Bristol

——, 1984b Neolithic Gloucestershire, in *Archaeology in Gloucestershire – from the earliest hunters to the industrial age* (ed A Saville), 80–112, Cheltenham

——, 1986a *The archaeology of the uplands – a rapid assessment of archaeological knowledge and practice*, London

——, 1986b *Archaeology in the uplands: what future for our past?*, London

——, 1987 *Prehistoric Britain*, London

Darvill, T C, and Timby, J R, 1985 Excavations at the Buckles, Frocester, 1984: second interim report, *Glevensis*, **19**, 21–8

Darvill, T C, Parker-Pearson, M, Smith, R W, and Thomas, R (eds), 1978 *New approaches to our past – an archaeological forum*, Southampton

de Brisay, K, 1975 The red hills of Essex, in de Brisay and Evans 1975, 5–11

de Brisay, K, and Evans, K A (eds), 1975 *Salt: the study of an ancient industry*, Colchester

Denford, G T, Farrell, A W, Gregson, C W, McGrail, S, and O'Connor, S, 1979 *Boat finds on land – a guide for archaeologists*, *Curr Archaeol*, **6**, 171–5

Dent, J, 1984 Skerne, *Curr Archaeol*, **8**, 251–3

Dickens, A G, 1951 *The register or chronicle of Butley Priory, Suffolk 1510–1535*, Winchester

Dimbleby, G W, 1962 *The development of British heathlands and their soils*, Oxford Forestry Memoir, **23**, Oxford

——, 1976 The history and archaeology of heaths, in *The southern heathlands: symposium held at Rogate Field Centre 4–6th October 1974* (eds J H P Sankey and H W Mackworth), London

——, 1978 Appendix I. Pollen analysis, in Christie 1978, 424–9

Dimbleby, G W, and Evans, J G, 1974 Pollen and land snails analysis of calcareous soils, *J Archaeol Sci*, **1**, 117–33

Dixon, P, 1976 *Barbarian Europe*, Oxford

DoE, 1983 *Criteria for the selection of Ancient Monuments*, Press Notice, **523**, London

——, 1985 *The use of conditions in planning permissions*, Circular, **1/85**, London

——, 1986 *Conservation and development: the British approach*, London

Doherty, J, and Pilkington, J, 1984 *Hampshire's countryside heritage 3: Rivers and wetlands*, Winchester

Dougill, W, 1936 *The English coast, its development and preservation*, London

Drewett, P, 1976 The excavation of four round barrows of the second millennium BC at West Heath, Harting, 1973–5, *Sussex Archaeol Collect*, **114**, 126–50

——, 1980 Sussex plough damage survey, in Hinchliffe and Schadla-Hall 1980, 69–73

——, 1985 The excavation of barrows V–IX at West Heath, Harting, 1980, *Sussex Archaeol Collect*, **123**, 35–60

Drury, P J, 1981 The production of brick and tile in medieval England, in Crossley 1981, 126–42

Eagles, B N, and Woodward, P J, 1984 Medieval timberwork at Bull Bridge, Wilton, *Wiltshire Archaeol Natur Hist Mag*, **79**, 237–8

Edlin, H L, 1949 *Woodland crafts in Britain*, London

Ehrenberg, M, 1980 The occurrence of Bronze Age metalwork in the Thames: an investigation, *Trans London Middlesex Archaeol Soc*, **31**, 1–15

Ellison, A, 1980 *Excavations at West Hill Uley: 1977–9 – 2nd interim report*, Comm Rescue Archaeol Avon Gloucestershire Somerset Occas Pap, **9**, Bristol

Emery, F V, 1962 Moated settlements in England, *Geography*, **47**, 378–88

Emmett, D D, 1979 Stone rows: the traditional view reconsidered, *Proc Devon Archaeol Soc*, **37**, 94–114

Erith, F H, 1971 The levelled long barrows, *Colchester Archaeol Group Annu Bull*, **14**, 35–6

ETB, 1983 *Leisure day-trips in Great Britain summer 1981 and 1982*, London, English Tourist Board

Evans, C, and Hodder, I, 1985 The Haddenham Project, *Fenland Res*, **2**, 18–23

Evans, J G, 1966 Late glacial and post-glacial subaerial deposits at Pitstone, Bucks, *Proc Geol Ass*, **77**, 347–64

——, 1968 Changes in the composition of land molluscan populations in north Wiltshire during the last 5000 years, in *Studies in the structure, physiology and ecology of molluscs*, Zoological Society London Symposia (ed V Fretter), **22**, 293–318, London

——, 1971 Habitat change on the calcareous soils of Britain: the impact of Neolithic man, in *Economy and settlement in Neolithic and early Bronze Age Britain and Europe* (ed D D A Simpson), 27–73, Leicester

——, 1975 *The environment of early man in the British Isles*, London

——, 1978 *An introduction to environmental archaeology*, London

——, 1979 The palaeo-environment of coastal blown-sand deposits in western and northern Britain, *Scot Archaeol Forum*, **9**, 16–26

Evans, J G, Pitts, M W, and Williams, D, 1982 An excavation at Avebury, Wiltshire, 1982, *Proc Prehist Soc*, **51**, 305–10

Evans, J G, Limbrey, S, and Cleere, H (eds), 1975 *The effect of man on the landscape: the Highland Zone*, CBA Res Rep, **11**, London

Evans, J H, 1953 Archaeological horizons in the north Kent marshes, *Archaeol Cantiana*, **64**, 103–46

Evelyn, J, 1706 *Silva, or a discourse on forest trees*, London

Farrell, L (ed), 1983 *Heathland management*, Focus on Nature Conservation, **2**, Banbury

Fasham, P (ed), 1975a *M3 Archaeology 1975*, Andover

——, 1975b An Iron Age site in Micheldever Wood, R27, in Fasham 1975a, 10–15

——, 1984 *Groundwater pumping techniques for excavation*, Inst Fld Archaeol Tech Pap, **1**, Birmingham

Fasham, P J, Schadla-Hall, R T, Shennan, S J, and Bates, P J, 1980 *Field walking for archaeologists*, Southampton

Faull, M L, and Moorhouse, S A, 1981 *West Yorkshire: an archaeological survey*, Wakefield

Feachem, R W, 1973 Ancient agriculture in the highlands of Britain, *Proc Prehist Soc*, **39**, 332–53

Feather, W S, and Manby, T G, 1970 Prehistoric chambered tombs of the Pennines, *Yorkshire Archaeol J*, **42**, 396–7

Feist, M J, 1978 *A study of management agreements*, Cheltenham

Fell, C, and Hildyard, E J, 1953 Prehistoric Weardale – a new survey, *Archaeol Aeliana*, 4 Ser, **31**, 98–115

Field, J, 1972 *English field names*, Newton Abbot

Field, N, nd *Fiskerton in the Iron Age*, Lincoln

Finberg, H P R, 1955 *Roman and Saxon Withington: a study in continuity*, Leicester Univ Department Local Hist Occas Pap, **8**, Leicester

Finch Smith, R, 1987 *Roadside settlements in lowland Roman Britain*, BAR, **157**, Oxford

Fleming, A, 1978 The prehistoric settlement of Dartmoor Part 1: south Dartmoor, *Proc Prehist Soc*, **44**, 97–124

——, 1982 Social boundaries and land boundaries, in *Ranking, resource and exchange* (eds C Renfrew and S Shennan), 52–5, Cambridge

——, 1983a Upland settlement in Britain: the second millennium and after, *Scot Archaeol Rev*, **2**, 171–6

——, 1983b The prehistoric landscape of Dartmoor Part 2: north and east Dartmoor, *Proc Prehist Soc*, **49**, 195–241

——, 1985 Dartmoor reaves, *Devon Archaeol*, **3**, 1–6

Fleming, A, and Ralph, N, 1982 Medieval settlement and land use on Holne Moor, Dartmoor: the landscape evidence, *Medieval Archaeol*, **26**, 101–37

Forde-Johnson, J, 1976 *Hillforts of the Iron Age in England and Wales*, Liverpool

Forestry Commission, 1974 *British Forestry*, Edinburgh

——, 1978 *The place of forestry in England and Wales*, Edinburgh

——, 1982 *Census of woodland trees 1979–82*, Edinburgh

——, 1984a *The Forestry Commission's objectives*, Policy and Procedure Pap, **1**, Edinburgh

——, 1984b *The Forestry Commission and recreation* Policy and Procedure Pap, **2**, Edinburgh

——, 1984c *The Forestry Commission and landscape design*, Policy and Procedure Pap, **3**, Edinburgh

——, 1984d *The Forestry Commission and conservation*, Policy and Procedure Pap, **4**, Edinburgh

——, 1985 *Forestry facts and figures 1984–5*, Edinburgh

Fowler, D D, 1982 Cultural resources management, *Advances in Archaeol Method and Theory*, **5**, 1–50

Fowler, G, 1950 A Romano-British village near Littleport, Cambridgeshire, *Proc Cambridge Antiq Soc*, **43**, 7–20

Fowler, P J, 1967 The archaeology of Fyfield and Overton Downs, Wiltshire, *Wiltshire Archaeol Natur Hist Mag*, **62**, 16–33

——, 1968 Conservation and the countryside, *Wiltshire Archaeol Natur Hist Mag*, **63**, 1–11

——, 1970 Old grassland: its archaeological significance and ecological importance, *Antiquity*, **44**, 57–9

——, 1971 Early prehistoric agriculture in western Europe: some archaeological evidence, in *Economy and settlement in Neolithic and early Bronze Age Britain and Europe* (ed D D A Simpson ed), 153–84, Leicester

184

——, 1977 Land management and the cultural resource, in Rowley and Breakell 1977, 131–42
——, 1980 Traditions and objectives in British field archaeology, 1953–78, *Archaeol J*, **137**, 1–21
——, 1983 *The farming of prehistoric Britain*, Cambridge
Fowler, P J, and Ellison, A B, 1977 Archaeology on Exmoor: its nature, assessment and management, *Exmoor Rev*, **18**, 78–84
Fowler, P J, and Thomas, A C, 1979 Lyonesse revisited: the early walls of Scilly, *Antiquity*, **53**, 175–89
Fraser, D, 1986 The role of archaeological record systems in the management of monuments, in Hughes and Rowley 1986
Frere, S S, 1967 *Britannia*, London
French, C, and Taylor, M, 1985 Desiccation and destruction: the immediate effects of dewatering at Etton, Cambridgeshire, *Oxford J Archaeol*, **4**, 139–56
Frere, S S, and St Joseph, J K S, 1983 *Roman Britain from the air*, Cambridge
Fry, G L A, and Cooke, A S, 1984 *Acid deposition and its implications for nature conservation in Britain*, Focus on Nature Conservation, **7**, Shrewsbury
Fulford, M, 1975 *New Forest Roman pottery*, BAR, **17**, Oxford
Garden History Society, 1984 *The conservation of historic gardens – Proceedings of a symposium held by the Garden History Society and the Ancient Monuments Society 9th May 1984*, Glastonbury
Gates, T, 1983 Unenclosed settlements in Northumberland, in *Settlement in North Britain 1000 BC – AD 1000* (eds J C Chapman and H C Mytum), BAR, **118**, 103–48, Oxford
Gelling, M, 1978 *Signposts to the past*, London
——(ed), 1983 *Offa's Dyke reviewed*, BAR, **114**, Oxford
Gelling, P S, and Stanford S C, 1965 Dark Age pottery or Iron Age ovens?, *Trans Proc Birmingham Warwickshire Archaeol Soc*, **82**, 77–91
Geraint Jenkins, J, 1974 *Nets and coracles*, Newton Abbot
Gillespie, R, 1984 *Radiocarbon user's handbook*, Oxford Univ Comm Archaeol Monogr, **3**, Oxford.
Gilyard-Beer, R, 1970 *Fountains Abbey, North Yorkshire*, London
Gimingham, C H, 1972 *Ecology of heathlands*, London
Godwin, H, 1943 Coastal peat beds of the British Isles and North Sea, *J Ecol*, **31**, 199–247
——, 1975 *History of the British flora*, 2 edn, Cambridge
——, 1978 *Fenland: its ancient past and uncertain future*, Cambridge
——, 1981 *The archives of the peat bogs*, Cambridge
Gold, J R, and Burgess, J (eds), 1982 *Valued environments*, London
Gosling, P, 1985 Archaeological conservation in practice, in Lambrick 1985a, 45–50
Gray, H L, 1915 *English field systems*, Harvard
Green, B, 1981 *Countryside conservation: the protection and management of amenity ecosystems*, London
Greeves, T, 1985 The Dartmoor tin industry. Some aspects of its field remains, *Devon Archaeol*, **3**, 31–40
Griffiths, F M, 1984 Archaeological investigations at Colliford Reservoir, Bodmin Moor, 1977–78, *Cornish Archaeol*, **23**, 47–140
Grinsell, L V, 1941 The round barrows of Wessex, *Proc Prehist Soc*, **7**, 73–113
——, 1980 The Cerne Abbas Giant: 1764–1980, *Antiquity*, **54**, 29–33
——, nd *The Stonehenge barrow groups*, Salisbury
Groube, L M, 1978 Priorities and problems in Dorset archaeology, in Darvill *et al* 1978, 29–52
Groube, L M, and Bowden, M C B, 1982 *The archaeology of rural Dorset, past present and future*, Dorset Natur Hist Archaeol Soc Monogr Ser, **4**, Dorchester
Gruffydd, J St B, 1977 *Protecting historic landscapes: gardens and parks*, Cheltenham
Guilbert, G, 1975 Ratlinghope – Still Hill Shropshire: earthworks, enclosures and cross dykes, *Bull Board Celtic Stud*, **26**, 363–73
Gurney, D A, 1985 *Phosphate analysis of soils: a guide for the field archaeologist*, Inst Fld Archaeol Tech Pap, **3**, Birmingham
Hadfield, M, 1973 Gardens and landscape parks, in *The National Trust Guide* (eds R Fedden and R Joekes), 227–62, London
——, 1979 *A history of British gardening*, London
Haigh J C B, Kisch, B K, and Jones, M U, 1983 Computer plot and excavated reality, in Maxwell 1983, 85–91
Hall, C, 1985 The passing of the past, *Countryman*, **90**, 15–21
Hall, D N, 1981 The Cambridgeshire Fenland: an intensive archaeological fieldwork survey, in *The evolution of marshland landscapes* (ed T Rowley), 52–73, Oxford
——, 1982 *Medieval fields*, Princes Risborough
Hampshire County Council, 1984 *Hampshire's countryside heritage policy*, Winchester
Hampton, J, and Palmer, R, 1977 Implications of aerial photography for archaeology, *Archaeol J*, **134**, 157–93
Hansford Worth, R, 1967 *Worth's Dartmoor*, Newton Abbot
Harding, A, 1984 *A . . . ical survey on Danby Rigg – 1984*, Durham
Harding, A F . . . *. . . imatic change in later prehistory*, Edinburgh
Harding, G, . . . *. . . sfield, Glevensis*, **12**, 27–8
Hart, C, 1971 *. . . trial archaeology of Dean*, Newton Abbot
Hart, C R, 19. . *. . . rth Derbyshire archaeological survey*, Chesterfield

Harte, J D C, 1985 *Landscape, land-use and the law: an introduction to the law relating to the landscape and its use*, London
Harvey, J, 1981 *Medieval gardens*, London
Haselgrove, C, Millett, M, and Smith, I (eds), 1985 *Archaeology from the ploughsoil*, Sheffield
Hatchards, nd *The Honourable Entertainment given to the Quenes Majestie at Elvetham 1591*, (reprint by Hatchards), London
Hatherly, J M, and Cantor, L M 1979–80 The medieval parks of Berkshire, *Berkshire Archaeol J*, **70**, 67–80
Hayfield, C (ed), 1980 *Fieldwalking as a method of archaeological research*, Dir Ancient Mon Hist Bldgs Occas Pap, **2**, London
Haynes, J S, 1983 *Historic landscape conservation*, Gloucestershire Papers in Local and Rural Planning, **20**, Gloucester
Hayes, R H, 1983 *Levisham Moor: archaeological investigations 1957–1978*, Helmsley
Hayes, T, 1976 A survey of Wark Forest, in Clack and Gosling 1976, 247–53
Hazel, V, 1983 *Hampshire's countryside heritage 4: Heathland*, Winchester
Hazelden, J, and Jarvis, M G, 1979 Age and significance of alluvium in the Windrush Valley, Oxfordshire, *Nature*, **282**, 291–2
HBMC, 1984a *Introduction: The Historic Buildings and Monuments Commission for England*, London
——, 1984b *England's archaeological resource: a rapid quantification of the national archaeological resource and a comparison with the schedule of ancient monuments*, London
——, 1984c *An analysis of support from Central Government (DAMHB) and the Historic Buildings and Monuments Commission (HBMC) for the recording of archaeological sites and landscapes in advance of their destruction between 1982 and 1984*, London
——, 1984d *The effects of the Ancient Monuments and Archaeological Areas Act 1979 as amended by the National Heritage Act 1983 on owners and occupiers of Scheduled Ancient Monuments*, London
——, 1984e *Management agreements for the preservation of ancient monuments*, London
——, 1986a *Rescue archaeology funding: a policy statement*, London
——, 1986b *Preservation by record: the work of the Central Excavation Unit 1975–85*, London
Helliwell, D R, 1984 *Economics of woodland management*, Chichester
Henderson, A H, 1979 Mesolithic material from the surface of Stannage Barrows, *Trans Hunter Archaeol Soc*, **10**, 365–9
Hendry, G, Bannister, N, and Tom, J, 1984 The earthworks of an ancient woodland, *Bristol Avon Archaeol*, **3**, 47–53
Heslop, D M, 1987 *The excavation of an Iron Age settlement at Thorpe Thewles, Cleveland, 1980–2*, CBA Res Rep, **65**, London
Hicks, S P, 1971 Pollen-analitical evidence for the effect of prehistoric agriculture on the vegetation of north Derbyshire, *New Phytol*, **70**, 647–68
Higham, N J, 1978 Dyke systems in northern Cumbria, *Bull Board Celtic Stud*, **28**, 142–56
Hinchliffe, J, 1980 Effects of ploughing on archaeological sites: assessment of the problem and some suggested approaches, in Hinchliffe and Schadla-Hall 1980, 11–17
Hinchliffe, J, and Schadla-Hall, T (eds), 1980 *The past under the plough*, Dir Ancient Mon Hist Bldgs Occas Pap, **3**, London
Hinton, D, 1977 *Alfred's kingdom*, London
H M Treasury, 1980 *Capital transfer tax and the National Heritage*, London
Hodgen, M, 1939 Domesday water mills, *Antiquity*, **13**, 261–79
Hodges, R, 1982 *Dark Age economics: the origins of towns and trade AD 600–1000*, London
Holden, E W, and Hudson, M A, 1981 Saltmaking in the Adur Valley, Sussex, *Sussex Archaeol Collect*, **119**, 117–48
Holleyman, G A, 1935 The Celtic field system in south Britain, *Antiquity*, **9**, 443–54
Hopkins, J J, 1983 Changes in the distribution and management of the Lizard heathlands, in Daniels 1983, 5
Hooper, M, 1975 Historical ecology, in *Landscape and documents* (eds A Rogers and T Rowley), London
Hoskins, W G, 1970 *The making of the English landscape*, Harmondsworth
Houlder, C H, 1979 The Langdale and Scarfell Pike axe factory sites: a field survey, in *Stone axe studies* (eds T H McK Clough and W Cummins), CBA Res Rep, **23**, 87–9, London
Hughes, M, and Rowley, L (eds), 1986 *The management and presentation of field monuments*, Oxford
Hughes, R C, 1980 Minimal cultivation: a non-plough approach to crop production, in Hinchliffe and Schadla-Hall 1980, 32–4
Hunter, J, 1977 Conserving the countryside legacy, *Country Life*, **161**, 1810–11
Hunter, M, 1975 *John Aubrey and the realm of learning*, London
Hussey, C, 1967 *English gardens and landscapes 1700–1750*, London
HWCC, 1984 *The strategy for Hadrian's Wall*, Newcastle upon Tyne
IUCN, 1980 *A world conservation strategy*, Gland, International Union for Conservation of Nature and Natural Resources
Jackson, A, 1978 *Forestry and archaeology: a study in survival of field monuments in south west Scotland*, Hertford

Jackson, D A, and Ambrose, T M, 1976   A Roman timber bridge at Aldwincle, Northamptonshire, *Britannia*, **7**, 39–72

Jacobi, R M, 1976   Britain inside and outside Mesolithic Europe, *Proc Prehist Soc*, **42**, 67–84

——, 1978a   Population and landscape in Mesolithic lowland England, in Limbrey and Evans 1978, 75–85

——, 1978b   The settlement of northern Britain in the 8th millennium BC, in *The post-glacial settlement of northern Europe* (ed P Mellars), 295–332, London

——, 1979   Early Flandrian hunters in the south-west, *Proc Devon Archaeol Soc*, **37**, 48–93

Jenkins, J, 1984   Protecting historic gardens, in Garden History Society 1984, 3–5

Jewell, P A, 1963   *The experimental earthwork on Overton Down, Wiltshire*, London

Jobey, G, 1981   Groups of small cairns and the excavation of a cairnfield on Millstone Hill, Northumberland, *Archaeol Aeliana*, 5 ser, **9**, 23–44

Johnson, N, 1981   Recent work of the Cornwall Committee for Rescue Archaeology, *Cornish Archaeol*, **20**, 215–16

——, 1983   The result of air and ground survey of Bodmin Moor, Cornwall, in Maxwell 1983, 5–13

Johnson, N, and David, A, 1982   Mesolithic site on Trevosa Head and contemporary geography, *Cornish Archaeol*, **21**, 67–103

Johnson, N, and Rose, P, 1983   *Archaeological survey and conservation in West Penwith, Cornwall*, Truro

Johnson, S, 1976   *The Roman forts of the Saxon Shore*, London

Jones, B, 1953   *Follies and grottoes*, London

Jones, C, 1973   *The conservation of chalk downland in Dorset*, Dorchester

Jones, G D B, 1982   The Solway frontier: interim report 1976–81, *Britannia*, **13**, 283–98

Jones, M, 1986   *England before Domesday*, London

Keeley, H C M (ed), 1984   *Environmental archaeology: a regional review*, 1, Dir Ancient Mon Hist Bldgs Occas Pap, **6**, London

——, 1987   *Environmental archaeology: a regional review*, **2**, HBMC Occas Pap, **1**, London

Kelly, M, and Osborne, P J, 1964   Two faunas and floras from the alluvium at Sustoke, Warwickshire, *Proc Linnaean Soc*, **176**, 37–65

Kerney, M P, Brown, E H, and Chandler, T J, 1964   The late glacial and post-glacial history of the chalk escarpment near Brook, Kent, *Phil Trans Roy Soc London B*, **248**, 135–204

Kirby, K J, 1984   *Forestry operations and broadleaf woodland conservation*, Focus on Nature Conservation 8, Shrewsbury

Lambert, J M, and Joyce, M, 1960   *The making of the Broads*, Roy Geogr Soc Res Ser, **3**, London

Lambrick, G, 1977   *Archaeology and agriculture*, Oxfordshire Archaeol Unit Survey, **4**, London

——, 1981   Thames floodplain survey, *CBA Group 9 Newsletter*, **12**, 129–34

——, 1983a   Thames floodplain survey, *CBA Group 9 Newsletter*, **13**, 147–8

——, 1983b   *The Rollright Stones*, Oxford

——(ed), 1985a   *Archaeology and nature conservation*, Oxford

——, 1985b   Archaeology and nature conservation in Oxfordshire, in Lambrick 1985a, 67–86

Lambrick, G, and McDonald, A, 1985   The archaeology and ecology of Port Meadow and Wolvercote Common, Oxford, in Lambrick 1985a 95–110

Lambrick, G, and Robinson, M A, 1979   *Iron Age and Roman riverside settlement at Farmoor, Oxfordshire*, CBA Res Rep, **32**, London

Lawson, A, 1981   The barrows of Norfolk, in *The barrows of East Anglia* (eds A J Lawson, E A Martin, and D Priddy), *E Anglian Archaeol*, **12**, 32–63, Norwich

Leach, P, and Thew, N, 1984   *A late Iron Age 'Oppidum' at Ilchester, Somerset: an interim assessment 1984*, Bristol, Western Archaeol Trust

Leavy, M J, Rowe, J, and Young, J D, 1986   *Management plans: a guide to their preparation and use*, Cheltenham

Leech, R, 1977   *The upper Thames valley in Gloucestershire and Wiltshire: an archaeological survey of the river gravels*, Committee for Rescue Archaeol Avon Gloucestershire Somerset Sur, **4**, Bristol

——, 1981   The Somerset Levels in the Romano-British period, in *The evolution of marshland landscapes* (ed T Rowley), 20 51, Oxford

Lennard, R, 1959   *Rural England 1086–1135*, London

Leslie, K C, 1971   Ashburnham Estate brickyards, 1840–1968, *Sussex Indust Hist*, **1**, 2–22

Lewis, N A, and Miles, D, 1985   Archaeology and nature conservation: problems and potential at Cherbury Camp, Oxfordshire, in Lambrick 1985a, 111–20

Limbrey, S, 1975   *Soil science and archaeology*, London

——, 1978   Changes in quality and distribution of the soils of lowland Britain, in Limbrey and Evans 1978, 21–6

Limbrey, S, and Evans, J G (eds), 1978   *The effect of man on the landscape: the Lowland Zone*, CBA Res Rep, **21**, London

Lineham, C D, 1966   Deserted sites and rabbit warrens on Dartmoor, Devon, *Medieval Archaeol*, **10**, 113–44

Linsley, S, and Falconer, K, 1986   Industrial age, in Darvill 1986a, 33–5

Lloyd, R, 1976   The demand for forest recreation, in Steele 1976, 93–108

Longley, D, 1980   *Runnymede Bridge 1976: excavations on the site of a late Bronze Age settlement*, Res Vol Surrey Archaeol Soc, **6**, Guildford

Loughlin, N, and Miller, K R, 1979   *A survey of archaeological sites in Humberside*, Hull

Lowenthal, D, and Binney, M (eds), 1981   *Our past before us: why do we save it?*, London

Loyn, H R, 1962   *Anglo-Saxon England and the Norman conquest*, London

Lynch, F M, 1972   Ring cairns and related monuments in Wales, *Scot Archaeol Forum*, **4**, 61–80

Lyne, M A B, and Jefferies, R S, 1979   *The Alice Holt, Farnham, Roman pottery industry*, CBA Res Rep, **30**, London

Mabey, R, 1980   *The common ground: a place for nature in Britain's future?*, London

MacEwen, M, and Sinclair, G, 1983   *New life for the hills*, London

Maclean, T, 1981 *Medieval English gardens*, Glasgow

Macready, S, and Thompson, F H (eds), 1985   *Archaeological field survey in Britain and abroad*, Soc Antiq London Occas Pap, **6**, London

MAFF, 1966   *Agricultural land classification*, Ministry of Agriculture, Fisheries and Food Tech Rep, **11**, London

——, 1977   *Getting down to drainage No 1: does your land need drainage?*, London

——, 1979   *Farming on ancient monuments*, London

——, 1982   *Agricultural statistics*, London

——, 1984   *Huccaby Demonstration Farm: draft management plan*, Leeds and Exeter

Manby, T G, 1976   Excavation of the Kilham Long Barrow, East Riding of Yorkshire, *Proc Prehist Soc*, **42**, 111–59

Manning, W H, 1964   The plough in Roman Britain, *J Roman Stud*, **54**, 54–65

Margary, I D, 1973   *Roman roads in Britain*, 3 edn, London

Margules, C, and Usher, M B (eds), 1980   *Management plans in the countryside*, London

Marples, M, 1949   *White horses and other hill figures*, London

Marsden, B, 1983   *Pioneers of prehistory*, Ormskirk

Martin, E, 1985   West Row, Mildenhall, Suffolk, *Fenland Res*, **2**, 66

Mathias, P, 1969   *The first industrial nation*, London

Matthews, W H, 1922   *Mazes and labyrinths*, London

Maxwell, G S (ed), 1983   *The impact of aerial reconnaissance on archaeology*, CBA Res Rep, **49**, London

May, J, 1976   *Prehistoric Lincolnshire*, Lincoln

McCrone, P, 1985   The archaeology of the Dartmoor woodlands, *Devon Archaeol Soc Newsletter*, **31**, 11

McDonald, G, 1982   The management of wet site archaeological resources, in *Proceedings of the ICOM waterlogged wood working group conference, Ottawa, 1981* (ed D W Gratton), 123–8, Ottawa

McDonnell, R R J, 1979   The upper Axe Valley: an interim statement, *Somerset Archaeol Natur Hist*, **123**, 75–82

——, 1980   Tidal fish weirs, West Somerset, *Somerset Archaeol Natur Hist*, **124**, 134–5

——, 1985   *Archaeological survey of the Somerset claylands*, Taunton

McGrail, S, 1978   *Log-boats of England and Wales*, BAR, **51**, Oxford

——, 1979   Prehistoric boats, timber and woodworking technology, *Proc Prehist Soc*, **45**, 159–163

McGrail, S, and Millett, M, 1985   The Hasholme log-boat, *Antiquity*, **59**, 117–20

McGrail, S, and O'Connor, S, 1979   The Giggleswick Tarn log-boat, *Yorkshire Archaeol J*, **51**, 41–9

Megaw, J V S, and Simpson, D D A, 1979   *Introduction to British prehistory*, Leicester

Mellars, P A, 1976   Fire, ecology, animal populations and man: a study of some ecological relationships in prehistory, *Proc Prehist Soc*, **42**, 15–46

Mercer, R J, 1970   The excavation of a Bronze Age hut-circle settlement, Stannon Down, St Breward, Cornwall, 1968, *Cornish Archaeol*, **9**, 17–46

——, 1980a   *Hambledon Hill: a Neolithic landscape*, Edinburgh

——, 1980b   Evaluation of modern ploughing threats to prehistoric sites, in Hinchliffe and Schadla-Hall 1980, 105 9

——, 1980c   *Archaeological field survey in northern Scotland*, **1**, Univ Edinburgh Department Archaeol Occas Pap, **4**, Edinburgh

——, 1981a   *Grimes Graves, Norfolk: excavations 1971–2*, DoE Archaeol Rep, **11**, London

——, 1981b   Excavations at Carn Brea, Illogan, Cornwall, 1970–73, *Cornish Archaeol*, **20**, 1–204

——(ed), 1981c   *Farming practice in British prehistory*, Edinburgh

——, 1982   Field survey: a route to research strategies, *Scot Archaeol Rev*, **1**, 91–7

Merryfield, D L, and Moore, P D, 1974   Prehistoric human activity and blanket peat initiation on Exmoor, *Nature*, **250**, 439–41

Miles, D (ed), 1982   *The Romano-British countryside – studies in rural settlement and economy*, BAR, **103**, Oxford

Millman, R, 1979   The future of historic landscapes, *Local Hist*, **13**, 456–67

Milne, R, 1977   Drilling to avoid ploughing up the past, *New Sci*, **73**, 572

Mingay, G E (ed), 1981   *The Victorian countryside*, London

Monaghan, J, 1982   An investigation of the pottery industry on the Upchurch Marshes, *Archaeol Cantiana*, **98**, 27–50

Moore, P D, 1973   The influence of prehistoric cultu. ...e initiation and spread of blanket bog in upland Wales, *Nature*,

Moorhouse, S, 1986   Medieval, in Darvill 1986a, 37–40

Morgan Evans, D, 1985   The management of historic landscapes, in Lambrick 1985a, 89–94

——, 1986   The management of archaeological sites, in Hughes and Rowley 1986, 9–16

Mortimer, J R, 1905   *Forty years' researches in British and Saxon burial mounds of East Yorkshire*, London

Muckelroy, K, 1978   *Maritime archaeology*, Cambridge

Murphy, P, 1984a   Prehistoric environments and economy, in *Aspects of East Anglian prehistory* (ed C Barringer), 13–30, Norwich

——, 1984b   Environmental archaeology in East Anglia, in Keeley 1984, 13–42

Musty, J, 1973   A preliminary account of the medieval pottery industry at Minety, north Wiltshire, *Wiltshire Archaeol Natur Hist Mag*, **68**, 79–88

Musty, J, Algar, D J, and Ewence, P F, 1969   The medieval pottery kilns at Laverstock, near Salisbury, Wiltshire, *Archaeologia*, **102**, 83–150

Mytum, H, 1986   Dark Age, in Darvill 1986a, 35–7

National Trust, 1983   *Fountains Abbey appeal*, London

NCC, 1977   *Blanket bogs*, Shrewsbury

——, 1981   *The conservation of lowland heathland*, Shrewsbury

——, 1982a   *The conservation of peat bogs*, Shrewsbury

——, 1982b   *The conservation of sand dunes*, Shrewsbury

——, 1982c   *The conservation of coastal shingle features*, Shrewsbury

——, 1982d   *The conservation of coastal cliffs and scarps*, Shrewsbury

——, 1982e   *The conservation of limestone pavement*, Shrewsbury

——, 1982f   *The conservation of semi-natural upland woodland*, Shrewsbury

——, 1982g   *Chalk grassland – its conservation and management*, Shrewsbury

——, 1983a   *The conservation of estuaries*, Shrewsbury

——, 1983b   *The conservation of rivers*, Shrewsbury

——, 1983c   *The conservation of lakes*, Shrewsbury

——, 1983d   *The conservation of mountain and moorland*, Shrewsbury

——, 1983e   *Handbook for the preparation of management plans*, Shrewsbury

——, 1983f   *The conservation of mountain and moorland*, Shrewsbury

——, 1983g   *The conservation of fens and marshes*, Shrewsbury

——, 1983h   *Fens*, Shrewsbury

——, 1984   *Nature conservation in Great Britain*, Peterborough

——, nd   *Nature conservation and river engineering*, Shrewsbury

Needham, S P, 1985   Neolithic and Bronze Age settlement on the buried floodplain of Runnymede, *Oxford J Archaeol*, **4**, 125–37

Newcomb, R M, 1979   *Planning the past: historical landscape resources and recreation*, Folkestone

NFU, 1984   *New directions for agricultural policy – the way forward*, National Farmers Union, London

O'Keefe, P J, and Prott, L V, 1984   *Law and the cultural heritage: 1 – Discovery and excavation*, Abingdon

Oldfield, F, Krawiecki, A, Maker, B, Taylor, J J, and Twigger, S, 1985   The role of mineral magnetic measurements in archaeology, in *Palaeoenvironmental investigations – Research design, methods and data analysis* (eds N R J Fieller, D D Guilbertson, and N G A Ralph), BAR, **S258**, 29–43, Oxford

O'Neil, H E, 1966   Sales' Lot Long Barrow, Withington, Gloucestershire 1962–1965, *Trans Bristol Gloucestershire Archaeol Soc*, **85**, 5–35

Ordnance Survey, 1973   *Field archaeology in Great Britain*, 5 edn, Southampton

O'Riordan, T, 1982   *Putting trust in the countryside*, Conservation and Development Programme for the UK Rep, **7**, London

Orme, B J, Coles, J M, Caseldine, A E, and Bailey, G N, 1981   Meare Village West 1979, *Somerset Levels Pap*, **7**, 12–69

Orrom, M H, 1976   Developing the recreational use of forests, in Steele 1976, 109–18

Palmer, N E, 1981   Treasure Trove and the protection of antiquities, *Modern Law Rev*, **44**, 178–87

Palmer, R, 1977   A computer method for transcribing information graphically from oblique aerial photographs to maps, *J Archaeol Sci*, **4**, 283–90

Palmer, S, 1970   The Mesolithic industries of Mother Siller's channel, Christchurch and the neighbouring areas, *Proc Hampshire Fld Club Archaeol Soc*, **27**, 9–32

Passmore, A H, and Pallister, J, 1967   Boiling mounds in the New Forest, *Proc Hampshire Fld Club Archaeol Soc*, **24**, 14–19

Peacock, D P S, 1969   Neolithic pottery production in Cornwall, *Antiquity*, **43**, 145–9

Pearce, S, 1985   Early medieval land-use on Dartmoor and its flanks, *Devon Archaeol*, **3**, 13–19

Pennington, W, 1974   *The history of British vegetation*, 2 edn, London

Peterkin, G F, 1977   *Woodland survey for nature conservation*, Nature Conservancy Council Chief Scientist's Team Notes, **2**, London

——, 1981   *Woodland conservation and management*, London

Phibbs, J L, 1980   *Wimpole Park, Cambridgeshire*, London

Phillips, C W (ed), 1970   *The Fenland in Roman times*, Roy Geogr Soc Res Ser, **5**, London

Phillips, P (ed), 1985   *The archaeologist and the laboratory*, CBA Res Rep, **58**, London

Piggott, C M, 1943   Excavation of fifteen barrows in the New Forest 1941–2, *Proc Prehist Soc*, **9**, 1–27

Piggott, S, 1950   *William Stukeley: an eighteenth century antiquary*, London

——, 1968   *The Druids*, London

——, 1976   *Ruins in a landscape: essays on antiquarianism*, Edinburgh

——, 1981   Early prehistory, in *Agrarian history of England and Wales*, **1**(i) (ed S Piggott), 1–59, Cambridge

Platt, C, 1976   *The English medieval town*, London

——, 1978   *Medieval England – a social history and archaeology from the Conquest to 1600 AD*, London

Polytechnic of North London, 1978   *Historic landscapes: identification, recording and management*, London

Postan, M M, 1975   *The medieval economy and society*, Harmondsworth

Prehistoric Society, 1984   *Prehistory, priorities and society: the way forward*, London

Prescott, R, 1983   *Hampshire's countryside heritage 6: Chalk grassland*, Winchester

Prince, H, 1967   *Parks in England*, Shalfleet Manor, Isle of Wight

Pryor, F M, 1983a   South-west Fen-edge survey 1982/3: an interim report, *Northamptonshire Archaeol*, **18**, 165

——, 1983b   Down the drain or how we discovered a Bronze Age crannog at Flag Fen, *Curr Archaeol*, **8**, 102–6

——, 1985a   Dyke survey: an imperfect approach to the invisible, *Archaeol Rev Cambridge*, **4**, 5–14

——, 1985b   Flag Fen, *Curr Archaeol*, **9**, 6–8

Pryor, F M, and Kinnes, I, 1982   A waterlogged causewayed enclosure in the Cambridgeshire Fens, *Antiquity*, **56**, 124–7

Quartermaine, J, and Claris, P, 1986   The Langdale axe factories, *Curr Archaeol*, **9**, 212–13

Quest, P, 1982   Capital transfer tax and historic landscapes, in *Conserving historic landscapes* (ed C Swainwick), 33–6, Castleton

Rackham, O, 1975   *Hayley Wood, its history and ecology*, Cambridge

——, 1976   *Trees and woodland in the British landscape*, London

——, 1977   Neolithic woodland management in the Somerset Levels: Garvin's, Walton Heath and Rowland's tracks, *Somerset Levels Pap*, **3**, 65–72

——, 1980   *Ancient woodland, its history, vegetation and uses in England*, London

——, 1986   *The history of the countryside*, London

Radley, J, Tallis, J H, and Switsur, V R, 1974   The excavation of three narrow-blade Mesolithic sites in the southern Pennines, England, *Proc Prehist Soc*, **40**, 1–19

Raistrick, A, 1937   Prehistoric cultivations at Grassington, West Yorkshire, *Yorkshire Archaeol J*, **33**, 166–74

Ramm, H G, McDowall, R W, and Mercer, E, 1970   *Sheilings and bastles*, London

Rankine, W F, and Dimbleby, G W, 1960   Further investigations at a Mesolithic site at Oakhanger, Selborne, Hants, *Proc Prehist Soc*, **26**, 246–62

Ratcliffe, D A (ed), 1977   *A nature conservation review*, Cambridge

RCHME, 1960   *A matter of time: an archaeological survey of the river gravels of England*, London

——, 1970   *An inventory of historical monuments in the County of Dorset: 3(2), Central Dorset*, London

——, 1976   *Ancient and historical monuments in the county of Gloucestershire 1: Iron Age and Romano-British monuments in the Gloucestershire Cotswolds*, London

——, 1978   *Survey of surveys 1978*, London

——, 1979   *An inventory of the historical monuments in the County of Northamptonshire: 2, Archaeological sites in central Northamptonshire*, London

——, 1981   *An inventory of the historical monuments in the County of Northamptonshire: 3, Archaeological sites in north-west Northamptonshire*, London

Reece, R, 1983   Continuity on the Cotswolds: some problems of ownership, settlement and hedge survey between Roman Britain and the Middle Ages, *Landscape Hist*, **5**, 11–19

Reid, C, 1913   *Submerged forests*, Cambridge

Renn, D, 1968   *Norman castles in Britain*, London

Repton, H, 1980   *Observations on the theory and practice of landscape gardening*, reprint edn, London

Reynolds, P J, 1979   *Iron Age farm: the Butser experiment*, London

——, 1985   *Iron Age agriculture revisited*, Wessex Lecture 1, CBA Regional Group 12, Salisbury

Riley, D A, 1982   *Aerial archaeology in Britain*, Princes Risborough

——, 1980   *Early landscape from the air: studies of cropmarks in South Yorkshire and north Nottinghamshire*, Sheffield

Rivet, A L F, 1964   *Town and country in Roman Britain*, 2 edn, London

——(ed), 1967   *The Iron Age in northern Britain*, Edinburgh

——, 1969   *The Roman villa in Britain*, London

Robinson, M A, and Lambrick, G H, 1984   Holocene alluviation and hydrology in the upper Thames basin, *Nature*, **308**, 809–14

Rodwell, W (ed), 1980   *Temples, churches and religion in Roman Britain* BAR, **77**, Oxford

Roe, D A, 1981   *The lower and middle Palaeolithic periods in Britain*, London

Ross, A, 1967   *Pagan Celtic Britain*, London

Rowley, T (ed), 1981   *The origins of open field agriculture*, London

Rowley, T, and Breakell, M (eds), 1977   *Planning and the historic environment, 2*, Oxford

Salisbury, C R, 1981   An Anglo-Saxon fish-weir at Colwick, Nottinghamshire, *Trans Thoroton Soc Nottinghamshire*, 26–36

——, 1985   The taming of the Trent, *East Midlands Archaeol*, **1**, 5–12

Salway, P, 1981   *Roman Britain*, Oxford

Savage, R, 1983   *The management of semi-natural woodland*, Winchester

Saville, A, 1980   *Archaeological sites in the Avon and Gloucestershire Cotswolds: an extensive survey of a rural archaeological resource with special reference to plough damage*, Committee for Rescue Archaeol Avon Gloucestershire Somerset Sur, **5**, Bristol

Sawyer, P H (ed), 1976   *Medieval settlement: continuity and change*, London

——, 1978   *From Roman Britain to Norman England*, London

Scaife, R G, and Burrin, P J, 1985   The environmental impact of prehistoric man as recorded in the upper Cuckmere Valley at Stream Farm, Chiddingly, *Sussex Archaeol Collect*, **123**, 27–34

Schadla-Hall, R T, 1986   Wet deposits under threat – losing the early post-glacial, *Rescue News*, **41**, 8

——, forthcoming   Recent investigations of the early Mesolithic landscape and settlement in the Vale of Pickering, North Yorkshire, in *Recent studies in the Mesolithic of north-western Europe* (eds M Zvelebil, H P Blankholm, and P Rowley-Conwy), Sheffield

Schiffer, M B, 1976   *Behavioural archaeology*, London

Schiffer, M B, and Gumerman, G J, 1977   *Conservation archaeology: a guide for cultural resource management studies*, London

Selkirk, A, 1973   Piercebridge, *Curr Archaeol*, **4**, 136–41

——, 1978   Otterburn, *Curr Archaeol*, **6**, 152–5

——, 1981   Littlecote, *Curr Archaeol*, **7**, 264–8

——, 1985   [summary of correspondence], *Curr Archaeol*, **9**, 95

Shackley, M, 1981   On the Palaeolithic archaeology of Hampshire, in *The archaeology of Hampshire* (eds S J Shennan and R T Schadla-Hall), 4–9, Winchester

——, 1985   *Using environmental archaeology*, London

Sheail, J, and Wells, T C E (eds), 1970   *Old grassland: its archaeological and ecological importance*, Abbots Ripton

Shennan, S J, 1985   *Experiments in the collection and analysis of archaeological survey data: the East Hampshire Survey*, Sheffield

Shirley, E P, 1867   *Some account of English deer parks: with notes on the management of deer*, London

Shoard, M, 1980   *The theft of the countryside*, Bath

Shotton, F W, 1978   Archaeological inferences from the study of alluvium in the lower Severn-Avon valleys, in Limbrey and Evans 1978, 27–31

Simmons, B B, 1980a   The Lincolnshire Fens, in Hinchliffe and Schadla-Hall 1978, 92–118

——, 1980b   Iron Age and Roman coasts around the Wash, in F Thompson 1980, 56–73

Simmons, I G, Dimbleby, G W, and Grigson, C, 1981   The Mesolithic, in Simmons and Tooley 1981, 82–124

Simmons, I, and Tooley, M (eds), 1981   *The environment in British prehistory*, London

Sinclair, G, and Bell, S, 1983   *The uplands landscape study*, London

Slater, F M, 1972   A history of the vegetation of Wem Moss, Shropshire, *Proc Birmingham Natur Hist Soc*, **22**, 92–118

Slater, T, 1978   Family, society and the ornamental villa on the fringes of English county towns, *J Hist Geogr*, **4**, 129–44

Smith, A G, 1981   The Neolithic, in Simmons and Tooley 1981, 125–209

Smith, C, 1979   *Fisherwick: the reconstruction of an Iron-Age landscape*, BAR, **61**, Oxford

Smith, G, 1984   Excavations on Goonhilly Down, the Lizard, 1981, *Cornish Archaeol*, **23**, 3–46

Smith, G, and Harris, D, 1982   The excavation of Mesolithic, Neolithic and Bronze Age settlements at Poldowrian, St Keverne, 1980, *Cornish Archaeol*, **21**, 23–66

Smith, I F, 1955   Late Beaker pottery from the Lyonesse surface and the date of the transgression, *Univ London Inst Archaeol Annu Rep*, **11**, 29–42

Smith, M A, 1959   Some Somerset hoards and their place in the Bronze Age of southern Britain, *Proc Prehist Soc*, **25**, 144–87

Smith, P D E, Allan, J P, Hamlin, A, Orme, B, and Wooton, B, 1983   The investigation of a medieval shell midden in Braunton Burrows, *Proc Devon Archaeol Soc*, **41**, 75–80

Sneed, P, 1980   The future of the past: some thoughts on public archaeology, conservation and cultural heritage resource management, in *Anthropological papers in memory of Earl H Swanson Jr* (ed D Lucille Herten), 112–16, Pocatello

Society for the Promotion of Roman Studies, 1985   *Priorities for the preservation and excavation of Romano-British sites*, London

Somerset County Council, 1983a   *Somerset Levels and Moors plan*, Taunton

——, 1983b   *Farming and archaeology – Somerset Levels and Moors plan*, Taunton

Sparks, B W, 1960   *Geomorphology*, London

Sparrow, C, 1982   Treasure Trove: a lawyer's view, *Antiquity*, **56**, 199–201

Spencer, P J, 1975   Habitat change in coastal and sand-dune areas: the molluscan evidence, in J G Evans *et al* 1975, 96–103

Spoor, G, 1980   Agronomic justification and techniques for subsoil disturbance, in Hinchliffe and Schadla-Hall 1980, 26–31

Spratt, D, 1982   *Prehistoric and Roman archaeology of north-east Yorkshire*, BAR, **104**, Oxford

Spratt, D, and Burgess, C (eds), 1985   *Upland settlement in Britain*, BAR, **143**, Oxford

Staines, S, 1979   Environmental change on Dartmoor, *Proc Devon Archaeol Soc*, **37**, 21–47

Standing, I, and Coates, S, 1979   Historical sites of industrial importance on Forestry Commission land in Dean, *Gloucestershire Soc Indust Archaeol J*, 16–20

Statham, D C, 1982   *The Bransdale Moor management plan*, Helmsley

Stead, I M, Bourke, J B, and Brothwell, D, 1986   *Lindow Man – the body in the bog*, London

Steane, J M, 1977   The development of Tudor and Stuart garden designs in Northamptonshire, *Northamptonshire Past Present*, **5**, 383–406

Steele, R C (ed), 1976   *Lowland forestry and wildlife conservation*, Monks Wood Experimental Station Symposium, **6**, London

Steers, J A, 1944   Coastal preservation and planning, *Geogr J*, **104**, 7–27

——, 1946   *The coastline of England and Wales*, Cambridge

Strong, R, Binney, M, and Harris, J, 1974   *The destruction of the country house 1875–1975*, London

Stroud, D, 1957   *Capability Brown*, London

——, 1962   *Humphry Repton*, London

Sudeley, Lord, 1969   Toddington and the Tracys, *Trans Bristol Gloucestershire Archaeol Soc*, **88**, 127–72

Sumner, H, 1917   *The ancient earthworks of the New Forest*, privately printed

Swanwick, C, 1982   *Conserving historic landscapes*, Castleton

Syson, L, 1965   *British water-mills*, London

Tate, W E, 1967   *The English village community and the enclosure movement*, London

Taylor, A F, and Woodward, P J, 1985   A Bronze Age barrow cemetery, and associated settlement at Roxton, Bedfordshire, *Archaeol J*, **142**, 72–149

Taylor, C C, 1966   Strip lynchets, *Antiquity*, **40**, 277–84

——, 1974   *Fieldwork in medieval archaeology*, London

——, 1975   *Fields in the English landscape*, London

——, 1980   The midlands: grassland and hedges – Paper presented to a professional seminar entitled The Past in the Modern Countryside: London, 21st May 1980

——, 1983a   *Village and farmstead: a history of rural settlement in England*, London

——, 1983b   *The archaeology of gardens*, Princes Risborough

Taylor, G G M, 1970   *Ploughing practice in the Forestry Commission*, London

Taylor, J A, 1976   Upland climates, in *The climate of the British Isles* (eds T J Chandler and S Gregory), London

Taylor, J J, 1976   *Bronze Age goldwork of the British Isles*, Cambridge

Thacker, C, 1979   *The history of gardens*, London

Thackray, D, 1985   Assessing the monuments: an overall view, *National Trust*, **46**, 24–5

——, 1986   Care and management of National Trust properties, in Hughes and Rowley 1986, 63–8

Thames Water Authority, 1979   *The environment and the river: a guide to good practice in carrying out river works*, Reading

Thomas, A C, 1970   Bronze age spade marks at Gwithian, Cornwall, in *The spade in northern and Atlantic Europe* (eds A Gailey and A Fenton), 10–17, Belfast

——(ed), 1983   *Research objectives in British archaeology*, London

——, 1985   *Exploration of a drowned landscape*, London

Thomas, A C, and Fowler, P J, 1985   Tintagel: a new survey of the Island, *RCHME Annu Rev*, 1984–5, 16–22

Thomas, A C, and Ratcliffe, J, 1984   *Preliminary report on the excavation of a chambered cairn, huts and field system at Bosiliack, Madron, West Cornwall*, Truro

Thompson, D, 1963   *Guide to Arbor Low together with notes on three other prehistoric sites in Derbyshire*, London

Thompson, F H (ed), 1980   *Archaeology and coastal change*, Soc Antiq London Occas Pap, **1**, London

Thompson, M W, 1977   *General Pitt Rivers: evolution and archaeology in the nineteenth century*, Bradford-on-Avon

Timber Growers UK, 1985   *The forestry and woodland code*, London

Tinsley, H M, 1981   The Bronze Age, in Simmons and Tooley 1981, 210–49

Tite, M S, 1972   *Methods of physical examination in archaeology*, London

Tittensor, R M, 1985   Conservation of our historic landscape heritage, *Folk Life*, **23**, 5–20

Todd, M, 1986   Roman and Romano-British Iron Age, in Darvill 1986a, 33–5

Tooley, M J, 1980   Theories of coastal change in north-west England, in F Thompson 1980, 74–86

Turner, J, 1981   The Iron Age, in Simmons and Tooley 1981, 250–81

Turner, M, 1980   *English parliamentary enclosure: its historical geography and economic history*, Folkestone

Turner, R C, 1986   Discovery and excavation of the Lindow bodies, in Stead *et al* 1986, 10–13

Turner, R C, and Briggs, C S, 1986   The bog burials of Britain and Ireland, in Stead *et al* 1986, 144–61

Underhill, T L, 1971   *Heaths and heather*, Newton Abbot

Vyner, B E, 1984   The excavation of a Neolithic cairn at Street House, Loftus, Cleveland, *Proc Prehist Soc*, **50**, 151–96

Wacher, J, 1974   *The towns of Roman Britain*, London

——, 1979   *The coming of Rome*, London

Wager, J F, 1981   *Conservation of historical landscapes in the Peak District National Park*, Bakewell

Wainwright, G J, 1979   *Gussage All Saints: an Iron Age settlement in Dorset*, DoE Archaeol Rep, **10**, London

——, 1984   The pressure of the past: Presidential Address, *Proc Prehist Soc*, **50**, 1–22

——, 1985   The preservation of ancient monuments, in Lambrick 1985a, 23–9

Wainwright, G J, and Cunliffe, B W, 1985   Maiden Castle: excavation, education, entertainment, *Antiquity*, **59**, 97–100

Wainwright, G J, and Longworth, I, 1971   *Durrington Walls, 1966–68*, Rep Res Comm Soc Antiq London, **29**, London

Walker, J S F (ed), 1984   *Blackstone Edge Roman road*, Manchester

Walsh, D, 1969   *Report of the Committee of Enquiry into the arrangements for the protection of field monuments 1966–1968*, London

Warren, H S, and Smith I F, 1954   Neolithic pottery from the submerged land surface of the Essex coast, *Univ London Inst Archaeol Annu Rep*, **10**, 26–33

Warren, H S, Piggott S, Clark, J D G, Leask, H G, Evans, E E, Childe, V G, and Grimes, W F, 1936   Archaeology of the submerged land-surface of the Essex coast, *Proc Prehist Soc*, **2**, 178–210

Watkins, C, and Wheeler, P T (eds), 1981   *The study and use of British woodlands*, Nottingham

Waton, P V, 1982   *A palynological study of the impact of man on the landscape of central southern England with special reference to the chalklands*, unpubl PhD thesis, Univ Southampton

——, 1983   The origins and past land-use of south-east Dorset heaths, in Daniels 1983, **4**

Webster, G, 1981   The excavation of a Romano-British rural establishment at Barnsley Park: Part I, *Trans Bristol Gloucestershire Archaeol Soc*, **99**, 21–78

Webster, G, Fowler, P, Noddle, B, and Smith, L, 1985   The excavation of a Romano-British rural establishment at Barnsley Park, Gloucestershire, 1961–1979: Part III, *Trans Bristol Gloucestershire Archaeol Soc*, **103**, 73–100

Webster, G, and Hobley, B, 1964   Aerial reconnaissance over the Warwickshire Avon, *Archaeol J*, **121**, 1–22

Wessex Water Authority, nd   *Environmental and conservation aspects relating to river works*, Bristol

Wheeler, R E M, and Wheeler, T V, 1932   *Report on the excavation of the prehistoric, Roman and post-Roman site in Lydney Park, Gloucestershire*, Rep Res Comm Soc Antiq London, **19**, Oxford

Whimster, R, 1977   Harlyn Bay reconsidered: the excavations of 1900–1905 in the light of recent work, *Cornish Archaeol*, **16**, 61–88

Whitaker, 1985   *Whitaker's almanack*, London

Whitaker, S F, 1980   Direct drilling, in Hinchliffe and Schadla-Hall 1980, 35–7

White, A J, 1984   Medieval fisheries in the Witham and its tributaries, *Lincolnshire Hist Archaeol*, **19**, 29–35

White, D A, 1982   *The Bronze Age cemeteries at Simons Ground, Dorset*, Dorset Natur Hist Archaeol Soc Monogr, **3**, Dorchester

Whitelock, D, 1930   *Anglo-Saxon wills*, Cambridge

Whitlock, R, 1979   *Historic forests of England*, Bradford-on-Avon

Whittle, A W R, 1977   *The earlier Neolithic of southern England and its continental background*, BAR, **S35**, Oxford

——, 1978   Resources and population in the British Neolithic, *Antiquity*, **52**, 34–42

Wilkinson, T J, and Murphy, P, 1984   *The Hullbridge Basin Survey 1984: interim report 5*, Chelmsford

—— and ——, 1986   Archaeological survey of an inter-tidal zone: the submerged landscape of the Essex coast, England, *J Fld Archaeol*, **13**, 177–94

Williams, C, 1985   *Mesolithic exploitation patterns in the central Pennines*, BAR, **139**, Oxford

Williams, D, 1977   The Romano-British black-burnished industry: an essay on characterization by heavy mineral analysis, in *Pottery and early commerce* (ed D P S Peacock), 163–220, London

Williams, M, 1970   *The draining of the Somerset Levels*, Cambridge

Wills, H, 1985   *Pillboxes: a study of UK defences 1940*, London

Wilson, D M (ed), 1976   *The archaeology of Anglo-Saxon England*, Cambridge

Wilson, D R, 1974   Romano-British villas from the air, *Britannia*, **5**, 251–61

——, 1975a   The evidence of air-photography, in J G Evans *et al* 1975, 108–11

——, 1975b   Causewayed camps and interrupted ditch systems, *Antiquity*, **49**, 178–85

——(ed), 1975c   *Aerial reconnaissance for archaeology*, CBA Res Rep, **12**, London

——, 1978   Pit alignments: distribution and function, in Bowen and Fowler 1978, 3–5

——, 1982   *Air photo interpretation for archaeologists*, London

——, 1984   The plan of *Viroconium Cornoviorum*, *Antiquity*, **58**, 117–20

Wilson, J, 1980   *Entertainments for Elizabeth I*, Woodbridge

Wilson, J, and Wilson, D, 1982   The site of the Elvetham entertainment, *Antiquity*, **54**, 46–7

Wilson, J D, 1974   The medieval deer parks of Dorset XIII, *Proc Dorset Natur Hist Archaeol Soc*, **95**, 76–80

Winbolt, S E, 1925   *Roman Folkestone*, London

Wood, E S, 1972   *A field guide to archaeology*, 3 edn, London

Wood, J B, and Warren, A, 1978   *A handbook for the preparation of management plans*, Discussion Papers in Conservation, **18**, London

Woodland Trust, 1984   *The Woodland Trust*, Grantham

Woods, A, 1984   *Upland landscape change: a review of statistics*, Cheltenham

Woodward, F, 1982   *Oxfordshire parks*, Oxfordshire Museums Service Publ, **16**, Woodstock

Wright, E V, 1978   Artefacts from the boat site at North Ferriby, Humberside, England, *Proc Prehist Soc*, **44**, 187–202

Wright, E V, and Wright, C W, 1947   Prehistoric boats from North Ferriby, East Yorkshire, *Proc Prehist Soc*, **13**, 114–38

Wymer, J, 1968   *Lower Palaeolithic archaeology in Britain as represented by the Thames Valley*, London

——, 1981   The Palaeolithic, in Simmons and Tooley 1981, 49–81

Yorke, F W B, 1955   *Ice-houses*, London

Young, C R, 1979   *The Royal Forests of medieval England*, Leicester